Contents

KU-266-014

access to history

Der
Dic
Ger

GEOFF LAY

SECOND

HODDER
EDUCATION
AN HACHETTE UK COMPANY

To Janet, my wife. Many thanks for your help and guidance

The Publishers thank OCR for permission to use a specimen exam question on page 396 from OCR's A Level History A specification H505 © OCR 2014. OCR have neither seen nor commented upon any model answers or exam guidance related to these questions.

The Publishers would like to thank the following for permission to reproduce copyright material:

Photo credits: p7 Library of Congress, LC-USZ62-103826; **p68** https://commons.wikimedia.org/wiki/File:Field_Marshal_Paul_von_Hindenburg.jpg; **p71** Library of Congress, LC-DIG-ggbain-36337; **p89** bpk/Kunstbibliothek, SMB; **p106** Bundesarchiv, Bild 119-2600/CC-BY-SA; **p109** https://commons.wikimedia.org/wiki/File:Papen_attach%C3%A90001.jpg; **p121** The Granger Collection/TopFoto; **p136** Bundesarchiv, Bild 102-13805/CC-BY-SA; **p137** ullsteinbild/TopFoto; **p140** Library of Congress, LC-USZ62-48839; **p153** Topham Picturepoint; **p167** Bundesarchiv, Bild 146-1968-101-20A/Heinrich Hoffmann/CC-BY-SA; **p179** Austrian Archives/Corbis; **p181** Bundesarchiv, Bild 102-12733/CC-BY-SA; **p200** Topham Picturepoint; **p218** Fine Art Images/HIP/TopFoto; **p245** Bundesarchiv, Bild 183-R99621/CC-BY-SA; **p247** Keystone/Hulton Archive/Getty Images; **p253** 'Ein Kampf, ein Wille, ein Ziel: Sieg um jeden Preis!', BANC PIC 2005.009:181--D, The Bancroft Library, University of California, Berkeley. Courtesy of The Bancroft Library, University of California, Berkeley ; **p291** akg-images; **p301** Haus der Geschichte der Bundesrepublik Deutschland; **p317** Bundesarchiv, B 145 Bild-F078072-0004/Katherine Young/CC-BY-SA; **p320** Archiv für Christlich-Demokratische Politik (ACDP)/CC BY-SA 3.0 de; **p327** Koch, Eric/Anefo-Nationaal Archief/CC BY-SA 3.0 nl; **p335** bpk/Kunstbibliothek, SMB/Knud Petersen; **p356** Bundesarchiv, Bild 183-J1231-1002-002/Spremberg, Joachim/CC-BY-SA; **p364** Haus der Geschichte der Bundesrepublik Deutschland; **p382** Deutsches Historisches Museum, Berlin; **p389** Edward Valachovic http://flickr.com/people/fauxaddress/Creative Commons Attribution-Share Alike 2.0 Generic licence.

Acknowledgements: listed on page vi.

Although every effort has been made to ensure that website addresses are correct at time of going to press, Hodder Education cannot be held responsible for the content of any website mentioned in this book. It is sometimes possible to find a relocated web page by typing in the address of the home page for a website in the URL window of your browser.

Hachette UK's policy is to use papers that are natural, renewable and recyclable products and made from wood grown in sustainable forests. The logging and manufacturing processes are expected to conform to the environmental regulations of the country of origin.

Orders: please contact Bookpoint Ltd, 130 Milton Park, Abingdon, Oxon OX14 4SB. Telephone: +44 (0)1235 827720. Fax: +44 (0)1235 400454. Lines are open 9.00a.m.–5.00p.m., Monday to Saturday, with a 24-hour message answering service. Visit our website at www.hoddereducation.co.uk

© Geoff Layton
Second edition © Geoff Layton 2015

First published in 2009 by
Hodder Education
An Hachette UK Company
Carmelite House, 50 Victoria Embankment
London EC4Y 0DZ

Impression number   10 9 8 7 6 5 4 3 2 1
Year   2019 2018 2017 2016 2015

Cover photo © Manfred Oesterle/Haus der Geschichte, Bonn
Produced, illustrated and typeset in Palatino LT Std by Gray Publishing, Tunbridge Wells
Printed and bound by CPI Group (UK) Ltd, Croydon CR0 4YY

A catalogue record for this title is available from the British Library

ISBN 978 1471839153

Contents

Dedication

Keith Randell (1943–2002)

The *Access to History* series was conceived and developed by Keith, who created a series to 'cater for students as they are, not as we might wish them to be'. He leaves a living legacy of a series that for over 20 years has provided a trusted, stimulating and well-loved accompaniment to post-16 study. Our aim with these new editions is to continue to offer students the best possible support for their studies.

Acknowledgements:

I have been very fortunate with the help of many who have given advice and encouragement in the preparation of this text; in particular Susan Price and my wife, Janet. I would like to thank them both.

The Publishers would like to thank the following for permission to reproduce material in this book: J. Noakes and G. Pridham, editors, *Nazism 1919–45*, volumes 1 and 2, University of Liverpool Press, 1988.

Allen Lane, *Hitler, 1889–36: Hubris* by Ian Kershaw, 1998. Arnold, *A History of Germany 1815–1990* by William Carr, 1991. Bachmann & Turner, *Weimar Eyewitness* by Egon Larsen, 1976. Berg, *The German Empire, 1871–1918* by Hans-Ulrich Wehler, 1985. C.H. Beck, *Das gespaltene Land. Leben in Deutschland 1945–1990. Texte und Dokumente zur Sozialgeschichte* by Christoph Kleßmann and Georg Wagner, editors, 1993. Cambridge University Press, *Drawing The Line: The American Decision to Divide Germany, 1944–9* by C. Eisenberg, 1996. German History in Documents and Images. GHIL Bulletin, *'A Very German Settlement'? The Post-1918 Settlement Revaluated* by C. Fischer, 2006. Hamish Hamilton, *German History in Marxist Perspective. The East German Approach* by A. Dorpalen, 1985. Harry S. Truman Library, 'The War Crimes Trials at Nuremberg'. Hurst & Blackett/Hutchinson, *Mein Kampf* by A. Hitler, 1939. Little, Brown, *Hitler's Willing Executioners* by Daniel Goldhagen, 1996. Longman, *From Bismarck to Hitler* by J.C.G. Röhl, 1970; *Hitler* by Ian Kershaw, 1991; *The Weimar Republic* by J.W. Hiden, 1974. Macmillan, *Stalin's Unwanted Child: The Soviet Union, The German Question and Founding of The GDR* by W. Loth, 1998; *The Meaning of Hitler* by Sebastian Haffner, 1979. Manchester University Press, *The Making of German Democracy, West Germany During The Adenauer Era, 1945–65* by Armin Grünbacher, 2010. *New Perspective*, volume 2, number 3 by Heinrich Metelmann, 1998. Oxford University Press, *Repainting The Little Red Schoolhouse: A History of Eastern German Education, 1945–1995* by J. Rodden, 2002. Routledge, *The Weimar Republic* by E. Kolb, 1988; *The Weimar Republic* by S.J. Lee, 1998. Secker & Warburg, *The Rise and Fall of The Third Reich* by W.H. Shirer, 1960. US Embassy in Germany. Walter de Gruyere, *The Conduct of Soviet Foreign Policy* by E.P. Hoffmann and F.J. Fleron, editors, 1980. Weidenfeld & Nicolson, *Account Settled* by H. Schacht, 1949; *Plotting Hitler's Death* by J. Fest, 1994; *Weimar: Why Did German Democracy Fail?* by Ian Kershaw, editor, 1990. Yad Vashem Studies, *Hitler's Role in The Final Solution* by Ian Kershaw, 2006.

CHAPTER 1

The creation of the Weimar Republic and its early years of crisis

The purpose of this chapter is to consider the events that occurred in Germany during the final days of the First World War and how they led to the German Revolution and the creation of the new democratic republic. These were dramatic and difficult times for German politicians and their people. The country was obliged to sign the Treaty of Versailles, imposed by the Allies, and that document was to mar the post-war years for its citizens. On top of that, Germany faced severe political and economic difficulties, resulting in the hyperinflation of 1923 when its currency became totally worthless. Not surprisingly, some Germans lost confidence in the government, which at times threatened the very existence of the republic. The following themes will be covered:

★ The collapse of Imperial Germany

★ The German Revolution

★ The National Assembly and Weimar constitution

★ The Treaty of Versailles

★ Threats from the extreme left

★ Threats from the extreme right

★ 'A republic without republicans'?

★ The economic crisis

★ The consequences of the Great Inflation

★ Stresemann's 100 days

The key debate on *page 55* of this chapter asks the question: What was the true nature of the German Revolution?

Key dates

1918	Sept.	Ludendorff conceded that Germany was defeated	1919	Feb.–May	Disturbances, strikes and riots in many parts of Germany
	Nov. 2–9	Grand Fleet mutiny at Kiel. Rebellions spread – soldiers' and workers' councils formed		June 28	Treaty of Versailles signed
				July 31	Weimar constitution adopted by the National Assembly
	Nov. 9	Kaiser abdicated and fled to Netherlands	1920	March	Kapp *putsch*
			1921	Aug. 26	Murder of Erzberger
		Ebert appointed chancellor Germany proclaimed a republic	1923	Jan. 11	Franco-Belgian occupation of the Ruhr (not ended until 1925)
	Nov. 11	Armistice signed with Allies at Compiègne		Jan.–Nov.	Period of hyperinflation
				Aug.–Nov.	Stresemann's 100 days
1919	Jan. 5–11	Spartacist uprising in Berlin		Nov. 9	Munich Beer Hall *putsch*
	Feb. 6	National Assembly met at Weimar	1924	April	Dawes Plan proposed and accepted

The collapse of Imperial Germany

▶ *What were the problems faced by Imperial Germany in 1918?*

▶ *What were the political changes caused by the October reform in Germany?*

When war broke out in 1914 it was assumed in Germany, as well as by all the Great Powers, that the conflict would not last very long. However, by late September 1918, after four years of bloody war, Germany faced military defeat. The reasons for its eventual collapse go right back to the early days of August 1914, but these developed over the years that followed:

- *Germany's failure to achieve rapid victory in the summer of 1914.* The German High Command's strategy was built on the notion of a quick victory in order to avoid a long drawn-out conflict with the **Allies**. By the autumn of 1914 the **Schlieffen Plan** had failed to gain a rapid victory.
- *Stalemate.* Germany was forced to fight the war on two fronts: the east and the west. The balance of military power resulted in a war of stalemate that put immense pressures on **Imperial Germany**. The situation was made particularly difficult for Germany by the Allies' naval blockade, which seriously limited the import of all supplies. And, although the German policy of **unrestricted submarine warfare** at first seriously threatened Britain, it did not decisively weaken it.
- *Strengths of the Allies.* Britain and France were major colonial powers and could call on their overseas empires for personnel, resources and supplies. Furthermore, from April 1917, the Allies were strengthened by the USA's entry into the war, which resulted in the mobilisation of 2 million men.
- *Limitations of the German war economy.* Imperial Germany was totally unprepared for the economic costs of a prolonged war. It made efforts to increase arms production, but the economy was seriously dislocated by the disruption to finance and the collapse of trade.
- *Failure of the final offensive, March 1918.* A chance for Germany to escape from the military defeat came when Russia signed for peace in the Treaty of Brest-Litovsk in March 1918. This immediately enabled Germany to launch a last major offensive on the Western Front. However, it was unable to maintain the momentum and, by August, German troops were being forced to retreat. At the same time its own allies, Austria, Turkey and Bulgaria, were collapsing.

The socio-economic effects of the First World War

In 1914 the vast majority of Germans supported the war and there were no signs of the country's morale and unity breaking down until the winter months of early 1917. Then, the accumulation of shortages, high prices and the

🔑 **KEY TERMS**

Allies The nations who were allied against Germany and Austria-Hungary during the First World War. They were Russia, France, Great Britain and later others, including the USA.

Schlieffen Plan Its purpose was to avoid a two-front war by winning victory on the Western Front before dealing with the threat from Russia. It aimed to defeat France within six weeks by a massive German offensive in northern France and Belgium.

Imperial Germany *Kaiserreich*. The title given to Germany from its unification in 1871 until 1918. Also referred to as the Second Reich (Empire).

Unrestricted submarine warfare Germany's policy of attacking all military and civilian shipping in order to sink supplies going to Britain.

black market, as well as the bleak military situation, began to affect the public mood. Social discontent thereafter grew markedly because of:

- *Food and fuel shortages.* The exceptionally cold winter of 1916–17 contributed to severe food and fuel shortages in the cities. It was nicknamed the 'turnip winter' because the failure of the potato crop forced the German people to rely heavily on turnips, which were normally used for animal fodder.
- *Civilian deaths.* The number of civilian deaths from starvation and hypothermia increased from 121,000 in 1916 to 293,000 in 1918.
- *Infant mortality.* The number of deaths of children under the age of one year increased by over 50 per cent in the course of the war years.
- *The influenza epidemic.* In 1918 Europe was hit by the 'Spanish flu', which killed between 20 million and 40 million people – a figure higher than the casualties of the First World War. It has been cited as the most devastating epidemic recorded, probably because people's resistance to disease was lowered by the decline in living conditions.
- *Inflation.* Workers were forced to work even longer hours, but wages fell below the inflation rate. Average prices doubled in Germany between 1914 and 1918, whereas wages rose by only 50–75 per cent.
- *Casualties.* About 2 million Germans were killed, with a further 6 million wounded, many suffering disability. The emotional trauma for all these soldiers and their families was not so easy to put into statistics.

Social discontent, therefore, grew markedly in the final two years of the war. Considerable anger was expressed against the so-called 'sharks' of industry, who had made vast profits from the war. Resentment grew in the minds of many within the middle class because they felt that their social status had been lowered as their income declined. Above all, opposition began to grow against the political leaders, who had urged **total war**. Faced with the worsening situation on the domestic front and the likelihood of defeat on the Western Front, the military leaders, Generals **Ludendorff** and Hindenburg, recognised the seriousness of Germany's position, and decided to seek peace with the Allies.

The October reform

Once Ludendorff came to appreciate that an Allied invasion of Germany would lead to destructive internal disturbances, he pushed for political change. Ever since Imperial Germany had been created in 1871, it had been an **autocracy**. Now Ludendorff wanted to change Germany into a **constitutional monarchy** through the **Kaiser**'s handing over political power to a civilian government. In other words, he aimed to establish a more democratic government, while maintaining the German monarchy.

Ludendorff's political turnaround had two aims. First, he wanted to secure for Germany the best possible peace terms from the Allies – it was believed that the Allied leaders would be more sympathetic to a democratic regime in

KEY TERMS

Black market
The underground economy where goods are sold at unregulated prices.

Total war Involves the whole population in war, economically and militarily.

Autocracy A system where one person (usually a hereditary sovereign) has absolute rule.

Constitutional monarchy Where the monarch has limited power within the lines of a constitution.

Kaiser Emperor. The last Kaiser of Germany was Wilhelm II, 1888–1918.

KEY FIGURE

Erich Ludendorff (1865–1937)
A talented energetic general, who virtually became military dictator of Germany 1916–18. He tried to direct the constitutional reform in October 1918, but failed and was dismissed. After the war he supported the Kapp *putsch* and the early activities of Hitler's Nazi Party, whose racial views he shared.

KEY TERMS

'Stab in the back' myth
The distorted view that the German Army had not lost the First World War and that unpatriotic groups, such as socialists and Jews, had undermined it. The myth severely weakened the Weimar democracy from the start.

Weimar Republic Took its name from the first meeting of the National Assembly in Weimar, which had moved from Berlin because of many disturbances. Weimar was chosen because it was a town with a great historical and cultural tradition.

Chancellor *Kanzler*. Prime minister of the German government.

Parliamentary democracy
A system of government where the political power is held by an elected parliament representing the people.

Reichstag The German parliament. Although created in 1871, it had limited powers until the October reforms of 1918.

Armistice A suspension of fighting pending a final peace settlement. Here, it refers to the document signed by German representatives led by Erzberger, on behalf of Ebert's government, and the Allies on 11 November 1918.

KEY FIGURE

Prince Max von Baden (1867–1929)

Last chancellor of Imperial Germany, 3 October to 9 November 1918.

Berlin. Secondly, he hoped the change would prevent the outbreak of political revolutionary disturbances. However, Ludendorff had a third and more cynical ulterior motive. He saw the need to shift the responsibility for Germany's defeat away from the military leadership and the conservative forces, which had dominated Imperial Germany, such as landowners and the army. Instead, he intended to put the responsibility and blame for the defeat on the new leadership. Here lay the origins of the **'stab in the back' myth**, which was later to play such a vital part in the history of the **Weimar Republic**. It was a theme soon taken up by sympathisers of the political right wing.

It was against this background that on 3 October 1918 **Prince Max von Baden**, a moderate conservative, was appointed **chancellor**. He had democratic views and also a well-established international reputation because of his work with the Red Cross. In the following month a series of constitutional reforms came into effect, which turned Germany into a **parliamentary democracy**:

- Wilhelm II gave up his powers over the army and the navy to the *Reichstag*.
- The chancellor and his government were made accountable to the *Reichstag*, instead of to the Kaiser.
- At the same time, **armistice** negotiations with the Allies were opened.

What pushed Germany, in such a short space of time, from political reform towards revolution was the widespread realisation that the war was lost. The shock of defeat, after years of hardship and optimistic propaganda, hardened popular opinion. By early November it was apparent that the creation of a constitutional monarchy would not defuse what had become a revolutionary situation.

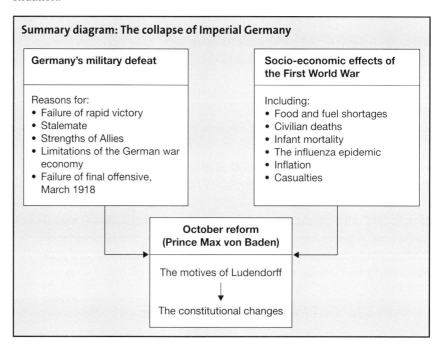

The German Revolution

▶ *How and why did the October reform fail to prevent the November revolution?*

▶ *Why were the consequences of the divisions in the left-wing movement so significant?*

On 29 October a mutiny began to spread among some sailors who refused to obey orders at Wilhelmshaven, near Kiel. Prince Max's government quickly lost control of the political situation and, by 2 November, sailors had taken charge of other major ports, such as Kiel and Hamburg. These takeovers had been prompted by a real fear among the sailors that their officers were planning a suicide attack on the British fleet, in order to restore the honour of the German navy. The news of the Kiel mutiny fanned the flames of discontent to other ports, Bremen and Lübeck, and soon throughout Germany. By 6 November numerous workers' and soldiers' councils, similar to the **soviets** that had been set up by the **Bolshevik Revolution** in Russia, were established in the major cities of Berlin, Cologne and Stuttgart. In **Bavaria**, the last member of the House of Wittelsbach, King Louis III, was deposed and the socialist Kurt Eisner proclaimed Bavaria an independent democratic **socialist republic**.

By the end of the first week of November it was clear that the October reforms had failed to impress the German people. The popular discontent was turning into a more fundamental revolutionary movement whose demands were for an immediate peace and the abdication of Kaiser Wilhelm II. The disturbances were prompted by:

- The realisation by troops and sailors that the war was lost and nothing was to be gained by carrying on.
- The sense of national shock when the news came of Germany's military defeat – propaganda and censorship had delayed the reality for too long.
- The increasing anger and bitterness over socio-economic conditions.

Prince Max would certainly have liked to preserve the monarchy, and possibly even Wilhelm II himself, but the Emperor's delusions that he could carry on without making any more political changes placed the chancellor in a difficult position. In the end, Prince Max became so worried by the revolutionary situation in Berlin that on 9 November he announced that the Kaiser would renounce the throne and that a left-wing provisional **coalition government** would be formed by Friedrich Ebert:

- 'provisional' as it was short term until a national election was held to vote for a National Assembly (parliament)
- 'coalition' as it was a combination of parties, the Social Democratic Party (SPD) and the Independent Social Democratic Party (USPD) (see page 6).

 KEY TERMS

Soviet A Russian word meaning an elected council. In Germany many of these councils were set up in 1918 and had the support of the more radical and revolutionary left-wing working class.

Bolshevik Revolution 'Bolshevik' means majority, which was used by Lenin as the leader of the majority Russian Socialist Party from 1903. In October 1917 Lenin and the Bolsheviks seized power to create a communist government.

Bavaria One of the oldest states in Europe and part of Imperial Germany, which maintained its kingdom until November 1918.

Socialist republic A system of government without a monarchy that aims to introduce social changes for collective benefit.

Coalition government Usually formed when a party does not have an overall majority in parliament; it then combines with more parties and shares government positions.

It was in this chaotic situation that **Philipp Scheidemann**, one of the provisional government's leaders, appeared on the balcony of the *Reichstag* building and proclaimed Germany a republic. (Actually, an hour later Germany was also declared a '**soviet republic**' by Karl Liebknecht – a statement crucial for the shaping of the next few months of the German Revolution.) It was only at this point in the evening of 9 November that the Kaiser, who was in Belgium, accepted the advice of leading generals to abdicate. However, in effect, the Kaiser did not formally abdicate, he simply walked away and went into exile voluntarily in the Netherlands.

The left-wing movement

A genuinely revolutionary situation existed in Germany in early November 1918. However, the revolutionary wave that swept Germany was not a united force. In fact, the left-wing movement behind it consisted of three main strands.

The SPD (German Social Democratic Party)

The SPD represented moderate socialist aims and was led by Friedrich Ebert and Philipp Scheidemann. It dated from 1875. In the election of 1912 it had become the largest party in the *Reichstag* with a membership of over a million. Its fundamental aim was to create a socialist republic, but being wholly committed to parliamentary democracy, it totally rejected anything that might have been likened to Soviet-style communism.

The Spartacists

On the extreme left stood the Spartacus League (otherwise known as the Spartacists), led by Karl Liebknecht and the Polish-born **Rosa Luxemburg**.

The Spartacists had been formed in 1905 as a minor faction of the SPD and by 1918 they had a national membership of about 5000. From 1914 the Spartacists had opposed the war and they were deeply influenced by Lenin and Bolshevism. They had come to believe that Germany should follow the same path as Communist Russia. The fundamental aim of the Spartacists was to create a soviet republic based on the rule of the **proletariat** through workers' and soldiers' councils.

The USPD (Independent German Social Democratic Party)

The USPD had been formed in 1917 as a breakaway group from the SPD. It was led by Hugo Haase and Karl Kautsky. Although the USPD was in a minority in the assembly in the *Reichstag*, it had a substantial following of 300,000 members.

The USPD demanded radical social and economic change as well as political reforms. However, as a political movement, it was far from united and internal divisions and squabbles seriously curtailed its influence. The main disagreement

Friedrich Ebert

1871	Born in Heidelberg of humble background and trained as a saddler
1889	Became a trade union organiser and SPD member
1912	Elected as a member of the *Reichstag*
1916	Chosen as leader of the SPD
1918	In November he was made chancellor of the provisional government when Imperial Germany collapsed. In November concluded the Ebert–Groener agreement
1919	Chosen as the country's first president, a position he held until his death
1925	Died at the age of 54 of a ruptured appendix

As a young apprentice Ebert became quickly involved in trade union work and his written and spoken skills were soon recognised by the SPD leadership. He quickly advanced through the party, covering a range of full-time political jobs, and in 1912 he entered the *Reichstag*. Although the First World War divided the SPD fundamentally, Ebert worked really hard to reconcile the different views in the party and in 1916 he was chosen as leader. However, it proved impossible to overcome the differences, which led a year later to the party splitting and the creation of the USPD.

When Germany collapsed in autumn 1918, Ebert wanted a democratic parliamentary government with a constitutional monarchy, but when events got out of hand the monarchy stood down and he accepted the chancellorship. It was a major success to manage to hold the first truly democratic German elections, which led to the National Assembly and the creation of the Weimar constitution. However, Ebert himself was attacked for endorsing the use of the army and the *Freikorps* to brutally suppress the more radical elements of the left.

From a humble background, Ebert was chosen to be the country's first president in February 1919, a position he held until his death. He oversaw the years of crisis and applied the emergency decrees of Article 48 with success (see pages 52–3). Yet, he became the focus of scurrilous criticism from the extreme right. He was a man of great integrity and decency, who was a patriot and served his office with distinction and correctness. His character and achievements shaped the development of Weimar.

was between those who sympathised with the creation of a parliamentary democracy and those who advocated a much more revolutionary democracy based on the workers' councils.

Ebert's coalition government

The different aims and methods of the socialist movement meant that there was a lack of unity in Ebert's coalition government. Moreover, it should also be remembered that German society was in a chaotic state of near collapse, so the leading political figures at the time had little room to manoeuvre when they had to make hasty and difficult decisions.

Ebert was a moderate and was frightened that the political situation in Germany could easily run out of control. In Table 1.1, overleaf, the nature of Ebert's major problems can be seen.

Table 1.1 Ebert's main problems

Socio-economic	Left-wing opposition	Right-wing opposition	Military
1. Inflation. Wages were falling behind prices, which was increasing social discontent	1. Strikes. From the autumn of 1918 the number of strikes increased markedly	1. *Freikorps*. A growing number of right-wing, nationalist soldiers were forming paramilitary units	1. Demobilisation. About 1.5 million soldiers had to be returned home to Germany
2. Shortages. From the winter of 1916–17 fuel and food shortages were causing real hardship in the cities	2. German communists. Inspired by the events of 1917–18 in Russia, communists aimed to bring about a revolution in Germany	2. The German Army. The army was generally conservative, but deeply embittered by the military defeat	2. Allied blockade. The Allies maintained the naval blockade even after the Armistice. Shortages, causing social distress, were not relieved until June 1919
3. Flu epidemic. The 'Spanish flu' killed thousands. It was the most serious flu epidemic of the twentieth century	3. Workers' and soldiers' councils. Hundreds of councils were created and many wanted changes to the army and industry	3. Nationalists. Nationalist-conservatives were deeply against the abdication of the Kaiser and did not support the creation of the new republic	3. Peace terms. The Armistice was when they agreed to stop fighting, but there was great public concern about the terms and actual effects of the peace treaty

Ebert's main worry was that the extreme left would gain the upper hand. He recognised the growing number of workers' councils and feared that they might threaten his policy of gradual change. He was determined to maintain law and order to prevent the country collapsing into civil war. He also feared that the return of millions of troops after the Armistice agreement, which was eventually signed on 11 November, would create enormous social and political problems. These were the main concerns in the minds of Ebert and the SPD leadership in the months that followed and were the main reasons why they made agreements with the army and industrialists.

Ebert–Groener agreement

On 10 November, the day after the declaration of the republic, General **Wilhelm Groener**, Ludendorff's successor, telephoned Chancellor Ebert, as later revealed in the former's memoirs:

SOURCE A

From the memoirs of General Groener written in the 1930s, quoted in J.C.G. Röhl, *From Bismarck to Hitler*, Longman, 1970, pp. 87–8.

In the evening [10 November 1918] I telephoned the Reich Chancellery and told Ebert that the Army put itself at the disposal of the government, that in return for this the Field Marshal and the officer corps expected the support of the government in the maintenance of order and discipline in the Army. The officer corps expected the government to fight against Bolshevism and was ready for the struggle. Ebert accepted my offer of an alliance …

At first, of course, we had to make concessions, for developments in the Army and in the homeland had taken such a turn as to make the vigorous issuing of commands by the High Command impossible for the time being. The task was to contain and render harmless the revolutionary movement.

The Ebert–Groener telephone conversation was very significant. The Supreme Army Command agreed to support the new government and to use troops to maintain the stability and security of the new republic. In return, Ebert promised to oppose the spread of revolutionary socialism and to preserve the authority of the army officers. The deal agreed has become known simply as the Ebert–Groener agreement.

Stinnes–Legien agreement

A few days later, on 15 November, Karl Legien, leader of the trade unions, and Hugo Stinnes, leader of the industrial employers, held another significant discussion. The Stinnes–Legien agreement was, in effect, a deal where the trade unions made a commitment not to interfere with private ownership and the free market, in return for workers' committees, an eight-hour working day and full legal recognition. Ebert's provisional government endorsed this because the German trade unions were a powerful movement and traditionally closely tied with the SPD.

These two agreements with the army and industry have been severely criticised over the years, particularly by the left wing. Critics have accused Ebert of having supported compromises with the forces of conservatism. The army was not reformed at all and it was not really committed to democracy. Employers resented the concessions and were unsympathetic to the Weimar system. Nevertheless, there is a counter-argument that Ebert and the SPD leadership were motivated by the simple desire to guarantee stability and a peaceful transition.

 **KEY FIGURE**

Wilhelm Groener (1867–1939)

Politician and soldier, who succeeded Ludendorff. Worked hard with Ebert to prevent revolutionary disturbances in Germany 1918–19. Committed to the Weimar Republic and served as defence minister 1928–32.

According to Groener in Source A, what did the two men agree on and why did the deal have important implications for the new republic?

Left-wing divisions

By the last days of 1918 it was clear that the SPD had become distanced from its political 'allies' on the left, and their conflicting aims resulted in fundamental differences over strategy and policies.

SPD

German Social Democratic Party. Moderate socialists.

The SPD government became increasingly isolated. It moved further to the political right and grew dependent on the civil service and the army to maintain effective government.

Aim

- To establish a socialist republic by the creation of parliamentary democracy.

Strategy

- To make arrangements for a democratic *Reichstag* election leading to a National Assembly.
- To introduce moderate changes, but to prevent the spread of communist revolution.

Policies

- To maintain law and order by running the country with the existing legal and police systems.
- To maintain the traditional German Army.
- To introduce welfare benefits.

Leaders

- Friedrich Ebert and Philipp Scheidemann.

USPD

The German Independent Social Democratic Party. Radical socialists.

In late December 1918 the USPD members of Ebert's government resigned over the shooting of some Spartacists by soldiers. However, the split had really emerged over the USPD's desire to introduce fundamental social and economic changes that the SPD did not want to adopt.

Aim

- To create a socialist republic governed by workers' and soldiers' councils in conjunction with a parliament.

Strategy

- To introduce radical social and economic changes.

Policies

- To reform the army fundamentally.
- To nationalise key industries (the transfer of private ownership to state ownership).
- To introduce welfare benefits.

Leaders

- Karl Kautsky and Hugo Haase.

Spartacists

Spartacus League. Revolutionary socialists.

On 1 January 1919 the Spartacists formally founded the *Kommunistische Partei Deutschlands*, the KPD – German Communist Party. It refused to participate in the parliamentary elections, preferring instead to place its faith in the workers' councils.

Aim

- To create a soviet republic based on the rule of the workers' and soldiers' councils.

Strategy

- To oppose the creation of a National Assembly and to take power by strikes, demonstrations and revolts leading to fundamental social and economic changes.

Policies

- To replace the army by local militias of workers.
- To carry out extensive nationalisation of industries and land.
- To introduce welfare benefits.

Leaders

- Rosa Luxemburg and Karl Liebknecht.

The Spartacist revolt

In January 1919 the Spartacists decided that the time was ripe to launch an armed rising in Berlin with the aim of overthrowing the provisional government in order to create a soviet republic. On 5 January they occupied public buildings, called for a general strike and formed a revolutionary committee. They denounced Ebert's provisional government and the coming elections, which in their eyes were betraying the revolution. However, they had little chance of success. There were three days of savage street fighting and over 100 were killed. The Spartacist coup was easily defeated and afterwards, controversially, Liebknecht and Luxemburg were brutally murdered while in police custody.

The uprising of January 1919 showed that the Spartacists were strong on policies, but detached from political realities. They had no real strategy and their 'revolutionaries' were mainly just workers with rifles. By contrast, the government led by the defence minister, **Gustav Noske**, had not only the backing of the army's troops, but also 120 'irregular' military-style groups, *Freikorps*, with about 400,000 soldiers. He placed his trust in the generals in charge to use unrestrained force against the disturbances.

These events created a very troubled atmosphere in the following few months. The elections for the National Assembly duly took place in January 1919 (see pages 12–15), although the continuation of strikes and street disorder in Berlin meant that, for reasons of security, the Assembly's first meeting was switched to the town of Weimar. More serious trouble in Bavaria in April resulted in a short-lived soviet-type republic being established there (see pages 31–2). The *Freikorps* brought the disturbances under control, though, in each case, at the cost of hundreds of lives. The infant republic had survived the traumas of its birth.

 KEY FIGURE

Gustav Noske (1868–1946)

Born a basket-maker, he became a trade unionist and SPD member. He was the first defence minister in the early Weimar governments 1918–20.

 **KEY TERM**

Freikorps 'Free corps'. They were right-wing, nationalist soldiers who acted as paramilitaries and were only too willing to use force to suppress communist activity.

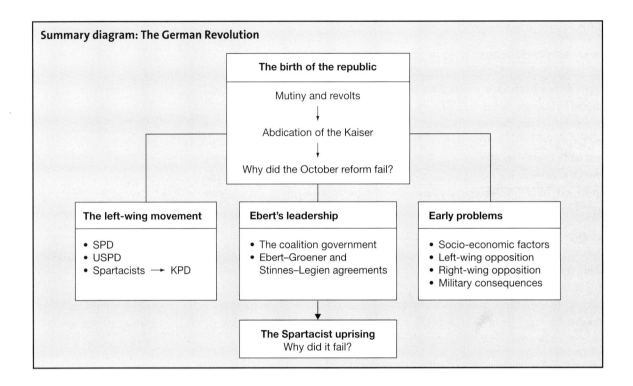

Summary diagram: The German Revolution

The birth of the republic

Mutiny and revolts

↓

Abdication of the Kaiser

↓

Why did the October reform fail?

The left-wing movement

- SPD
- USPD
- Spartacists → KPD

Ebert's leadership

- The coalition government
- Ebert–Groener and Stinnes–Legien agreements

Early problems

- Socio-economic factors
- Left-wing opposition
- Right-wing opposition
- Military consequences

The Spartacist uprising
Why did it fail?

③ The National Assembly and Weimar constitution

▶ *Were the elections for the National Assembly and Weimar constitution an achievement for democracy?*

▶ *How fundamental were the changes brought about by the German Revolution?*

Despite the disturbances across Germany in the months after the collapse of Imperial Germany, the new republic was still able to hold its first elections for a National Assembly on 19 January 1919. Most political parties took the opportunity to retitle themselves, but new names did not disguise the fact that there was considerable continuity in the structure of the party system (see Table 1.2).

Table 1.2 The major political parties in the Weimar Republic

BVP: *Bayerische Volkspartei* (Bavarian People's Party)	Leader: Heinrich Held	The BVP was a regional party formed from elements of the ZP in 1919 in order to uphold Bavaria's local interests. It was conservative, but generally supported the republic
DDP: *Deutsche Demokratische Partei* (German Democratic Party)	Leaders: Walther Rathenau (see page 35) and Hugo Preuss	Formed from the National Liberals in the old *Reichstag*, it attracted support from the professional middle classes, especially the intellectuals and some of the businessmen. The party supported the democratic republic and was committed to constitutional reform
DNVP: *Deutschnationale Volkspartei* (German National People's Party)	Leaders: Karl Helfferich and Alfred Hugenberg (see page 68)	The DNVP was a right-wing party formed from the old conservative parties and some of the racist, anti-Semitic groups, such as the Pan-German League. It was monarchist and anti-republican. Generally, it was closely tied to the interests of heavy industry and agriculture, including landowners and small farmers
DVP: *Deutsche Volkspartei* (German People's Party)	Leader: Gustav Stresemann (see page 71)	A new party founded by Stresemann, who was a conservative and monarchist. At first suspicious of the Weimar Republic and voted against the new constitution. From 1921, under Stresemann's influence, the DVP became a supporter of parliamentary democracy. It attracted support from the Protestant middle and upper classes
KPD: *Kommunistische Partei Deutschlands* (German Communist Party)	Leader: Ernst Thälmann (see page 106)	The KPD was formed in January 1919 by the extreme left wing (Spartacists). It was anti-republican in the sense that it opposed Weimar-style democracy and supported a revolutionary overthrow of society. Most of its supporters were from the working class and it was strengthened by the defection of many USPD members in 1920
NSDAP: *Nationalsozialistische Partei Deutschlands* (National Socialist German Workers' Party – Nazi Party)	Leader: Adolf Hitler (see page 140)	Extreme right-wing party formed in 1919. It was anti-republican, anti-Semitic and strongly nationalist. Until 1930 it remained a fringe party with support from the lower middle classes
SPD: *Sozialdemokratische Partei Deutschlands* (German Social Democratic Party)	Leaders: Friedrich Ebert (see page 7) and Philipp Scheidemann	The moderate wing of the socialist movement, it was very much the party of the working class and the trade unions. It strongly supported parliamentary democracy and was opposed to the revolutionary demands of the more left-wing socialists
USPD: *Unabhängige Sozialdemokratische Partei Deutschlands* (Independent German Social Democratic Party)	Leaders: Karl Kautsky and Hugo Haase	The USPD broke away from the SPD in April 1917. It included many of the more radical elements of German socialism and, therefore, sought social and political change. About half its members joined the KPD during 1919–20 while by 1922 most of the others had returned to the ranks of the SPD
ZP: *Zentrumspartei* (Centre Party)	Leaders: Matthias Erzberger (see page 35) and Heinrich Brüning (see page 106)	The ZP had been created in the nineteenth century to defend the interests of the Roman Catholic Church. It continued to be the major political voice of Catholicism and enjoyed a broad range of supporters from aristocratic landowners to Christian trade unionists. Most of the ZP was committed to the republic. From the late 1920s it became more sympathetic to the right wing

The election results (see Figure 1.1) quickly led to the creation of the National Assembly on 6 February.

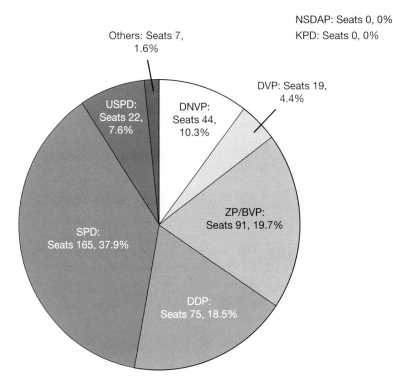

Figure 1.1 *Reichstag* election result January 1919. Turnout was 83 per cent and the total number of seats was 423.

In many respects the results represented a major success for the forces of parliamentary democracy:

- The high turnout of 83 per cent in the election suggested faith in the idea of democracy.
- 76.1 per cent of the electorate voted for pro-democratic parties.
- The solid vote for the three main democratic parties: the SPD, the DDP and the ZP, made it straightforward to form a coalition government, which became known as the 'Weimar Coalition'.

However, it should be borne in mind that:

- Although the DNVP gained only 10.3 per cent, it had backing from important conservative supporters, for example, landowners, army officers and industrialists.
- The DVP and its leader, Stresemann, did not support the Weimar Republic in 1919 because they wanted Germany to have a constitutional monarchy.

The Weimar constitution

Back in November 1918, Ebert had invited the liberal lawyer Hugo Preuss to draw up a new **constitution** for Germany, and a draft was outlined by the time the National Assembly was established in February 1919. Preuss worked closely on the draft with a constitutional committee of 28 members over the next six months, although their discussions were deeply overshadowed by the dispute about the Treaty of Versailles (see pages 21–9).

The proposals for the new constitution were influenced by the long-established democratic ideas of Britain and the USA. Nevertheless, Germany's particular circumstances and traditions were not ignored as, for example, in the introduction of **proportional representation** (PR) and the creation of a **federal structure**. Eventually, on 31 July 1919, the *Reichstag* voted strongly in favour of the constitution (262 for and 75 against) and on 11 August President Ebert ratified it.

The key terms of the constitution

The main features of the constitution are outlined below and in Figure 1.2 (page 16).

Definition

Germany was declared a 'democratic state', although it retained the title of 'Reich' (empire). It was a republic (all monarchies were ended). It had a federal structure with seventeen *Länder* (regional states), for example, Prussia, Bavaria and Saxony.

President

The people elected the president every seven years. He enjoyed considerable powers, such as:

- The right to dissolve the *Reichstag*.
- The appointment of the chancellor. (Although the president was not obliged, he tended to choose as chancellor the leader of the largest party in the *Reichstag*. In order to form a workable coalition government, it was necessary for the chancellor to negotiate with the leaders of other political parties.)
- The position of supreme commander of the armed forces.
- The capacity to rule by decree at a time of national emergency (**Article 48**) and to oversee the *Reichstag*.

These powers created a very complex relationship between the powers of the president and those of the *Reichstag* and chancellor.

KEY TERMS

Constitution The principles and rules that govern a state.

Proportional representation A system that allocates parliamentary seats in proportion to the total number of votes.

Federal structure Where power and responsibilities are shared between central and regional governments, for example, the USA.

Article 48 Gave the Weimar president the power in an emergency to rule by decree.

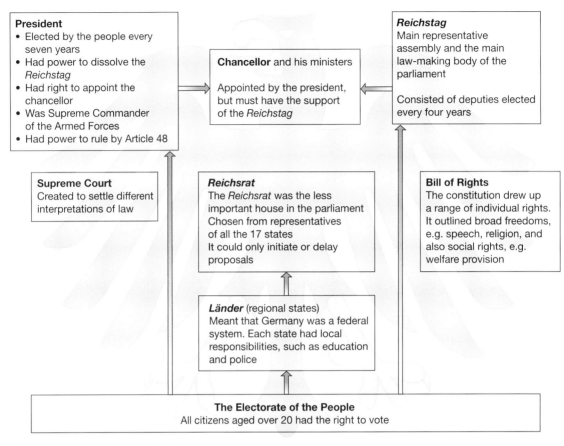

President
- Elected by the people every seven years
- Had power to dissolve the *Reichstag*
- Had right to appoint the chancellor
- Was Supreme Commander of the Armed Forces
- Had power to rule by Article 48

Chancellor and his ministers

Appointed by the president, but must have the support of the *Reichstag*

Reichstag
Main representative assembly and the main law-making body of the parliament

Consisted of deputies elected every four years

Supreme Court
Created to settle different interpretations of law

Reichsrat
The *Reichsrat* was the less important house in the parliament
Chosen from representatives of all the 17 states
It could only initiate or delay proposals

Bill of Rights
The constitution drew up a range of individual rights. It outlined broad freedoms, e.g. speech, religion, and also social rights, e.g. welfare provision

Länder (regional states)
Meant that Germany was a federal system. Each state had local responsibilities, such as education and police

The Electorate of the People
All citizens aged over 20 had the right to vote

Figure 1.2 The Weimar constitution.

Parliament

There were two houses in the German parliament:

- The *Reichstag* was the main representative assembly and law-making body of the parliament. It consisted of deputies elected every four years on the basis of a system of proportional representation (PR). The PR system allocated members to parliament from the official list of political party candidates. They were distributed on the basis of one member for every 60,000 votes in an electoral district.
- The *Reichsrat* was the less important house in the parliament. It was made up of representatives from all of the seventeen state regional governments (*Länder*), which all held local responsibilities such as education, police and so on. But the *Reichsrat* could only initiate or delay proposals, and the *Reichstag* could always overrule it.

Bill of Rights

The constitution also drew up a range of individual rights. It outlined broad freedoms, for example:

- personal liberty and the right to free speech
- freedom from censorship
- equality before the law of all Germans
- religious freedom (and no state Church was allowed).

In addition to this, the Bill of Rights upheld a range of social rights, for example to provide welfare and the protection of labour.

Supreme Court

In order to settle different interpretations of law, a Supreme Court was created.

The issues

Since the Weimar Republic lasted only fourteen crisis-ridden years, it is hardly surprising that its written constitution has been the focus of considerable attention. Some historians have gone so far as to argue that the real causes of the collapse of the republic and the success of the Nazis can be found in its clauses. Such claims are based on three aspects of the constitution:

- The introduction of PR.
- The relationship between the president and the *Reichstag* and, in particular, the emergency powers available to the president under Article 48.
- The fact that the traditional institutions of Imperial Germany were allowed to continue.

Proportional representation (PR)

The introduction of PR became the focus of criticism after 1945 because, it was argued, it had encouraged the formation of many new, small splinter parties, for example, the Nazis. This made it more difficult to form and maintain governments.

In Weimar Germany it was virtually impossible for one party to form a majority government, and so coalitions were required – sometimes of three and even four parties. Furthermore, it was argued that all the negotiations and compromises involved in forming governments contributed to the political instability of Weimar. It is for these reasons that many critics of Weimar felt that a voting political system based on two major parties, like in Britain (or the USA), which favoured the so-called **'first past the post'** model, would have created more political stability.

Having said this, it is difficult to see how an alternative voting system, without PR, could have made for a more effective parliamentary democracy in early twentieth-century Germany. The main problem was the difficulty of creating coalitions among the main parties, which had been well established in the nineteenth century. The parties were meant to reflect the different political, religious and geographical views, and so a system of PR was the only fair way. By comparison, the existence of all the splinter parties was a relatively minor issue.

 **KEY TERM**

'First past the post'
An electoral system that simply requires the winner to gain one vote more than the second placed candidate. In a national election it tends to give the most successful party disproportionately more seats than its total vote merits.

There is also the view that, after the economic and political crisis of 1929–33 (see pages 98–112), PR encouraged the emergence of political extremism. However, it now seems clear that the changes in the way people voted and the way they changed their allegiance from one party to another were just too volatile to be kept in check. It may also have been the case that a 'first past the post' system would have actually helped the rise of Nazism and communism.

The relationship between the president and the *Reichstag*

The relationship created between the *Reichstag* and the president in the Weimar constitution was meant to have a fair system of checks and balances, but this was very complex. It was intended to lessen the fears that an unrestricted parliament would become too powerful. Fear of an over-powerful parliament was strong on the right wing, and within liberal circles. It therefore aimed to create a presidency that could provide leadership 'above the parties' and limit the powers of the *Reichstag*. The president's powers were seen as amounting to those of a substitute emperor. When the power of the president is compared with the authority of the *Reichstag*, it seems that the attempt to prevent too much power being placed in the hands of one institution resulted in massive power being granted to another. As a result, there was uncertainty in constitutional matters from the start.

The framers of the constitution struggled to keep a balance of power between the president and the *Reichstag*. Was the ultimate source of authority in the democratic republic vested in the representative assembly of the people – the *Reichstag* – or in the popularly elected head of state – the president?

Article 48

Matters were made more difficult by the powers conferred upon the president by Article 48. This provision provided the head of state with the authority to suspend civil rights in an emergency and restore law and order by the issue of presidential decrees. The intention was to create the means by which government could continue to function in a crisis. However, the effect was to override the power of the *Reichstag* in what the historian Gordon Craig referred to as 'a constitutional anomaly'. Fears of the emergency powers were actively expressed by some deputies in the constitutional debate of 1919, and they later assumed a particular importance during the crisis that brought Hitler to power in 1933 (see pages 125–7). However, it should be remembered that in the crisis of 1923 the presidential powers were used as intended and to very good effect (see pages 52–3).

The continuity of traditional institutions

Although the Weimar constitution introduced a wide range of democratic rights and civil liberties, it made no provision to reform the old traditional institutions of Imperial Germany, such as:

- The civil service was well educated and professional, but tended to conform to the conservative values of Imperial Germany.
- The judiciary continued to enjoy its traditional independence under the Weimar constitution, but the hearts of many judges did not lie with the Weimar Republic.
- The army enjoyed great status and many of the generals were socially linked with the **Junkers**. It sought to maintain its influence after 1918 and was generally not sympathetic to democratic Germany. It was the only real authority that had military capacity.
- Universities were very proud of their traditional status and generally more sympathetic to the old political ideas and rules.

In Weimar's difficult early years effective use was made of the established professional skills and educated institutions of the state. However, the result was that powerful conservative forces were able to exert great influence. This was at odds with the left wing's wishes to extend civil rights and to create a modern, democratic society. So, while the spirit of the Weimar constitution was democratic and progressive, many of the institutions remained dedicated to the values of Imperial Germany.

What kind of revolution?

By mid-1919 a degree of stability had returned to Germany. The revolution had run its course and the Weimar Republic had been established. However, serious doubts remain about the nature and real extent of these revolutionary changes.

Undoubtedly, there existed the possibility of revolution in Germany as the war came to an end. The effects of war and the shock of defeat shook the faith of large numbers of people used to the old order. Imperial Germany could not survive, so Wilhelm II and the other princes stood down and parliamentary democracy was introduced. These were important changes.

Moreover, it should be remembered that the new constitution was a great improvement upon the previous undemocratic constitution of Imperial Germany and a very large majority voted in favour of it. Indeed, Weimar was initially seen as 'the most advanced democracy in the world'. What the constitution could not control were the conditions and circumstances in which it had to operate; the Weimar Republic had other, more serious, issues than just the constitution, such as the Treaty of Versailles and its socio-economic problems. It seems unrealistic to imagine that any piece of paper could have resolved all of Germany's problems after 1918. The Weimar constitution had weaknesses, but it was not fatally flawed.

In the end, however, the German Revolution was strictly limited in scope. Society was left almost untouched by these events, for there was no attempt to reform the key institutions:

- The civil service, judiciary and army all remained essentially intact.

 **KEY TERM**

Junkers The landowning aristocracy, especially those from eastern Germany.

Democracy and Dictatorships in Germany 1919–63

- Similarly, the power and influence of Germany's industrial and commercial leaders remained unchanged.
- There were no changes in land ownership.

Certainly, plans were outlined for the improvement of working conditions and the beginnings of a **welfare state** by the government, but the SPD leadership hoped that all the changes would follow in the wake of constitutional reform. As it was, the divisions on the left really played into the hands of the conservative forces, who became increasingly influential in German politics. In the words of the historian M. Hughes (1988), 'it is more accurate to talk of a potential revolution which ran away into the sand rather than the genuine article'.

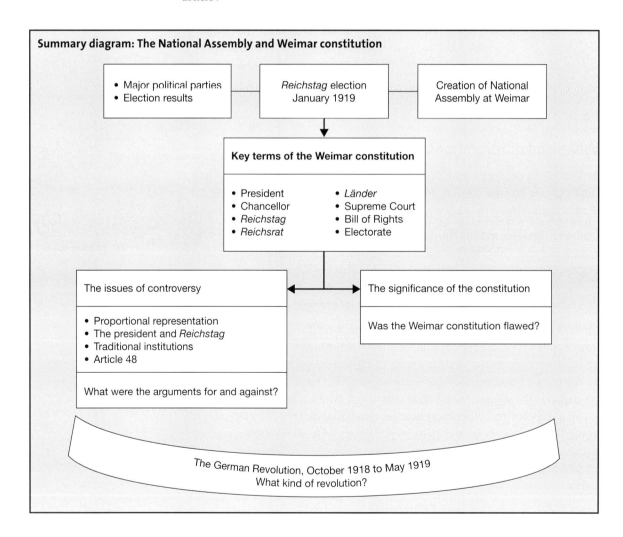

KEY TERM

Welfare state The idea of the state playing a key role in the protection and promotion of the economic and social well-being of its people.

Summary diagram: The National Assembly and Weimar constitution

- Major political parties
- Election results

Reichstag election January 1919

Creation of National Assembly at Weimar

Key terms of the Weimar constitution

- President
- Chancellor
- *Reichstag*
- *Reichsrat*
- *Länder*
- Supreme Court
- Bill of Rights
- Electorate

The issues of controversy

- Proportional representation
- The president and *Reichstag*
- Traditional institutions
- Article 48

What were the arguments for and against?

The significance of the constitution

Was the Weimar constitution flawed?

The German Revolution, October 1918 to May 1919
What kind of revolution?

The Treaty of Versailles

▶ *What were the most significant terms of the Treaty of Versailles?*

▶ *Why has the Treaty of Versailles been so controversial?*

KEY TERMS

For most Germans the **Paris Peace Settlement** of 1919 was a far more controversial issue than the new constitution. It had been generally assumed among German public opinion that the peace treaty would be fair. This was partly because defeat had never really been expected, even as late as the summer of 1918, and partly because it was generally assumed that it would be based mainly on US President Wilson's Fourteen Points (see below).

It soon became clear that the peace treaty would not be open for discussion with Germany's representatives. When the draft terms were presented in May 1919 there was national shock and outrage in Germany. In desperation, the first Weimar government led by Scheidemann resigned. The Allies were not prepared to negotiate, which obliged an embittered *Reichstag* finally to accept the Treaty of Versailles by 237 votes to 138 in June. This was because Germany simply did not have the military capacity to resist. Therefore, on 28 June 1919 the German representatives, led by Hermann Müller, signed the treaty in the Hall of Mirrors at Versailles near Paris.

The aims of the 'Big Three'

The Treaty of Versailles was a compromise, but only in the sense that it was a compromise *between* the Allied powers. So the really decisive negotiations were between the so-called 'Big Three':

- Woodrow Wilson, president of the USA
- Georges Clemenceau, prime minister of France
- David Lloyd George, prime minister of Great Britain.

Woodrow Wilson

Woodrow Wilson has traditionally been portrayed as an idealist, as he had a strong religious background. Initially, he had been an academic, but he was drawn into politics when he had campaigned against corruption. At first he had opposed the USA's entry into the war. Once he had declared war against Germany in April 1917 he drew up the Fourteen Points in the hope of creating a more just world. His main aims were:

- to reduce armaments
- to apply the principle of **self-determination**
- to create a **League of Nations** in order to maintain international peace.

Paris Peace Settlement
The meeting by the Allies in Paris, 1919–20, which resulted in five peace treaties with the defeated enemies and the creation of the League of Nations. The Versailles Treaty was signed with Germany on 28 June 1919, and the St-Germain Treaty with Austria-Hungary on 10 September 1919.

Self-determination The right of people of the same nation to decide their own form of government. In effect, it is the principle of each nation ruling itself. Wilson believed that it was integral to the peace settlement and would lead to long-term peace.

League of Nations
The international body to encourage disarmament and to prevent war.

Buffer state The idea of separating two rival countries by leaving a space between them. Clemenceau believed that the creation of an independent Rhineland state could prevent long-established Franco-German aggression (although Wilson believed this was at odds with self-determination).

Reparations Payment of money (and gold) and the transfer of property and equipment from the defeated to the victor after war.

Plebiscite A vote by the people on one specific issue – like a referendum.

Georges Clemenceau

Georges Clemenceau was an uncompromising French nationalist. Germany had invaded France twice in his lifetime and he was deeply influenced by the devastation from the war in northern France. He was motivated by revenge and he was determined to gain financial compensation and to satisfy France's security concerns. His main aims were:

- to annex the Rhineland and to create a '**buffer state**'
- to impose major disarmament on Germany
- to impose heavy **reparations** on Germany in order to weaken it and to get recompense for the damage of the war in order to finance rebuilding.

David Lloyd George

David Lloyd George was a pragmatist. He was keen to uphold British national interests and initially he played on the idea of revenge. However, he recognised that there would have to be compromise. In particular, he saw the need to restrain Clemenceau's revenge. His main aims were:

- to guarantee British military security – especially, to secure naval supremacy
- to keep communism at bay
- to limit French demands because he feared that excessively weakening Germany would have serious economic consequences for the European economy.

The terms of the Treaty of Versailles

The key terms of the Treaty of Versailles can be listed under the following headings: territorial arrangements, war guilt, reparations, disarmament and maintaining peace.

Territorial arrangements

- Eupen-Malmedy. Subject to a **plebiscite**, the districts of Eupen and Malmedy to be handed over to Belgium.
- Alsace-Lorraine. Germany to return these provinces to France. (Mainly French speaking and with some rich iron deposits. Previously annexed by Germany in 1871.)
- North Schleswig. Subject to plebiscite, Germany to hand over North Schleswig to Denmark.
- West Prussia and Posen. Germany to surrender West Prussia and Posen to Poland, thus separating East Prussia from the main part of Germany and creating the 'Polish Corridor'. (Mixed population, but mainly Polish except for the big towns.)
- Upper Silesia. A plebiscite to be held in the province of Upper Silesia. (As a result, in 1921 it was divided between Poland and Germany, which caused great acrimony as the population was mixed and the area rich in resources.)

- Danzig and Memel. The German coastal cities of Danzig (Gdańsk in Polish) and Memel made international 'free cities' under the control of the League of Nations.
- Austria. The reunification (**Anschluss**) of Germany with Austria was forbidden in order to prevent making a stronger Germany. (Although the empires of Germany and Austria had been independent states, they were both German speaking and there had been demands for some kind of union after 1918.)
- Kiel Canal and rivers. All major rivers to be open for all nations and to be run by an international commission.
- Saar area. Placed under the control of the League of Nations for fifteen years, which was 'administered' by France. (A very rich industrial area, but mainly German. Voted to return to Germany in 1935.)
- Rhineland. The Rhineland to be **demilitarised** from the French frontier to a line 50 km (32 miles) east of the Rhine. (The Rhineland remained part of Germany, but no fortifications allowed and no military forces to be garrisoned within the area.)
- Germany's colonies. All German colonies distributed as **mandates**, under control of countries supervised by the League of Nations, for example Britain took responsibility for German East Africa.

KEY TERMS

Anschluss Usually translated as 'union'. Although the population of Austria was wholly German, the Versailles Treaty outlawed any political union between Germany and Austria.

Demilitarisation The removal of military personnel, weaponry or forts.

Mandates The name given by the Allies to the system created in the peace settlement for the supervision of all the former colonies of Germany (and Turkey) by the League of Nations.

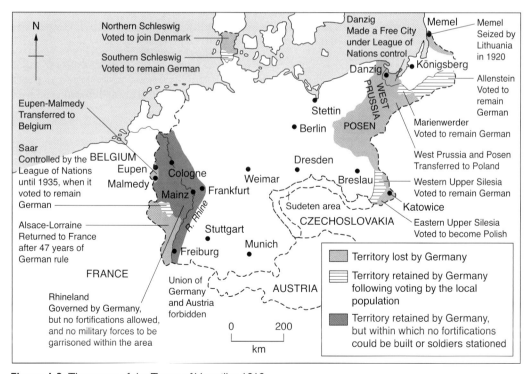

Figure 1.3 The terms of the Treaty of Versailles 1919.

Table 1.3 German losses resulting from the Treaty of Versailles

Type of loss	Percentage of loss
Territory	13%
Population	12% (6.5 million)
Agricultural production	15%
Iron ore	48%
Coal	15%

War guilt

Germany was forced to sign the War Guilt clause (Article 231). It read:

SOURCE B

From Article 231 of the Versailles Treaty, 1919.

The Allied Governments affirm and Germany accepts the responsibility of Germany and her allies for causing all the loss and damage to which the Allied governments and their peoples have been subjected as a result of the war imposed by the aggression of Germany and her allies.

❓ Why did the Allies impose the clause in Source B and why was it accepted by the German delegation?

Reparations

- Reparations sum was to be fixed later by the Inter-Allied Reparations Commission (IARC). In 1921 the sum was fixed at £6600 million.
- Germany to make substantial payments in kind, for example timber. Also all coal production in the Saar region was to be given to France.

Disarmament

- Germany to abolish **conscription** and to reduce its army to 100,000. No tanks or big guns were allowed.
- Rhineland demilitarised zone (see above).
- Germany allowed no military aircraft.
- German navy limited to six battleships, six cruisers, twelve destroyers and twelve torpedo boats. No submarines were allowed. (The German fleet surrendered to Britain in 1918, but sank its own ships at Scapa Flow on 28 June 1919.)

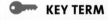 **KEY TERM**

Conscription Compulsory enlistment to the armed services by the state. Germany inherited from Prussia the tradition of a large conscript army with a high standard of military readiness.

Maintaining peace

The treaty also set out the Covenant of the League of Nations, which included the aims and organisation of the League. Germany had to accept the League, but it was initially not allowed to join.

The *Diktat*

No other political issue produced such total agreement within Weimar Germany as the rejection and condemnation of the Treaty of Versailles. The treaty's terms were seen as unfair and were simply described as a ***Diktat***. Germany's main complaints were as follows:

- The treaty was considered to be very different from Wilson's Fourteen Points. Most obviously, many Germans found it impossible to understand how and why the guiding principle of self-determination was *not* applied in a number of cases. They viewed the following areas as 'German', but excluded from the new German state and placed under foreign rule: Austria, Danzig, Posen and West Prussia, Memel, Upper Silesia, Sudetenland and Saar.
- Similarly, the loss of Germany's colonies was not in line with the fifth of Wilson's Fourteen Points, which had called for 'an impartial adjustment of all colonial claims'. Instead, they were passed on to the care of the Allies as mandates.
- Germany found it impossible to accept the War Guilt clause (Article 231), which was the Allies' justification for demanding the payment of reparations. Most Germans argued that Germany could not be held solely responsible for the outbreak of the war. They were convinced that the war had been fought for defensive reasons because their country had been threatened by 'encirclement' from the Allies in 1914.
- Germans considered the Allied demand for extensive reparations as totally unreasonable. Worryingly, the actual size of the reparations payment was not stated in the Treaty of Versailles – it was left to be decided at a later date by the IARC. From a German viewpoint this amounted to their being forced to sign a 'blank cheque'.
- The imposition of the disarmament clauses was seen as grossly unfair, as Britain and France remained highly armed and made no future commitments to disarm. It seemed as if Germany had been **unilaterally disarmed**, whereas Wilson had spoken in favour of universal disarmament.
- Germany's treatment by the Allies was viewed as undignified and unworthy of a great power. For example, Germany was excluded from the League of Nations but, as part of the treaty, was forced to accept the rules of its Covenant. This simply hardened the views of those Germans who saw the League as a tool of the Allies rather than as a genuine international organisation.

The Allies maintained a military blockade on Germany until the treaty was signed. This had significant human consequences such as increasing food shortages. Furthermore, the Allies threatened to take further military action if Germany did not co-operate.

 **KEY TERMS**

Diktat A dictated peace. The Germans felt that the Treaty of Versailles was imposed without negotiation.

Unilateral disarmament The disarmament of one party. Wilson pushed for general (universal) disarmament after the war, but France and Britain were more suspicious. As a result, only Germany had to disarm.

? How did the German cartoon in Source C condemn the Treaty of Versailles?

A cartoon drawn in July 1919 from the German newspaper *Kladderatsch*, which portrays Georges Clemenceau as a vampire.

Versailles: a more balanced view

In the years 1919–45 most Germans regarded the Treaty of Versailles as a *Diktat*. In Britain, too, there developed a growing sympathy for Germany's position. However, this was not the case in France, where the treaty was generally condemned as being too lenient. It was only after the Second World War that a more balanced view of the Treaty of Versailles emerged. As a result, recent historians have tended to view the peacemakers of 1919 more sympathetically. Earlier German criticisms of the treaty are no longer as readily accepted as they once were.

Of course, at the Paris peace conferences, Allied statesmen were motivated by their own national self-interests, and the representatives of France and Britain were keen to achieve these at the expense of Germany. However, it is now recognised that it was the situation created by the war that shaped the terms of the treaty and not just anti-German feeling. The aims and objectives of the various Allies differed and achieving agreement was made more difficult by the complicated circumstances of the time. It should be remembered that the Paris Peace Settlement was not solely concerned with Germany; Austria-Hungary, Bulgaria and Turkey were forced to sign separate treaties. In addition, other problems had to be dealt with. For example, Britain had national interests to look after in the Middle East as a result of the collapse of the Turkish Empire. At the same time, the Allies were concerned by the threat of Soviet Russia and were motivated by a common desire to contain the Bolshevik menace.

In the end, the Treaty of Versailles was a compromise. It was not based on Wilson's Fourteen Points as most Germans thought it would be, but equally it was not nearly so severe as certain sections of Allied opinion had demanded. It should be borne in mind that:

- Clemenceau, the French representative, was forced to give way over most of his country's more extreme demands, such as the creation of an independent Rhineland and the **annexation** of the Saar.
- The application of self-determination was not nearly so unfair as many Germans believed:
  - Alsace-Lorraine would have voted to return to France anyway, as it had been French before 1871.
  - Plebiscites were held in Schleswig, Silesia and parts of Prussia to decide their future.
  - Danzig's status under the League was the result of Woodrow Wilson's promise to provide 'Poland with access to the sea'.
  - The eastern frontier provinces of Posen and West Prussia were rather more mixed in ethnic make-up than Germans were prepared to admit (in these provinces Germans predominated in the towns, whereas the Poles did so in the countryside – which made it very difficult to draw a clear frontier line).
  - Austria and Sudetenland had never been part of Germany before 1918, anyway.
- Germany was not physically occupied during the war and, as a result, the real damage was suffered on foreign soil (France and Belgium).
- The Treaty of Versailles appeared relatively moderate in comparison to the severity of the terms imposed by the Germans on the Russians at the Treaty of Brest-Litovsk in 1918, which annexed large areas of Poland and the Baltic states.

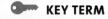 **KEY TERM**

Annexation Taking over of another country against its will.

The significance of the Treaty of Versailles

The historical significance of the Treaty of Versailles goes well beyond the debate over its fairness. It raises the important issue of its impact on the Weimar Republic and whether it acted as a serious handicap to the establishment of long-term political stability in Germany.

The economic consequences of reparations were undoubtedly a genuine concern. The English economist John Maynard Keynes feared in 1919 that the reparations would fundamentally weaken the economy of Germany, with consequences for the whole of Europe. However, Germany's economic potential was still considerable. It had potentially by far the strongest economy in Europe and still had extensive industry and resources. As will be seen later (pages 43–7), the republic's economic problems cannot be blamed on the burden of reparations alone. It should also be noted that by 1932, because reparations had been scaled back, Germany actually received more in loans under the Dawes Plan (see pages 72–3) than it paid in reparations.

It is not really possible to maintain that the treaty had weakened Germany politically. In some respects, Germany in 1919 was in a stronger position than in 1914. The great empires of Russia, Austria-Hungary and Turkey had gone, creating a power vacuum in central and eastern Europe that could not be filled, at least in the short term, by a weak and isolated Soviet Russia or by any other state. In such a situation, cautious diplomacy might have led to the establishment of German power and influence at the heart of Europe. However, on another level, the treaty might be considered more to blame for Weimar's weakness because, in the minds of many Germans, it was regarded as the real cause of the country's problems and they really believed that it was totally unfair. During the war German public opinion had been strongly shaped by nationalist propaganda and then deeply shocked by the defeat. Both the Armistice and Versailles were closely linked to the 'stab in the back' myth that the German Army had not really lost the First World War in 1918 (see page 4). It may have been a myth, but it was a very powerful one.

As a result, although the war had been pursued by Imperial Germany, it was the new democracy of Weimar that was forced to take the responsibility and the blame for the First World War. Therefore, Weimar democracy was deeply weakened by Versailles, which fuelled the propaganda of the republic's opponents over the years. Even for sympathetic democrats like Hugo Preuss, Versailles only added to their belief that the gains of the revolution had been undone. In this way the Treaty of Versailles contributed to the internal political and economic difficulties that emerged in Germany after 1919.

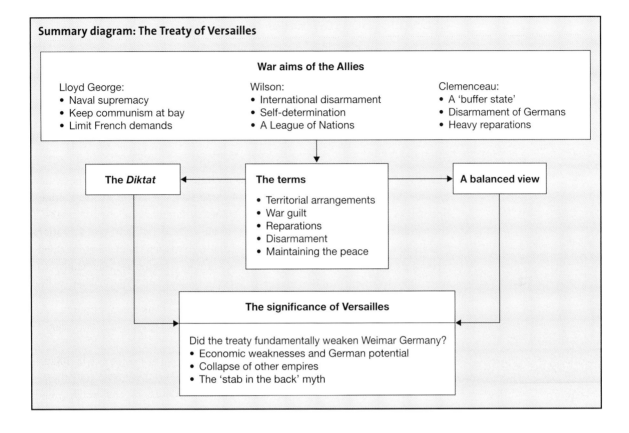

Summary diagram: The Treaty of Versailles

War aims of the Allies

Lloyd George:
- Naval supremacy
- Keep communism at bay
- Limit French demands

Wilson:
- International disarmament
- Self-determination
- A League of Nations

Clemenceau:
- A 'buffer state'
- Disarmament of Germans
- Heavy reparations

The *Diktat*

The terms
- Territorial arrangements
- War guilt
- Reparations
- Disarmament
- Maintaining the peace

A balanced view

The significance of Versailles
Did the treaty fundamentally weaken Weimar Germany?
- Economic weaknesses and German potential
- Collapse of other empires
- The 'stab in the back' myth

⑤ Threats from the extreme left

▶ *How serious was the opposition of the extreme left to the Weimar Republic?*

After the German Revolution of 1918–19 the left-wing movement (see pages 6–11) at first remained in a state of confusion:

- The moderate socialists of the SPD were committed to parliamentary democracy.
- The Communists (the KPD) pressed for a workers' revolution.
- The USPD stood for the creation of a radical socialist society, but within a democratic framework.

This situation became clearer when, in 1920, the USPD disbanded and the vast majority of its members joined either the KPD or the SPD. So, from that time there were two left-wing alternative parties, but with fundamental differences.

KPD opposition to Weimar

The KPD believed that the establishment of parliamentary democracy fell a long way short of its real aims. It wanted the revolution to proceed on Marxist lines (see box on page 31) with the creation of a one-party communist state and the major restructuring of Germany both socially and economically. As a result of the 1917 Russian Revolution, many German communists were encouraged by the political unrest to believe that international revolution would spread throughout Europe.

The KPD's opposition to the republic was nothing less than a complete rejection of the Weimar system. It was not prepared to be part of the democratic opposition or to work within the parliamentary system to bring about desired changes. The differences between the moderate and extreme left were so basic that there was no chance of political co-operation between them, let alone a coming together into one socialist movement. The extreme left was totally committed to a very different vision of German politics and society, whereas the moderate left was one of the pillars of Weimar democracy.

Revolutionary disturbances

The KPD was indeed a reasonable political force in the years 1919–23. It enjoyed the support of ten to fifteen per cent of the electorate and there were continuous revolutionary disturbances – protests, strikes and uprisings (see Table 1.4).

Table 1.4 Major communist uprisings 1919–23

Date	Place	Action	Response
January 1919	Berlin	Spartacist uprising to seize power (see page 11)	Crushed by German Army and *Freikorps*
March 1919	Bavaria	Creation of soviet republic 'Red Bavaria' (see below)	Crushed by the *Freikorps*
March 1920	Ruhr	Formation of the Ruhr Army by 50,000 workers to oppose the Kapp *putsch* (see pages 35–7)	Crushed by German Army and *Freikorps*
March 1921	Merseburg and Halle	'March Operation'. Uprising of strikes organised by the KPD	Put down by police
Summer 1923	Saxony and Thuringia	'The German October'. A wave of strikes and the creation of an SPD/KPD state government. Plans for a military uprising by the communists (see below)	Overthrown by German Army

KEY TERM

Putsch The German word for an uprising. Normally, a *putsch* means the attempt by a small group to overthrow the government.

The most significant disturbances were 'Red Bavaria' and the 'German October'.

Marxism

Karl Marx (1818–83) was a German revolutionary who expressed his ideology in two major books, *The Communist Manifesto* and *Capital*, in which he outlined his scientific analysis of human society. He claimed that history was a continuous struggle of the classes between those who had economic and political power and those who did not. This continuous process of class struggle was known as the dialectic.

Marxists in the nineteenth century were inspired by the belief that the industrial age would culminate in a revolution in which the proletariat (working classes) would overthrow the bourgeoisie (industrial classes) by revolution and create a classless society.

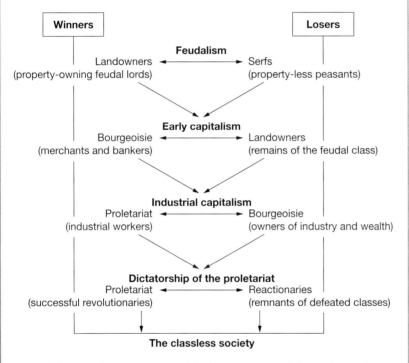

Figure 1.4 A visual representation of the Marxist notion of the workings of the dialectic.

Red Bavaria

After the collapse of the Bavarian monarchy (see page 5), the USPD leader Kurt Eisner took the political lead there. However, he struggled to unite the socialist parties to implement reforms and was assassinated on 21 February 1919. In the wake of this, confusion broke out. A Bavarian Soviet Republic with a 'Red Army' of workers was set up by Eugen Leviné and proposed radical political and

KEY TERMS

White Terror The 'Whites' were seen as the opponents to the Reds. The term 'White Terror' originated from the suppression of the soviet republic in Bavaria in May 1919, although it became a general name for the murders and violence of 1919–22.

Red threat A 'Red' was a loose term used to describe anyone sympathetic to the left. It originated from the Bolshevik use of the red flag in Russia, which in turn had been based on its use in the French Revolution.

economic changes. Yet, after a month, the *Freikorps* and the army moved in and brutally crushed the republic with 1000 deaths in May, which became known as the **White Terror**. This traumatic episode in a conservative, agricultural Catholic area shifted politics to the right wing and it became a haven for extremists.

The 'German October'

In the crisis of 1923 (see pages 52–4), left-wing revolutionary actions came to a head in central Germany. The KPD and SPD had formed coalitions in the regional governments of Saxony and Thuringia, but the communists went further and made military preparations for an uprising with 'Proletarian Hundreds' (defence units). In response, Stresemann's government, by rapid and determined action, foiled the plan for the 'German October' revolution – the army crushed the units and the regional governments were re-created without communists.

The Red threat?

These actions by the extreme left gave the impression that Germany was really facing a Bolshevik-inspired **Red threat** and, as a result of right-wing propaganda, many Germans began to have exaggerated fears about the possibility of impending revolution.

Yet, looking back, it is clear that the extreme left posed much less of a threat to Weimar than was believed. Despite all the disturbances, the revolutionary left was never really likely to seize political power. The main reasons for their failure lay in a combination of their own weaknesses and the effective resistance of the Weimar governments:

- Bad co-ordination. Even during the chaos and uncertainty of 1923, the extreme left proved incapable of mounting a unified attack on Weimar democracy.
- Poor leadership. The extreme left suffered at the hands of the *Freikorps*, which removed some of its ablest and most spirited leaders, for example, Liebknecht and Luxemburg (see page 11). The later leadership suffered from internal divisions and disagreements on tactics.
- Concessions. The Weimar governments played on the differences within the extreme left by making concessions which split it, for example, over the Kapp *putsch* in March 1920 (see pages 35–7).
- Repression. The authorities systematically repressed the rebels with considerable brutality.

In the end, the extreme left was just not powerful enough to lead a revolution against the Weimar Republic.

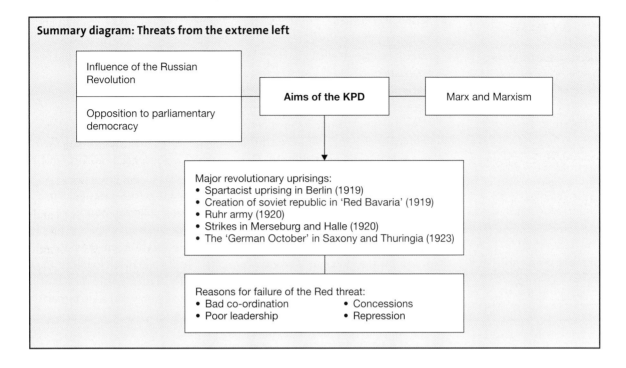

Summary diagram: Threats from the extreme left

Influence of the Russian Revolution

Opposition to parliamentary democracy

Aims of the KPD

Marx and Marxism

Major revolutionary uprisings:
- Spartacist uprising in Berlin (1919)
- Creation of soviet republic in 'Red Bavaria' (1919)
- Ruhr army (1920)
- Strikes in Merseburg and Halle (1920)
- The 'German October' in Saxony and Thuringia (1923)

Reasons for failure of the Red threat:
- Bad co-ordination
- Poor leadership
- Concessions
- Repression

6 Threats from the extreme right

▶ *What were the aims and objectives of the extreme right?*

▶ *Who were the plotters in the Kapp* putsch *and the Munich Beer Hall* putsch, *and why did they both fail?*

Opposition from the extreme right was very different both in its form and in its extent to that of the extreme left. On the right wing there was a very mixed collection of opponents to the republic and their resistance found expression in different ways.

The ideology of the extreme right

In contrast to Marxist socialism, the extreme right did not really have an alternative organised ideology (apart from a shared intense nationalism). It was simply drawn together by a growing belief in the following:

- Anti-democracy. It was united by its rejection of the Weimar system and its principles. It aimed to destroy the democratic constitution because it was seen as weak, which it believed had contributed to Germany's problems.
- **Anti-Marxism**. Even more despised than democracy was the fear of communism. It was seen as a real threat to traditional values and the ownership of property and wealth – and when Russian communism was established, it reinforced the idea that communism was anti-German.

 **KEY TERM**

Anti-Marxism Opposition to the ideology of Karl Marx.

🔑 **KEY TERMS**

Authoritarianism A broad term meaning government by strong non-democratic leadership.

Nationalism In general, the belief in – and support for – a national identity. The spirit of German nationalism helped to unify the German states in the nineteenth century. But many nationalists wanted to create a Greater Germany of all German speakers.

'November criminals' Those who signed the November Armistice and a term of abuse to vilify all those who supported the democratic republic.

Völkisch Nationalistic views associated with racism (especially anti-Semitism).

Anti-Semitism Hatred of Jews. It became the most significant part of Nazi racist thinking. For Hitler, the 'master-race' was the pure Aryan (the people of northern Europe). The lowest race for Hitler was the Jews.

Reactionary Opposing change and supporting a return to traditional ways.

- **Authoritarianism**. The extreme right favoured the restoration of some authoritarian, dictatorial regime – although in the early 1920s there was no real consensus on what kind of strong government and leadership would be established.
- **Nationalism**. Nationalism was at the core of the extreme right, but Germany's national pride had been deeply hurt by the events of 1918–19. Not surprisingly, from the time of the Treaty of Versailles, this conservative-nationalist response reinforced the ideas of the 'stab in the back' myth and the **'November criminals'**. The war, it was argued, had been lost not because of any military defeat suffered by the army, but as a result of the betrayal by unpatriotic forces within Germany. These were said to include pacifists, socialists, democrats and Jews. Right-wing politicians found a whole range of scapegoats to take the blame for German acceptance of the Armistice. Worse still, these 'November criminals' had been prepared to overthrow the monarchy and establish a republic. To add insult to injury, they had accepted the 'shameful peace' of Versailles. The extreme right accepted such interpretations, distorted as they were. They not only served to remove any responsibility from Imperial Germany, but also acted as a powerful stick with which to beat the leaders of Weimar Germany.

Organisations of the extreme right

The extreme right appeared in various forms. It included a number of political parties and was also the driving force behind the activities of various paramilitary organisations.

DNVP

The DNVP (German National People's Party) was a coalition of nationalist-minded old imperial conservative parties and included such groups as the Fatherland Party and the Pan-German League. From the very start, it contained extremist and racist elements. Although it was still the party of landowners and industrialists, it had a broad appeal among some of the middle classes. It was by far the largest party in the *Reichstag* on the extreme right and was able to poll 15.1 per cent in the 1920 election.

Racist nationalism

The emergence of racist nationalism, or *völkisch* nationalism, was clearly apparent before 1914, but the effects of the war and its aftermath increased its attraction for many on the right. By the early 1920s there were probably about 70 relatively small splinter nationalist parties, which were also racist and **anti-Semitic**, for example the Nazi Party.

Bavaria became a particular haven for such groups, since the regional state government was sufficiently **reactionary** to tolerate them. One such group was the German Workers' Party, originally founded by Anton Drexler. Adolf Hitler joined the party in 1919 and within two years had become its leader. However, during the years 1919–24, regional and policy differences divided such groups and attempts to unify the nationalist right ended in failure. When, in 1923, Hitler and the Nazis attempted to organise an uprising with the Munich Beer Hall *putsch*, it ended in fiasco (see pages 37–9). It was not until the mid-1920s that Hitler began to bring the different groups together under the leadership of the NSDAP.

Freikorps

The *Freikorps* that flourished in the post-war environment attracted the more brutal and ugly elements of German militarism. As a result of the demobilisation of the armed forces there were nearly 200 **paramilitary units** around Germany by 1919.

The *Freikorps* were employed by the government in a crucial role to suppress the threats from the extreme left but became a law unto themselves. Since the *Freikorps* were anti-republican and committed to the restoration of authoritarian rule, they had no respect for the Weimar governments and were quite prepared to use acts of violence and murder to intimidate others. Indeed, after their bloody action in 'Red Bavaria' (see pages 31–2), they became key players in the 'White Terror'.

Consul Organisation

From 1920 the Weimar governments tried to control the actions of the *Freikorps*, but a new threat emerged from the right wing in the form of political assassination. In the years 1919–22 there were 376 political murders: 22 by the left and 354 by the right. The most notorious terrorist gang was known as the 'Consul Organisation' because it was responsible for the assassination of a number of key republican politicians:

- **Matthias Erzberger**. Murdered because he was a Catholic and a member of the ZP who had signed the Armistice.
- **Walther Rathenau**, foreign minister 1921–2 (who drew up the Rapallo Treaty with the **USSR**). Murdered because he was Jewish and was committed to democracy.
- Karl Gareis, leader of the USPD. Murdered on 9 June 1921 because he was a committed socialist.

Extreme right uprisings

Hostility from the extreme right against Weimar democracy came to a head with two uprisings: the Kapp *putsch* and the Munich Beer Hall *putsch*.

The Kapp *putsch*

The *Freikorps* played a central role in the first attempt by the extreme right wing to seize power from the constitutional government. This was because by early

KEY TERMS

Paramilitary units Informal military squads.

USSR Soviets had been introduced in 1917. At first, Russia was named Soviet Russia (RSFSR) and then renamed the USSR, the Union of Soviet Socialist Republics, in 1922.

KEY FIGURES

Matthias Erzberger (1875–1921)

A democrat and strong Catholic member of the ZP. Proposed the peace resolution in 1917 and signed the Armistice on 11 November 1918. Finance minister in the Weimar governments of 1919–20, but forced to resign following the infamous legal case. Assassinated by paramilitaries.

Walther Rathenau (1867–1922)

Jewish businessman and politician, who rose to prominence in the First World War. Pro-democrat and founder of the DDP in 1919. Served as minister of reconstruction and later foreign minister. Assassinated by the Consul Organisation as he was seen as a traitor and a Jew.

KEY FIGURES

**Wolfgang Kapp
(1858–1922)**

Prussian civil servant who helped to found the right-wing German Fatherland Party. Campaigned for the restoration of the monarchy, but the *putsch* was a fiasco.

**Hans von Seeckt
(1866–1936)**

German general and monarchist who became head of army command 1920–6. His attitude towards the republic was ambivalent, although he served it better than many other generals.

? According to Source D, why did Seeckt take no action in the Kapp *putsch*? What were the implications of his decision?

1920 there was considerable unease within the ranks of the *Freikorps* at the demands to reduce the size of the German Army according to the terms of the Versailles Treaty (see page 24).

When it was proposed to disband two brigades of the army, the Ehrhardt Marine Brigade and the Baltikum that were stationed in the Berlin area, **Wolfgang Kapp** and General Lüttwitz decided to exploit the situation. They encouraged 12,000 troops to march on Berlin and seize the main buildings of the capital virtually unopposed, where they installed a new government.

Significantly, the German Army did not provide any resistance to this *putsch*. In spite of requests from Ebert and the chancellor to put down the rebellious forces, the army was not prepared to become involved with either side. Although it did not join those involved in the *putsch*, it failed to support the legitimate government. General **von Seeckt**, the senior officer in the Defence Ministry, spoke to many colleagues and reputedly declared the following on the outbreak of the *putsch* on 13 March 1920:

SOURCE D

Seeckt's words, quoted in William Carr, *A History of Germany 1815–1990*, fourth edition, Arnold, 1991, p. 263.

Troops do not fire on troops. So, you perhaps intend, Herr Minister, that a battle be fought before the Brandenburger Tor between troops that have fought side by side against a common enemy? When Reichswehr *[Reich defence force] fires on* Reichswehr *then all comradeship within the officers corps will have vanished.*

The army's decision to put its own interests before its obligation to defend the government forced the latter to flee the capital and move to Stuttgart. However, the *putsch* collapsed. Before leaving Berlin, the SPD members of the government had called for a general strike, which paralysed the capital and quickly spread to the rest of the country. After four days, Kapp and his government exerted no real authority and they fled the city.

The aftermath of the Kapp *putsch*

At first sight, the collapse of the Kapp *putsch* could be viewed as a major success for the Weimar Republic. In the six days of crisis, it had retained the backing of the people of Berlin and had effectively withstood a major threat from the extreme right. However, what is significant is that the Kapp *putsch* had taken place at all. In this sense, the Kapp *putsch* highlights clearly the weakness of the Weimar Republic. The army's behaviour at the time of the *putsch* was typical of its right-wing attitudes and its lack of sympathy for the republic. During the months after the coup, the government failed to confront this problem.

The army leadership had revealed its unreliability. Yet, amazingly, at the end of that very month Seeckt was made chief of the army command (1920–6). He was appointed because he enjoyed the confidence of his fellow officers, even though his support for the republic was lukewarm. Under Seeckt's influence, the organisation of the army was remodelled and its status redefined:

- Seeckt imposed very strict military discipline and recruited new troops, increasingly at the expense of the *Freikorps*.
- Seeckt was determined to uphold the independence of the army. He believed it held a privileged position that placed it beyond direct government control. For example, he turned a blind eye to the Versailles disarmament clauses in order to increase the size of the army, with more modern weapons.

Many within its ranks believed that the army served some higher purpose to the nation as a whole. It had the right to intervene as it saw fit without regard to its obligations to the republic. All this suggests that the aftermath of the Kapp *putsch*, the Ebert–Groener Pact (see page 9) and the constitution's failure to reform the structure of the army had made it a '**state within a state**'.

The judiciary also continued with the old political values that had not changed since imperial times. It enjoyed the advantage of maintaining its independence from the Weimar constitution, but it questioned the legal rights of the new republic and reached some dubious and obviously biased decisions. Those involved in the *putsch* of 1920 never felt the full rigour of the law:

- Kapp died awaiting trial.
- Lüttwitz was granted early retirement.
- Only one of the 705 prosecuted was actually found guilty and sentenced to five years' imprisonment.

The Munich Beer Hall *putsch*

Although the Munich Beer Hall *putsch* was one of the threats faced by the young republic in 1923, the event is also a crucial part of the rise of Hitler and the Nazis. So the details of the events also relate to Chapter 4 on pages 87–9.

The government of Bavaria (of which Munich was the regional capital) was under the control of the ultra-conservative Gustav von Kahr, who blamed most of Germany's problems on the national government in Berlin. Like Hitler, he wished to destroy the republican regime, although his long-term aim was the creation of an independent Bavaria. By October 1923 General von Lossow, the army's commander in Bavaria, had fallen under von Kahr's spell and had even begun to disobey orders from the defence minister from Berlin. So it was both of these ultra-conservatives who plotted with Hitler and the Nazis to 'March on Berlin' (see Table 1.5, overleaf).

KEY TERM

State within a state
A situation where the authority and government of the state are threatened by a rival power base.

Table 1.5 The plotters in the Munich Beer Hall *putsch*

Name	Position	Background/attitude	Involvement
Erich von Ludendorff	Retired general	Took part in Kapp *putsch*. Opposed to democracy (see also pages 3–4)	Collaborated with Hitler and supported the *putsch* on 8–9 November
Gustav von Kahr	Leader of the Bavarian state government	Deeply anti-democratic and sympathetic to many of the right-wing extremists. Committed to the restoration of the monarchy in an independent Bavaria	Planned with Hitler and Lossow to seize power, but became wary. Forced to co-operate with Hitler's rally on 8 November, though did not support the *putsch* on 9 November
Otto von Lossow	Commander of the Bavarian section of the German Army	Despised Weimar democracy and supported authoritarian rule. Very conservative	Planned with Hitler and Kahr to seize power, but became wary. Forced to co-operate in the rally on 8 November, though did not support the *putsch* on 9 November
Adolf Hitler	Leader of the Nazi Party	Extremist: anti-Semitic, anti-democratic and anti-communist. Backed by the Nazi SA (see page 140)	Planned and wholly committed to seize power. Forced the hands of Kahr and Lossow and carried on with the *putsch* on 9 November
Hans von Seeckt	General and chief of the army command, 1920–6	Unsympathetic to democracy and keen to preserve the interests of the army, but suspicious of Hitler and the Nazis (see pages 36–7)	Initially ambiguous attitude in early November. But in the crisis he used his powers to command the armed forces to resist the *putsch*

By the first week of November 1923, Kahr and Lossow, fearing failure, decided to abandon the plan. However, Hitler was not so cautious and preferred to press on rather than lose the opportunity. On 8 November, when Kahr was addressing a large audience in one of Munich's beer halls, Hitler and the Nazis took control of the meeting and declared a 'national revolution'. Under pressure, Kahr and Lossow co-operated and agreed to proceed with the uprising. However, the tables were turned when Seeckt used his powers to command the armed forces to resist the *putsch*.

When, on the next day, the Nazis attempted to take Munich, they had insufficient support and the Bavarian police easily crushed the *putsch*. Fourteen Nazis were killed and an injured Hitler was arrested on a charge of treason.

The aftermath of the Munich Beer Hall *putsch*

On one level, the inglorious result of the Nazi *putsch* was encouraging for Weimar democracy. It withstood a dangerous threat in what was a difficult year. Most significantly, Seeckt and the army did not throw in their lot with the Nazis, which upset Hitler so much that he described Seeckt as a 'lackey of the Weimar Republic'. However, once again it was the dealings of the judiciary that raised so much concern:

- Hitler was sentenced to a mere five years (the minimum stipulation for treason). His imprisonment at Landsberg provided quite reasonable conditions and he was released after less than ten months.
- Ludendorff was acquitted on the grounds that although he had been present at the time of the *putsch*, he was there 'by accident'!

The judiciary in Weimar Germany

Although the judiciary enjoyed independence under the Weimar constitution, the hearts of many judges did not lie with the Weimar Republic. As was seen with the legal cases after the two *putsches*, they were biased and tended to favour the extreme right and condemn the extreme left. Indeed, during the years 1919–22:

- Out of the 354 right-wing assassins only 28 were found guilty and punished, but no one was executed.
- Of the 22 left-wing assassins, ten were sentenced to death.

SOURCE E

In what ways does the cartoonist in Source E try to deride the judiciary? And what concerns does he raise about the trial and the sympathies of the German judiciary for Weimar Germany?

In a 1924 cartoon about the trial of Hitler and Ludendorff, a judge says: 'High treason? Rubbish! The worst we can charge them with is breaking by-laws about entertaining in public.'

Summary diagram: Threats from the extreme right

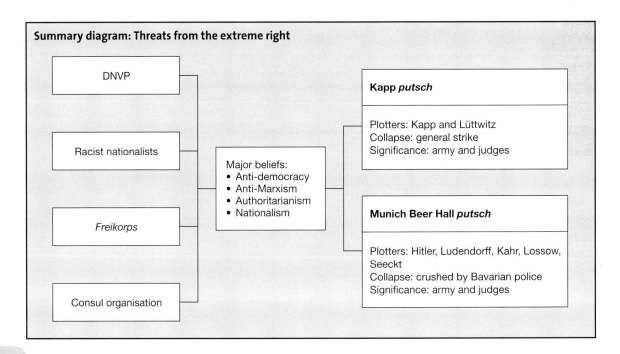

DNVP

Racist nationalists

Freikorps

Consul organisation

Major beliefs:
• Anti-democracy
• Anti-Marxism
• Authoritarianism
• Nationalism

Kapp *putsch*

Plotters: Kapp and Lüttwitz
Collapse: general strike
Significance: army and judges

Munich Beer Hall *putsch*

Plotters: Hitler, Ludendorff, Kahr, Lossow, Seeckt
Collapse: crushed by Bavarian police
Significance: army and judges

7 'A republic without republicans'?

> ▶ *Why did it become increasingly difficult for the new republic to function as a democracy?*

The optimism of the first election of the republic (see page 14) gave way to concerns in the election of June 1920. The results can be seen in Table 1.6 and they raise several key points:

- The combined support for the three main democratic parties declined dramatically:
  - 1919: 76.1 per cent
  - 1920: 48.0 per cent
    (The figures do not include the DVP under the leadership of Stresemann, which voted against the Weimar constitution at first, but became committed to the republic from 1921.)
- The performance for each of the pro-democratic parties was as follows:
  - the SPD declined sharply from 37.9 to 21.7 per cent
  - the DDP declined catastrophically from 18.5 to 8.3 per cent
  - the ZP dropped down slightly from 19.75 to 18.0 per cent.
- The support for the extreme left and right increased, especially the DNVP:
  - the DNVP increased from 10.3 to 15.1 per cent
  - the KPD/USPD increased from 7.6 to 20.0 per cent.

Table 1.6 Weimar *Reichstag* election results 1919–20 (see major political parties on page 13)

	Turnout	NSDAP	DNVP	DVP	ZP/BVP	DDP	SPD	USPD/KPD	Others
January 1919									
Seats	423	–	44	19	91	75	165	22	7
%	83	–	10.3	4.4	19.7	18.5	37.9	7.6	1.6
June 1920									
Seats	459	–	71	65	85	39	102	88	9
%	79.2	–	15.1	13.9	18.0	8.3	21.2	20.0	2.9

The Weimar Republic faced overt opposition not only from both the extremes but also from its democratic supporters, who struggled with the practical problem of creating and maintaining workable government coalitions. In the four years 1919–23 Weimar had six governments, the longest of which lasted just eighteen months (see Table 1.7, overleaf).

Table 1.7 Governments of the Weimar Republic 1919–23

Period in office	Chancellor	Make-up of the coalition
1919	Philipp Scheidemann	SPD, ZP, DDP
1919–20	Gustav Bauer	SPD, ZP, DDP
1920	Hermann Müller	SPD, Centre, DDP
1920–1	Konstantin Fehrenbach	ZP, DDP, DVP
1921–2	Joseph Wirth	SPD, DDP, ZP
1922–3	Wilhelm Cuno	ZP, DDP, DVP

Conclusion

The success of the democratic parties in the *Reichstag* elections of January 1919 at first disguised some of Weimar's fundamental problems in its political structure. But opposition to the republic ranged from indifference to brutal violence and, as early as 1920, democratic support for Weimar began to switch to the extremes. This is shown by the results of the first election after the Treaty of Versailles.

The extent of the opposition from the extreme right to democracy was not always appreciated. Instead, President Ebert and the Weimar governments overestimated the threat from the extreme left and they came to rely on the forces of reaction for justice and law and order. This was partly because the conservative forces successfully exploited the image of the left as a powerful threat. So, in many respects, it was the persistence of the old attitudes in the major traditional national institutions that represented the greatest long-term threat to the republic. The violent forces of counter-revolution, as shown by the *putsches* of Kapp and Hitler, were too weak and disorganised to seize power in the early years. But the danger of the extreme right was just below the surface; it was the real growing threat to Weimar democracy.

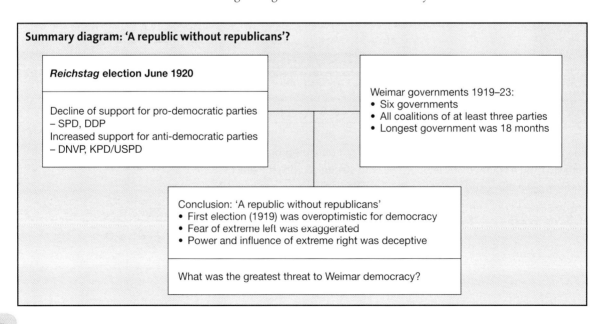

Summary diagram: 'A republic without republicans'?

Reichstag election June 1920

Decline of support for pro-democratic parties – SPD, DDP
Increased support for anti-democratic parties – DNVP, KPD/USPD

Weimar governments 1919–23:
• Six governments
• All coalitions of at least three parties
• Longest government was 18 months

Conclusion: 'A republic without republicans'
• First election (1919) was overoptimistic for democracy
• Fear of extreme left was exaggerated
• Power and influence of extreme right was deceptive

What was the greatest threat to Weimar democracy?

The economic crisis

▶ *How did the First World War weaken the German economy?*

▶ *Why did Germany suffer hyperinflation?*

In the twenty years before the First World War the German economy grew immensely. By 1914 it had become arguably the most powerful economy on the continent and it was in a position to compete with Britain's supremacy. These strengths were based on:

- extensive natural resources, for example, coal and iron ore
- an advanced and well-developed industrial base, for example, engineering, chemicals, electrical equipment
- a well-educated population, with special technical skills
- an advanced banking system.

However, the result of four years of total war seriously dislocated the German economy. So, although the economy still had many natural strengths and great potential, by 1919 it faced fundamental economic problems. The most notable of these were:

- The loss of resources from such territories as the Saar, Alsace-Lorraine and Silesia, which resulted in a sixteen per cent decline in coal production, thirteen per cent decline in arable agricultural land and 48 per cent loss of iron ore (see page 24).
- The cost of paying reparations (set at £6600 million in 1921).
- The growing increase in prices. Between 1914 and 1918 the prices of basic goods increased nearly four-fold.
- The increase in national debt to 144,000 million marks by 1919 compared with 5000 million marks in 1914.

Significantly, Germany had always depended on its ability to export to achieve economic growth. However, between 1914 and 1918 world trade had collapsed and even after 1919 it remained very sluggish.

Causes of the Great Inflation

Germany's growing economic problems came to a head in 1923 when prices soared and money values spiralled down. This is referred to as **hyperinflation**, which had dramatic effects. And it led to 1923 becoming an extraordinary year:

SOURCE F

From Egon Larsen, *Weimar Eyewitness*, Bachmann & Turner, 1976, pp. 54–5.

You went into a cafe and ordered a cup of coffee at the prices shown on the blackboard over the service hatch: an hour later, when you asked for the bill, it had gone up by a half or even doubled … Bartering became more and more widespread.

 KEY TERM

Hyperinflation In Germany in 1923, it meant that prices spiralled out of control because the government increased the amount of money being printed. As a result, it displaced the whole economy.

What picture emerges from these anecdotes of 1923 in Source F? Of what value is this source to a historian?

Professional people including lawyers accepted food in preference to cash fees. A haircut cost a couple of eggs, and craftsmen such as watchmakers displayed in their shop windows: 'Repairs carried out in exchange for food' … In the summer of that inflation year my grandmother found herself unable to cope. So she asked one of her sons to sell her house. The old woman decided to keep the money under her mattress – with the result that nothing was left except a pile of worthless paper when she died a few months later.

Although prices had been rising since the early months of the war, many Germans came to assume that this was a result of the Treaty of Versailles and particularly the reparations. Others blamed the situation on the financial greed and corruption of the Jews. However, with hindsight, it is clear that the fundamental cause of the inflation was the huge increase in the amount of paper money in circulation, as a result of the government's printing more and more notes to pay off the interest on its massive debts. The causes of the Great Inflation can be divided into three phases:

- The long term: the military demands of the First World War (1914–18) led to an enormous increase in financial costs.
- The medium term: the costs of introducing social reforms and welfare and the pressure to satisfy the demands for reparation payments from 1921.
- The short term: the French occupation of the Ruhr in 1923 resulted in financial and political crisis.

Long term

Not surprisingly, Germany had made no financial provision for a long drawn-out war. However, despite the increasing cost of the war, the Kaiser's government had decided, for political reasons, against increases in taxation. Instead, it had borrowed massive sums by selling **war bonds** to the public. When this proved insufficient from 1916, it simply allowed the national debt to grow bigger and bigger.

The result of Imperial Germany's financial policies was that by the end of 1918 only sixteen per cent of war expenditure had been raised from taxation – 84 per cent had been borrowed. Victory would doubtless have allowed Imperial Germany to settle its debts by claiming reparations from the Allies, but defeat meant the reverse.

Another factor was that although the war years had seen almost full employment, the economy had concentrated on the supply of military weapons. Since production was necessarily military based, it did not satisfy the growing requirements of the civilian consumers. Consequently, the high demand for, and the shortage of, consumer goods began to push prices up.

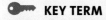 **KEY TERM**

War bonds To pay for the war, Imperial Germany encouraged people to invest in government funds in the belief that they were helping to finance the war and their savings would be secure.

The Weimar Republic had to cope with the massive costs of war. By 1919, Germany's finances were described by the modern-day historian Volker Berghahn as 'an unholy mess'.

Medium term

The government of the Weimar Republic (like any government with a large deficit) could control inflation only by narrowing the gap between the government's income and expenditure through:

- increasing taxation in order to raise its income
- cutting government spending to reduce its expenditure.

However, in view of Germany's domestic situation neither of these options was particularly attractive, as both would alienate the people and cause political and social difficulties, such as increased unemployment and industrial decline.

From 1919 the Weimar government, guided by Erzberger, the finance minister, extensively increased taxation on profits, wealth and income. However, it decided not to go so far as aiming to **balance the budget**. It decided to adopt a policy of **deficit financing** in the belief that it would:

- give the people more money to spend and so increase the demand for goods and thereby create work
- overcome the problems of demobilising millions of returning troops – a booming economy would ensure there were plenty of jobs for the returning soldiers and sailors
- cover the cost of public spending on an extensive welfare state, for example, health insurance, housing and benefits for the disabled and orphans (see pages 60–1).

Unfortunately, an essential part of this policy was to allow inflation to continue.

The reparations issue should be seen as only a contributory factor to the inflation. It was certainly not the primary cause. Nevertheless, the sum drawn up by the Reparations Commission added to the economic burden facing the Weimar government because the reparation payments had to be in **hard currency**, like dollars and gold (not inflated German marks). In order to pay their reparations, the Weimar governments proceeded to print larger quantities of marks and sell them to obtain the stronger currencies of other countries. This was not a solution. It was merely a short-term measure that had serious consequences. The value of the mark went into sharp decline and inflation climbed even higher (see Table 1.8, overleaf).

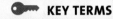 **KEY TERMS**

Balanced budget
A financial programme in which a government does not spend more than it raises in revenue.

Deficit financing
The financial policy of a government to spend more than it receives as revenue, in order to stimulate the economy. In this way, it gives the people more money to spend and so, in theory, increases the demand for goods and thereby creates work.

Hard currency A currency that the market considers to be strong because its value does not depreciate. In the 1920s the hardest currency was the US dollar.

Table 1.8 The Great Inflation: exchange rate and wholesale prices

Date	Exchange rate of German marks against the dollar	Wholesale price index. The index is created from a scale of prices starting with 1 for 1914
1914 July	4.2	1
1919 January	8.9	2
1920 January	14.0	4
1921 January	64.9	14
1922 January	191.8	37
1923 January	17,792	2,785
1923 July	353,412	74,787
1923 September	98,860,000	23,949,000
1923 November	200,000,000,000	750,000,000,000

Short term

Germany had already been allowed to postpone several instalments of its reparations payments in early 1922, but an attempt to resolve the crisis on an international level by calling the Genoa Economic Conference was ill fated. When, in July 1922, the German government made another request for a 'holiday' from making reparations payments, the final stage of the country's inflationary crisis set in.

The French government, at this time led by Raymond Poincaré, suspected German intentions and was determined to secure what was seen as France's rightful claims. Therefore, when in December 1922 the Reparations Commission declared Germany to be in default, Poincaré ordered French and Belgian troops to occupy the industrial Ruhr, to make Germany pay in kind for what it had not paid in capital.

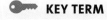 **KEY TERM**

Passive resistance Refusal to work with occupying forces.

The government, led by Wilhelm Cuno, embarked on a policy of **passive resistance**. It urged the workers to go on strike and refuse to co-operate with the French authorities, although it also promised to carry on paying their wages. At the same time, the government was unable to collect taxes from the Ruhr area and the French prevented the delivery of coal to the rest of Germany, thus forcing the necessary stocks of fuel to be imported.

In this situation, the government's finances collapsed and the mark fell to worthless levels. By autumn 1923 it cost more to print a bank note than the note was worth and the *Reichsbank* was forced to use newspaper presses to produce sufficient money. The German currency ceased to have any real value and the German people had to resort to barter.

Conclusion

The fundamental cause of the Great Inflation is to be found in the mismanagement of Germany's finances from 1914 onwards. Certainly, the inflationary spiral did not increase at an even rate and there were short periods, as in the spring of 1920 and the winter of 1920–1, when it did actually slacken. However, at no time was there willingness by the various German governments to bring spending and borrowing back within reasonable limits.

Until the end of 1918 the cost of waging war was the excuse, but in the immediate post-war period the high levels of debt were allowed to continue. It has been argued by some that the inflation remained quite modest in the years 1914–22 and perhaps acceptable in view of all the various difficulties facing the new government. However, the payment of reparations from 1921 simply added to an already desperate situation and the government found it more convenient to print money than to tackle the basic problems facing the economy.

By the end of 1922 hyperinflation had set in. Cuno's government made no effort to deal with the situation. Indeed, it could be said that Cuno deliberately deepened the economic crisis and played on the nationalist fervour brought about by the popular decision to encourage passive resistance. It was only in August 1923, when the German economy was on the verge of complete collapse, that a new coalition government was formed under Gustav Stresemann. He found the will to introduce an economic policy which was aimed at controlling the amount of money in circulation.

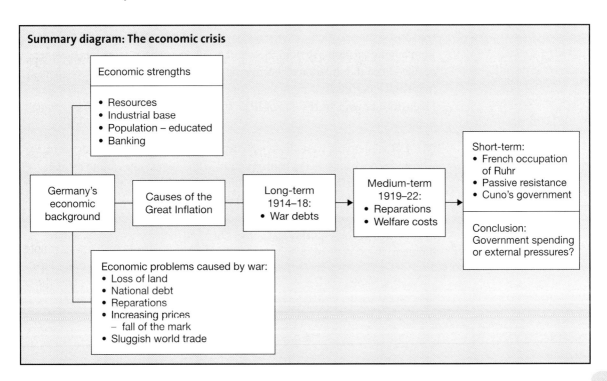

Summary diagram: The economic crisis

- Economic strengths
  - Resources
  - Industrial base
  - Population – educated
  - Banking
- Germany's economic background
- Causes of the Great Inflation
- Long-term 1914–18:
  - War debts
- Medium-term 1919–22:
  - Reparations
  - Welfare costs
- Short-term:
  - French occupation of Ruhr
  - Passive resistance
  - Cuno's government
- Conclusion: Government spending or external pressures?
- Economic problems caused by war:
  - Loss of land
  - National debt
  - Reparations
  - Increasing prices
    - fall of the mark
  - Sluggish world trade

9 The consequences of the Great Inflation

▶ *Why did some Germans lose and some win?*

▶ *How disastrous was the inflation?*

It has been claimed that the worst consequence of the inflation was the damage done to the German middle class. Stresemann himself said as much in 1927. Later on in the 1930s it was generally assumed that the reason a large proportion of the middle class voted for the Nazis was because of their economic sufferings in 1923. In the light of recent historical research, such assumptions have come to be questioned and a much more complex interpretation has emerged about the impact of the inflation on the whole of society.

The key to understanding who gained and who lost during the period of the hyperinflation lies in considering each individual's savings and their amount of debt. However, it was not always clearly linked to class differences. So what did this mean in practice?

Winners and losers

The real winners were those sections of the community who were able to pay off their debts, mortgages and loans with inflated and worthless money. This obviously worked to the advantage of such groups as businessmen and homeowners, which included members of the middle class. Those who recognised the situation for what it was exploited it by making massive gains from buying up property from those financially desperate. Some businessmen profited from the situation by borrowing cheaply and investing in new industrial enterprises. Among these, one of the most notorious examples was Hugo Stinnes who, by the end of 1923, controlled twenty per cent of German industry.

At the other extreme were those who depended on their savings. Any German who had money invested in bank accounts with interest rates found its real value had eroded. Most famously, millions who had bought and invested in war bonds now could not get their money back. The bonds were worth nothing. Those living on fixed incomes, such as pensioners, found themselves in a similar plight. Their savings quickly lost value, since any increase was wiped out by inflation.

Table 1.9 Financial winners and losers

Financial winners and losers	Explanation of gains or losses
Mortgage holders	Borrowed money was easily paid off in valueless money
Savers	Money invested was eroded
Exporters	Sales to foreign countries were attractive because of the rate of exchange
Those on fixed incomes	Income declined in real terms dramatically
Recipients of welfare	Depended on charity or state. Payments fell behind the inflation rate
Long-term renters/landlords	Income was fixed in the long term and so it declined in real terms
The German state	Large parts of the government debt were paid off in valueless money (but not reparations)

The material impact of the hyperinflation has recently been the subject of considerable historical research in Germany and, as a result, our understanding of this period has been greatly increased and many previous conclusions have been revised. However, it should be remembered that the following discussion of the effects of the hyperinflation on whole classes deals with broad categories, for example, region and age, rather than individual examples. Two people from the same social class could be affected in very different ways depending on their individual circumstances.

Peasants

In the countryside the peasants coped reasonably well as food remained in demand. They depended less on money for the provision of the necessities of life because they were more self-sufficient.

Mittelstand

The **Mittelstand**, including shopkeepers and craftsmen, also seem to have done reasonably good business, especially if they were prepared to exploit the demands of the market.

Industrial workers

Workers' **real wages** and standard of living improved until 1922. It was in the chaos of 1923 that, when the trade unions were unable to negotiate wage settlements for their members, wages could not keep pace with the rate of inflation and a very real decline took place. However, as they had fewer savings, they lost proportionally less than those living on saved income. Unemployment did go up to 4.1 per cent in 1923, but it was still at a relatively low level.

 **KEY TERMS**

Mittelstand Translated as 'the middle class', but in Germany it represents the lower middle classes: shopkeepers, craft workers and clerks. Traditionally independent and self-reliant, but increasingly squeezed out between the power and influence of big business and industrial labour.

Real wages The actual purchasing power of income when set against prices.

Civil servants

The fate of public employees is probably the most difficult to analyse. Their income fell sharply in the years 1914–20, but they made real gains in 1921–2. They suffered again in the chaos of 1923 because they depended on fixed salaries, which fell in value before the end of each month. They tended to gain – if they were buying a property on a mortgage – but many had been attracted to buying the war bonds and so lost out.

Retired

Elderly people generally suffered badly because they depended on fixed pensions and savings.

Businessmen

Generally, they did well because they bought up property with worthless money and they paid off mortgages. They also benefited if they made sales to foreign countries, as the rate of exchange was very attractive.

The human consequences

By merely listing the financial statistics of the Great Inflation, there is a danger of overlooking the very real human dimension. Government records show clearly that the mortality rate of the larger towns increased, mainly because of the deteriorating diet which led to diseases like scurvy and dropsy.

Even more interesting were the effects on behaviour, as people began to resort to desperate measures:

- a decline in law and order and an increase in crime
- a decline in 'morality', for example, more prostitution
- a growth in the number of suicides
- an increase in prejudice and a tendency to find scapegoats, for example, Jews.

It has often been suggested that such social problems contributed to people's lack of faith in the republican system. The connection is difficult to prove, as it is not easy to assess the importance of morality and religious codes in past societies. However, it would be foolish to dismiss out of hand their effects on German society and its traditional set of values. At the very least, the loss of some old values led to increased tensions. Even more significantly, when another crisis developed at the end of the decade, the people's confidence in the ability of Weimar to maintain social stability was eventually lost. In that sense, the inflation of 1923 was not the reason for the Weimar Republic's decline, but it caused psychological damage that continued to affect the republic in future years.

Conclusion

Traditionally, the Great Inflation has been portrayed as a catastrophe with damaging consequences that paved the way for the collapse of the Weimar Republic and the rise of Nazism. However, a number of economic historians from the 1980s have perceived the issue differently.

The historian C-L. Holtfrerich maintains that in the years up to the end of 1922 Weimar's economic policy amounted to a 'rational strategy … in the national interest'. His interpretation is that by not reducing the budget deficits, the Weimar Republic was able to maintain economic growth and increase production. He argues that the German economy compared favourably with other European economies that also went into recession in 1920–1:

- Low unemployment. Whereas Britain had an unemployment rate of seventeen per cent in 1921, Germany had nearly full employment with only 1.8 per cent unemployed.
- Rising wage levels. The real wages of industrial workers increased between 1918 and 1922.
- Growing foreign investment. Foreigners' capital, particularly from the USA, provided an important stimulus to economic activity.
- Industrial production. This nearly doubled from 1919 to 1922 (albeit from a low base because of the war).

Holtfrerich does not accept that the policy was a disaster. In fact, he sees it as the only way that could have ensured the survival of the Weimar Republic. He argues that, in the early years of 1921–2, any policy that required cutting back spending would have resulted in the most terrible economic and social consequences – and perhaps even the collapse of the new democracy. In this sense, the inflation up to 1923 was actually beneficial.

This interpretation remains controversial and many have found it difficult to accept. Holtfrerich has been criticised for drawing an artificial line at 1922 – as if the years up to 1922 were those of modest and 'good' inflation, whereas the year 1923 marked the start of hyperinflation with the problems arising from that date. This seems a rather doubtful way of looking at the overall development of the Great Inflation, bearing in mind the long-term build-up and the nature of its causes. It also tends to separate the inflation from the drastic measures that were eventually required to solve it. Finally, an assessment of the Great Inflation must consider other important factors, such as the social and psychological. There is always a danger for economic historians to rely largely on a study of economic and financial data.

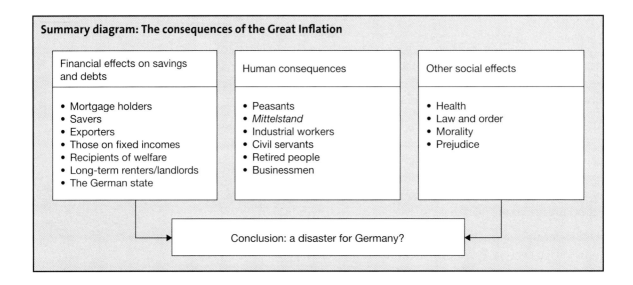

Summary diagram: The consequences of the Great Inflation

Financial effects on savings and debts	Human consequences	Other social effects
• Mortgage holders • Savers • Exporters • Those on fixed incomes • Recipients of welfare • Long-term renters/landlords • The German state	• Peasants • *Mittelstand* • Industrial workers • Civil servants • Retired people • Businessmen	• Health • Law and order • Morality • Prejudice

Conclusion: a disaster for Germany?

⑩ Stresemann's 100 days

▶ *How did the Weimar Republic survive the crisis of 1923?*

In the summer of 1923 the problems facing the Weimar Republic came to a head and it seemed close to collapse:

- The German currency had collapsed and hyperinflation had set in.
- French and Belgian troops were occupying the Ruhr.
- The German government had no clear policy on the occupation, except for passive resistance.
- There were various left-wing political disturbances across the country: in Saxony the creation of an SPD/KPD regional state government resulted in an attempted communist uprising.
- The ultra-conservative state government in Bavaria was defying the national government: this finally resulted in the Munich Beer Hall *putsch* (see pages 36–40).

Timeline 1923: Weimar's year of crisis

- 11 January: Franco-Belgian occupation of the Ruhr (not ended until 1925)
- 13 January: passive resistance proclaimed by the German government
- January to November: period of hyperinflation
- 12 August: Stresemann made chancellor of Germany. State of emergency declared
- August to November: Stresemann's 100 days

- Autumn: 'German October' uprising in Saxony: overthrown by army
- 9 November: Munich Beer Hall *putsch*
- 15 November: introduction of *Rentenmark*
- 30 November: international committee created under chairman Charles S. Dawes to reorganise reparations

Yet, only a few months later, a semblance of calm and normality returned. The Weimar Republic's remarkable survival illustrates the telling comment of the historian D. Peukert that even 1923 shows 'there are no entirely hopeless situations in history'.

Stresemann's achievements

It is important to recognise that, during the summer of 1923, things had just been allowed to slide under the chancellor, Cuno. Nevertheless, the appointment of Gustav Stresemann as chancellor in August 1923 resulted in the emergence of a politician who was actually prepared to take difficult political decisions. Stresemann led a broad coalition of DVP, DDP, ZP and SPD and aimed to resolve Germany's economic plight and also tackle the problem of her weakness internationally.

Within a few weeks Stresemann introduced a series of crucial initiatives:

- First, in September, he called off the 'passive resistance' in the Ruhr and promised to resume the payment of reparations. He needed to conciliate the French in order to evoke some international sympathy for Germany's economic position.
- Under the guidance of finance minister Hans Luther, the government's expenditure was sharply cut in order to reduce the deficit. Over 700,000 public employees were sacked.
- The leading financial expert Hjalmar Schacht was appointed to oversee the introduction of a new German currency. In December 1923 the trillions of old German marks were replaced and a new stable currency, the *Rentenmark*, was established.
- Stresemann evoked some sympathy from the Allies for Germany by the 'miracle of the *Rentenmark*' and his conciliatory policy. He therefore asked the Allies to hold an international conference to consider Germany's economic plight and, as a result, the Dawes Committee was established. Its report, the Dawes Plan, was published in April 1924. It did not reduce the overall reparations bill, but for the first five years it fixed the payments in accordance with Germany's ability to pay (see pages 72–3).
- The extremists of the left and the right were defeated (see pages 32 and 39).

The survival of Weimar

Although Stresemann's resolute action in tackling the problems might help to explain why the years of crisis came to an end, on its own it does not help us to understand why the Weimar Republic was able to come through. The republic's survival in 1923 was in marked contrast to its collapse ten years later when challenged by the Nazis.

Why, then, did the republic not collapse during the crisis-ridden months before Stresemann's emergence on the political scene? The following factors provide clues to an answer:

- Popular anger was directed more towards the French and the Allies than towards the Weimar Republic itself.
- Despite the effects of inflation, workers did not suffer to the same extent as they did during the mass unemployment of the 1930s.
- Some businessmen did very well out of the inflation, which made them tolerant of the republic.

If these suggestions about public attitudes towards the republic are correct, then it seems that, although there was distress and disillusionment in 1923, hostility to the Weimar Republic had not yet reached unbearable levels – as it was to do ten years later.

Moreover, in 1923 there was no obvious political alternative to Weimar. The extreme left had not really recovered from its divisions and suppression in the years 1918–21 and in its isolated position it did not enjoy enough support to overthrow Weimar. The extreme right, too, was not yet strong enough. It was similarly divided and had no clear plans. The failure of the Kapp *putsch* served as a clear warning of the dangers of taking hasty action and was possibly the reason why the army made no move in 1923.

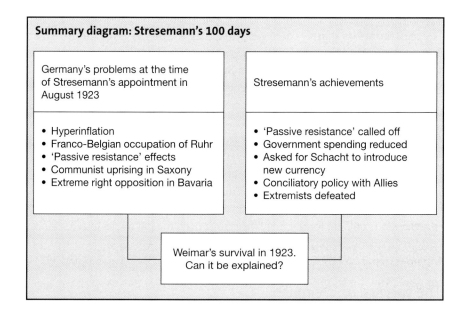

Summary diagram: Stresemann's 100 days

Germany's problems at the time of Stresemann's appointment in August 1923

- Hyperinflation
- Franco-Belgian occupation of Ruhr
- 'Passive resistance' effects
- Communist uprising in Saxony
- Extreme right opposition in Bavaria

Stresemann's achievements

- 'Passive resistance' called off
- Government spending reduced
- Asked for Schacht to introduce new currency
- Conciliatory policy with Allies
- Extremists defeated

Weimar's survival in 1923. Can it be explained?

Key debate

▶ *What was the true nature of the German Revolution?*

At first, Weimar itself was not a subject of extensive research by historians. If it was, they concentrated on the final years regarding its collapse and the Nazi seizure of power. It was not really until the 1950s (in the wake of the Nazi defeat and the division of Germany in 1949 into two politically very different regimes) that the German Revolution 1918–19 became the focus of more academic debate.

An achievement? The liberal democratic view

Most historians in West Germany, such as E. Eyck and K.D. Erdmann, assumed that there had only ever been two possible options available to Germany at the end of the war: the people were torn between a communist dictatorship and a parliamentary republic in the style of Weimar. In this light, Ebert's decisions were portrayed as those of a heroic figure whose actions had created a parliamentary democracy and saved Germany from Bolshevism. Erdmann succinctly states that there was a clear choice between: 'social revolution in line with forces demanding for a **proletarian dictatorship**, or a parliamentary republic in line with the conservative elements like the German officer corps'.

A tragic disaster? The Marxist view

In contrast, historians in communist East Germany viewed the German Revolution as an unsuccessful proletarian revolution. Partly this was because the masses had not yet been sufficiently organised, because the Communist Party was not founded until early 1919. In addition, they saw the actions of the SPD betraying the left-wing movement. Even worse, they felt that Ebert had decided to collaborate with the traditional forces of the army and industry. In their view, the real heroes were the Spartacists, who had stuck to their true revolutionary ideas and died on the barricades in Berlin.

EXTRACT 1

From A. Dorpalen, *German History in Marxist Perspective. The East German Approach*, Hamish Hamilton, 1985, pp. 314–15.

To anyone viewing revolutions as engines of social progress, Ebert's concern with restoring order carried little conviction. It seemed a manoeuvre to salvage the old power apparatus in open betrayal of the revolution and the government's own supporters. In its blind struggle against the revolution … the new regime did not purge the bureaucracy of its non-democratic elements, but retained the old imperial officials right up to the minister level. In the same vein, Ebert entered an alliance with the old militarist forces – those mortal enemies of the nation – thus shielding the officer corps from all revolutionary aspirations inside and outside the Army. Similarly the government sanctioned a pact between labour unions and the private capitalist employers.

 **KEY TERM**

Proletariat dictatorship
The Marxist theory of a state in which the working class controls power.

 In Extract 1, what are the criticisms of Ebert and the SPD?

A failed compromise? The revised view of social historians

Yet, the view of an influential group of social historians in the 1970s in West Germany was that the social base for change in Germany was wider than it had been previously believed. The analysis by Kolb and Rürup about the workers' councils movement has shown that very few fell under the control of the extreme revolutionary left. The vast majority were led by the SPD with USPD support and that the threat from the revolutionary communists was grossly exaggerated. They may well have been vocal in putting forward their revolutionary plans, but their actual base of support was minimal. So, according to their interpretations, the revolution still amounted to little more than a political and constitutional revolution, which fell short of bringing about any radical changes in the social and economic structure of Germany. The historian H.U. Wehler sees the revolution as an uneasy compromise between two elements – the 'revolution from above' and the 'revolution from below'. As a result, the conservative traditional forces managed to control and manipulate events. More cautiously, H.A. Winkler claims:

EXTRACT 2

From H.A. Winkler, quoted in E. Kolb, *The Weimar Republic*, Routledge, 1988, p. 145.

First: the governing Social Democrats could not, without provoking chaos, avoid some degree of co-operation with leading elements of the old regime. Secondly: the extent of that co-operation … was considerably greater than the situation required. In other words, if the Social Democrats had shown a greater degree of political will, they could have altered more and would not have had to preserve so much.

? According to Extract 2, what was wrong with the level of co-operation shown between the SPD and the old order?

'A Very German Revolution'? In opposition to the received view

More recently, the New Zealand historian C. Fischer has come to criticise the long-established dominant view that the German Revolution had failed to achieve fundamental social change. He proposes that it is too simple to denounce the revolution as a weak compromise, judged by some social historians as a failure when matched against the model of normal revolutions. Instead, he believes that in the circumstances of Germany's defeat and the financial costs imposed, the revolution was not a feeble compromise – in his view it was in many respects a remarkable achievement.

EXTRACT 3

From C. Fischer, 'A Very German Settlement'? The Post-1918 Settlement Revaluated, GHIL Bulletin, 2006, pp. 31–2.

1918 was, indeed, a very German revolution but then, on the whole, countries tend to get the revolutions they have earned. On those terms Germany's revolutionary settlement was sufficiently practical yet visionary to offer the country a viable future, for it represented a readiness on each side to accommodate the other, and thus was a triumph of moderation over utopian extremism in all its forms.

In spite of this, Weimar failed, but in 1920 the reasons for this lay as much in the future as in Germany's historical legacy, and international forces would play as great a part in this disaster as domestic factors.

> According to Extract 3, what was so successful about the German Revolution?

Chapter summary

By the late summer of 1918 it was clear to the military leadership that the war was lost. Ludendorff then initiated proposals with the October reform in the hope of preserving Imperial Germany. Yet, they were not enough to satisfy the people; the social discontent led rapidly to populist opposition and the abdication of the Kaiser and the declaration of a republic. Clearly, therefore, the German Revolution was a crucial historical development. By summer 1919, Ebert's new regime had stood up for a parliamentary democracy and successfully held national elections. Moreover, the Weimar constitution was passed convincingly and the government had overcome some powerful opposition from the revolutionary left wing.

From the very start the republic was still threatened from the extreme left and the extreme right. Both sides could not tolerate the democracy and were quite prepared to resort to various forms of political violence. As for the Treaty of Versailles, the terms were not actually so damning. However, their severity as perceived in the German mind added fuel to Weimar's critics, especially from the influence of powerful conservative institutions, such as the army and the judiciary.

On top of that, the hyperinflation brought things to a head in 1923. Although a minority of the population was able to pay off their debts with borrowed money in useless notes, those with savings and set incomes were hit very badly.

Yet, quite surprisingly, Weimar did survive 1923 – in contrast to the 1930s. In his 100 days Stresemann showed resolution with his political and economic initiatives, while the political extremists revealed their limitations. The question was whether after the trauma of those years the new republic really could stabilise and develop into a mature democracy.

Refresher questions

Use these questions to remind yourself of the key material covered in this chapter.

1 What was the 'stab in the back' myth and why was it so significant?

2 How and why did the October reform fail to prevent revolution in November?

3 In what ways was the left-wing movement divided?

4 What were the main problems faced by Ebert's government?

5 Why did the Spartacist revolt fail?

6 What are the arguments for and against the terms of the Weimar constitution?

7 Did the Treaty of Versailles fundamentally weaken Weimar Germany?

8 Was the failure of the extreme left caused by its own weaknesses?

9 What did the extreme right stand for and how did it manifest this?

10 Explain the significance of the *Reichstag* election result of 1920.

11 Why did Weimar democracy struggle to form workable governments?

12 Why did the democratic parties lose votes in 1920 compared to 1919?

13 Were Germany's debts from the First World War the major cause of the hyperinflation?

14 Why were there some winners and some losers in the inflation?

15 How did Weimar manage to survive the crisis of 1923?

 Question practice

ESSAY QUESTIONS

1 Assess the reasons for the outbreak of the German Revolution.

2 How serious were the economic problems for the Weimar Republic?

3 Which of the following was the greater threat to the stability of the Weimar Republic? i) The Weimar constitution. ii) The Treaty of Versailles. Explain your answer with reference to both i) and ii).

4 'The main threat to the Weimar Republic in the period 1919–23 was the extreme right.' How far do you agree with this statement?

INTERPRETATION QUESTION

1 Read the interpretation and then answer the question that follows. 'It is no longer acceptable to blame the ultimate failure of the Republic on the Treaty of Versailles.' (From J. Hiden, *The Weimar Republic*, 1996.) Evaluate the strengths and limitations of this interpretation, making reference to other interpretations that you have studied.

CHAPTER 2

Weimar's 'golden years'

It is generally held that after the turmoil of the early 1920s, the years 1924–9 were a time of recovery and stability in German history. Indeed, it is quite common to refer to the period as the 'golden twenties'. The purpose of this chapter is to consider the accuracy of this picture by examining the following sections:

★ The German economic recovery
★ Political stability
★ Stresemann's foreign policy achievements
★ Culture
★ Weimar 1924–9: an overview

Key dates

1922		Treaty of Rapallo	**1926**		Germany joined the League of Nations
1923–9		Stresemann as foreign minister	**1928**	**May**	Müller's Grand Coalition created
1924	**April**	Dawes Plan		**Aug.**	Kellogg–Briand Pact
1925	**Feb. 28**	Death of Ebert	**1929**	**June**	Young Plan proposals (adopted in March 1930)
	April	Hindenburg elected president			
	Oct.	Locarno Conference		**Oct.**	Death of Stresemann

 1 # The German economic recovery

▶ *How much did the Weimar economy really recover in the 'golden twenties'?*

It is often claimed that after the hyperinflation, the introduction of the new currency – the *Rentenmark* – and the measures brought about by the Dawes Plan ushered in five years of economic growth and affluence. Certainly the period stands out between the economic chaos of 1922–3 and the **Great Depression** of 1929–33. So, for many Germans looking back from the end of the 1920s, it seemed as if Germany had made a remarkable recovery.

 **KEY TERM**

Great Depression
The severe economic crisis of 1929–33 started in the USA by the Wall Street Crash; marked by mass unemployment, falling prices and a lack of spending.

The strengths of the German economy

In spite of the loss of resources as a result of the Treaty of Versailles, heavy industry was able to recover reasonably quickly and, by 1928, production levels had reached those of 1913. This was the result of the use of more efficient methods of production, particularly in coal-mining and steel manufacture, and also because of increased investment. Foreign bankers were particularly attracted by Germany's high interest rates. Large American corporations, such as Ford and General Motors, invested massively in factories with more efficient methods of mass production.

At the same time, German industry had the advantage of being able to lower costs because of the growing number of **cartels**, which had better purchasing power than smaller industries. For example, IG Farben, the chemicals giant, became the largest manufacturing enterprise in Europe, while Vereinigte Stahlwerke combined the coal, iron and steel interests of Germany's great industrial companies and grew to control nearly half of all production.

Between 1925 and 1929 German **exports** rose by 40 per cent. Such economic progress brought social benefits as well. Hourly wage rates rose every year from 1924 to 1930 and by as much as five to ten per cent in 1927 and 1928.

Social welfare

Although the state of Imperial Germany had introduced social care in the 1880s, the Weimar Republic made striking improvements in the provision of welfare. The Weimar constitution incorporated basic social rights and aimed to address social provision through the creation of a welfare state. Significantly, in the hope of creating a more equal society, Erzberger, as finance minister, had aimed clearly to offset the costs by implementing a series of **progressive taxes**, including increasing taxes on capital and an increase in the highest income tax from four per cent to 60 per cent.

KEY TERMS

Cartel An arrangement between businesses to control the market by exercising a joint monopoly.

Exports Goods sold to foreign countries.

Progressive tax A tax system in which those who earn higher incomes pay a higher percentage of their income than those with lower incomes.

Social legislation

- Working conditions. As a result of the Stinnes–Legien agreement (see page 9) various laws were introduced restricting the maximum working week to 48 hours and a state scheme for compulsory arbitration in strikes.
- War victims. Benefits and pensions for widows and the wounded were included from 1920 in the welfare scheme.
- National Youth Welfare Law (1922). Programmes for the young from poor backgrounds were established, as well as provision for youth clubs and sports facilities.

- Health and pensions. The new National Insurance Code extended welfare in various laws (1923–5):
  - more standardised pensions
  - an improved health insurance scheme provided by doctors and insurance funds
  - accident insurance for occupational diseases, for example in the chemical industry and the mines.
- Unemployment. The Unemployment Insurance Law of 1927 created a system covering 17 million workers which offered benefits at 75 per cent of pay for three-quarters of a year (the largest scheme in the world).

Table 2.1 Public health

Before 1914	After 1920
Deaths from tuberculosis in 1913: 143 in 10,000 Deaths from pneumonia in 1913: 119 in 10,000 4.8 doctors per 10,000 people in 1909 63.1 hospital beds per 10,000 people in 1910	Deaths from tuberculosis in 1928: 87 in 10,000 Deaths from pneumonia in 1928: 93 in 10,000 7.4 doctors per 10,000 people in 1930 90.9 hospital beds per 10,000 people in 1930

In addition, large state subsidies were provided for the construction of local amenities such as parks, schools, sport facilities, council houses and especially hospitals and health care (see Table 2.1). Over 2 million houses were built between 1924 and 1931 – and a further 200,000 renovated – so that the figure of homelessness was reduced by 60 per cent in the decade. All these developments, alongside the more obvious signs of wealth, for example the increase in the number of cars, supported the view that the Weimar Republic's economy was enjoying boom conditions. However, revenue did not match expenditure, meaning that the social costs had serious financial implications for the economy of the Weimar Republic (see pages 62–3).

The weaknesses in the German economy

From the statistics for 1924–9 it is easy to get an impression that there was a 'golden age'. However, the actual rate of German recovery was less clear:

- The economic growth was uneven, and in 1926 production actually declined. In overseas trade, the value of **imports** always exceeded that of exports.
- Unemployment never fell below 1.3 million in this period. And even before the effects of the USA's financial crisis began to be felt, the number of unemployed workers averaged 1.9 million in 1929.
- In agriculture, grain production was still only three-quarters of its 1913 figure and farmers, many of whom were in debt, faced falling incomes. By the late 1920s, income per head in agriculture was 44 per cent below the national average.

Fundamental economic problems

The economic indicators listed above suggest that the German economy had fundamental problems in this period and it is therefore important to appreciate the broader view by looking at the following points:

- *World economic conditions did not favour Germany.* Traditionally, Germany had relied on its ability to export to achieve economic growth, but world trade did not return to pre-war levels. German exports were hindered by protective **tariffs** in many parts of the world. They were additionally handicapped by the loss of valuable resources in territories such as Alsace-Lorraine and Silesia (see pages 22–3) as a result of the Versailles Treaty.

 **KEY TERMS**

Imports Goods purchased from foreign countries.

Tariffs Taxes levied by an importing nation on foreign goods coming in, and paid by the importers.

- *German agriculture.* The German peasantry made up one-third of the national population and found itself in difficulties because of worldwide pressures. The fall in world prices from the mid-1920s placed a great strain on farmers, who were simply failing to make a profit. Support in the form of government financial aid and tariffs could help only partially to reduce the problem. This decline in income reduced the spending power of a large section of the population and this led to a fall in demand within the economy as a whole.
- *The changing balance of the population.* From the mid-1920s, there were more school leavers because of the high pre-war birth rate. The available workforce increased from 32.4 million in 1925 to 33.4 million in 1931. This meant that, even without a recession, there was always likely to be an increase in unemployment in Germany.
- *Savings and investment discouraged.* Savers had lost a great deal of money in the Great Inflation and, after 1924, there was less enthusiasm to invest money again. As a result, the German economy came to rely on investors from abroad, for example the USA, who were attracted by the prospect of higher interest rates than those in their own countries. Germany's economic well-being became ever more dependent on foreign investment.
- *Government finances raised concern.* Although the government succeeded in balancing the budget in 1924, from 1925 it was in ongoing debt. It continued to spend increasing sums of money and by 1928 public expenditure had reached 26 per cent of **GNP**, which was double the pre-war figure. Such a situation did not provide the basis for solid future economic growth.

'A sick economy'?

It has been suggested that the problems faced by the German economy before the world **depression** of 1929 were disguised by the flood of foreign capital and by the development of an extensive social welfare system. The German economy was in a poor state because:

- foreign loans made it liable to suffer from any problems that arose in the world economy
- investment was too low to encourage growth
- the cost of the welfare state could be met only by the government's taking on increasing debts
- the agricultural sector faced serious problems from the mid-1920s and various sectors of the German economy had actually started to slow down from 1927.

KEY TERMS

GNP Gross national product is the total value of all goods and services in a nation's economy (including income derived from assets abroad).

Depression An economic downturn marked by mass unemployment, falling prices and a lack of spending.

The Deutsche Bank reported in 1928:

SOURCE A

From the annual report of the Deutsche Bank, quoted in Ian Kershaw, editor, *Weimar: Why Did German Democracy Fail?*, Weidenfeld & Nicolson, 1990, p. 163.

[It referred to] … the complete inner weakness of our economy. It is so overloaded with taxes required by the excessively expensive apparatus of the state, with over-high social payments, and particularly with the reparations sum now reaching its 'normal' level [as laid down by the Dawes Plan] that any healthy growth is constricted. Development is only possible to the extent that these restrictive chains are removed.

What weaknesses did the Deutsche Bank identify in the economy? To what extent is Source A of value to a historian?

Whether the above weaknesses are enough to support the view of Weimar Germany as 'an abnormal, in fact a sick economy', as claimed by the historian K. Borchardt, remains controversial, and it is hard to assess what might have happened without the world economic crisis. However, it is interesting that Stresemann wrote in 1928, 'Germany is dancing on a volcano. If the short-term credits are called in, a large section of our economy would collapse.' So, on balance, the evidence suggests that by 1929 the Weimar Republic was facing serious difficulties and was already heading for a major economic downturn of its own making.

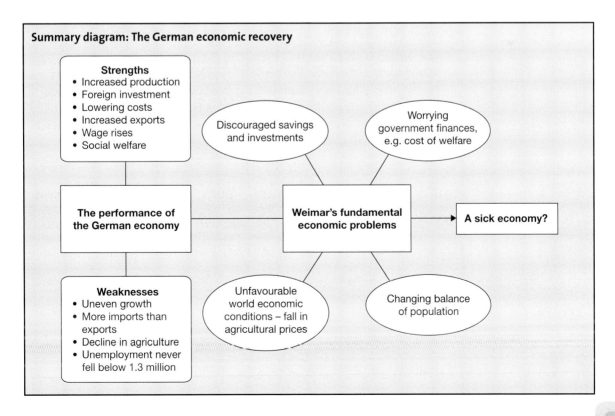

Summary diagram: The German economic recovery

Strengths
- Increased production
- Foreign investment
- Lowering costs
- Increased exports
- Wage rises
- Social welfare

Discouraged savings and investments

Worrying government finances, e.g. cost of welfare

The performance of the German economy

Weimar's fundamental economic problems

A sick economy?

Weaknesses
- Uneven growth
- More imports than exports
- Decline in agriculture
- Unemployment never fell below 1.3 million

Unfavourable world economic conditions – fall in agricultural prices

Changing balance of population

(2) Political stability

▶ *How politically stable was Weimar in the years 1924–9?*

The election results during the middle years of the Weimar Republic gave grounds for cautious optimism about its survival (see Table 2.2). The extremist parties of both left and right lost ground and altogether they polled less than 30 per cent of the votes cast:

● The DNVP peaked in December 1924 with 103 seats (20.5 per cent of the vote) and fell back to 73 (14.2 per cent) in May 1928.
● The Nazis lost ground in both elections and were reduced to only twelve seats (2.6 per cent) by 1928.
● The KPD, although recovering slightly by 1928 with 54 seats (10.6 per cent), remained below their performance of May 1924 and well below the combined votes gained by the KPD and USPD in June 1920 (see page 41).

In comparison, the parties sympathetic to the republic maintained their share of the vote and the SPD made substantial gains, winning 153 seats (29.8 per cent) in 1928. As a result, following the 1928 election, a 'Grand Coalition' of the SPD, DDP, DVP and ZP was formed under Hermann Müller, the leader of the SPD. It enjoyed the support of over 60 per cent of the *Reichstag* and it seemed as if democracy was at last beginning to emerge in Weimar politics.

Coalition politics

The election of 1928 must not be regarded as typical in Weimar history, and it should not hide the basic weaknesses of the German parliamentary system. These included not only the problems created by proportional representation (see page 17), but also the ongoing difficulty of creating and maintaining coalitions from the various parties. In such a situation each party tended to put its own self-interests before those of the government.

Table 2.2 Weimar *Reichstag* election results 1924 and 1928. (See also major political parties on page 13)

	Turnout	NSDAP	DNVP	DVP	ZP/BVP	DDP	SPD	KPD	Others
May 1924									
Seats	472	32	95	45	81	28	100	62	29
%	77.4	6.5	19.5	9.2	15.6	5.7	20.5	12.6	10.3
December 1924									
Seats	493	14	103	51	88	32	131	45	29
%	78.8	3.0	20.5	9.2	17.3	6.3	26.0	9.0	7.8
May 1928									
Seats	491	12	73	45	78	25	153	54	51
%	75.6	2.6	14.2	8.7	15.2	4.9	29.8	10.8	14.0

The parties tended to reflect their traditional interests: religion and class. So attempts to widen their appeal made little progress. As a result, the differences between the main parties meant that opportunities to form workable coalitions were very limited:

- There was never any possibility of a coalition including both the SPD and the DNVP because the former believed in parliamentary democracy whereas the latter fundamentally rejected the Weimar political system.
- The Communists, KPD, remained totally isolated.
- A right–centre coalition of Centre, DVP and DNVP created a situation in which the parties tended to agree on domestic issues, but disagree on foreign affairs.
- On the other hand, a broad coalition of SPD, DDP, DVP and Centre meant that these parties agreed on foreign policy, but differed on domestic issues.
- A minority government of the political centre, including the DDP, DVP and Centre, could only exist by seeking support from either the left or right. It was impossible to create a coalition with a parliamentary majority that could also consistently agree on both domestic and foreign policy.

In this situation, there was little chance of democratic government being able to establish lasting political stability. Of the seven governments between 1923 and 1930 (see Table 2.3), only two had majorities and the longest survived for just 21 months. In fact, the only reason governments lasted as long as they did was that the opposition parties were also unable or unwilling to unite. More often than not, it was conflicts within the parties that formed the coalition governments that led them to collapse.

Table 2.3 Governments of the Weimar Republic 1923–30

Period in office	Chancellor	Make-up of the coalition
1923–4	Wilhelm Marx	Centre, DDP, DVP
1924–5	Wilhelm Marx	Centre, DDP, DVP
1925	Hans Luther	Centre, DVP, DNVP
1926	Hans Luther	Centre, DDP, DVP
1926	Wilhelm Marx	Centre, DDP, DVP
1927–8	Wilhelm Marx	Centre, DDP, DNVP
1928–30	Hermann Müller	SPD, DDP, Centre, DVP

The responsibility of the parties

The attitude of the Weimar Republic's political parties towards parliamentary government was irresponsible. This may well have been a legacy from the imperial years. In that time the parties had expressed their own narrow interests in the knowledge that it was the Kaiser who ultimately decided policy. However, in the 1920s, parliamentary democracy needed the political parties to show a more responsible attitude towards government. The evidence suggests that no such attitude existed, even in the most stable period of the republic's history.

The SPD

Until 1932 the SPD remained the largest party in the *Reichstag*. However, although firm in its support of the republic, the party was divided between its desire to uphold the interests of the working class and its commitment to democracy. Some members, and especially those connected with the trade unions, feared that joining coalitions with other parties would lead to a weakening of their principles. Others, the more moderate, wanted to participate in government in order to influence it. At the same time, the party was hindered by the old argument between those committed to a more extreme left-wing socialist programme and those who favoured moderate, gradual reform.

As a result, during the years of the republic 1920–28, the SPD did not join any of the fragile government coalitions. This obviously weakened the power base of those democratic coalitions from 1924 to 1928. The SPD remained the strongest party during those years: although it was committed to democracy, it was not prepared to take on the responsibility of government until 1928.

The Centre Party

It, therefore, fell to the Centre Party to provide real political leadership in Weimar politics. The ZP electoral support was solid and the party participated in all the coalition governments from 1919 to 1932 by taking ministerial posts. However, its support did not increase because its appeal was restricted to traditional Catholic areas. Further, its social and economic policies, which aimed at bridging the gaps between the classes, led to internal quarrels.

In the early years, such differences had been put to one side under the strong left-wing leadership of Matthias Erzberger and Josef Wirth. However, during the 1920s, the party moved decisively to the right and the divisions within the party widened. In 1928, the leadership eventually passed to Ludwig Kaas and Heinrich Brüning, who appealed more to the conservative partners of the coalition than to the liberal or social democratic elements. This was a worrying sign both for the future of the Centre Party and for Germany itself.

The liberal parties

The position of the German liberals was not a really strong one. The DDP and DVP joined in all the coalition governments of this period, and in Gustav Stresemann, the leader of the DVP, they possessed the republic's only really capable statesman. However, this hid some worrying trends. Their share of the vote, although constant in the mid-1920s, had nearly halved from 22 per cent in 1920 to fourteen per cent by 1928. Indeed, Stresemann addressed the DVP executive committee in these terms on 26 February 1928:

SOURCE B

From Stresemann's speech to the DVP in 1928, quoted in S.J. Lee, *The Weimar Republic*, Routledge, 1998, p. 75.

Let us not fool ourselves about this: we are in the midst of a parliamentary crisis that is already more than a crisis of conscience. The crisis has two roots: one the caricature that has become the parliamentary system in Germany; secondly the complete false position of parliament in relation to its responsibilities to the nation.

> What are the main points of Stresemann's political message in Source B? And why is the context – time and audience – of the source so significant?

The reasons for the liberals' eventual collapse after 1930 were already established beforehand. This decline was largely a result of the divisions within both parties. The DDP lacked clear leadership and its membership was involved in internal bickering over policy. The DVP was also divided and, despite Stresemann's efforts to bring unity to the party, conflict remained. It is not really surprising that moves to bring about some kind of united liberal party came to nothing. As a result, German liberalism failed to gain popular support; and after 1929 its position declined dramatically.

The DNVP

One promising feature of German party politics came unexpectedly from the conservative DNVP. Since 1919, the DNVP had been totally opposed to the republic and it had refused to take part in government. In electoral terms, it had enjoyed considerable success, and in December 1924, gained 103 seats (20.5 per cent). However, as the republic began to recover after the 1923 crisis, it became increasingly clear that the DNVP's hopes of restoring a more right-wing government were diminishing. The continuous opposition policy meant that the party had no real power and achieved nothing. Some influential groups within the DNVP realised that if they were to have any influence on government policy, then the party had to be prepared to participate in government. As a result, in 1925 and 1927, the DNVP joined government coalitions. This more sympathetic attitude towards the Weimar Republic was an encouraging development.

The more conciliatory policy was not popular with all groups within the party. When, in the 1928 election, the DNVP vote fell by a quarter, the more extreme right wing asserted its influence. Significantly, it elected **Alfred Hugenberg**, an extreme nationalist, as the new leader. Hugenberg was Germany's greatest media tycoon: he owned 150 newspapers and a publishing house, and had interests in the film industry. He utterly rejected the idea of a republic based on parliamentary democracy. He now used all his resources to promote his political message. The DNVP reverted to a programme of total opposition to the republic and refused to be involved in government. A year later, his party was working closely with the Nazis against the Young Plan (see pages 76 and 101).

🔑 KEY FIGURE

Alfred Hugenberg (1865–1951)

A civil servant, banker, industrialist and major media proprietor of the 1920s. He was appointed leader of the DNVP in 1928 and then funded Hitler's political campaign.

President Hindenburg

A presidential election was due in 1925. It was assumed that President Friedrich Ebert would be re-elected, so his unexpected death in February 1925 created political problems. There was no clear successor in the first round of the election and so a second round was held. It did result in the choice of Hindenburg as president, but the figures clearly underlined the divisions in German society (see Table 2.4).

Table 2.4 Presidential election, second round, 26 April 1925

Candidate (party)	Votes (millions)	Percentage
Paul von Hindenburg (DNVP)	14.6	48
Wilhelm Marx (ZP)	13.7	45
Ernst Thälmann (KPD)	1.9	6

The appointment of President Hindenburg has remained controversial. On the one hand, on Hindenburg's coming to power there was no immediate swing to the right. The new president proved totally loyal to the constitution and carried

Paul von Hindenburg

1847	Born of a Prussian noble family in Posen and served his whole career in the Prussian Army
1914	Won the victory of the Battle of Tannenberg on the Eastern Front
1916	Promoted to field marshal and military dictator 1916–18
1918	Accepted the defeat of Germany and retired
1925	Elected president of Germany
1930–2	Appointed Brüning, Papen and Schleicher as chancellor
1932	Re-elected president
1933	Persuaded to appoint Hitler as chancellor
1934	Died. Granted a national funeral

Hindenburg was regularly promoted, but his career was seen as 'steady rather than exceptional'. In 1914 he was recalled from retirement and his management of the campaign on the Eastern Front earned him distinction. However, Hindenburg did not have great military skills and was outshone in his partnership with Ludendorff. During the years 1916–18 the two men were effectively the military dictators of Germany.

Although Hindenburg served as president of Germany (1925–34), he accepted the post only reluctantly. He was not a democrat and looked forward to the return of the monarchy. Nevertheless, he took up the responsibility of his office and performed his duties correctly.

From 1930 his significance increased in the political crisis. As president, he was responsible for the appointment of all the chancellors from 1930 to 1934 and he became a crucial player in the political intrigue of the competing forces. Given his authority, Hindenburg was held ultimately responsible for the events that ended with the appointment of Hitler, but he was very old and easily influenced by Papen and Schleicher (see pages 102 and 109). He had no respect for Hitler, but he did not have the will and determination to make a stand against Nazism.

out his presidential duties with correctness. Those nationalists who had hoped that his election might lead to the restoration of the monarchy, or the creation of a military-type regime, were disappointed. Indeed, it has been argued that Hindenburg as president acted as a true substitute kaiser or **Ersatzkaiser**. In that sense, the status of Hindenburg as president at last gave Weimar some respectability in conservative circles.

On the other hand, it is difficult to ignore the pitfalls resulting from the appointment of an old man. In his heart, Hindenburg had no real sympathy for the republic or its values. Those around him were mainly made up of anti-republican figures, many of them from the military. He preferred to include the DNVP in government and, if possible, to exclude the SPD. From the start, Hindenburg's view was that the government should move towards the right, although it was really only after 1929 that the serious implications of his outlook became fully apparent for Weimar democracy. As the historian A.J. Nicholls, writing in 1968, put it: 'he refused to betray the republic, but he did not rally the people to its banner'.

KEY TERM

Ersatzkaiser 'Substitute emperor'. After Marshal Hindenburg was elected president, he provided the *Ersatzkaiser* figure required by the respectable right wing – he was a conservative, a nationalist and a military hero.

The limitations of the political system

During this period the parliamentary and party political system in Germany failed to make any real progress. It just coped as best it could. Government carried out its work but with only limited success. There was no *putsch* from left or right and the anti-republican extremists were contained. Law and order were restored and the activities of the various paramilitary groups were limited.

However, these were only minor and very negative successes and, despite the good intentions of certain individuals and groups, there were no signs of any real strengthening of the political structure. Stable government had not been established. This is not surprising when it is noted that one coalition government collapsed in 1926 over a minor issue about the use of the national flag and the old imperial flag. Another government fell over the creation of religious schools.

Even more significant for the future was the growing contempt and cynicism shown by the people towards party politics. This was particularly connected with the negotiating and bargaining involved in the creation of most coalitions. The turnout of the elections declined in the mid-1920s compared to 1919 and 1920. There was also an increasing growth of small fringe parties. The apparent stability of these years was really a deception, a mirage. It misled some people into believing that a genuine basis for lasting stable government had been achieved. It had not.

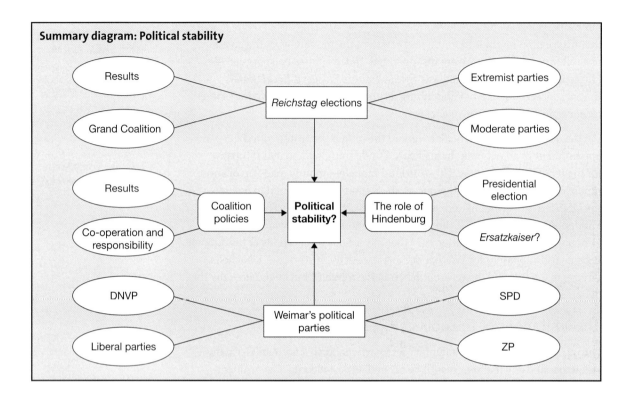

Summary diagram: Political stability

3 # Stresemann's foreign policy achievements

▶ *What were Stresemann's aims in foreign policy?*

▶ *To what extent was Stresemann successful?*

Before 1921–2 there was little to suggest that Stresemann was to become the mainstay of Weimar democracy. In the years before 1914 his nationalism found expression in his support of the Kaiser's **Weltpolitik**, and from the start of the First World War Stresemann was an ardent supporter of the **Siegfriede**. He campaigned for 'unrestricted submarine warfare' and opposed supporters of peace. By 1918 his support for the military regime and the Treaty of Brest-Litovsk had earned him the title of 'Ludendorff's young man' (see page 3). And when the war came to an end in defeat, Stresemann was deliberately excluded from the newly created DDP and, so, was left no real option but to form his own party, the DVP. At first, his party was hostile to the revolution of 1918 and the republic and campaigned for the restoration of the monarchy.

Gustav Stresemann

1878	Born in Berlin, the son of a publican and brewer
1914–18	Nationalist and supporter of Ludendorff and Hindenburg
1919	Formed the DVP and became its leader, 1919–29
1921	Despite opposing Weimar democracy at first, he and the DVP decided to support it
1923	'Stresemann's 100 days' as chancellor of Germany
1923–9	Foreign minister in all governments
1926	Awarded the Nobel Peace Prize
1929	Died of a stroke at the age of 51

Having graduated with an economics degree from Berlin University and having run a successful business career, Stresemann was elected, at 29, the youngest member of the *Reichstag*. He was a committed monarchist and nationalist who strongly supported the expansionist policies of Imperial Germany.

Stresemann was appalled by Germany's defeat and, in his heart, he remained a monarchist who hoped to create a constitutional monarchy. In 1919 he formed the DVP and opposed the Weimar Republic. However, by 1921 he came to recognise the political reality and finally committed himself and his party to the republic.

In the 1923 crisis Stresemann was made chancellor, and it is generally recognised by historians that it marked the climax of his career. All the problems were confronted: the occupation of the Ruhr, the hyperinflation and the opposition from left- and right-wing extremists. Although his term in office lasted for just three months (which became known as 'Stresemann's 100 days'), it laid the basis for the recovery of 1924–9.

Stresemann was foreign minister in all the Weimar governments 1923–9; in effect he was the architect of Weimar foreign policy. He showed a strength of character and a realism which allowed him to negotiate with the Allies and to improve Germany's international position. Nevertheless, he failed to generate real domestic support for Weimar. Indeed, his long-term reputation remains arguable, as he failed to revise the Versailles Treaty fundamentally. It is also questionable whether he could have saved the Weimar Republic from Nazism.

Indeed, it was only after the failed Kapp *putsch* and the murders of Erzberger and Rathenau (page 35) that Stresemann led his party into adopting a more sympathetic approach towards the Weimar Republic. His sudden change of heart has provided plenty of evidence for those critics who have regarded his support of the Weimar Republic as sham. This charge is not entirely fair. Despite the conservatism of his early years, Stresemann's subsequent career shows that he was a committed supporter of constitutional government.

Stresemann's ideal was a constitutional monarchy. But that was not to be. By 1921 he had become convinced that the republic and its constitution provided Germany with its only chance of preventing a dictatorship of either left or right. This was a realistic assessment of the situation and the reason why he was referred to as a ***Vernunftrepublikaner***, a rational republican, rather than a committed one.

 **KEY TERM**

Vernunftrepublikaner
'A rational (pragmatic) republican'. Used in the 1920s to define those people who really wanted Germany to have a constitutional monarchy but who, out of necessity, came to support the democratic Weimar Republic.

Stresemann's foreign policy aims

From the time he became responsible for foreign affairs at the height of the 1923 crisis, Stresemann's foreign policy was shaped by a deep understanding of the domestic and international situations. He recognised, unlike many nationalists, that Germany had been militarily defeated and not simply 'stabbed in the back'. He also rejected the solutions of those hardliners who failed to understand the circumstances that had brought Germany to its knees in 1923.

Stresemann's main aims were to free Germany from the limitations of Versailles and to restore his country to the status of a great power, the equal of Britain and France. Offensive action was ruled out by Stresemann and so his only choice was diplomacy. As he once remarked, he was backed up only by the power of German cultural traditions and the German economy. So, at first, he worked towards his main aims in the 1920s by pursuing the following objectives:

- To recognise that France did rightly have security concerns and that France also controlled the balance of power on the continent. He regarded Franco-German friendship as essential to solving outstanding problems.
- To play on Germany's vital importance to world trade in order to earn the goodwill and co-operation of Britain and the USA. The sympathy of the USA was also vital so as to attract American investment into the German economy.
- To maintain the Rapallo-based friendship with the USSR. He rejected out of hand those 'hardliners' who desired an **alliance** with Soviet Russia and described them as the 'maddest of foreign policy makers'. Stresemann's strategy was in the tradition of Wirth's **fulfilment**.
- To encourage co-operation and peace, particularly with the Western powers of Britain and France. This was in the best interests of Germany to make it the leading power in Europe once again.

The Dawes Plan

The starting point of Stresemann's foreign policy was the issue of reparations. As chancellor, he had called off 'passive resistance' and agreed to resume the payment of reparations. The result of this was the US-backed Dawes Plan (see Figure 2.1), which was described as 'a victory for financial realism'. Despite opposition from the right wing it was accepted in April 1924.

Although the Dawes Plan left the actual sum to be paid unchanged, the monthly instalments over the first five years were calculated according to Germany's capacity to pay. Furthermore, it provided for a large loan to Germany to aid economic recovery. For Stresemann, its advantages were many:

- For the first time since the First World War, Germany's economic problems received international recognition.
- Germany gained credit for the cash-starved German economy by means of the loan and subsequent investments.
- It resulted in a French promise to evacuate the Ruhr during 1925.

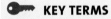
KEY TERMS

Alliance An agreement where members promise to support the other(s) if one or more of them is attacked.

Fulfilment The policy of conforming to the terms of the Versailles Treaty, while aiming for a moderate revision of the terms. It was initiated by Joseph Wirth in 1921–2 and later pursued by Stresemann.

THE DAWES PLAN 1924

The reorganisation of German currency
- One new *Rentenmark* was to be worth one billion of the old marks.
- The setting up of a German national bank, the *Reichsbank*, under Allied supervision.

An international loan of 800 million gold marks to aid German economic recovery
- The loan was to be financed mainly by the USA.

New arrangements for the payment of reparations
- Payment to be made annually at a fixed scale over a longer period.

Figure 2.1 The Dawes Plan 1924.

In the short term, the Dawes Plan was a success. The German economy was not weakened, since it received twice as much capital from abroad as it paid out in reparations. The mere fact that reparations were being paid regularly contributed to the improved relations between France and Germany during these years. However, the whole system was dangerously dependent on the continuation of American loans, as can be seen in Figure 2.2. In attempting to break out of the crisis of 1923, Stresemann had linked Germany's fortunes to powerful external forces, which had dramatic effects after 1929.

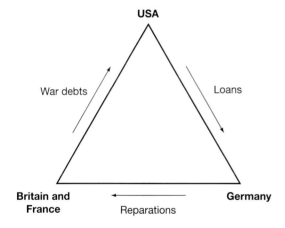

Figure 2.2 The reparations triangle in the 1920s.

The Locarno Pact

The ending of the occupation of the Ruhr and the introduction of the Dawes Plan showed that the Great Powers were prepared to take Germany's interests seriously. However, Stresemann continued to fear that Anglo-French friendship could lead to a military alliance. In order to ease this concern, Stresemann proposed an international security pact for Germany's western frontiers. Although France was at first hesitant, Britain and the USA both backed the idea.

In October 1925 a series of treaties was signed which became known as the Locarno Pact. The main points were:

- A **mutual guarantee agreement** accepted the Franco-German and Belgian–German borders. These terms were guaranteed by Britain and Italy. All five countries renounced the use of force, except in self-defence.
- The demilitarisation of the Rhineland was recognised as permanent.
- **Arbitration treaties** between Germany, Poland and Czechoslovakia agreed to settle future disputes peacefully – but the existing frontiers were not accepted as final.

To see the territories affected by the Treaty of Locarno, refer to the map on page 23.

The Locarno treaties represented an important diplomatic development. Germany was freed from its isolation by the Allies and was again treated as an equal partner. Stresemann had achieved a great deal at Locarno at very little cost. He had confirmed the existing frontiers in the west, since Germany was in no position to change the situation. In so doing he had also limited France's freedom of action since the occupation of the Ruhr or the annexation of the Rhineland was no longer possible. Moreover, by establishing the beginnings of a solid basis for Franco-German understanding, Stresemann had lessened France's need to find allies in eastern Europe. The Poles viewed the treaties as a major setback, since Stresemann had deliberately refused to confirm the frontiers in the east.

Further diplomatic progress

Stresemann hoped that further advances would follow Locarno, such as the restoration of full German rule over the Saar and the Rhineland, a reduction in reparations and a revision of the eastern frontier. However, although there was further diplomatic progress in the years 1926–30 it remained limited:

- Germany had originally been excluded from the League of Nations (see page 24) but, in 1926, it was invited to join the League and was immediately recognised as a permanent member of the Council of the League.
- Two years later, in 1928, Germany signed the Kellogg–Briand Pact, a declaration that outlawed 'war as an instrument of national policy'. Although of no real practical effect, it showed that Germany was co-operating with 68 nations.
- In 1929 the Allies agreed to evacuate the Rhineland earlier than intended, in return for a final settlement of the reparations issue. The result was the Young Plan, which further revised the scheme of payments. Germany now agreed to continue to pay reparations until 1988, although the total sum was reduced to £1850 million, only one-quarter of the figure demanded in 1921 (see page 24).

The Treaty of Berlin

Although Stresemann viewed friendship with the West as his priority, he was not prepared to drop the Rapallo Treaty. He was still determined to stay on good terms with the USSR. As a result, the two countries signed the Treaty of Berlin in April 1926 in order to continue the basis of a good Russo-German relationship. This was not double-dealing by Stresemann, but was simply a recognition that Germany's defence needs in the heart of Europe meant that it had to have understanding with both the East and the West. The treaty with the Soviet Union therefore reduced strategic fears on Germany's Eastern Front and placed even more pressure on Poland to give way to German demands for frontier changes. It also opened up the possibility of a large commercial market and increased military co-operation.

Assessment of Stresemann: success or failure?

In 1926 Stresemann was awarded the Nobel Peace Prize (along with his British and French counterparts, Aristide Briand and Austen Chamberlain). Only three years later, at the early age of 51, he died suddenly of a stroke.

Stresemann has always been the focus of debate. He has been regarded by some as a fanatical nationalist and by others as a 'great European' working for international reconciliation. He has been praised for his staunch support of parliamentary government, but condemned for pretending to be a democrat. He has also been portrayed as an idealist on the one hand and an opportunist on the other.

SOURCE C

How does the cartoonist portray Stresemann in Source C?

'He looks to the right, he looks to the left – he will save me.' (The little boy is the 'German Michael' – a stereotype for the naïve German.) A cartoon drawn in 1923 about Stresemann.

Stresemann achieved a great deal in a short time to change both Germany's domestic and international positions. Moreover, the improvement had been achieved by peaceful methods. When one also considers the dire situation he inherited in 1923 with forces, both internal and external, stacked against him, it is perhaps not surprising that his policy has been described as 'astonishingly successful' (E. Kolb) and he has been referred to as 'Weimar's greatest statesman' (J. Wright).

Nevertheless, it should be borne in mind that the circumstances in the years 1924–9 were working strongly in Stresemann's favour. M. Walsdorff in 1971 was more critical of Stresemann for failing to achieve his fundamental aims to revise Versailles. He argues, first, that Stresemann overestimated his ability to establish friendly relations with other powers. Second, he suggests that the limits and slow pace of the changes had resulted in a dead end – and there was no hint of any revision of the Polish frontier.

Also, Stresemann's policies failed to generate broad enough domestic support for Weimar. The right wing was always totally against 'fulfilment' and, although a minority, they became increasingly loud and influential so that, by the time of Stresemann's death, the nationalist opposition was already mobilising itself against the Young Plan (see pages 101–2). Even more significantly, it seems that the silent majority had not really been won over by Stresemann's policy of conciliation. Consequently, by 1929 his policy had not had time to establish itself and generate sufficient support to survive the difficult circumstances of the 1930s.

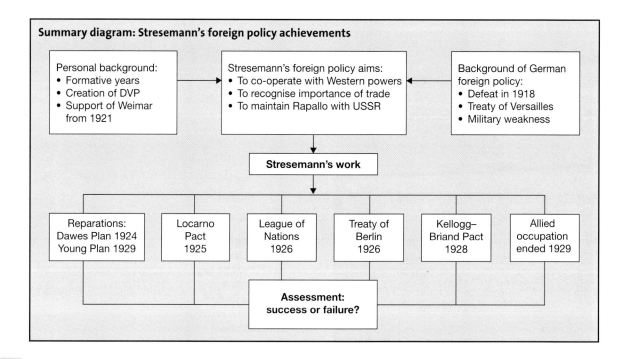

Summary diagram: Stresemann's foreign policy achievements

Culture

▶ *In what ways were the 1920s a culturally rich period?*

▶ *Why was there a conflict of cultures in Weimar Germany?*

The Weimar years witnessed an explosion of culture that affected many aspects of German life. Its roots pre-dated 1914, but Imperial Germany had in the main been conservative, authoritarian and conformist. In contrast, in the wake of the war and defeat, the Weimar Republic became a more liberal society that upheld **toleration** and reduced censorship. This also coincided with dramatic changes in communication – the emergence of film and the radio. All this encouraged many cultural artists to express themselves openly in Weimar Germany and contributed to the label of the 'golden years', as described by William Shirer, the European correspondent of the American newspaper, the *Chicago Tribune*:

> *A wonderful ferment was working in Germany. Life seemed more free, more modern, more exciting than in any place I had ever seen. Nowhere else did the arts or the intellectual life seem so lively … In contemporary writing, painting, architecture, in music and drama, there were new currents and fine talents.*

The new cultural ferment

The term generally used to reflect the cultural developments in Weimar Germany was **Neue Sachlichkeit**. It can be translated as 'new practicality' or 'new functionalism', which means essentially a desire to show reality and objectivity. These words are best explained by looking at some of the major examples of different art forms.

Art

Artists in favour of the 'new objectivity' broke away from the traditional nostalgia of the nineteenth century. They wanted to understand ordinary people in everyday life – and through their art they aimed to comment on the state of society. This approach was epitomised by Georg Grosz and Otto Dix, whose paintings and caricatures in a seedy and aggressive style had strong political and social messages.

Architecture and design

One of the most striking artistic developments in Weimar Germany was the Bauhaus school led by the architect Walter Gropius, which was established in 1919 in the town of Weimar itself. The Bauhaus movement was a new style that influenced all aspects of design – furniture, urban planning, pottery, textiles and graphics. Its approach was functional and it emphasised the close relationship between art and technology, which is underlined by its motto 'Art and Technology – a new unity'. It used materials such as steel, cement and plastic, in geometric designs. It was profoundly resisted among more conservative circles.

KEY TERMS

Toleration Acceptance of alternative political, religious and cultural views.

Neue Sachlichkeit 'New functionalism'. A form of art that developed in post-war Germany which tried to express reality with a more objective view of the world.

Literature

It is impossible to categorise the rich range of writing which emerged in Weimar Germany. Not all writers were **expressionists** influenced by the *Neue Sachlichkeit*. For example, the celebrated Thomas Mann, who won the Nobel Prize for literature, was not part of that movement. In fact, the big sellers were the authors who wrote traditional nostalgic literature – such as Hans Grimm. In the more *avant garde* style were the works of Arnold Zweig and Peter Lampel, who explored a range of social issues growing out of the distress and misery of working people in the big cities. Two particular books to be remembered are: the pacifist *All Quiet on the Western Front*, published in 1928 by Erich Maria Remarque, an ex-soldier critical of the First World War; and *Berlin Alexanderplatz*, written by Alfred Döblin, which examined the life of a worker in Weimar society.

Theatre

In drama, *Neue Sachlichkeit* developed into what was called *Zeittheater* (theatre of the time), which introduced new dramatic methods often with explicit left-wing sympathies – and were most evident in the plays of Bertolt Brecht and Erwin Piscator. They used innovative techniques such as banners, slogans, film and slides, and adopted controversial methods to portray characters' behaviour in their everyday lives.

Mass culture

The 1920s were a time of dramatic changes that saw the emergence of a modern mass culture. Germany was no exception. It saw the development of mass communication methods and international influences, especially from the USA, such as jazz music and consumerism.

Film

During the 1920s, the German film industry became the most advanced in Europe and there were more cinemas in the country than elsewhere in Europe. German film-makers were also well respected for their high-quality work. Most notable of the films of the time were:

- *Metropolis* (1926) by the film-maker Fritz Lang: a sci-fi classic that raised frightening issues about the direction of modern industrialised society.
- *Fridericus Rex* (*King Frederick the Great*, 1922): a traditional, patriotic epic.
- *Blue Angel* (1930), with the young actress Marlene Dietrich: the first big German 'talkie', which openly played on female glamour and touched on sexual issues.

However, although the German film market was very much dominated by the organisation UFA, run by Alfred Hugenberg (see page 67), from the mid-1920s American 'movies' quickly made an exceptional impact. The popular appeal of the comedy of Charlie Chaplin shows that Weimar culture was part of an international mass culture and was not exclusively German.

Radio

Radio also emerged very rapidly as another mass medium. The German Radio Company was established in 1923 and, in the following year, a radio network and nine companies were set up to serve different regions across the country. By 1932, despite the depression, one in four Germans owned a radio.

Cabaret

Berlin had all the traditional features of high culture but in the 1920s a vibrant nightlife also developed. Cabaret clubs opened up with a permissiveness that mocked the conventions of the old Germany: satirical comedy, jazz music and women dancers (and even wrestlers) in varying degrees of nudity. At parties there was an interest in sexual experimentation that included transvestism and homosexuality.

The conflict of cultures

It is easy to assume that Weimar was an exciting and vibrant era which celebrated its liberal creativity and culture. However, there were some respected conservative intellectuals, like Arthur Möller and Oswald Spengler, who condemned the new democratic and industrial society. Moreover, many of the writers in the 1920s opposed pacifism and proudly glorified the sacrifices of the First World War.

Much of the reaction against *Neue Sachlichkeit* simply reflected the broader doubts and tensions in Weimar society. Berlin was not typical of Germany, but it left a very powerful impression – both positive and negative. Some could enjoy and appreciate the cultural experimentation, but most Germans were horrified by what they saw as the decline in established moral and cultural standards.

It has also been suggested that Weimar culture never established a genuinely tolerant attitude. The *avant garde* and the conservatives were clearly at odds with each other. Ironically, although both sides took advantage of the freedoms and permissiveness of Weimar liberalism, they still remained critical of each other. Weimar society was becoming increasingly **polarised** before the onset of the political and economic crisis in 1929.

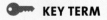 **KEY TERM**

Polarisation The division of society into distinctly opposite views (the comparison is to the north and south poles).

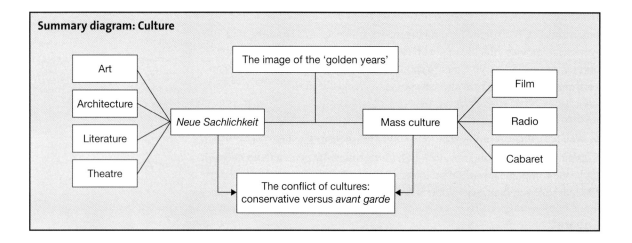

Summary diagram: Culture

- Art
- Architecture
- Literature
- Theatre

→ Neue Sachlichkeit

The image of the 'golden years'

Mass culture
- Film
- Radio
- Cabaret

The conflict of cultures: conservative versus avant garde

5 Weimar 1924–9: an overview

▶ *To what extent had Weimar stabilised in the years 1924–9?*

The years 1924–9 marked the high point of the Weimar Republic. By comparison with the periods before and after, these years do appear stable. The real increase in prosperity experienced by many, and the cultural vitality of the period, gave support to the view that these years were indeed the 'golden years'. However, historians have generally tended to question this stability because it was in fact limited in scope. This is the reason why the historian D. Peukert describes these years as a 'deceptive stability'.

A weak economy?

Germany's economic recovery was built on poor foundations that created a false idea of prosperity. Problems persisted in the economy and they were temporarily hidden only by an increasing reliance on credit from abroad. Consequently, Germany's economy became tied up with powerful external forces over which it had no control. Hindsight now allows historians to see that, in the late 1920s, any disruption to the world's trade or finance markets was bound to have a particularly damaging effect on the uncertain German economy.

A divided society?

German society was still divided by deep class differences that prevented the development of national agreement and harmony. The introduction of the state scheme for compulsory arbitration in strikes in 1919 did not fully overcome concerns between employers and their workers. Its procedure was used as a matter of course, whereas the intention had been that it would be the exception, not the rule. As a result, there was arbitration in some 76,000 industrial disputes between 1924 and 1932. In 1928 workers were locked out from their place of work in the Ruhr ironworks when the employers refused to accept the arbitration award. It was the most serious industrial confrontation of the Weimar period. A compromise solution was achieved, but it showed the extent of bitterness and division in industrial relations, even before the start of the depression. Ironically, even social welfare, which was meant to be integrating for society, was not so well received: the employers were concerned at the growing cost of their contributions, while the peasantry grew resentful as they did not benefit.

A fractured political system?

Tension was also evident in the political sphere, where the parliamentary system had failed to build on the changes of 1918–19. The original ideals of the constitution had not been developed and there was little sign that it had produced a stable and mature system. In particular, the main democratic parties had still not recognised the necessity of working together in a spirit of compromise. It was not so much the weaknesses of the constitution, but the failure to establish a shared political outlook that led to its instability. Even the successes of Stresemann in the field of foreign affairs were offset by the fact that significant numbers of his fellow countrymen rejected his policy out of hand and pressed for a more hardline approach.

In reality, the middle years of the Weimar Republic were stable only in comparison with the periods before and after. The fundamental problems inherited from the war and the years of crisis had not been fully resolved. In that sense, Weimar's condition in 1929 raised the question: was it strong enough to withstand a storm?

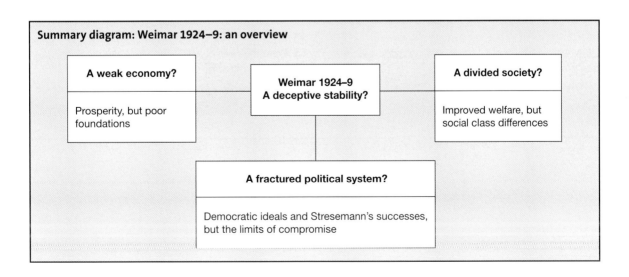

Summary diagram: Weimar 1924–9: an overview

A weak economy?
Prosperity, but poor foundations

**Weimar 1924–9
A deceptive stability?**

A divided society?
Improved welfare, but social class differences

A fractured political system?
Democratic ideals and Stresemann's successes, but the limits of compromise

Chapter summary

In contrast to the chaotic early years of crisis, the 'golden age' afterwards can be seen as a welcome improvement. The restoration of a solid currency with the *Rentenmark* and the decline of political extremists were significant factors in creating a calmer environment. However, all the features of the 'recovery' or the 'stability' were relative. The economy did grow markedly, but the prosperity was built on poor foundations, especially because of the dependence on US loans. The democratic governments did manage to function more effectively and Stresemann could trumpet his diplomatic successes, but the compromises were not generally celebrated. Cultural life thrived, but although welfare improved, the fundamental class divisions in society were not overcome. Therefore, by the end of the decade, it is questionable whether the economic social and political changes amounted to real long-term success for the Weimar Republic.

Refresher questions

Use these questions to remind yourself of the key material covered in this chapter.

1 What were the strengths and the weaknesses of the German economy in the 'golden twenties'?

2 Did Weimar's social welfare provision make Germany a more equal society?

3 Was the Weimar economy fundamentally sick?

4 Did the *Reichstag* results of 1924–8 suggest optimism for the Weimar Republic?

5 What were the problems/weaknesses faced by the main parties: a) SPD, b) ZP, c) liberal parties and d) DNVP?

6 Why did the political parties find it so difficult to co-operate?

7 Was the appointment of Hindenburg as president a good or a bad sign for Weimar democracy?

8 What were Stresemann's aims and objectives?

9 What were the strengths and weaknesses of the Dawes Plan?

10 Why were the Locarno treaties so significant?

11 Did Stresemann fail or succeed?

12 What was *Neue Sachlichkeit* and how did it express itself?

13 In what ways did Weimar culture reach out to ordinary people?

14 Who reacted against *Neue Sachlichkeit* and why?

15 Were the years of Weimar's golden age a time of deceptive stability?

Question practice

ESSAY QUESTIONS

1 Assess the reasons why Weimar Germany in the 1920s was seen as a culturally rich age.

2 How important was the part played by Gustav Stresemann in the establishment of stability within Germany between 1923 and 1929?

3 'By 1929 the Weimar Republic had a good chance of survival.' How far do you agree with this statement?

4 Assess the view that the years 1924–9 were a period of economic recovery for Weimar Germany.

INTERPRETATION QUESTION

1 Read the interpretation that follows and answer both parts of the question. Some historians have claimed that 'Stresemann was Weimar's greatest statesman'. (From J.R. Wright, *Gustav Stresemann: Weimar's Greatest Statesman*, 2004.) a) Explain how this interpretation can be supported. b) Explain how this interpretation can be challenged.

CHAPTER 3

The collapse of Weimar democracy and the rise of Nazism

In the 1920s Nazism took root, yet Hitler and the Nazi Party enjoyed a rather chequered history. It was the onset of the world depression which precipitated a political and economic crisis in Germany. This chapter prompts two key inextricably linked questions: 'Why did Weimar democracy fail?' and 'Why did the Nazis take power?' These issues will be examined in the following sections:

★ Hitler and the creation of the Nazi Party

★ Nazi ideology

★ Nazi fortunes in the 1920s

★ The world economic crisis

★ The breakdown of parliamentary government

★ Brüning: presidential government

★ Papen's 'Cabinet of Barons'

★ The death of Weimar democracy

★ The Nazi mass movement

★ Nazi political methods

★ Political intrigue and the appointment of Hitler

★ Conclusion

The key debate on *page 129* of this chapter asks the question: Was the creation of the Nazi dictatorship an inevitable product of German history?

Key dates

1929	Oct.	Wall Street Crash and onset of the world depression	1932	April	Re-election of Hindenburg as president of Germany
1930	March	Collapse of Müller's government and Brüning appointed as chancellor		May	Resignation of Brüning. Papen appointed as chancellor
	Sept.	*Reichstag* election: Nazis emerged as second largest party		July	*Reichstag* election: Nazis emerged as largest party
	Dec.	Brüning's economic measures imposed by presidential decree		Sept.	*Reichstag* passed a massive vote of no confidence in Papen's government
1931	July	Five leading German banks failed		Dec.	Papen dismissed and replaced by Schleicher as chancellor
1932	Jan.	Unemployment peaked at 6.1 million	1933	Jan. 30	Schleicher dismissed and Hitler appointed as chancellor

1 Hitler and the creation of the Nazi Party

▶ *How did Hitler become involved in politics?*

▶ *Why did the Beer Hall* putsch *fail?*

There was little in the background of Adolf Hitler to suggest that he would become a powerful political figure. Hitler was born at Braunau-am-Inn in 1889 in what was then the **Austro-Hungarian Empire**. He failed to impress at school and, after the death of his parents, he moved to Vienna in 1907. There he applied unsuccessfully for a place as a student at the Academy of Fine Arts. For the next six years he led an aimless and unhappy existence in the poorer districts of the city. It was not until he joined the Bavarian Regiment on the outbreak of war in 1914 that he found a real purpose in life. He served bravely throughout the war and was awarded the military decoration of Iron Cross, first class.

When the war ended Hitler was in hospital recovering from a British gas attack. By the time he had returned to Bavaria in early 1919 he had already framed in his mind the core of what was to become National Socialism:

- fervent German nationalism
- support of authoritarianism and opposition to democracy and socialism
- a racially inspired view of society which exhibited itself most obviously in a rabid anti-Semitism and a veneration of the German **Volk** as the master race.

Such a mixture of ideas in a man whose personal life was much of a mystery – he had no close family and few real friends – has excited some historians to resort to psychological analysis leading to extraordinary speculation. Did his anti-Semitism originate from contracting syphilis from a Jewish prostitute? Could his authoritarian attitude be explained by his upbringing at the hands of an old and repressive father? Or perhaps the influences came from further afield. One clue to his fierce anti-Semitism could be his encounters with **White Russian** *émigrés* who had fled Russia after the 1917 Bolshevik Revolution. They were extreme right-wing nationalists who saw Bolshevism as a part of a Jewish conspiracy for world domination. Many of them had been members of the notoriously violent Black Hundreds organisation, which had been involved in the worst of the **pogroms** in tsarist Russia. Yet, such suggestions are all highly speculative and do not really help to explain the key question of how and why Hitler became such an influential political force.

The creation and emergence of the Nazi Party

It was because of Hitler's committed right-wing attitudes that he was employed in the politically charged atmosphere of 1919 as a kind of spy by the Bavarian section of the German Army. One of his investigations brought him into contact

KEY TERMS

Austro-Hungarian Empire A large multinational empire in central Europe that existed from 1867 to 1918. It was created from the Empire of Austria and the Kingdom of Hungary.

Volk Often translated as 'people', although it tends to suggest a nation with the same ethnic and cultural identities and with a collective sense of belonging.

White Russians Opponents of the Bolsheviks after the creation of the Soviet state.

Pogrom A state-organised or encouraged massacre of innocent people. The term originated from the massacres of Jews in Russia.

Anti-capitalism Rejects an economic system based on private property and profit.

with the DAP (*Deutsche Arbeiterpartei* – German Workers' Party), which was not a movement of the revolutionary left, as Hitler had assumed on hearing its name, but one committed to nationalism, anti-Semitism and **anti-capitalism**. Hitler joined the tiny party and immediately became a member of its committee. His energy, oratory and propaganda skills soon made an impact on the small group and it was Hitler who, with the party's founder, Anton Drexler, drew up the party's 25-points programme in February 1920 (see Source A). At the same time, it was agreed to change the party's name to the NSDAP, the National Socialist German Workers' Party. (For an analysis of Nazi ideology, see pages 90–4.)

By mid-1921 it was clear that Hitler was the driving force behind the party. Although he still held only the post of propaganda chief, it was his powerful speeches that had impressed local audiences and had helped to increase party membership to 3300. He encouraged the creation of the armed squads to protect party meetings and to intimidate the opposition, especially the communists. It was his development of early propaganda techniques – the Nazi salute, the swastika, the uniform – that had done so much to give the party a clear and easily recognisable identity.

? In what ways did the NSDAP programme in Source A attempt to appeal to the fears and prejudices of the German people?

SOURCE A

From the programme of the NSDAP, quoted in J. Noakes and G. Pridham, editors, *Nazism 1919–45*, volume 1, Liverpool University Press, 2000, p. 314.

1. We demand the union of all Germans in a Greater Germany on the basis of the right of national self-determination.

2. We demand equality of rights for the German People in its dealings with other nations, and the revocation of the peace treaties of Versailles and Saint Germain.

3. We demand land and territory (colonies) to feed our people and to settle our surplus population.

4. Only members of the Volk (nation) may be citizens of the State. Only those of German blood, whatever their creed may be members of the nation. Accordingly no Jew may be a member of the nation. …

7. We demand that the State shall make it its primary duty to provide a livelihood for its citizens. If it should prove impossible to feed the entire population, non-citizens must be deported from the Reich. …

10. It must be the first duty of every citizen to perform physical or mental work. The activities of the individual must not clash with the general interest, but must proceed within the framework of the community and be for the general good. …

14. We demand profit sharing in large industrial enterprises.

15. We demand the extensive development of insurance for old age. …

18. We demand the ruthless prosecution of those whose activities are injurious to the common interest. Common criminals, usurers, profiteers must be punished with death, whatever their creed or race. …

25. We demand the creation of a strong central power of the Reich.

Alarmed by Hitler's increasing domination of the party, Drexler and some other members of the committee tried to limit his influence. However, it was here, for the first time, that Hitler showed his political ability to manoeuvre and to gamble. He was by far the most influential speaker and the party knew it, so, shrewdly, he offered to resign. In the ensuing power struggle he was quickly able to mobilise support at two meetings in July 1921. He was invited back triumphant. Embarrassed, Drexler resigned and Hitler became chairman and *Führer* (leader) of the party.

Having gained supreme control over the party in Munich, Hitler aimed to subordinate all the other right-wing groups under his party's leadership and certainly, in the years 1921–3, the party was strengthened by a number of significant developments:

- The armed squads were organised and set up as the *Sturm Abteilung*, **SA**, in 1921 as a paramilitary unit led by Ernst Röhm (see page 145). It was now used to organise planned thuggery and violence.
- The party established its first newspaper in 1921, the *Völkischer Beobachter* (the *People's Observer*).
- In 1922 Hitler won the backing of Julius Streicher, who previously had run a rival right-wing party in northern Bavaria. Streicher also published his own newspaper, *Der Stürmer*, which was overtly anti-Semitic with a range of seedy articles devoted to sex and violence.
- Hitler was also fortunate to win the support of the influential Hermann Göring, who joined the party in 1922 (see page 136). He was born into a Bavarian landowning family, while his wife was a leading Swedish aristocratic. They made many very helpful social contacts in Munich, which gave Hitler and Nazism respectability.

By 1923 the party had a membership of about 20,000. Hitler certainly enjoyed an impressive personal reputation and, as a result, Nazism successfully established an influential role on the extreme right in Bavaria. However, despite Nazi efforts, it still proved difficult to control all the radical right-wing political groups, which remained independent organisations across Germany. The Nazi Party was still very much a fringe party, limited to the region of Bavaria.

The Beer Hall *putsch* 1923

The successful takeover of power by **Mussolini** in Italy in October 1922, combined with the developing internal crisis in Germany, convinced Hitler that the opportunity to seize power had arrived. Indeed, a leading Nazi introduced

KEY TERM

SA *Sturm Abteilung.* Became known in English as the stormtroopers. They supported the radical socialist aspects of Nazism. They were also referred to as the Brownshirts after the colour of their uniform.

KEY FIGURE

Benito Mussolini (1883–1945)

Journalist and at first a strong socialist. Became leader of the National Fascist Party in 1919 and seized power in the 'March on Rome' in 1922. During 1925–43 he ruled Italy as a dictator known as *Il Duce* (the leader).

Hitler at one of his speeches in Munich by saying: 'Germany's Mussolini is called Adolf Hitler'. However, the Nazis were far too weak on their own to stage any kind of political takeover and Hitler was still seen merely as a 'drummer' who could stir up the masses for the national movement. It was the need for allies which led Hitler into negotiations with Kahr and the Bavarian state government, and the Bavarian section of the German Army under Lossow (see pages 37–9).

It was with these two men that Hitler plotted to 'March on Berlin' (in the style of Mussolini's coup which, only the previous year, had become known as the 'March on Rome'). They aimed to mobilise all the military forces from Bavaria – including sections of the German Army, the police, the SA and other paramilitaries – and then, by closing in on Berlin, to seize national power. With hindsight, Hitler's plan was unrealistic and doomed because:

- He grossly overestimated the level of public support for a *putsch* – despite the problems faced by Weimar's democratic government in 1923 (see page 52).
- He showed a lack of real planning.
- He relied too heavily on the promise of support from Ludendorff.
- Most significantly, at the eleventh hour, Kahr and Lossow, fearing failure, decided to hold back.

Hitler was not so cautious and preferred to press on rather than lose the opportunity. On 8 November, when Kahr was addressing a large audience in one of Munich's beer halls, Hitler and the Nazis took control of the meeting, declared a 'national revolution' and forced Kahr and Lossow to support it. The next day Hitler, Göring, Streicher, Röhm (and Ludendorff) marched into the city of Munich with 2000 SA men, but they had no real military backing and the attempted take-over of Munich was easily crushed by the Bavarian police. Fourteen Nazis were killed and Hitler was arrested on a charge of treason.

Timeline: the Nazi Party in the 1920s

1919		Creation of German Workers' Party (DAP) by Anton Drexler
1920	Feb.	Party name changed to NSDAP (National Socialist German Workers' Party)
		25-Points party programme drawn up by Drexler and Hitler
1923	Nov. 8–9	Beer Hall *putsch* in Munich
1924		Hitler in Landsberg prison. *Mein Kampf* written
1925	Feb.	NSDAP refounded in Munich
1926	Feb.	Bamberg Conference: Hitler's leadership of the party re-established
1928	May	Nazis win just twelve seats in *Reichstag* election

The consequences

In many respects, the *putsch* was a farce. Hitler and the *putschists* were arrested and charged with treason and the NSDAP was banned. However, Hitler gained significant political advantages from the episode:

- He turned his trial into a great propaganda success both for himself and for the Nazi cause. He played on all his rhetorical skills and evoked admiration for his patriotism. For the first time he made himself a national figure.
- He won the respect of many other right-wing nationalists for having had the courage to act.
- The leniency of his sentence – five years, the minimum stipulated by the Weimar constitution and actually reduced to ten months – seemed like an act of encouragement on the part of the judiciary.
- He used his months in prison to write and to reassess his political strategy, including dictating ***Mein Kampf***.

KEY TERM

Mein Kampf 'My struggle'. The book written by Hitler in 1924, which expresses his political ideas.

SOURCE B

In Source B, how are Hitler and Ebert portrayed?

'Hitler's entry into Berlin.'
A cartoon published by the *Simplicissimus* magazine in April 1924, just after Hitler's trial.

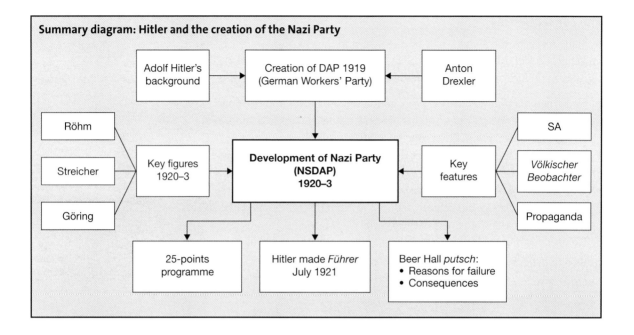

Summary diagram: Hitler and the creation of the Nazi Party

Nazi ideology

▶ *What were the main elements of Nazi thinking?*

▶ *Was Nazism an original German ideology?*

Nazism always emphasised the importance of action over thought. However, while in Landsberg prison, Hitler dictated the first part of *Mein Kampf* which, in the following years, became the bible of National Socialism. Together with the 25-points programme of 1920 (see pages 86–7), it provided the basic framework of Nazi ideology.

Racism

Hitler's ideas were built on his concept of race. He believed that humanity consisted of a hierarchy of races and that life was no more than 'the survival of the fittest'. He argued that **Social Darwinism** necessitated a struggle between races, just as animals fought for food and territory in the wild. Furthermore, he considered it vital to maintain racial purity, so that the blood of the weak would not undermine the strong.

It was a crude philosophy, which appears even more simplistic when Hitler's analysis of the races is considered. The *Herrenvolk* (master-race) was the **Aryan** race and was exemplified by the Germans. It was the task of the Aryans to remain pure and to dominate the inferior races. At the lower end of his racial

KEY TERMS

Social Darwinism
A philosophy that portrayed the world as a 'struggle' between people, races and nations. Hitler viewed war as the highest form of 'struggle' and was deeply influenced by the theory of evolution based on natural selection.

Aryan Defined by the Nazis as the non-Jewish people of northern Europe. Technically, refers to people whose language has an Indian/European root.

pyramid Hitler placed the Slavs, Gypsies and 'Negroes', and the particular focus of his hatred, the Jews. In the following extract from *Mein Kampf* Hitler writes:

SOURCE C

From A. Hitler, *Mein Kampf*, Hurst & Blackett/Hutchinson, 1939, p. 248. (See also the 25-points programme, page 86: points 4 and 7.)

The adulteration of the blood and racial deterioration conditioned thereby are the only causes that account for the decline of ancient civilisations; for it is never by war that nations are ruined, but by the loss of their powers of resistance, which are exclusively a characteristic of pure racial blood. In this world everything that is not of sound stock is like chaff. Every historical event in the world is nothing more, nor less, than a manifestation of the instinct of racial self-preservation, whether for weal or woe [for better or for worse].

According to Hitler in Source C, what were the reasons for the rise and fall of nations?

Anti-Semitism

Hitler's anti-Semitism was violent and irrational. The Jew became the universal scapegoat for the Nazis, responsible for all Germany's problems past and present. Hitler saw the Jewish community as a kind of cancer within the German political body – a disease that had to be cut out. However, he was the product, not the creator, of a society that was permeated by such prejudices. There was a long tradition of anti-Semitism in European history. It was not the preserve of the Nazis, and it certainly had never been a purely German phenomenon. It was rooted in the religious hostility of Christians towards the Jews (as being responsible for the death of Christ) that could be traced back to medieval Europe. There had emerged in Germany, in the course of the nineteenth century, a more clearly defined anti-Semitism based on racism and national resentment. By 1900 a number of specifically anti-Semitic *völkisch* political parties were winning seats in the *Reichstag* and, although they were comparatively few, their success shows that anti-Semitic ideas were becoming more prevalent and generally more respectable.

Anti-democracy

In Hitler's opinion there was no realistic alternative to strong dictatorial government. Ever since his years in Vienna he had viewed parliamentary democracy as weak and ineffective. It went against the German historical traditions of militarism and the power of the state. Furthermore, it encouraged the development of an even greater evil, communism.

More specifically, Hitler saw Weimar democracy as a betrayal. In his eyes, it was the democratic and socialist politicians of 1918, 'the November criminals', who had stabbed the German Army in the back, by accepting the Armistice and establishing the republic (see pages 4 and 34). Since then Germany had lurched from crisis to crisis.

KEY TERMS

Führerprinzip
'The leadership principle'. Hitler upheld the idea of a one-party state, built on an all-powerful leader.

Lebensraum 'Living space'. Hitler's aim to create an empire by establishing German supremacy over the eastern lands in Europe.

In place of democracy Hitler wanted an all-embracing one-party state that would be run on the **Führerprinzip**, which rejected representative government and liberal values. Thus, the masses in society were to be controlled for the common good, but an individual leader was to be chosen in order to rouse the nation into action, and to take the necessary decisions. (See also the 25-points programme, page 87: point 25.)

Nationalism

A crucial element in Nazi thinking was an aggressive nationalism, which developed out of the particular circumstances of Germany's recent history. The Armistice of 1918 and the subsequent Treaty of Versailles had to be overturned, and the lost territories had to be restored to Germany (see pages 22–4). But Hitler's nationalism called for more than a mere restoration of the 1914 frontiers. It meant the creation of an empire (Reich) to include all those members of the German *Volk* who lived beyond the frontiers of Imperial Germany: the Austrian Germans; the Germans in the Sudetenland; the German communities along the Baltic coast; all were to be included within the borderlands of Germany.

Yet, Hitler's nationalist aims did not end there. He dreamed of a Greater Germany, a superpower, capable of competing with the British Empire and the USA. Such an objective could be achieved only by territorial expansion on a grand scale. This was the basis of Hitler's demand for **Lebensraum** for Germany. Only by the conquest of Poland, the Ukraine and Russia could Germany obtain the raw materials, cheap labour and food supplies so necessary for continental supremacy. The creation of his 'New Order' in eastern Europe also held one other great attraction: namely, the destruction of the USSR, the centre of world communism. In *Mein Kampf* Hitler wrote:

? According to Source D, what were Hitler's main political aims?

SOURCE D

Extract from A. Hitler, *Mein Kampf*, Hurst & Blackett/Hutchinson, 1939, p. 17. (See also the 25-points programme, page 86: points 1, 2 and 3.)

The German people must be assured the territorial area which is necessary for it to exist on earth ... People of the same blood should be in the same Reich. The German people will have no right to engage in a colonial policy until they shall have brought all their children together in one state. When the territory of the Reich embraces all the Germans and finds itself unable to assure them a livelihood, only then can the moral right arise, from the need of the people, to acquire foreign territory ... Germany will either become a World Power or will not continue to exist at all. ... The future goal of our foreign policy ought to be an Eastern policy, which will have in view the acquisition of such territory as is necessary for our German people.

The socialist aspect of Nazism

A number of points in the 1920 programme demanded socialist reforms and, for a long time, there existed a faction within the party that emphasised the anti-capitalist aspect of Nazism, for example:

- profit-sharing in large industrial enterprises
- the extensive development of insurance for old age
- the nationalisation of all businesses.

Hitler accepted these points in the early years because he recognised their popular appeal but he never showed any real commitment to such ideas. As a result, they were the cause of important differences within the party and were not really dropped until Hitler had fully established his dominant position by 1934. (See also the 25-points programme, page 86: points 10, 14 and 15.)

What Hitler and Goebbels later began to promote was the concept of the *Volksgemeinschaft* (people's community). This remained the vaguest element of the Nazi ideology, and is therefore difficult to define precisely. First, it was intended to overcome the old differences of class, religion and politics. But secondly, it aimed to bring about a new collective national identity by encouraging people to work together for the benefit of the nation and by promoting 'German values'. Such a system could of course benefit only those who racially belonged to the German *Volk* and who willingly accepted the loss of individual freedoms in an authoritarian system (see also page 193).

KEY TERM

Volksgemeinschaft
'A people's community'. Nazism stressed the development of a harmonious, socially unified and racially pure community.

The ideology of National Socialism

Early historians and biographers of Hitler simply saw him as a cynical opportunist motivated by the pursuit of power. Others have now generally come to view him as a committed political leader influenced by certain key ideas that he used to lay the basis of a consistent Nazi programme.

However, to describe Hitler's thinking, or Nazism, as an ideology is really to flatter it. An 'ideology' suggests a coherent thought-through system or theory of ideas as found, for example, in Marxism. Nazism lacked coherence and was intellectually superficial and simplistic. It was not genuinely a rational system of thought, just a random collection of ideas. It was not in any positive sense original – every aspect of Hitler's thinking was to be found in the nationalist and racist writings of the nineteenth century:

- His nationalism was an outgrowth of the fervour generated in the years leading up to Germany's unification of 1871.
- His idea of an all-German Reich was a simple repetition of the demands for the 'Greater Germany' made by those German nationalists who criticised the limits of the 1871 unification.

- Even the imperialism of *Lebensraum* had already found expression in the programme of 'Germanisation' supported by those writers who saw the German race as somehow superior.
- The growing veneration for the *Volk* had gone hand-in-hand with the development of racist ideas, and in particular of anti-Semitism.

Thus, even before Hitler and other leading Nazis were born, the core of what would become Nazism was already current in political circles. It was to be found in the cheap and vulgar pamphlets sold to the masses in the large cities; in the political programme of respectable pressure groups, such as the **Pan-German League**; within the corridors of Germany's great universities; and in the creative works of certain cultural figures, such as the composer Richard Wagner.

Despite these links, one must avoid labelling Nazi ideology as the logical result of German intellectual thinking. This would be to ignore, for example, the strong socialist tradition in Germany. Moreover, it is well to remember that a number of countries, but especially Britain and France, also witnessed the circulation of very similar nationalist ideas at this time. In that sense, nationalism and racism were products of nineteenth-century European history. Nazi ideology was not original, nor should it be assumed that it was an inevitable result of Germany's past alone.

 **KEY TERM**

Pan-German League
A movement founded in the late nineteenth century, which campaigned for the uniting of all Germans into one country.

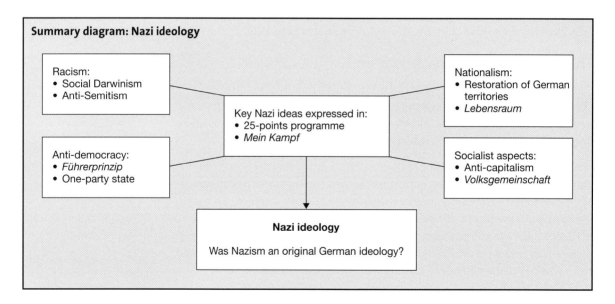

Nazi fortunes in the 1920s

▶ *In what ways was the Nazi Party revitalised and how strong was it by 1929?*

When Hitler left prison in December 1924 the future for Nazism looked bleak. The party was in disarray; its leading members were split into factions and the membership was in decline. More significantly, the atmosphere of crisis that had prevailed in the early years of the republic had given way to a period of political and economic calm (see pages 59–69). Nevertheless, the party was officially refounded on 27 February 1925 and at the same time Hitler wrote a lengthy editorial for the *Völkischer Beobachter* with the heading 'A new beginning'.

Strategy and leadership

In Landsberg prison Hitler, reflecting on the failure of the 1923 *putsch*, became convinced of two vital points: first, that he must re-establish his own absolute control over the party, and secondly, that an armed coup was no longer an appropriate tactic. Therefore, a new policy was necessary, as Hitler reputedly said in prison in 1924:

> *we shall have to hold our noses and enter the* Reichstag *against the Catholic and Marxist deputies. If out-voting them takes longer than our shooting them, at least the result will be guaranteed by their own Constitution! Any lawful process is slow.*

However, the party remained deeply divided in a number of ways:

- Not everyone agreed with the new policy of legality.
- Traditional regional hostilities continued to exist, particularly between the party's power base in Bavaria and the branches in northern Germany.
- Most importantly, policy differences had become more pronounced between the nationalist and anti-capitalist wings of the party.

For over a year Hitler struggled with this internal friction. The problem was highlighted by the power and influence of **Gregor Strasser** and also his brother Otto. Gregor Strasser joined the NSDAP in 1920 and stood loyally next to Hitler in the Munich *putsch*, but he epitomised the opposing standpoint within the party. He favoured the more socialist anti-capitalist policies for the workers and he was in effect the leader of the movement in northern Germany.

Eventually, in February 1926, the ideological and personality differences within the party came to a head at a special party conference in Bamberg. On the one hand, it was a significant victory for Hitler, as he mobilised sufficient support to re-establish his supremacy. The Nazi Party was to be run according to the *Führerprinzip* and there was to be no place for disagreements. On the other hand, the party declared that the original 25 points of the programme with its socialist elements remained unchangeable. So, although Hitler had cleverly

 **KEY FIGURE**

Gregor Strasser (1892–1934)

Strasser was always a supporter of the anti-capitalist 'left-wing' socialist faction and, in effect, second to Hitler until 1932. An inspiring political speaker, he also had the administrative skills to develop the party's mass movement. He was expelled from the party in 1932 and murdered in the Night of the Long Knives (see page 147).

outmanoeuvred his greatest threat and he had re-established a degree of unity within the party, there were still significant rivalries and differences.

The creation of the party structure

The most significant development in the years before the Great Depression lay in the reorganisation of the party structure. The whole of Germany was divided into regions (*Gaue*), which reflected the electoral geography of Weimar's system of proportional representation. The control of each region was placed in the hands of a **Gauleiter**, who then had the responsibility of creating district (*Kreis*) and branch (*Ort*) groups. In this way, a vertical party structure was created throughout Germany, which did not detract from Hitler's own position of authority as leader.

Perhaps the most renowned of the *Gauleiters* was the holder of the Berlin post, Josef Goebbels. Goebbels had originally been a sympathiser of Strasser's socialist ideas, but from 1926 he transferred his support to Hitler. He was then rewarded by being given the responsibility for winning over the capital, a traditionally left-wing stronghold of the SPD. He showed a real interest in propaganda and created the newspaper *Der Angriff* (*The Attack*), but was not appointed chief of party propaganda until 1930 (see pages 119–23).

The Nazis also founded a number of new associated Nazi organisations that were geared to appeal to the specific interests of particular groups of Germans. Among these were:

- the **Hitler Youth**
- the Nazi Teachers' Association
- Union of Nazi Lawyers
- the Order of German Women.

Strasser was mainly responsible for building up an efficient party structure and this was reflected in its increasing membership during these years (see Table 3.1).

One other significant initiative in these years was the creation of the **SS**, *Schutz Staffel*. It was set up in 1925 as an elite body of black-shirted guards, sworn to absolute obedience to the *Führer*. In 1929 it had only 200 members. At first, it was just Hitler's personal bodyguard, although, when it was placed under the control of Himmler later that year, it soon developed its own identity.

The *Reichstag* election of May 1928

By 1928 it can be seen clearly that the party had made progress and was really an effective political machine, most obviously because:

- The structure was effectively organised.
- The membership had increased four-fold since 1925.
- Hitler's leadership was authoritative and secure (despite the ongoing challenge from the Strasser faction).

KEY TERMS

Gauleiter 'Leader of a regional area'. The Nazi Party was organised into 35 regions from 1926.

Hitler Youth *Hitler Jugend* (*HJ*). Nazi youth organisation.

SS *Schutz Staffel* (protection squad). Became known as the Blackshirts, named after the uniform.

Table 3.1 NSDAP membership

Year	Membership numbers
1925	27,000
1926	49,000
1927	72,000
1928	108,000

As a result, the Nazi Party had also successfully absorbed many of the other right-wing racist groups in Germany.

Such advances, however, could not compensate for Nazi disappointment after the *Reichstag* election in May 1928. When the votes were counted, the party had won only 2.6 per cent of the vote and a mere twelve seats (see page 64). It seemed as if Hitler's policy of legality had failed to bring political success, whereas in the favourable socio-economic circumstances Weimar democracy had managed to stabilise its political position. So, Nazism may have taken root, but there was no real sign that it could flourish in Germany.

If this evidence confirmed the belief of many that Hitler was nothing more than an eccentric without the personal leadership to establish a really broad national appeal, there was just one development which ran counter to this. In the election, the party made significant gains in the northern part of Germany among the rural middle and lower-middle classes of areas such as Schleswig-Holstein.

This trend was reflected in the regional state elections of 1929, which suggested that the fall in agricultural prices was beginning to cause discontent – demonstrations and protests were giving way to bankruptcies and violence. Most significantly, in the province of Thuringia, in central Germany, the Nazi Party trebled its vote in regional elections and broke the ten per cent barrier for the first time, recording 11.3 per cent. Such figures suggested that the Nazis could exploit the increasingly difficult economic times of the Great Depression.

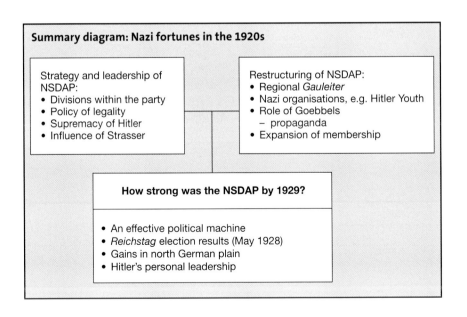

Summary diagram: Nazi fortunes in the 1920s

Strategy and leadership of NSDAP:
- Divisions within the party
- Policy of legality
- Supremacy of Hitler
- Influence of Strasser

Restructuring of NSDAP:
- Regional *Gauleiter*
- Nazi organisations, e.g. Hitler Youth
- Role of Goebbels
  – propaganda
- Expansion of membership

How strong was the NSDAP by 1929?

- An effective political machine
- *Reichstag* election results (May 1928)
- Gains in north German plain
- Hitler's personal leadership

The world economic crisis

> ▶ *What were the political, economic and social effects of the world economic crisis on Germany?*

There is no dispute among historians that the economic crisis known as the Great Depression was an event of major significance. Its effects were felt throughout most of the world.

Germany undoubtedly felt it in a particularly savage way. It suffered the consequences of the **Wall Street Crash** more than any other country. Almost immediately the American loans and investment dried up and this was quickly followed by demands for the repayment of those short-term loans. At the same time, the crisis caused a further decline in the price of food and raw materials as the industrialised nations reduced their imports. As demand for exports collapsed, so world trade slumped. In this situation, German industry could no longer pay its way. Without overseas loans and with its export trade falling, prices and wages fell and the number of bankruptcies increased.

> ### KEY TERM
>
> **Wall Street Crash**
> The collapse of share prices on the New York Stock Exchange in October 1929.

Table 3.2 Economic effects of the world economic crisis on Germany

Economic effects	Key features
Trade	
Slump in world trade. Demand for German exports fell rapidly, for example steel, machinery and chemicals	Exports value fell by 55% 1929 = £630 million 1932 = £280 million
Employment	
Workers laid off – mass unemployment	Number of registered unemployed (annual averages) 1929 = 1.8 million 1932 = 5.6 million
Industry	
Industrial production declined sharply	Production (1928 = 100%) 1929 = 100% 1932 = 58%
Agriculture	
Wages and incomes fell sharply. Many farms sold off	Agricultural prices (1913 = 100%) 1927 = 138% 1932 = 77%
Finance	
Banking sector dislocated by loss of confidence	Five major banks collapsed in 1931; 50,000 businesses bankrupted

It is, however, all too easy to put Germany's economic crisis down to the Wall Street Crash. It should be borne in mind that there were fundamental weaknesses in the German economy *before* the crash:

- The **balance of trade** was in the red, that is, it was in debt.
- The number of unemployed averaged 1.9 million in 1929.
- Many farmers were already in debt and had been facing falling incomes since 1927.
- German government finances from 1925 were continually run in deficit.

Although the Wall Street Crash contributed to Germany's economic problems, it is probable that the German economy faced a chance of a serious depression without it. This suggests that the world economic crisis should really be seen as simply the final push that brought the Weimar economy crashing down. In that sense, it could be said that the Wall Street Crash was merely the occasion, not the cause of Germany's economic crisis.

The human effects of the Great Depression

During the winter of 1929–30 unemployment rose above 2 million, and only twelve months after the crash it had reached 3 million. By January 1932 it stood at 6.1 million, which did not substantially fall until the spring of 1933. On their own, such figures can provide only a limited understanding of the effects of a depression of this magnitude. Unemployment figures, for example, do not take into account those who did not register. Nor do they record the extent of part-time working throughout German industry.

Most significantly, statistics fail to convey the extent of the human suffering that was the consequence of this disaster because the depression in Germany affected virtually everyone; few families escaped its effects.

Many manual industrial workers, both skilled and unskilled, faced the prospect of long-term unemployment. For their wives, there was the impossible task of trying to feed families and keep homes warm on the money provided by limited social security benefits. However, such problems were not to be limited to the working class. This depression dragged down the middle classes. From the small shopkeepers to the well-qualified professionals in law and medicine, people struggled to survive in a world where there was little demand for their goods and services. For such people, the decline in their economic position and the onset of poverty were made more difficult by the loss of pride and respectability.

The situation in the countryside was no better than in the towns. As world demand fell further, the agricultural depression deepened, leading to widespread rural poverty. For some **tenant farmers** there was even the ultimate humiliation of being evicted from their homes, which had often been in their families for generations.

KEY TERMS

Balance of trade
The difference in value between exports and imports. If the value of the imports is above that of exports, the balance of the payments has a deficit that is often said to be 'in the red'.

Tenant farmer A farmer who works land owned by someone else and pays rent either in cash or in a share of the produce.

Today it is difficult to appreciate the scale of the suffering that struck the German people in the early 1930s. The city of Cologne could not pay the interest on its debts, banks closed their doors and, in Berlin, large crowds of unemployed youngsters were kept occupied with open-air games of chess and cards. To many ordinary respectable Germans it seemed as if society itself was breaking down uncontrollably. It is not surprising that many people lost faith in the Weimar Republic, which seemed to offer no end to the misery, and began to see salvation in the solutions offered by political extremists. This was why the economic crisis in Germany quickly degenerated into a more obvious political crisis.

The political implications

The impact of the depression in Germany was certainly more severe than in either Britain or France, but it was on a par with the American experience. By 1932 in Germany, one in three workers was unemployed and industrial production had fallen by 42 per cent of its 1929 level. In the USA, the comparable figures were one in four and 46 per cent. However, in Germany the economic crisis quickly became a political crisis, simply because there was a lack of confidence that weakened the republic's position in its hour of need. Britain, France and the USA were all well-established democracies and did not face the possibility of a wholesale collapse of their political systems.

Taken together, these two points suggest that the depression hastened the end of the Weimar Republic, but only because its economy was already in serious trouble, and the democratic basis of its government was not sufficiently well established.

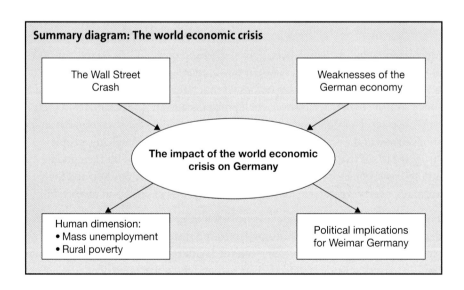

Summary diagram: The world economic crisis

- The Wall Street Crash
- Weaknesses of the German economy
- **The impact of the world economic crisis on Germany**
- Human dimension:
  - Mass unemployment
  - Rural poverty
- Political implications for Weimar Germany

The breakdown of parliamentary government

▶ *Why did the Grand Coalition eventually break up?*

▶ *How did the leadership of Brüning weaken democracy?*

In 1929 the German government was in the hands of Hermann Müller's Grand Coalition, which had been formed after the general election of May 1928 (see page 64). Yet, at the time when unity and firm government were required, the Weimar Republic was torn apart by the re-emergence of the emotive issue of reparations.

The Young Plan and the National Opposition

The Dawes Plan successfully overcame the reparations crisis by rescheduling payments but, from the outset, it was seen as a temporary measure until Germany regained its economic strength (see pages 72–4). In 1929 the Inter-Allied Reparations Commission (see page 24) formed a committee of financiers under the chairmanship of the US banker Owen Young and its report suggested a new scheme of payments. Germany was to continue paying reparations until 1988, but the final sum was reduced to £1850 million (only one quarter of the figure demanded in 1921). So, after some negotiation, the German government accepted the Young Plan. However, in German right-wing circles, Stresemann's diplomacy was seen as another betrayal of national interests to the Allies. In their view, any payment of reparations was based on the 'lie' of the war guilt clause and the new scheme, therefore, had to be opposed.

A national committee, created by Alfred Hugenberg, the leader of the DNVP (see page 67), was formed to fight the Young Plan. Hugenberg now used all his media resources to promote his message. Moreover, he generated support from a wide variety of other right-wing nationalist factions:

- *Stahlhelm* (the largest ex-servicemen's organisation), led by Franz Seldte.
- The Pan-German League.
- Some leading industrialists, for example Fritz Thyssen.
- Hitler and the Nazi Party.

Together this **National Opposition** drafted a 'Law against the Enslavement of the German People', which denounced any reparations and demanded the punishment of collaborating ministers. The proposal gained enough signatures for it to be made the issue of a national referendum in December 1929. In the end, the National Opposition won only 5.8 million votes, a long way short of the 21 million required by the constitution for success.

 KEY TERM

National Opposition
A title given to various political forces that was forged out of the Young Plan in 1929 to oppose all reparations payments.

The campaign of the National Opposition had stirred nationalist emotions. It had brought together many right-wing opponents of the republic. For Hitler, the campaign also showed clear-cut benefits:

- The party membership grew to 130,000 by end of 1929.
- Nazism really gained a national standing for the first time.
- The main party rally at Nuremberg had been a great propaganda success on a much more grandiose scale than any before.
- Hitler made influential political contacts on the extreme right wing.
- It brought the opportunity of having access to Hugenberg's media empire.

The collapse of Müller's Grand Coalition

Müller's coalition government successfully withstood the attack from the National Opposition. However, it was not so successful in dealing with its own internal divisions. Müller, a Social Democrat, struggled to hold the coalition together, and it was an issue of finance which finally brought down the government in March 1930.

The sharp increase in unemployment had created a large deficit in the new national insurance scheme (see page 60) and the four major parties in the coalition could not agree on how to tackle it. The SPD, as the political supporters of the trade unions, wanted to increase the contributions and to maintain the levels of welfare payments. The DVP, on the other hand, had strong ties with big business and insisted on reducing benefits. Müller could no longer maintain a majority and he had no option but to tender the resignation of his government.

The appointment of Heinrich Brüning

President Hindenburg granted the post of chancellor to Heinrich Brüning. At first sight, this appeared an obvious choice, since he was the parliamentary leader of the ZP, the second largest party in the *Reichstag*. However, with hindsight, it seems that Brüning's appointment marked a crucial step towards the end of true parliamentary government. This was for two reasons.

First, he was manoeuvred into office by a select circle of political intriguers, who surrounded the ageing President Hindenburg:

- Otto Meissner, the president's state secretary
- Oskar von Hindenburg, the president's son
- Major General **Kurt von Schleicher**, a leading general.

All three were conservative nationalists and had limited faith in the democratic process. Instead, they looked to the president and the emergency powers of Article 48 of the constitution as a means of creating a more authoritarian government. In Brüning, they saw a respectable, conservative figure who could offer firm leadership.

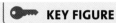 **KEY FIGURE**

Kurt von Schleicher (1882–1934)

Professional soldier and civil servant. Defence minister in Papen's presidential government and chancellor from December 1932 to January 1933. Murdered in the Night of the Long Knives (see page 147).

Secondly, Brüning's response to the growing economic crisis led to a political constitutional crisis. His economic policy was to propose cuts in government expenditure, so as to achieve a balanced budget and prevent the risk of reviving inflation. However, the budget was rejected in the *Reichstag* by 256 votes to 193 in July 1930. When, despite this, Brüning put the proposals into effect by means of an emergency decree, signed by the president according to Article 48, the *Reichstag* challenged the decree's legality and voted for its withdrawal. Deadlock had been reached. Brüning therefore asked Hindenburg to dissolve the *Reichstag* and to call for an election in September 1930.

Nazi breakthrough

Brüning had hoped that in the developing crisis the people would be encouraged to support the parties of the centre-right, from which a coalition could be formed. However, the election results proved him wrong (see Table 3.3).

Table 3.3 *Reichstag* election results for 1928 and 1930. (See also major political parties on page 13.)

	Turnout	NSDAP	DNVP	DVP	ZP/BVP	DDP	SPD	USPD/KPD	Others
May 1928									
Seats	491	12	73	45	78	25	153	54	51
%	75.6	2.6	14.2	8.7	15.2	4.9	29.8	10.8	14.0
September 1930									
Seats	577	107	41	30	87	20	143	77	72
%	82.0	18.3	7.0	4.5	14.8	3.8	24.5	13.1	13.8

The key features about the performance of the political parties are as follows:

- Nazis: with 107 seats and 18.3 per cent, the NSDAP became the second largest political party in Germany.
- Nationalists: the vote of the DNVP was halved from 14.2 to 7 per cent, largely benefiting the Nazis.
- Middle-class democratic parties: the DDP and the DVP lost twenty seats between them.
- Left-wing parties: the vote of the SPD declined from 29.8 to 24.5 per cent, although in contrast the vote of the KPD, the Communists, increased from 10.8 to 13.1 per cent.

As a result of the 1928 *Reichstag* election being so disappointing, not even Hitler could have expected the dramatic gains of 1930. Nevertheless, there are several key factors to explain the Nazi breakthrough:

- Since 1928 the Nazi leaders had deliberately directed their propaganda at rural and middle-class/lower middle-class audiences. Nazi gains were at the expense of the DNVP, DVP and DDP.

- Nazi success cannot just be explained by these 'protest votes'. Nearly half of the Nazi seats were won by the party's attracting 'new' voters:
  - The electorate had grown by 1.8 million since the previous election because a new generation of voters had been added to the roll.
  - The turnout had increased from 75.6 to 82 per cent.

It would seem that the Nazis had not only picked up a fair proportion of these young first-time voters, but also persuaded many people who had not previously participated in elections to support their cause.

The implications of the 1930 *Reichstag* election were profound. It meant that the left and right extremes had made extensive gains against the pro-democratic parties. This now made it very difficult for proper democratic parliamentary government to function.

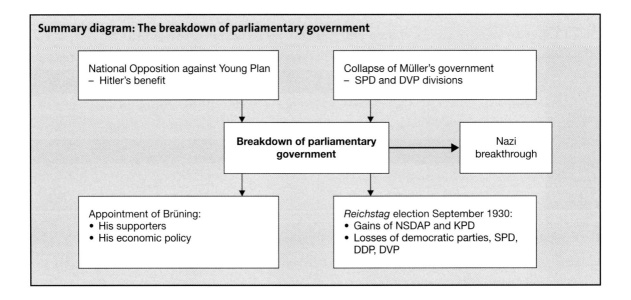

Summary diagram: The breakdown of parliamentary government

National Opposition against Young Plan – Hitler's benefit

Collapse of Müller's government – SPD and DVP divisions

Breakdown of parliamentary government

Nazi breakthrough

Appointment of Brüning:
- His supporters
- His economic policy

Reichstag election September 1930:
- Gains of NSDAP and KPD
- Losses of democratic parties, SPD, DDP, DVP

6 Brüning: presidential government

▶ *How did parliamentary democracy turn into presidential government?*

▶ *Was Brüning economically incompetent, or simply a victim of circumstances?*

Brüning's political position after the election was undoubtedly difficult. His plan of reinforcing his parliamentary support from the centre-right had not succeeded. Instead, he faced the committed opposition of the more powerful extremes of both left and right. However, Brüning was not dismissed as chancellor; he still enjoyed the support of Hindenburg and his government was 'tolerated' by the SPD. Although the SPD did not join the government, it resolved not to oppose in parliament the emergency decrees of Article 48 because of the threat now facing the republic from the extremists.

In this way, true parliamentary democracy gave way to 'presidential government' with some backing from the *Reichstag*. From 1930 to 1932 Brüning remained as chancellor and he governed Germany by the use of Article 48 through President Hindenburg. He was almost a semi-dictator, as can be seen from his growing use of presidential decrees (see Table 3.4).

Table 3.4 Presidential government 1930–2

	1930	1931	1932
Presidential decree laws (Article 48)	5	44	66
Reichstag **laws**	98	34	5
Sitting days of the *Reichstag*	94	42	13

Economic policy

Brüning's economic policy was at least consistent in pursuing his aims:

- to balance the budget
- to prevent the chance of restarting inflation
- to get rid of the burden of German reparations

Throughout his two years in office, his main measures were imposed by presidential decree:

- to cut spending drastically
- to raise taxes.

This lowered demand, which led to a worsening of the slump. Most obviously, there was a large increase in the number of unemployed and a serious decline in welfare state provision. Soon he was mocked with the title 'the Hunger Chancellor'.

Many historians have condemned Brüning's economic regime for sticking to its policy of reducing expenditure, for seriously worsening the situation and enabling the rise of the Nazis. He was criticised particularly for his failure in the summer of 1931 to introduce economic measures, such as **public works** in the construction industry. These might just have been enough to lessen the worst effects of the depression during 1932.

It could be argued that Brüning had limited economic alternatives. This was because the German economy had entered the depression with such severe weaknesses from the 1920s (see pages 61–3) that economic failure was unavoidable. On these grounds, therefore, it could be argued that no chancellor would have been in a position to expand the economy and that Brüning was at the mercy of other forces.

 **KEY TERM**

Public works Employment schemes financed by the state to provide jobs.

Heinrich Brüning

1885	Born into a Catholic trading family
1904–11	Attended Munich University and awarded a doctorate in economics
1915–18	Volunteered in the war and won the Iron Cross, first class
1924–33	Elected to the *Reichstag* as ZP deputy – and party leader from 1929
1930	Appointed as chancellor by Hindenburg in March
	His July budget was rejected by the *Reichstag*, resulting in the *Reichstag* election of September 1930
1932	Proposed land reform of the Prussian estates
	Dismissed as chancellor by Hindenburg
1934	Fled to the Netherlands and emigrated to the USA
1970	Died in the USA

Brüning was a political and economic conservative. He was very much on the right wing of the ZP, with a hostility towards socialism, which made it difficult for him to work with the left-wing parties when he became the party leader. In his heart, he remained a monarchist and hoped to amend the Weimar constitution to make it a more authoritarian system.

The significance of Brüning's career is almost completely concentrated into the two years of his chancellorship. He certainly did not sympathise with the Nazis, but his policies and decisions have been heavily criticised because:

- He called for the *Reichstag* election in September 1930 and misread the political consequences.
- He remained committed to the economic programme of balancing the budget, which resulted in enormous economic and political pressures.
- He relied on Hindenburg for the emergency decrees – and he failed to recognise his overdependence on the president.

In his defence, he was a man of integrity and a victim of exceptional circumstances. His historical reputation is perhaps overshadowed by the later development of the Nazi dictatorship.

Brüning's fall from power

In the spring of 1932, Hindenburg's first seven-year term of office as president came to an end. Brüning committed himself to securing Hindenburg's re-election and after frenetic campaigning Hindenburg was re-elected on the second ballot. He gained 19.3 million votes (53 per cent) compared with Hitler's 13.4 million (36.8 per cent). However, it was a negative victory. Hindenburg had been chosen only because he was the sole alternative between Hitler and the KPD candidate, **Ernst Thälmann**. Also, despite losing, Hitler had doubled the Nazi vote and had projected an even more powerful personal image. Moreover, Hindenburg showed no real gratitude to Brüning and, at the end of May 1932, the president forced his chancellor to resign because of the following factors:

- the banking crisis
- land reform
- intrigue.

The banking crisis

The collapse of the major bank, the Danat, and several others in June 1931 revived fears of financial crisis. By the end of the year unemployment was

 KEY FIGURE

Ernst Thälmann (1886–1944)

KPD leader 1925–33. *Reichstag* member 1924–33. Unquestioning supporter of the Soviet line. Held in concentration camp until his murder in 1944.

approaching 5 million people and there were demonstrations in the streets. In October 1931 the National Opposition (see pages 101–2) was reborn as the Harzburg Front. It brought together a range of right-wing political, military and economic forces who demanded the resignation of Brüning and a new *Reichstag* election. The Front arranged a massive rally to denounce Brüning, but in the winter of 1931–2 the chancellor still enjoyed the support of Hindenburg.

Land reform

Brüning aimed to issue an emergency decree to turn some *Junker* estates in east Prussia into 600,000 allotments for unemployed workers. Landowners saw this as a threat to their property interests and dubbed it 'agrarian bolshevism'.

Intrigue

Brüning's unpopularity over land reform spurred on the group of right wingers, led by Kurt von Schleicher, who probably pushed for the resignation of the chancellor with the aim of creating a right-wing government.

Brüning could be viewed as an innocent sacrifice who was removed by Hindenburg without consultation with the *Reichstag*. However, it should be borne in mind that he had only survived as chancellor because he enjoyed the personal backing of the president. Brüning had agreed to the creation of presidential government based on the powers granted by Article 48 of the constitution, but he was not astute enough to recognise the precarious nature of his own position. He depended solely on retaining the confidence of the president. This makes it harder to sympathise with him when he became the victim of the intrigue of the presidential court.

Assessment of Brüning

Brüning was an honest, hard-working and honourable man who failed. He was not really a committed democrat, but neither was he sympathetic to Nazism, an important point to remember. In many respects, Brüning was making good progress towards his aims, when he was dismissed:

- He succeeded in ending the payment of reparations, which were cancelled at Lausanne in 1932 at the height of the depression.
- He sympathised with the reduction of the democratic powers of the *Reichstag*.

However:

- He was not astute enough to appreciate how dangerous and unstable the economic crisis had become in Germany by 1932.
- Neither did he realise how insecure was his own position. For as long as Brüning retained the confidence of Hindenburg, presidential government protected his position.

With no real hope of improvement in the economic crisis, it is not surprising that large sections of the population looked to the Nazis to save the situation.

Rule of law Governing a country according to its laws.

Brüning would have nothing to do with Hitler and the Nazis and he continued to uphold the **rule of law**. Sadly, presidential rule had made Germany become accustomed to rule by decree. In this way, democracy was undermined and the path was cleared for more extreme political parties to assume power. In the end, it is hard to escape the conclusion that Brüning's chancellorship was a dismal failure, and, in view of the Nazi tyranny that was soon to come, a tragic one.

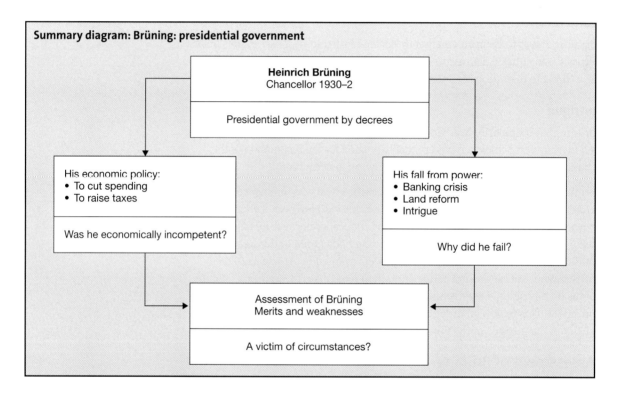

Summary diagram: Brüning: presidential government

Heinrich Brüning
Chancellor 1930–2

Presidential government by decrees

His economic policy:
• To cut spending
• To raise taxes

Was he economically incompetent?

His fall from power:
• Banking crisis
• Land reform
• Intrigue

Why did he fail?

Assessment of Brüning
Merits and weaknesses

A victim of circumstances?

⑦ Papen's 'Cabinet of Barons'

▶ *What was Papen's political aim in 1932?*

▶ *Why was the* Reichstag *election of July 1932 so politically significant?*

Schleicher now sought to use his influence with Hindenburg by recommending Franz von Papen as the new chancellor (see opposite). If many greeted the choice of Papen with disbelief, it was his very lack of ability which appealed to Schleicher, who saw the opportunity to influence events more directly through him. As an aristocrat, Papen had good connections with high society; as a Catholic, he was a member of the ZP, although his political views mirrored those of the nationalists. His outlook quickly formed the basis for a close friendship with Hindenburg.

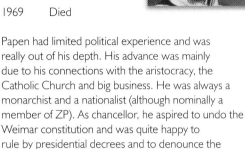

Franz von Papen

1879	Born into a Catholic aristocratic family
1913–18	Cavalry officer and diplomat
1932	In May he was appointed chancellor to head his 'Cabinet of Barons'
	Dissolved the *Reichstag*, with serious consequences
	Removed the Prussian state government in July
	Defeated by a vote of no confidence in the *Reichstag* in September
1933	Appointed as vice-chancellor in Hitler's coalition
1934	Resigned after the Night of the Long Knives
1946	Found not guilty of war crimes in the Nuremberg trials
1969	Died

Papen had limited political experience and was really out of his depth. His advance was mainly due to his connections with the aristocracy, the Catholic Church and big business. He was always a monarchist and a nationalist (although nominally a member of ZP). As chancellor, he aspired to undo the Weimar constitution and was quite happy to rule by presidential decrees and to denounce the state government of Prussia. Despite pursuing his personal ambitions he was quickly outmanoeuvred by Hitler.

Papen was politically ambitious, but his understanding and experience of politics were limited (he did not even hold a seat in the *Reichstag*). The new cabinet was called a non-party government of 'national concentration', although it was soon nicknamed the 'Cabinet of Barons'. It was a presidential government dominated by aristocratic landowners and industrialists – like Papen, many were not even members of the *Reichstag*. In order to strengthen the government, Papen and Schleicher wanted to secure political support from the Nazis. Hitler agreed not to oppose the new government in return for two concessions:

- The dissolution of the *Reichstag* and the calling of fresh elections.
- The end of a government ban on the SA and SS, introduced after violence during the presidential campaign.

Papen and Schleicher hoped that this agreement with the Nazis would result in the creation of a right-wing authoritarian government with some popular support in the form of the Nazis. The *Reichstag* was therefore dissolved and an election was arranged for 31 July 1932.

Reichstag election: July 1932

The election campaign was brutal, as street violence once again took hold in the large cities. In the month of July alone 86 people died as a result of political fights. Yet, such bloodshed provided Schleicher and Papen with the excuse to abolish the most powerful regional state government in Germany: Prussia. This government of Prussia had long been a coalition of the SPD and the ZP and had been the focus of right-wing resentment since the creation of the republic. So, on 20 July 1932, it was simply removed by Papen, who declared a state of emergency and appointed himself as Reich commissioner of Prussia. This was of immense significance:

- It was an arbitrary and unconstitutional act.
- It replaced a parliamentary system with a presidential authoritarian government.
- Democrats – especially the SPD and the trade unions – gave in without any real opposition. Their passive response shows how far the forces of democracy had lost the initiative.

Many on the right wing congratulated Papen on the Prussian coup. However, it did not win him any additional electoral support. When the election results came in (see Table 3.5), it was again the Nazis who had cause to celebrate, which raised serious implications for the country, as reported by a Reich minister in Source E.

SOURCE E

From a report by ex-Reich minister Dr Külz in a memorandum, quoted in J.W. Hiden, *The Weimar Republic*, Longman, 1974, pp. 101–2.

Looked at politically, objectively, the result of the election is so fearful because it seems that the present election will be the last normal Reichstag election for a long time to come … The elected Reichstag is totally incapable of functioning …

If things are faced squarely and soberly the situation is such that more than half the German people have declared themselves against the present state, but have not said what sort of state they would accept. Thus, any organic development is for the moment impossible. As the lesser of many evils to be feared, I think, would be the open assumption of dictatorship by the present government.

? Explain why the author in Source E states that the 'Reichstag is totally incapable of functioning'. Refer also to the details in Table 3.5.

Table 3.5 *Reichstag* election results 1928–32. (See also major political parties on page 13.)

	Turnout	NSDAP	DNVP	DVP	ZP/BVP	DDP	SPD	KPD	Others
May 1928									
Seats	491	12	73	45	78	25	153	54	51
%	75.6	2.6	14.2	8.7	15.2	4.9	29.8	10.8	14.0
September 1930									
Seats	577	107	41	30	87	20	143	77	72
%	82.0	18.3	7.0	4.5	14.8	3.8	24.5	13.1	13.8
July 1932									
Seats	608	230	37	7	97	4	133	89	11
%	84.1	37.3	5.9	1.2	15.7	1.0	21.6	14.3	2.9

It is worth bearing in mind the following key features about the performance of the political parties:

- Nazis: with 230 seats and 37.3 per cent of the vote the NSDAP became the largest political party in Germany.
- Nationalists: the vote of the DNVP fell further to 5.9 per cent.
- Middle-class democratic parties: the DDP and the DVP collapsed disastrously. They polled only 2.2 per cent of the vote and gained just eleven seats between them.
- Left-wing parties: the vote of the SPD declined further to 21.6 per cent, although in contrast the vote of the KPD increased to 14.3 per cent.

In electoral terms the gains of the Nazis could be explained by:

- the collapse of the DDP and DVP vote
- the decline of the DNVP
- a small percentage of disgruntled workers changing from SPD to NSDAP
- the support for the 'other parties' falling from 13.8 to 2.9 per cent, which suggests that their loyalty transferred to the Nazis
- the turnout increasing to 84 per cent, which indicated the same trend as in September 1930 that the party was attracting even more 'new voters'.

Two further points are worth remembering about the *Reichstag* election of July 1932. First, only 39.5 per cent voted for the pro-democratic parties; and secondly, added together, the percentage of votes for the KPD and NSDAP combined to 51.6 per cent. These two political facts are telling indeed. The German people had voted to reject democracy.

Table 3.6 Germany's governments 1928–33

Chancellor	Dates in office	Type of government
Hermann Müller (SPD)	May 1928–March 1930	Parliamentary government. A coalition cabinet of SPD, ZP, DDP and DVP
Heinrich Brüning (ZP)	March 1930–May 1932	Presidential government dependent on emergency decrees. A coalition cabinet from political centre and right
Franz von Papen (ZP, but very right wing)	May 1932–December 1932	Presidential government dependent on emergency decrees. Many non-party cabinet members
General Kurt von Schleicher (Non-party)	December 1932–January 1933	Presidential government dependent on emergency decrees. Many non-party cabinet members
Adolf Hitler (NSDAP)	1933–45	Coalition cabinet of NSDAP and DNVP, but gave way to Nazi dictatorship

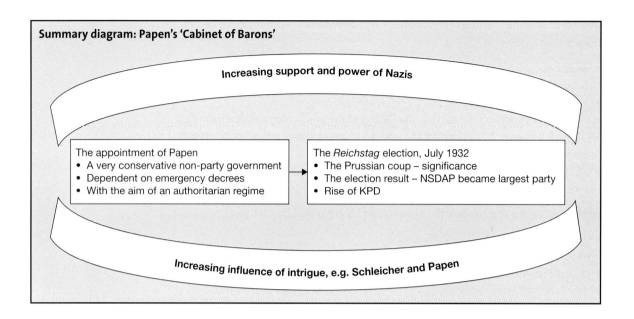

Summary diagram: Papen's 'Cabinet of Barons'

Increasing support and power of Nazis

The appointment of Papen
- A very conservative non-party government
- Dependent on emergency decrees
- With the aim of an authoritarian regime

The *Reichstag* election, July 1932
- The Prussian coup – significance
- The election result – NSDAP became largest party
- Rise of KPD

Increasing influence of intrigue, e.g. Schleicher and Papen

 # The death of Weimar democracy

▶ *When and why did democracy die?*

It is now clear that Weimar democracy was almost dead well *before* the establishment of the Nazi dictatorship. The problem for the historian is trying to determine when the Weimar Republic expired and why.

Three fundamental weaknesses of the Weimar Republic stand out.

The hostility of Germany's vested interests

From the very start, the Weimar Republic faced the hostility of Germany's established elites. Following military defeat and the threat of revolution, this opposition was at first limited. However, the fact that so many key figures in German society and business rejected the idea of a democratic republic was a major problem for Weimar. They worked against the interests of Weimar and hoped for a return to the pre-war situation. This was a powerful handicap to the successful development of the republic in the 1920s and, in the 1930s, it was to become a decisive factor in its final collapse.

Ongoing economic problems

The republic was also troubled by an almost continuous economic crisis that affected all levels of society. It inherited the enormous costs of the First World War followed by the burden of post-war reconstruction, Allied reparations and the heavy expense of the new welfare benefits. So, even though the inflation crisis of 1923 was overcome, problems in the economy were disguised and remained unresolved. These were to have dramatic consequences with the onset of the world economic crisis in 1929.

Limited base of popular support

Weimar democracy never enjoyed widespread political support. There was never total acceptance of, and confidence in, its system and its values. From the republic's birth its narrow base of popular support was caught between the extremes of left and right. But, as time went by, Weimar's claims to be the legitimate government became increasingly open to question. Sadly, Weimar democracy was associated with defeat and the humiliation of the Treaty of Versailles and reparations. Its reputation was further damaged by the crisis of 1922–3. Significantly, even the mainstays of the Weimar Republic had weaknesses:

- The main parties of German liberalism, DDP and DVP, were losing support from 1924.
- The ZP and DNVP were both moving to the political right.
- Even the loyalty and the commitment of the SPD to democracy have to be balanced against its failure to join the coalitions in the mid-1920s and its conflict with its left-wing partner, the KPD.

In short, a sizeable proportion of the German population never had faith in the existing constitutional arrangements and, as the years passed, more were looking for change.

The changing phases of the Weimar Republic

These unrelenting pressures meant that Weimar democracy went through a number of phases:

- The difficult circumstances of its birth in 1918–19 left it handicapped. It was in many respects, therefore, a major achievement that it survived the problems of the period 1919–23.
- The years of relative stability from 1924 to 1929 amounted to only a short breathing space and did not result in any strengthening of the Weimar system. On the eve of the world economic crisis it seemed that Weimar's long-term chances of survival were already far from good.
- In the end, the impact of the world depression, 1929–33, intensified the pressures that brought about Weimar's final crisis.

In the view of some historians, Weimar had been a gamble with no chance of success. For others, the republic continued to offer the hope of democratic survival right until mid-1932, when the Nazis became the largest party in the July *Reichstag* election. However, the manner of Brüning's appointment and his decision to rule by emergency decree created a particular system of presidential government. This fundamentally undermined the Weimar system and was soon followed by the electoral breakthrough of the Nazis. From this time, democracy's chance of surviving was very slim indeed. Democracy lived on with ever increasing weakness before it reached its demise in July 1932. However, in truth, democratic rule in Weimar Germany was terminal from the summer of 1930.

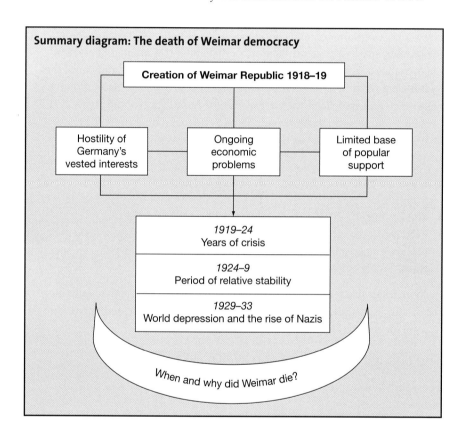

Summary diagram: The death of Weimar democracy

Creation of Weimar Republic 1918–19

Hostility of Germany's vested interests

Ongoing economic problems

Limited base of popular support

1919–24
Years of crisis

1924–9
Period of relative stability

1929–33
World depression and the rise of Nazis

When and why did Weimar die?

9 The Nazi mass movement

▶ *Who voted for the Nazis and why?*

The point is often made that Hitler and the Nazis never gained an overall majority in *Reichstag* elections. However, such an occurrence was very unlikely because of the number of political parties in Weimar Germany and the operation of the proportional representation system. Considering this, Nazi electoral achievements by July 1932 were very impressive. Only one other party on one other occasion had polled more: the SPD in the revolutionary atmosphere of January 1919 (see page 14). Nazism had become a mass movement with which millions identified and, as such, it laid the foundations for Hitler's coming to power in January 1933. Who were these Nazi voters and why were they attracted to the Nazi cause?

The results of the elections 1928–32 show the changing balance of the political parties (see page 110), although really these figures on their own are limited in what they show us about the nature of Nazi support. The graph and table in Figure 3.1 reveal a number of significant points about the kind of people who actually voted for the Nazis. From this it seems fairly clear that the Nazis made extensive gains from those parties with a middle-class and/or a Protestant identity. By contrast, it is apparent that the Catholic parties, the Communist Party and, to a large extent, the Social Democrats were able to withstand the Nazi electoral gains.

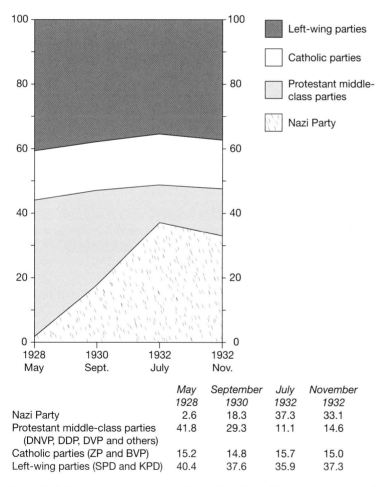

	May 1928	September 1930	July 1932	November 1932
Nazi Party	2.6	18.3	37.3	33.1
Protestant middle-class parties (DNVP, DDP, DVP and others)	41.8	29.3	11.1	14.6
Catholic parties (ZP and BVP)	15.2	14.8	15.7	15.0
Left-wing parties (SPD and KPD)	40.4	37.6	35.9	37.3

Figure 3.1 Percentage of vote gained by each major political grouping in the four *Reichstag* elections 1928–32.

Geography and denomination

These political trends are reflected in the geographical base of Nazi support, which was generally higher in the north and east of the country and lower in the south and west. Across the North German Plain, from East Prussia to Schleswig-Holstein, the Nazis gained their best results and this seems to reflect the significance of two important factors: religion and urbanisation.

In the predominantly Catholic areas (see Figure 3.2) the Nazi breakthrough was less marked, whereas the more Protestant regions were more likely to vote Nazi. Likewise, the Nazis fared less well in the large industrial cities, but gained greater support in the more rural communities and in residential suburbs.

The Nazi vote was at its lowest in the Catholic cities of the west, such as Cologne and Düsseldorf. It was at its highest in the Protestant countryside of the north and north-east, such as Schleswig-Holstein and Pomerania. Therefore, Bavaria, a strongly Catholic region, and the birthplace of Nazism, had one of the lowest Nazi votes. Such a picture does not of course take into account the exceptions created by local circumstances. For instance, parts of the province of Silesia, although mainly Catholic and urbanised, still recorded a very high Nazi vote. This was probably the result of nationalist passions generated in a border province, which had lost half its land to Poland.

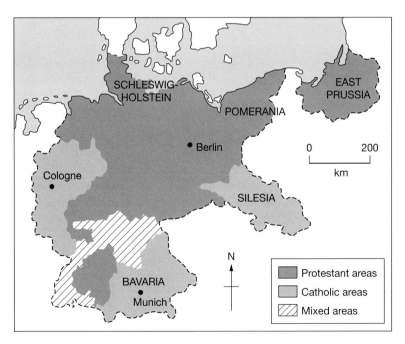

Figure 3.2 Regional divisions by religion.

Class

Nazi voters also reflected the rural/urban division in terms of their social groupings. It therefore seems that the Nazis tended to win a higher proportion of support from:

- the peasants and farmers
- the *Mittelstand* (the lower-middle classes, such as artisans, craftsmen and shopkeepers)
- the established middle classes, such as teachers, **white-collar workers** and public employees.

Also, actual Nazi membership lists (see Figure 3.3 and Table 3.7) reveal clearly that a significantly higher proportion of the middle-class subsections tended to join the Nazi Party than the other classes, that is government officials/employees, the self-employed and white-collar workers. It is worth bearing in mind two other points. First, although the working class did join the Nazi Party in smaller proportions, it was still the largest section in the NSDAP. Secondly, although it seems that the peasantry tended to vote for the Nazis, the figures show they did not join the NSDAP in the same proportion.

> **KEY TERM**
>
> **White-collar workers**
> Workers not involved in manual labour.

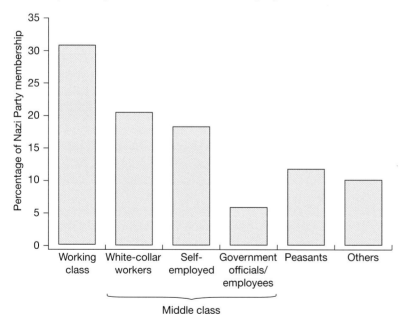

Figure 3.3 Nazi Party members in 1932.

Table 3.7 German society as a whole in 1933 (percentage)

| | Middle class | | | | |
Working class	White-collar workers	Self-employed	Government officials/employees	Peasants	Others
46.3	12.4	9.6	4.8	20.7	6.2

The appeal of Nazism

It is clear that more of the Protestants and the middle classes voted for Nazism in proportion to their percentage in German society. The real question is: why were Catholics or socialists not so readily drawn to voting for the Nazis?

- First, both Catholicism and socialism represented well-established ideologies in their own right and both opposed Nazism on an intellectual level.
- Secondly, the organisational strength of each movement provided an effective counter to Nazi propaganda. For socialism, there was the trade union structure; for Catholicism, there was the Church hierarchy, extending right down to the local parish priest.
- Thirdly, both movements had suffered under the Imperial German regime. As so often happens, persecution strengthened commitment. It was, therefore, much harder for the Nazis to break down the established loyalties of working class and Catholic communities, and their traditional **associationism**, or identity, remained strong. In contrast, the Protestants, the farmers and the middle classes had no such loyalties. They were therefore more likely to accept the Nazi message.

KEY TERM

Associationism Having a strong identity or affiliation with a particular group.

The 'politics of anxiety'

What was common among many Nazi voters was their lack of faith in, and lack of identity with, the Weimar system. They believed that their traditional role and status in society were under threat. For many of the middle classes the crisis of 1929–33 was merely the climax of a series of disasters since 1918. Hitler was able to exploit what is termed 'the politics of anxiety', as expressed by the historian T. Childers in his book *The Nazi Voter* (1983):

> [By 1930] the NSDAP had become a unique phenomenon in German electoral politics, a catch-all party of protest, whose constituents, while drawn primarily from the middle class electorate were united above all by a profound contempt for the existing political and economic system.

In this way, Hitler seemed able to offer to many Germans an escape from overwhelming crisis and a return to former days.

Young people

Another clearly identifiable group of Nazi supporters was the youth of Germany. The depression hit at the moment when young adults from the pre-war baby-boom came of age and, however good their qualifications, many had little chance of finding work. In a study of Nazi Party membership, 41.3 per cent of those who joined before 1933 had been born between 1904 and 1913, despite this age group representing only 25.3 per cent of the total population. Equally striking, of the young adults aged 20–30 who became members of political parties, 61 per cent joined the Nazis. Thus, it was the young who filled the ranks of the SA – often unemployed, disillusioned with traditional politics and without hope for the future. They saw Nazism as a movement for change, not a source of respectability. Equally, the SA activities gave them something to do. All ages were prepared to vote for the Nazis, but the younger members of society were actually more likely to become involved by joining the party.

Nazism: the people's party

The previous analysis should not obscure the fact that the Nazis still boasted a broader cross-section of supporters than any other political party. Unlike most of the other parties, the Nazis were not limited by regional, religious or class ties. So, by 1932, it is fair to say that the NSDAP had become Germany's first genuine *Volkspartei* or broad-based people's party. This point was made in a recent study of voting habits that suggests the Nazis became a mass party only by making inroads into the working-class vote. Hitler therefore succeeded in appealing to *all* sections of German society; it is simply that those from Protestant, rural and middle-class backgrounds supported the party in much greater numbers.

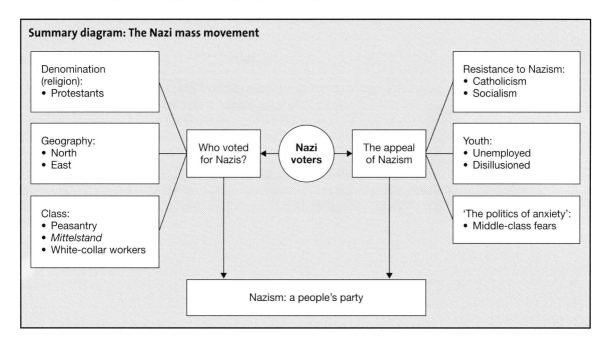

Summary diagram: The Nazi mass movement

10 Nazi political methods

▶ *In what ways did Goebbels develop propaganda?*
▶ *Did Nazi violence advance the rise of Nazism?*

It would be wrong to assume that voters for the Nazi Party were simply won over by the appeal of a radical political ideology at a time of economic crisis. There were still various fringe parties on the extreme right, which publicised similar messages. What made the Nazis stand out for the voters was their revolutionary political style. Or, to use present-day jargon, it was the presentation and packaging of the party and its programme.

Propaganda

From his earliest days in politics Hitler had shown an uncanny, but cynical awareness of the power of propaganda. In 1924 in *Mein Kampf* he had written:

> *The receptive powers of the masses are very restricted, and their understanding is feeble. On the other hand, they quickly forget. Such being the case, all-effective propaganda must be confined to a few bare essentials and those must be expressed as far as possible in stereotyped formulas.*

Such thinking was to remain the basis of Nazi propaganda, and there can be little doubt that its implementation in the years 1929–33 played a vital part in Nazi success.

The whole process of Nazi propaganda was highly organised. From April 1930 Josef Goebbels was promoted and put in complete charge of the party's propaganda machine, which reached right down to branch level. In this way, information and instructions could be sent out from party headquarters and adapted to local circumstances. It also allowed the party to target its money and efforts in the key electoral districts. Finally, it encouraged feedback from the grassroots in order to share good ideas and put them into practice.

Canvassing

Posters and leaflets had always played an important role in Nazi electioneering, but Goebbels was able to initiate a new approach. He practised mass politics on a grand scale. The electorate was deluged with material that had a range of propaganda techniques and an increasingly sophisticated application. He showed a subtlety in his understanding of psychology, as shown by the following directive issued by his propaganda office during the presidential campaign of 1932:

According to Sources F and G, in what ways does Goebbels expect the poster to have an impact?

SOURCE F

From a directive by the Nazi Reich Propaganda Department to all regional departments, quoted in J. Noakes and G. Pridham, editors, *Nazism 1919–45*, volume 1, Liverpool University Press, 2000, p. 73.

... Hitler Poster. The Hitler poster depicts a fascinating Hitler head on a completely black background. Subtitle: white on black – 'Hitler'. In accordance with the Führer's wish this poster is to be put up only during the final days (of the campaign). Since experience shows that during the final days there is a variety of coloured posters, this poster with its completely black background will contrast with all the others and will produce a tremendous effect on the masses ...

SOURCE G

'Our Last Hope'. Nazi poster of the 1932 presidential election.

Goebbels correctly recognised the need to direct propaganda according to people's social and economic interests. Specific leaflets were produced for different social groups, and Nazi speakers paid particular attention to the concerns of the individual clubs and societies they addressed. In this way, the Nazi propaganda message was tailored to fit a whole range of people. For example:

- To appeal to farmers and peasants by offering special benefits to offset the collapse of agricultural prices.
- To appeal to the unemployed and the industrial workers by aiming to overcome the depression and offering 'bread' and 'work'.

- To appeal to the *Mittelstand*, for example, by limiting the control of large department stores.
- To appease the industrialists by playing down the fear of nationalisation and the state control of the economy.

Technology

Modern technology was also exploited. Loudspeakers, radio, film and records were all used. Expensive cars and aeroplanes were hired, not only for the practical purpose of transporting Hitler quickly to as many places as possible, but also to project a statesman-like image. In 1932 three major speaking programmes were organised for Hitler, called 'Flight over Germany'. At a local level the political message was projected by the party arranging social events and entertainment such as sports, concerts and fairs.

Mass suggestion

It was in the organisation of the mass rallies that the Nazis showed their mastery of propaganda. The intention was to create an atmosphere so emotional that all members of the crowd would succumb to the collective will. This is the idea of **mass suggestion** and every kind of device was used to heighten the effect: uniforms, torches, music, salutes, flags, songs and anthems, and speeches from leading personalities. Many people have since described how they were converted as a result of such meetings.

Unifying themes and scapegoats

In order to project itself as a mass people's party, Nazism tried to embrace and bring together many of the disparate elements in Germany. This was partly achieved by Goebbels, who showed an astute ability to play on social and psychological factors to influence people (see Figure 3.4). Three key unifying themes dominated Nazi propaganda:

- The *Führer* cult. Hitler was portrayed as a messiah-type figure, who could offer strong authoritarian leadership and a vision for Nazi Germany's future.
- The *Volksgemeinschaft* (national community). To appeal to the people for the development of a unifying movement regardless of class.
- German nationalism. To play on German nationalism and to exploit the discontent since the First World War. To make Germany great again.

Through these themes, Nazi propaganda successfully portrayed itself as both revolutionary and reactionary. The party aimed to destroy the republic, while at the same time promising a return to a glorious bygone age.

In addition, Nazism cynically played on the idea of 'scapegoats'. It focused on several identifiable groups, which were denounced and blamed for Germany's suffering:

- The 'November criminals'. The politicians responsible for the Armistice and the creation of the republic became representative of all negative aspects associated with Weimar democracy.

KEY TERM

Mass suggestion
A psychological term suggesting that large groups of people can be unified simply by the atmosphere of the occasion. Hitler and Goebbels used their speeches and large rallies to particularly good effect.

- Communists. By playing on the fears of communism – the KPD was a sizeable party of thirteen to seventeen per cent in 1930–2 – and the increasing threat of Communist USSR.
- Jews. It was easy to exploit the long-established history of anti-Semitism in Europe as a whole, and in Germany in particular (although they only made up less than one per cent of the German population).

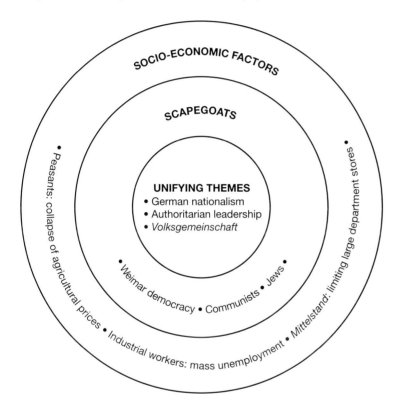

Figure 3.4 Nazi propaganda.

Violence

There was one other strand to the political style of this Nazi revolution: the systematic encouragement and use of violence. Weimar politics had been a bloody affair from the start, but the growth of the SA and SS unleashed an unprecedented wave of violence, persecution and intimidation.

The growth of unemployment resulted in a phenomenal expansion of the SA, led by Röhm, in 1921–3 and 1930–4. Understandably, many people joined as members of the SA out of desperation, for food and accommodation, although much of it was just thuggery. The SA mainly was responsible for the violence against the opposition, especially the communists. All this helped to destabilise the already difficult situation in Germany and, in the wake of the presidential election (see page 106), the SA was actually banned for three months. However, it was restored by the new chancellor, Papen, in June 1932. During the campaign of July 1932 there were 461 political riots in Prussia alone: battles between communists and Nazis on 10 July left ten people dead; a week later, nineteen died after the Nazis marched through a working-class suburb of Hamburg.

Such violent activities were encouraged by the Nazi leadership as control of the streets was seen as essential to the expansion of Nazi power. The ballot box of democracy remained merely a means to an end, and, therefore, other non-democratic tactics were considered legitimate in the quest for power. The Nazis poured scorn on rational discussion and fair play. For them, the end did justify the means. For their democratic opponents, there was the dilemma of how to resist those who exploited the freedoms of a democratic society merely to undermine it.

The Stennes' revolt

Despite the Nazi violence, Hitler became increasingly keen to maintain the policy of legality. He felt that it was important to keep discipline, so he could maintain the image of a party that could offer firm and ordered government. The SA had generally supported the radical socialist aspects of Nazism, and yet Hitler was concerned increasingly with appealing to the middle-class conservative Nazi voters. The most serious disagreement between the SA and the party leadership has become known as the Stennes' revolt, in February 1931.

Walther Stennes, the leader of the Berlin SA, rebelled against the orders of Hitler and Goebbels to act legally and to limit the violence. Hitler defeated the revolt with a small purge, but it underlined the fact that the relationship between the party leadership and the SA was at times very difficult. These differences were not really resolved until the infamous **Night of the Long Knives** in 1934 (see pages 144–8).

KEY TERM

Night of the Long Knives
A crucial turning point that took place on 30 June 1934 when Hitler arranged for the SS to purge the SA leadership. About 200 victims were murdered, including Röhm, Strasser and Schleicher.

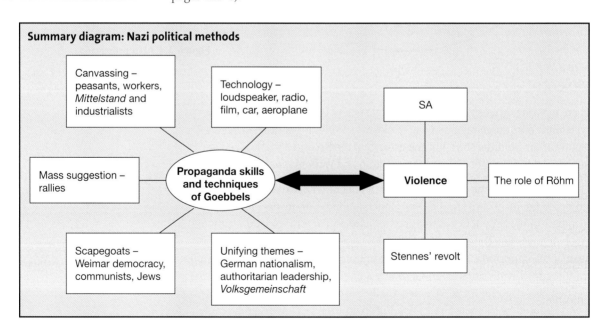

Summary diagram: Nazi political methods

- Canvassing – peasants, workers, *Mittelstand* and industrialists
- Technology – loudspeaker, radio, film, car, aeroplane
- Mass suggestion – rallies
- **Propaganda skills and techniques of Goebbels**
- Scapegoats – Weimar democracy, communists, Jews
- Unifying themes – German nationalism, authoritarian leadership, *Volksgemeinschaft*
- SA
- **Violence**
- The role of Röhm
- Stennes' revolt

Political intrigue and the appointment of Hitler

▶ *Why did Papen and Schleicher fail?*

▶ *Why did President Hindenburg eventually appoint Hitler as chancellor?*

The political strength of the Nazi Party following the July 1932 *Reichstag* elections was beyond doubt (see page 110). However, there still remained the problem for Hitler of how to translate this popular following into real power. He was determined to take nothing less than the post of chancellor for himself. This was unacceptable to both Schleicher and Papen, who were keen to have Nazis in the cabinet, but only in positions of limited power. Therefore, the meeting between Hitler, Papen and Hindenburg on 13 August ended in deadlock.

Papen's failure

As long as Papen retained the sympathy of Hindenburg, Hitler's ambitions would remain frustrated. Indeed, a leading modern historian, Jeremy Noakes, describes the period from August to December 1932 as 'the months of crisis' for the Nazis, since 'it appeared the policy of legality had led to a cul-de-sac'. Party morale declined and some of the wilder SA members again became increasingly restless.

On the other hand, Papen was humiliated when on 12 September the *Reichstag* passed a massive vote of 'no confidence' in his government (512 votes to 42). Consequently, he dissolved the new *Reichstag* and called for yet another election. In some respects Papen's reading of the situation was sound. The Nazis were short of money, their morale was low and the electorate was growing tired of repeated elections. These factors undoubtedly contributed to the fall in the Nazi vote on 6 November to 11.7 million (33.1 per cent), which gave them 196 seats. However, Papen's tactics had not achieved their desired end, since the fundamental problem of overcoming the lack of majority *Reichstag* support for his cabinet remained. Hitler stood firm: he would not join the government except as chancellor.

In his frustration, Papen began to consider a drastic alternative; the dissolution of the *Reichstag*, the declaration of **martial law** and the establishment of a presidential dictatorship. However, such a plan was completely opposed by Schleicher, who found Papen's growing political desperation and his friendship with President Hindenburg additional causes for concern. Schleicher still believed that the popular support for the Nazis could not be ignored, and that Papen's plan would give rise to civil commotion and perhaps civil war. When he informed Hindenburg of the army's lack of confidence in Papen, the President was forced, unwillingly, to demand the resignation of his friendly chancellor.

 KEY TERM

Martial law Government and control by military authorities over the civilian population.

Schleicher's failure

Schleicher at last came out into the open. Over the previous two years he had been happy to play his role behind the scenes, but he now decided to become the dominant player when he gained the favour of Hindenburg and was appointed chancellor on 2 December.

Schleicher's aims, rather ambitiously, were to achieve political stability and restore national confidence by creating a more broadly based government. He had a two-pronged strategy:

- First, to gain some support from elements of the political left, especially the trade unions, by suggesting a programme of public works.
- Second, to split the Nazis and attract the more socialist wing of the Nazi Party, under Gregor Strasser, by offering him the position of vice-chancellor.

With these objectives Schleicher, therefore, intended to project himself as the chancellor of national reconciliation. However, his political manoeuvres came to nothing.

First, the trade unions remained deeply suspicious of his motives and, encouraged by their political masters from the SPD, broke off negotiations. Moreover, the idea of public works alienated some of the landowners and businessmen. Secondly, although Schleicher's strategy of offering Strasser the post of vice-chancellor was a very clever one, in the end it did not work. Strasser responded positively to Schleicher's overtures and he was keen to accept the post, but the appointment exacerbated the fundamental differences between Hitler and Strasser and led to a massive row. Hitler retained the loyalty of the party's leadership and Strasser was left isolated and promptly forced to resign from the party. This marked a major defeat to the radical Nazis.

Nevertheless, the incident had been a major blow to party morale, and tensions remained high in the last few weeks of 1932, as the prospect of achieving power seemed to drift away.

Hitler's success

Hitler's fortunes did not begin to take a more favourable turn until the first week of 1933. Papen had never forgiven Schleicher for dropping him and was determined to regain political office. He recognised that he could achieve this only by convincing Hindenburg that he could muster majority support in the *Reichstag*. Consequently, secret contacts were made with Nazi leaders, which culminated in a meeting on 4 January 1933 between Papen and Hitler. Here, it was agreed in essence that Hitler should head a Nazi–Nationalist coalition government with Papen as vice-chancellor.

Backstairs intrigue to unseat Schleicher now took over. Papen looked for support for his plan from major landowners, leaders of industry and the army. It was only now that the conservative establishment thought that they had identified an escape from the threat of communism and the dangerous intrigues of Schleicher. But, above all, Papen had to convince the president himself. Hindenburg, undoubtedly encouraged by his son, Oskar, and his state secretary, Meissner, eventually gave in. Schleicher had failed in his attempt to bring stability. In fact, he had only succeeded in frightening the powerful vested interests with his ambitious plans.

Hindenburg finally agreed, on the advice of Papen, to withdraw his support for Schleicher and to appoint Hitler as chancellor, in the mistaken conviction that Hitler could be controlled and used in the interests of the conservative establishment. Papen believed that Hitler would be a chancellor in chains and so, two days later, on 30 January 1933, Hindenburg agreed to sanction the creation of a Nazi–Nationalist coalition.

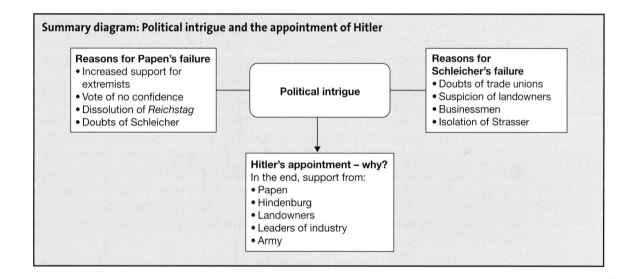

Summary diagram: Political intrigue and the appointment of Hitler

Reasons for Papen's failure
- Increased support for extremists
- Vote of no confidence
- Dissolution of *Reichstag*
- Doubts of Schleicher

Political intrigue

Reasons for Schleicher's failure
- Doubts of trade unions
- Suspicion of landowners
- Businessmen
- Isolation of Strasser

Hitler's appointment – why?
In the end, support from:
- Papen
- Hindenburg
- Landowners
- Leaders of industry
- Army

12 Conclusion

▶ *Why was Weimar replaced by Hitler and the Nazis?*

The Great Depression transformed the Nazis into a mass movement. Admittedly, 63 per cent of Germans never voted for them, but 37 per cent of the electorate did, so that the Nazis became by far the strongest party in a multi-party democracy. The depression had led to such profound social and economic hardship that it created an environment of discontent, which was easily exploited by the Nazis' style of political activity. Indeed, it must be questionable whether Hitler would have become a national political figure without the severity of that economic downturn. However, his mixture of racist, nationalist and anti-democratic ideas was readily received by a broad spectrum of German people, and especially by the disgruntled middle classes.

Yet, other extreme right-wing groups with similar ideas and conditions did not enjoy similar success. This is partially explained by the impressive manner in which the Nazi message was communicated: the use of modern propaganda techniques, the violent exploitation of scapegoats – especially Jews and communists – and the well-organised structure of the party apparatus. All these factors undoubtedly helped but, in terms of electoral appeal, it is impossible to ignore the powerful impact of Hitler as a charismatic leader with a cult following. Furthermore, he exhibited extraordinary political acumen and ruthlessness when he was involved in the detail of political infighting.

Nevertheless, the huge popular following of the Nazis, which helped to undermine the continued operation of democracy, was insufficient on its own to give Hitler power. In the final analysis, it was the mutual recognition by Hitler and the representatives of the traditional leaders of the army, the landowners and industry that they needed each other, which led to Hitler's appointment as chancellor of a coalition government on 30 January 1933.

Ever since September 1930 every government had been forced to resort almost continuously to the use of presidential emergency decrees because they lacked a popular mandate. In the chaos of 1932 the only other realistic alternative to including the Nazis in the government was some kind of military regime – a presidential dictatorship backed by the army, perhaps. However, that, too, would have faced similar difficulties. Indeed, by failing to satisfy the extreme left and the extreme right there would have been a very real possibility of civil war. A coalition with Hitler's Nazis, therefore, provided the conservative elites with both mass support and some alluring promises: a vigorous attack on Germany's political left wing; and rearmament as a precursor to economic and political expansion abroad. For Hitler, the inclusion of Papen and Hugenberg gave his cabinet an air of conservative respectability.

In the end, Hitler became chancellor because the political forces of the left and centre were too divided and too weak, and because the conservative right wing was prepared to accept him as a partner in government in the mistaken belief that he could be tamed. With hindsight, it can be seen that 30 January 1933 was decisive. The dictatorship did not start technically until the completion of the 'legal revolution' in February–March 1933 (see pages 134–40), but Hitler was already entrenched in power and, as one historian has claimed, now he 'could only be removed by an earthquake'.

Key debate

> ▶ *Was the creation of the Nazi dictatorship an inevitable product of German history?*

From the very outset, the establishment of the Nazi dictatorship presented observers not only with profound political and economic questions, but also with serious moral ones. Even many years later, objective historians cannot help but bring a small degree of subjectivity to their interpretations.

Left-wing Marxists: Nazism, the result of crisis capitalism

In the 1930s many left-wing analysts sought to explain the unexpected rise of Nazism (and the rise of fascism in Italy). They came to believe that there was a close connection between the advance of Nazism and the crisis of capitalism faced by Germany in 1929–33. Consequently, big business lost faith in the Weimar Republic and supported the Nazis, who were seen as mere 'agents' for the controlling capitalists who sought to satisfy their desire for profits.

Anti-German determinists: Hitler, the result of German history

Left-wing arguments were matched by some equally strong views from critics of Germany. Clearly, anti-German feelings can be put down to the impact of wartime propaganda in Britain. Nevertheless, some academic historians after the Second World War portrayed Nazism as the natural product of German history. The renowned English historian A.J.P. Taylor wrote in *The Course of German History* in 1945: 'It was no more a mistake for the German people to end up with Hitler than it is an accident when a river flows into the sea.'

The culmination of this kind of anti-German determinist view was probably reached with the publication in 1959 of William Shirer's *Rise and Fall of the Third Reich*. This monumental work, written by an American journalist who had worked as a correspondent in Germany between 1926 and 1941, had a profound impact on the general public. He argued that Germany's political evolution, its cultural and intellectual heritage, and the people's national character all contributed to the inevitable success of Hitler. He wrote:

EXTRACT I

From W.H. Shirer, *The Rise and Fall of the Third Reich*, Secker & Warburg, 1960, pp. 122–3.

Acceptance of autocracy, of blind obedience, to the petty tyrants who ruled as princes, became ingrained in the German mind. The idea of democracy, or rule by parliament … did not sprout in Germany. This political backwardness of Germany … set Germany apart from and behind the other countries of the West. There was no natural growth of a nation. This has to be borne in mind if

In Shirer's view in Extract 1, what were the main reasons for the failure of Weimar democracy?

one is to comprehend the disastrous road this people subsequently took and the warped state of mind which settled over it …

There thus arose quite artificially a state born of no popular force nor even an idea except that of conquest, and held together by the absolute power of the ruler, by narrow minded bureaucracy which did his bidding and by a ruthless disciplined Army … The State, which was run with the efficiency and soullessness of a factory, became all; the people were little more than cogs in the machinery …

Gerhard Ritter: Nazism, the result of a 'moral crisis' in Europe

Not surprisingly, the implicit anti-German sentiments were not kindly received in Germany. As a consequence, there emerged in the post-war decade in West Germany a school of thought that emphasised the 'moral crisis of European society' epitomised by Ritter, who focused on the European circumstances in which Nazism had emerged. In his view, it was hard to believe that Germany's traditions, such as the power of the Prussian state, or its rich cultural history could have contributed to the emergence of Hitler. Instead, Ritter emphasised the events and developments since 1914 in Europe as a whole. It was the shock given to the traditional European order by the First World War that created the environment for the emergence of Nazism. The decline in religion and standards of morality, a tendency towards corruption and materialism and the emergence of mass democracy were all exploited by Hitler to satisfy his desire for power.

Structuralists: Nazism, a response to Germany's social and economic 'structures'

The 1960s witnessed a phenomenal growth in research on the Third Reich, partly due to the release of the German archives by the Western Allies. By the late 1960s and early 1970s, historians such as Martin Broszat and Hans Mommsen had started to exert a major influence on our understanding of the rise of Hitler and the Third Reich, and they have been dubbed as **structuralists**.

In essence, the structuralist interpretation has emphasised Germany's continuities from the 1850s to 1945. It argues that Germany's society and economy had remained dominated by authoritarian forces, such as the armed services and the bureaucracy, and had not really developed democratic institutions. As a result, the power and influence of such conservative vested interests continued to rule Germany – even after the creation of the Weimar Republic – and these conservatives sympathised with the Nazi movement, which provided the means to uphold a right-wing authoritarian regime. Hans-Ulrich Wehler wrote:

EXTRACT 2

From Hans-Ulrich Wehler, *The German Empire, 1871–1918*, Berg, 1985, pp. 230–1.

No judgement on Weimar's chances of survival can skirt round the problem that after a little more than a dozen years the downward spiral to Brüning's authoritarian regime began only to be followed by the successful National Socialist 'seizure of power' in 1933. The latter undoubtedly represented a convergence of certain trends in German history …

Since continuity in the imperial bureaucracy and the Army, in the educational system and the political parties, in the economy and its pressure groups, and so on, were largely preserved, one thing at least was assured: the traditional power elites were able to depute the stirrup holders for Hitler … In the concrete circumstances which prevailed, however, the Führer could never, at any rate, have climbed into the saddle without the stirrups to help him. Viewed in this light, the costs of the decision taken in 1918–19 began in 1933, to assume undreamt-of dimensions which were eventually to involve the whole world.

> According to Wehler in Extract 2, which institutions made it possible for Hitler to gain power?

Internationalists: Nazism, a result of Hitler's ideology and his evil genius

Some historians have continued to argue that there is no escape from the central importance of Hitler the individual in the Nazi seizure of power. Indeed, **intentionalists**, such as Klaus Hildebrand and Eberhard Jäckel, believe that the personality and ideology of Hitler remain so essential that Nazism can be equated with the term 'Hitlerism'. This is because, although the intentionalists accept the special circumstances created by Germany's history, they emphasise the pivotal role of Hitler, who was a brilliant **demagogue** with masterly political skills which enabled him to outmanoeuvre the other elites.

Ian Kershaw: Hitler's coming to power, the result of miscalculation

The latest interpretation from Kershaw, arguably the leading British historian of Nazi Germany, goes well beyond the framework of mere biography. He deliberately tries to balance structuralist and intentionalist views. Kershaw recognises the circumstances of the time, such as the xenophobic nationalism, the defeat of the war and Weimar's difficult conditions, which allowed the 'Austrian drifter' to emerge. Yet, most significantly, he emphasises that the appointment of Hitler was not inevitable, but the result of multiple miscalculations. Even until the very last moment at 11 o'clock on 30 January 1933, there was a possibility that a Hitler chancellorship might not materialise. He writes:

 **KEY TERMS**

Intentionalists Historians who interpret history by emphasising the role (intentions) of people who shape history.

Demagogue A leader who plays on the prejudices of the masses with populist emotions.

? How and why does Kershaw argue in Extract 3 that there was no inevitability in Hitler's rise to power?

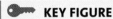

KEY FIGURE

Otto von Bismarck (1815–98)

Chancellor of Prussia from 1862 and then of Germany 1871–90. A conservative nationalist who recognised the need for changes to strengthen Imperial Germany.

EXTRACT 3

From Ian Kershaw, *Hitler*, Longman, 1991, p. 38.

*There was no inevitability about Hitler's triumph in January 1933. Five years earlier, the Nazi Party had been a fringe irritant in German politics, but no more … External events, the Young Plan to adjust German reparations payments, the Wall Street Crash and Brüning's entirely unnecessary decision to have an election in summer 1930 – put the Nazis on the political map. Though democracy had by that time an unpromising future, a Nazi dictatorship seemed far less likely than some other form of authoritarian dictatorship or even a reversion to a **Bismarckian** style of government, possibly under a restored monarchy. In bringing Hitler to power, chances and conservative miscalculation played a larger role than any actions of the Nazi leader himself.*

Chapter summary

Hitler emerged from an obscure background. He and the party were the clear products of the difficulties of post-war Germany. Nazi ideology grew out of an uncompromising rejection of Weimar democracy and socialism; instead, fervent nationalism and racism, especially anti-Semitism, were embraced.

The strategy of seizing power in the Munich *putsch* of 1923 was a disaster and Hitler's imprisonment could have ended his political ambitions once and for all. Nevertheless, once he was released, the party was revitalised. The restructuring of the many Nazi organisations and the dynamic propaganda led by Goebbels helped to lay better foundation stones for the party. Yet, the Nazis made a limited impression in the 1920s; it was really the world depression which destabilised the fragile Weimar Republic.

The socio-economic impact was very severe in Germany and resulted in increasingly desperate political measures. Brüning's resorting to the use of presidential decrees marked a crucial turning point in the breakdown of German democracy. The political crisis was exacerbated further by the electoral success of the Nazis in becoming the largest party. Therefore, when the governments of Papen and Schleicher collapsed, Hitler was appointed as chancellor by Hindenburg in the mistaken belief that Hitler could be controlled and used in the interests of the conservative establishment.

Refresher questions

Use these questions to remind yourself of the key material covered in this chapter.

1 How did Hitler manage to turn the failure of the Beer Hall *putsch* to his advantage?

2 Explain each of these elements of Nazi thinking: a) racism, b) anti-democracy, c) nationalism and d) socialist aspects.

3 How original was Nazi ideology?

4 Had the Nazi Party taken root in the 1920s?

5 How did the economic crisis affect the lives of the German people?

6 Why did the economic crisis turn into a political one in 1930?

7 To what extent was Brüning a failure?

8 Which social groups tended to vote Nazi? And why?

9 Why has Nazism been described as a 'people's party'?

10 In what ways did Goebbels develop Nazi propaganda?

11 How did violence help to advance the rise of Nazism?

12 Why did the Papen and Scheicher governments fail to achieve political stability?

13 Why did President Hindenburg eventually appoint Hitler as chancellor?

14 Why was Weimar replaced by Hitler and the Nazis?

 Question practice

ESSAY QUESTIONS

1 To what extent is it accurate to describe the Nazi Party as weak in the years before 1929?

2 Assess the reasons for the appeal of the Nazi Party to German voters between 1930 and 1932.

3 'The Weimar Republic was swept away in an economic catastrophe.' To what extent do you agree with this statement?

4 Which of the following was of greater importance for Hitler's accession to power? i) Popular support. ii) Backstairs intrigue. Explain your answer with reference to both i) and ii).

INTERPRETATION QUESTION

1 Read the interpretation that follows and answer both parts of the question. Some historians have claimed that 'There was nothing inevitable about Hitler's triumph in January 1933.' (From I. Kershaw, *Hitler: 1889–1936 Hubris*, 2000.) a) Explain how this interpretation can be supported. b) Explain how this interpretation can be challenged.

CHAPTER 4

Nazi consolidation of power 1933–4

Although Hitler was legally appointed as chancellor, he did not have dictatorial powers. The purpose of this chapter is to understand how, by the summer of 1934, Germany became a one-party state under the leadership of Hitler. It is important to recognise the range of competing political forces and the significance of the turning points in the Nazi consolidation of power. These are considered in the following sections:

★ The Nazi 'legal revolution'
★ Co-ordination: *Gleichschaltung*
★ The Night of the Long Knives
★ A Nazi revolution?

Key dates

1933	Jan. 30	Hitler appointed as chancellor
	Feb. 27	*Reichstag* fire: communists blamed
	March 5	Last elections according to the Weimar constitution
	March 21	Day of Potsdam
	March 23	Enabling Law passed

1933	July 14	All political opposition to NSDAP declared illegal
1934	June 30	The Night of the Long Knives; purge of the SA
	Aug. 2	Death of Hindenburg: Hitler merged the posts of chancellor and president to become *Führer*

 The Nazi 'legal revolution'

► *What were the political strengths and weaknesses of Hitler?*
► *How did Hitler create a dictatorship in two months?*

Although Hitler had been appointed chancellor, his power was by no means absolute. Hindenburg had not been prepared to support Hitler's appointment until he had been satisfied that the chancellor's power would remain limited. Such was Papen's confidence about Hitler's restricted room for manoeuvre that he boasted to a friend, 'In two months we'll have pushed Hitler into a corner so hard that he'll be squeaking.'

Hitler's limitations as chancellor

At first sight, the confidence of the conservatives seemed to be justified, since Hitler's position was weak in purely constitutional terms:

- There were only two other Nazis in the cabinet of twelve: **Wilhelm Frick**, as minister of the interior, and Göring (see page 136) as a minister, but with no specific responsibility. There were, therefore, nine other non-Nazi members of the cabinet, all from conservative-nationalist backgrounds, such as the army, industry and landowners.
- Hitler's coalition government did not have a majority in the *Reichstag*, suggesting that it would be difficult for the Nazis to introduce any dramatic legislation.
- The chancellor's post, as the previous twelve months had clearly shown, was dependent on the whim of President Hindenburg, and he openly resented Hitler. Hindenburg had made Hitler chancellor, but he could as easily sack him.

Hitler was very much aware of the potential power of the army and the trade unions. He could not alienate these forces, which could break his government. The army could arrange a military coup or the trade unions could organise a general strike, as they had done in 1920 (see page 37).

Hitler's strengths as chancellor

Within two months, the above restraints were overcome by Hitler. Moreover, power was to be achieved by carrying on with the policy of legality, which the party had pursued since 1925. Hitler already possessed several key strengths when he became chancellor:

- He was the leader of the largest political party in Germany, which was why the policy of ignoring him had not worked. During 1932 it had led only to the ineffectual governments of Papen and Schleicher. Therefore, political realism forced the conservatives to work with him. They probably needed him more than he needed them. The alternative to Hitler was civil war or a communist coup – or so it seemed to many people at the time.
- More importantly, the Nazi Party had now gained access to the resources of the state. For example, Göring not only had a place in the cabinet but was also minister of the interior in Prussia, with responsibility for the police. It was a responsibility that he used blatantly to harass opponents, while ignoring Nazi crimes. Goebbels (see page 167), likewise, exploited the propaganda opportunities on behalf of the Nazis. 'The struggle is a light one now', he confided in his diary, '… since we are able to employ all the means of the state. Radio and press are at our disposal.'
- Above all, however, Hitler was a masterly political tactician. He was determined to achieve absolute power for himself whereas Papen was really politically naïve. It soon became clear that 'Papen's political puppet' was too clever to be strung along by a motley collection of ageing conservatives.

KEY FIGURE

Wilhelm Frick (1877–1946)

Trained as a lawyer and an early member of NSDAP. Minister of the interior 1933–43 but lost influence after his dismissal. Executed in the Nuremberg trials.

Hermann Göring

1893   Born in Bavaria, the son of the German South West Africa governor

1923   Took part in the Munich *putsch* and injured

1933   Joined Hitler's cabinet as minister without portfolio

        Used the *Reichstag* fire to discredit the communists. Exploited the terror to impose the dictatorship

1934   Helped to organise the Night of the Long Knives

1935   Commander-in-chief of the new *Luftwaffe* (air force)

1936   Appointed director of the Four-Year Plan

1940–5   Retained most of his offices. Increasingly isolated within the Nazi leadership

1946   Killed himself an hour before his execution at the Nuremberg trials

Göring came from a well-to-do family and with this status and the contacts provided by his aristocratic first wife, he was able to give Nazism a more respectable image in high society. He was popular because of his witty and charming conversation.

Göring played a crucial role in the rise of Nazism and during the early years of the Third Reich. His approach was uncompromising and brutal. During 1933–4 he organised the infiltration of the German police by the SA and SS and willingly used violence and murder to secure Nazi power. He was deeply involved in the *Reichstag* fire (see page 138) and the Night of the Long Knives (see pages 144–8). From 1936 he overtook Schacht and became in effect economic dictator.

Göring acquired a host of titles and posts, and in 1939 he was officially named as Hitler's successor. However, he became increasingly resented by other leading Nazis for his ambition and greed. After the failure of the *Luftwaffe* to win the Battle of Britain (1940) he was more isolated within the leadership and his influence declined.

The *Reichstag* election, 5 March 1933

Hitler lost no time in removing his strings. Within 24 hours of his appointment as chancellor, new *Reichstag* elections had been called. He felt that new elections would not only increase the Nazi vote, but also enhance his own status.

The campaign for the final *Reichstag* elections held according to the Weimar constitution had few of the characteristics expected of a democracy: violence and terror dominated, with meetings of the socialists and communists being regularly broken up by the Nazis. In Prussia, Göring used his authority to enrol an extra 50,000 into the police; nearly all were members of the SA and SS. Altogether 69 people died in street fights during the five-week campaign.

The Nazis also used the atmosphere of hate and fear to great effect in their election propaganda. Hitler set the tone in his 'Appeal to the German People' of 31 January 1933. He blamed the prevailing poor economic conditions on democratic government and the terrorist activities of the communists. He cultivated the idea of the government as a peaceful 'national uprising' determined to restore Germany's pride and unity. In this way, he played on the deepest desires of many Germans, but never committed himself to the details of a political and economic programme.

SOURCE A

In what ways does the cartoonist convey the nature of Hitler's political dilemma in Source A?

'Not the most comfortable seat.' A US cartoon drawn soon after Hitler's appointment as chancellor in 1933.

Another key factor was the improved Nazi financial situation. At a meeting on 20 February with twenty leading industrialists, Hitler was promised 3 million *Reichsmarks*. With such financial backing and Goebbels' exploitation of the media, the Nazis were confident of securing a parliamentary majority.

The *Reichstag* fire

As the campaign moved towards its climax, one further bizarre episode strengthened the Nazi hand. On 27 February the *Reichstag* building was set on fire, and a young Dutch communist, Marinus van der Lubbe, was arrested in incriminating circumstances. At the time, it was believed by many that the incident was a Nazi plot to support the claims of a communist coup, and thereby to justify Nazi repression. However, to this day the episode has defied satisfactory explanation. A major investigation in 1962 concluded that van der Lubbe had acted alone; a further eighteen years later Berlin authorities posthumously acquitted him; whereas in his recent biography of Hitler, Ian Kershaw remains convinced that van der Lubbe acted on his own in a series of three attempted arsons within a few weeks. So, it is probable that the true explanation will never be known. The real significance of the *Reichstag* fire is the cynical way it was exploited by the Nazis to their advantage.

On the next day, 28 February, Frick drew up, and Hindenburg signed, the 'Decree for the Protection of People and State'. In a few short clauses, most civil and political liberties were suspended and the power of central government was strengthened. The justification for the decree was the threat posed by the communists. Following this, in the final week of the election campaign, hundreds of anti-Nazis were arrested and the violence reached new heights.

Election result

In this atmosphere of fear, Germany went to the polls on 5 March. The election had a very high turnout of 88 per cent – a figure this high suggests the influence and intimidation of the SA, corruption by officials and an increased government control of the radio.

Somewhat surprisingly, the Nazis increased their vote from 33.1 per cent to only 43.9 per cent, thereby securing 288 seats. Hitler could claim a majority in the new *Reichstag* only with the help of the 52 seats won by the Nationalists. It was not only disappointing; it was also a political blow, since any change in the existing Weimar constitution required a two-thirds majority in the *Reichstag*.

The Enabling Law, March 1933

Despite this constitutional hurdle, Hitler decided to propose to the new *Reichstag* an Enabling Law that would effectively do away with parliamentary procedure and legislation and instead transfer full powers to the chancellor and his government for four years. In this way, the dictatorship would be grounded in legality. However, the successful passing of the law needed a two-thirds majority, which depended on gaining the support or abstention of some of the other major political parties.

A further problem was that the momentum built up within the lower ranks of the Nazi Party was proving increasingly difficult for Hitler to contain in the regional areas. Members were impatiently taking the law into their own hands and this gave the impression of a '**revolution from below**', as was highlighted by Rudolf Diels, the first head of the **Gestapo**, in his memoirs:

SOURCE B

From Rudolf Diels, *Lucifer Ante Portas*, 1950, p. 200, quoted in J. Noakes and G. Pridham, editors, *Nazism 1919–45*, volume 1, University of Liverpool Press, 1988, p. 147.

The uprising of the Berlin SA electrified the remotest parts of the country … In Silesia, the Rhineland, Westphalia and the Ruhr area unauthorised arrests, insubordination to the police, forcible entry into public buildings, disturbances of the work of the authorities, the smashing up of dwellings and night raids had begun before the Reichstag fire at the end of February.

It was no longer possible to tell which public or private spheres had been penetrated by the SA, and scarcely possible to guess the purposes for which it allowed itself to be hired, and employed. There was hardly a single business undertaking which had not employed an 'old fighter' of the SA for protection against the dangers of coordination, denunciation, and threats. They were present everywhere as self-appointed directors, special commissars and SA delegates.

The 'revolution from below' threatened to destroy Hitler's image of legality, and antagonise the conservative vested interests and his DNVP coalition partners. Such was his concern that a grandiose act of reassurance was arranged that became known as the Day of Potsdam. On 21 March, at Potsdam garrison church, Goebbels orchestrated the ceremony to celebrate the opening of the *Reichstag*. In the presence of Hindenburg, the Crown Prince (the son of Kaiser Wilhelm II) and many of the army's leading generals, Hitler symbolically aligned National Socialism with the forces of the old Germany.

Two days later the new *Reichstag* met in the Kroll Opera House to consider the Enabling Law, and on this occasion the Nazis revealed a very different image. The communists (those not already in prison) were refused admittance, while the deputies in attendance faced a barrage of intimidation from the ranks of the SA who surrounded the building.

The Nazis still required a two-thirds majority to pass the law and, on the assumption that the SPD would vote against, they needed the backing of the ZP. Hitler thus promised in his speech of 23 March to respect the rights of the Catholic Church and to uphold religious and moral values. These were false promises, which the ZP deputies deceived themselves into believing. In the end

KEY TERMS

Revolution from below
The radical elements in the party wanted to direct the Nazi revolution from a more local level rather than from the leadership in Berlin.

Gestapo *Geheime Staats Polizei*. The secret state police. A key policing organisation for surveillance and repression.

How does Diels in Source B challenge the Nazi claim of the peaceful national uprising?

only the Social Democrats voted against, and the Enabling Law was passed by 444 to 94 votes.

Germany had succumbed to what K.D. Bracher in the 1950s has called the 'legal revolution'. Within the space of a few weeks Hitler had legally dismantled the Weimar constitution. The way was now open for him to create a one-party dictatorship.

Adolf Hitler

1889	Born in Braunau-am-Inn, Austria. Left school with no real qualifications
1914–18	Served in the German Army and awarded the Iron Cross, first class
1921	Appointed leader of the NSDAP
1923–4	Beer Hall *putsch*. Sentenced to five years in prison for treason; wrote *Mein Kampf*
1925–33	Restructured the party and committed the party to a 'legality policy'
1933	Appointed German chancellor by Hindenburg
	Given dictatorial powers by the Enabling Law
1934	Ordered the purge of the SA, known as the Night of the Long Knives
	Death of Hindenburg: Hitler assumed the joint offices of chancellor and president and the title of *Führer*
1938	Blomberg–Fritsch crisis. Purge of army generals and other leading conservatives
1939	Ordered the invasion of Poland on 1 September (resulting in the declaration of war by Britain and France)
1941	Ordered the invasion of the USSR on 22 June
1944	Survived assassination attempt in the Stauffenberg Bomb Plot
1945	Killed himself in the ruins of Berlin

Hitler's outlook on life was shaped by his unhappy years in Vienna (1907–13) when he failed to become an art student. It was here, too, that the core of his political ideas was established: anti-Semitism, German nationalism, anti-democracy and anti-Marxism. Hitler found a real purpose only in the war of 1914–18.

His nationalism and the camaraderie of the troops gave him direction, but the shock of Germany's surrender confirmed his prejudices.

In post-war Germany Hitler was drawn to the NSDAP, which remained a fringe political party in Bavaria in the 1920s. The depression created the environment in which he could exploit his political skills: his charisma, his rhetoric and his advanced use of propaganda. Nevertheless, although he became the leader of the largest party by 1932, he was only invited to be chancellor in January 1933 as part of a coalition with other nationalists and conservatives.

The Nazi dictatorship was established with immense speed and Hitler was personally given unlimited powers. He was portrayed as the all-powerful dictator, but there has been great debate about his direction of daily affairs (see pages 152–6). Nevertheless, Hitler's leadership controlled German events through:

- creating a one-party state
- supporting the racial policy that culminated in genocide
- pursuing an expansionist foreign policy.

Below the surface Hitler's regime was chaotic, but the cult of the *Führer* was upheld by Goebbels' propaganda machine, as well as by the diplomatic and military successes of 1935–41. However, winter 1942–3 marked the 'turn of the tide' and Hitler, increasingly deluding himself, refused to consider surrender. It was only when the Red Army closed in on Berlin that the spell of the *Führer*'s power was finally broken – by Hitler killing himself in his bunker.

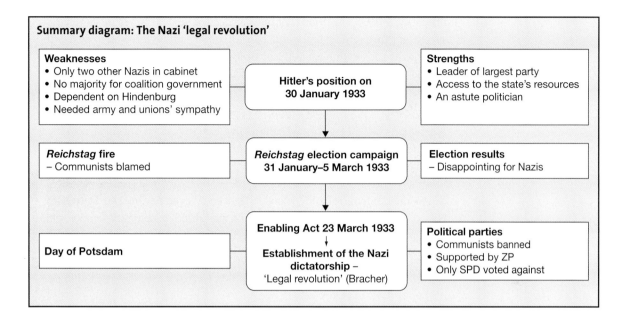

Summary diagram: The Nazi 'legal revolution'

Weaknesses		Strengths
• Only two other Nazis in cabinet • No majority for coalition government • Dependent on Hindenburg • Needed army and unions' sympathy	**Hitler's position on 30 January 1933**	• Leader of largest party • Access to the state's resources • An astute politician
***Reichstag* fire** – Communists blamed	***Reichstag* election campaign 31 January–5 March 1933**	**Election results** – Disappointing for Nazis
Day of Potsdam	**Enabling Act 23 March 1933** ↓ **Establishment of the Nazi dictatorship –** 'Legal revolution' (Bracher)	**Political parties** • Communists banned • Supported by ZP • Only SPD voted against

② Co-ordination: *Gleichschaltung*

▶ *What was* Gleichschaltung?

▶ *In what ways did Nazism achieve co-ordination?*

The Enabling Law was the constitutional foundation stone of the Third Reich. In purely legal terms the Weimar constitution was not dissolved until 1945, and the Enabling Law provided a legal basis for the dictatorship, which evolved from 1933 (see pages 138–9). The intolerance and violence used by the Nazis to gain power could now be used as tools within government by Hitler and the party.

The degeneration of Weimar's democracy into the Nazi state system is usually referred to as ***Gleichschaltung*** or co-ordination. It applied to the Nazifying of German society and structures and specifically to the establishment of the dictatorship, 1933–4. To some extent it was generated by the power and freedom exploited by the SA at the local level – a 'revolution from below', but it was also directed by the Nazi leadership from the political centre in Berlin – a 'revolution from above'. These two political forces attempted to 'co-ordinate' as many aspects of German life as possible along Nazi lines. However, differences over the exact long-term goals of National Socialism laid the foundations for future conflict within the party (see pages 144–8).

Co-ordination has been viewed rather neatly as the 'merging' of German society with party associations and institutions in an attempt to Nazify life in Germany. At first, many of these Nazi organisations had to live alongside existing bodies, but they gradually replaced them. In this way, much of Germany's educational and social life became increasingly controlled (see also pages 192–229).

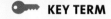 **KEY TERM**

Gleichschaltung 'Bringing into line' or 'co-ordination'.

Primarily, in 1933, the priority of the Nazi leadership was to secure its *political* supremacy through the process of 'co-ordination'. It therefore had to deal with agencies at odds with Nazi political aspirations, such as the regional states, the independent trade unions and the political parties.

The regional states (*Länder*)

The regions had a very strong tradition in German history. This obstructed Nazi desires to create a fully unified country. Nazi activists had already exploited the climate of February–March 1933 to intimidate opponents and to infiltrate regional state governments. Indeed, their 'political success' rapidly degenerated into terror and violence that seemed even beyond the control of Hitler, who called for restraint because he was afraid of losing the support of the conservatives. The situation was resolved in three legal stages:

- First, a law of 31 March 1933 dissolved regional parliaments (*Landtage*) and reformed them with acceptable majorities, allowing the Nazis to dominate them.
- Secondly, a law of 7 April 1933 created Reich governors (*Reichstatthalter*), who more often than not were the local party *Gauleiter* with full powers.
- Finally, in January 1934 regional state parliaments were abolished. The governments of all the states were subordinated to the Ministry of the Interior in Berlin central government.

By early 1934 the federal principle of government was as good as dead. Even the Nazi Reich governors existed simply 'to execute the will of the supreme leadership of the Reich'.

The trade unions

Germany's trade union movement was powerful because of its mass membership and its strong connections with socialism and Catholicism. In 1920 it had clearly shown its industrial muscle when a general strike defeated the Kapp *putsch* (see pages 36–7). German organised labour was hostile to Nazism so posed a major threat to the stability of the Nazi state.

Yet, by May 1933 it was a spent force. The depression had already severely weakened it by reducing membership and lessening the will to resist. However, the trade union leaders deluded themselves that they could work with the Nazis and thereby preserve a degree of independence and at least the structure of trade unionism. Their hope was that:

- in the short term, trade unionism would continue to serve its social role to help members
- in the long term, it could provide the framework for development in industrial relations in the post-Nazi era.

However, the labour movement was deceived by the Nazis.

The Nazis surprisingly declared 1 May (the traditional day of celebration for international socialist labour) a national holiday, which gave the impression to the trade unions that perhaps there was some scope for co-operation. This proved to be the briefest of illusions. On the following day, trade union premises were occupied by the SA and SS, union funds were confiscated and many of the leaders were arrested and sent to the early concentration camps such as Dachau.

Independent trade unions were then banned and in their place all German workers' organisations were absorbed into the German Labour Front (*Deutscher Arbeitsfront*, DAF), led by Robert Ley. DAF became the largest organisation in Nazi Germany with 22 million members, but it acted more as an instrument of control than as a genuine representative body of workers' interests and concerns (see pages 194–5). Also, it lacked the most fundamental right to negotiate wages and conditions of work. So, by the end of 1933, the power of the German labour movement had been decisively broken.

Political parties

The process of *Gleichschaltung* could never allow the existence of other political parties. Nazism openly rejected democracy and any concessions to alternative opinions. Instead, it aspired to establish authoritarian rule within a one-party state. This was not difficult to achieve:

- The communists had been outlawed since the *Reichstag* fire (see page 138).
- Soon after the destruction of the trade unions the assets of the Social Democrats were seized and they were then officially banned on 22 June.
- Most of the major remaining parties willingly agreed to dissolve themselves in the course of late June 1933 – even the Nationalists (previously coalition partners to the Nazis) obligingly accepted.
- Finally, the Catholic Centre Party decided to give up the struggle and followed suit on 5 July 1933.

Thus, there was no opposition left when a decree of 14 July formally proclaimed 'The Law against the Establishment of Parties', which made the Nazi Party the only legal political party in Germany.

The success of *Gleichschaltung*

By the end of 1933 the process of *Gleichschaltung* was well advanced in many areas of public life in Germany, although far from complete. In particular, it had made limited impression on the role and influence of the army, big business and the Churches (although an agreement was made with the papacy in July 1933, see page 204). Also, the civil service and education had only been partially co-ordinated. This was mainly due to Hitler's determination to shape events through the 'revolution from above' and to avoid antagonising such powerful vested interests. Yet, there were many in the lower ranks of the party who had contributed to the 'revolution from below' and who now wanted to extend the process of *Gleichschaltung*. It was this internal party conflict which laid the basis for the bloody events of June 1934.

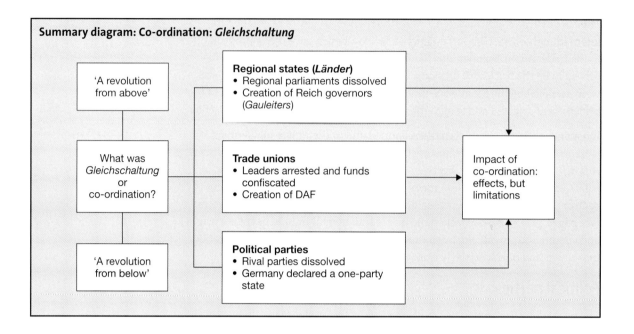

Summary diagram: Co-ordination: *Gleichschaltung*

'A revolution from above'

What was *Gleichschaltung* or co-ordination?

'A revolution from below'

Regional states (*Länder*)
• Regional parliaments dissolved
• Creation of Reich governors (*Gauleiters*)

Trade unions
• Leaders arrested and funds confiscated
• Creation of DAF

Political parties
• Rival parties dissolved
• Germany declared a one-party state

Impact of co-ordination: effects, but limitations

 ③ # The Night of the Long Knives

▶ *When and why did Hitler decide to crush the SA?*

Within six months of coming to power Hitler had indeed turned Germany into a one-party dictatorship. However, in a speech on 6 July 1933 to the Reich governors, Hitler warned of the dangers of a permanent state of revolution. He therefore formally declared an end to the revolution and demanded that 'the stream of revolution must be guided into the safe channel of evolution'.

Hitler was caught in a political dilemma. He was increasingly concerned that the behaviour of party activists was beyond his control. This was likely to create embarrassment in his relations with the more conservative forces whose support he still depended on, for example big business, civil service and, above all, the army. Hitler's speech amounted to a clear-cut demand for the party to accept the realities of political compromise and the necessity of change from above.

The position of the SA

Hitler's appeal failed to have the desired effect. If anything, it reinforced the fears of many party members that the Nazi leadership was prepared to dilute National Socialist ideology. Such concerns came in particular from within the ranks of the SA giving rise to calls for '**a second revolution**'.

 **KEY TERM**

A second revolution
The aims of Röhm and the SA were for social and economic reforms and the creation of a 'people's army' which would merge the German Army and the SA. These aims were more attractive to 'left-wing socialist Nazis' or 'radical Nazis'.

Table 4.1 SA membership 1931–4

	1931	1932	1933	1934
Membership figures	100,000	291,000	425,000	3,000,000
SA membership grew at first because of the large number of unemployed young men, but from 1933 many joined simply as a way to advance themselves.				

The growing SA (see Table 4.1) represented the radical, left wing of the Nazi Party and to a large extent it reflected a more working-class membership, often young and unemployed. It placed far more emphasis on the socialist elements of the party programme than Hitler ever did and saw no need to hold back simply to satisfy the elites. After its vital role in winning the political battle on the streets before 1933, many members were embittered and frustrated over the limited nature of the Nazi revolution. They were also disappointed by their own lack of personal gain from this acquisition of power.

Such views were epitomised by the SA leader, **Röhm**, who openly called for a genuine 'National Socialist Revolution'. Röhm was increasingly disillusioned by the politics of his old friend Hitler and recognised that the developing confrontation would decide the future role of the SA in the Nazi state. In a private interview in early 1934 with a local party boss, Rauschning, Röhm gave vent to his feelings and his ideas: 'Adolf is a swine. He will give us all away. He only associates with the reactionaries now … Getting matey with the East Prussian generals. They're his cronies now.'

Röhm did not want SA marches and rallies to degenerate into mere propaganda shows now that the street-fighting was over. He wanted a more political role for the SA, amalgamating it with the army into a people's militia – of which he would be the commander. He also had hopes for more fundamental social and economic reforms.

The power struggle between the SA and the army

Röhm's plan was anathema to the German Army, which saw its traditional role and status directly threatened. Hitler was therefore caught between two powerful, but rival, forces. Both could create considerable political difficulties for him.

The SA consisted of 3 million committed Nazis (see Table 4.1), with Hitler's oldest political friend leading it. It had fought for Hitler in the 1923 Munich *putsch* and in the battle of the streets, 1930–3. The SA was far larger than the army, but the army was the one organisation that could unseat Hitler. The officer class was suspicious of Hitler and had close social ties with many of the other powerful interests, for example the civil service and *Junkers*. Moreover, the army alone possessed the military skills vital to the success of his foreign policy aims. However large, the SA could never match the discipline and professional expertise of the army.

 **KEY FIGURE**

Ernst Röhm (1887–1934)

An early member of NSDAP who helped to form the SA and favoured the 'radical Nazis'. He was a homosexual and a heavy drinker, and enjoyed the blood and violence of war and political street battles. By 1931 he had turned the SA into a powerful force. He was arrested and murdered in the Night of the Long Knives.

Political realities dictated that Hitler had to retain the backing of the army but, in the winter of 1933–4, he was still loath to engineer a showdown with his old friend, Röhm. He tried to conciliate Röhm by bringing him into the cabinet. He also called a meeting in February between the leaders of the army, the SA and the SS to seek an agreement about the role of each within the Nazi state. However, the tension did not ease. Röhm and the SA resented Hitler's apparent acceptance of the privileged position of the army, while the unrestrained actions and ill discipline of the SA increased dissatisfaction among the generals.

The purge

The developing crisis came to a head in April 1934 when it became apparent that President Hindenburg did not have much longer to live. The implications of this were profound, as Hitler wanted to assume the presidency without opposition. He certainly did not want a contested election, and had no sympathy for those who wanted to restore the monarchy. Hitler's hand was forced by the need to secure the army's backing for his succession to Hindenburg.

The support of the army had become the key to the survival of Hitler's regime in the short term, while in the long term it offered the means to fulfil his ambitions in foreign affairs. Any personal loyalty Hitler felt for Röhm and the SA was finally put to one side. The army desired their elimination and an end to the talk of a 'second revolution' and a 'people's army'. By agreeing to this, Hitler could gain the favour of the army generals, secure his personal position and remove an increasingly embarrassing millstone from around his neck.

Without primary written evidence it is difficult to establish the exact details of the events in June 1934. However, it seems highly probable that, at a meeting on the battleship *Deutschland* in April 1934, Hitler and the two leading generals, **Blomberg** and Fritsch, came to an agreed position against Röhm and the SA. Furthermore, influential figures within the Nazi Party, in particular Göring and Himmler, were also manoeuvring behind the scenes. They were aiming for a similar outcome in order to further their own ambitions by removing a powerful rival. Given all that, Hitler probably did not decide to make his crucial move to solve the problem of the SA until mid-June, when Papen gave a speech calling for an end to SA excesses and criticised the policy of co-ordination. Not surprisingly, these words caused a real stir and were seen as a clear challenge. Hitler now recognised that he had to satisfy the conservative forces – and that meant destroying the power of the SA immediately.

On 30 June 1934, the Night of the Long Knives, Hitler eliminated the SA as a political and military force once and for all. Röhm and the main leaders of the SA were shot by members of the SS, although the weapons and transport were actually provided by the army. There was no resistance of any substance. In addition, various old scores were settled: Schleicher, the former chancellor, and Strasser, the leader of the radical socialist wing of the Nazi Party, were both killed. Altogether it is estimated that 200 people were murdered.

 **KEY FIGURE**

Werner von Blomberg (1878–1946)

Member of the general staff. Appointed as minister of defence in 1933 and later war minister and commander-in-chief of the armed forces 1935–8. Forced to resign in 1938.

From a very different perspective, the *Völkischer Beobachter* (*People's Observer*), the Nazi newspaper, reported on the cabinet meeting held two days earlier on 3 July:

SOURCE C

From the *Völkischer Beobachter* (*People's Observer*), 5 July 1934, quoted in J. Noakes and G. Pridham, editors, *Nazism 1919–45*, volume 1, Liverpool University Press, 1988, p. 182.

… The Reich Chancellor began by giving a detailed account of the origin and suppression of the high treason plot. The Reich Chancellor stressed that lightning action had been necessary otherwise many thousands of people would have been in danger of being wiped out.

Defence Minister General von Blomberg thanked the Führer in the name of the Cabinet and the Army for his determined and courageous action, by which he had saved the German people from civil war. The Führer had shown greatness as a statesman and a soldier. This had aroused in the hearts of the members of the cabinet and of the whole German people a vow of service, devotion and loyalty in this grave hour.

The Reich Cabinet then approved a law on measures for the self-defence of the State. Its single paragraph reads: 'The measures taken on 30 June and 1–2 July to suppress the acts of high treason are legal, being necessary for the self-defence of the State.'

> Using your historical knowledge, is there any evidence supporting the claim in Source C that there was a 'high treason plot'? What is the significance of the 'self-defence' law approved on 3 July?

The significance of the Night of the Long Knives

It would be difficult to overestimate the significance of the Night of the Long Knives. In one bloody action, Hitler overcame the radical left in his own party, and neutralised the conservative right of traditional Germany. By the summer of 1934, the effects of the purge could be seen clearly:

- The German Army had endorsed the Nazi regime in Blomberg's public vote of thanks to Hitler on 1 July. German soldiers agreed to take a personal oath of loyalty to Hitler rather than to the state (see page 174).
- The SA was virtually disarmed and played no further political role in the Nazi state. Just as Röhm had feared, its major role was to attend propaganda rallies as a showpiece force.
- More significantly for the future, the incident marked the emergence of the SS. German generals had feared the SA, but they failed to recognise the SS as the party's elite institution of terror.
- Above all, Hitler had secured his own personal political supremacy. His decisions and actions were accepted, so in effect he had managed to legalise murder. He told the *Reichstag* that 'in this hour, I was responsible for the fate of the German nation and thereby the supreme judge'. From that moment, it was clear that the Nazi regime was not a traditional authoritarian one, like Imperial Germany 1871–1918; it was a personal dictatorship with frightening power.

When Hindenburg died on 2 August, there was no political crisis. Hitler merged the offices of chancellor and president, and took the new official title of *Führer.* The Nazi regime had been stabilised and the threat of a 'second revolution' had been completely removed.

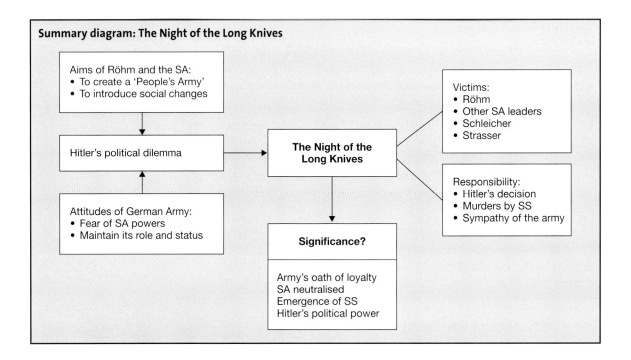

4 A Nazi revolution?

▶ *Did Germany undergo a political revolution in the years 1933–4?*

Between 1933 and 1934 Hitler and the Nazis effectively established a dictatorship. This was achieved through a range of key factors:

- *Terror.* The Nazis used violence – increasingly without legal restriction, for example the arrest of the communists and the Night of the Long Knives. Nazi organisations also employed violence at a local level to intimidate opposition.
- *Legality.* The use of law by the Nazis gave a legal justification for the development of the regime, for example the Emergency Decree of 28 February 1933, the Enabling Law and the dissolution of the parties.
- *Deception.* Hitler misled powerful groups in order to destroy them, for example the trade unions and the SA.

- *Propaganda.* The Nazis successfully cultivated powerful images – especially when Goebbels took on responsibility for the Propaganda Ministry. Myths were developed about Hitler as a respectable statesman, for example the Day of Potsdam (see page 139).
- *Weaknesses of the opposition.* In the early Weimar years, the left had considerable potential power, but it became divided between the Social Democrats and the Communists – and was marred by the economic problems of the depression.
- *Sympathy of the conservative right.* Many of the traditional vested interests, for example the army and the civil service, were not wholly committed to Weimar and they really sympathised with a more right-wing authoritarian regime. They accepted the Night of the Long Knives.

The word revolution should be used with caution. It means a fundamental change – an overturning of existing conditions. If Germany had undergone a 'political revolution' in the course of 1933–4, the evidence must support the idea that there was a decisive break in the country's political development.

Arguments for

At first sight the regime created by the Nazis by the end of 1934 seems the very opposite of the Weimar Republic. However, Weimar democracy had ceased to function effectively well before Hitler became chancellor. The strength of the anti-democratic forces had threatened the young democracy from the very start, so that it was never able to establish strong roots. Yet, even by comparison with pre-1918 Germany, the Nazi regime had wrought fundamental changes:

KEY TERM

Autonomy The right of self-government.

- the destruction of the **autonomy** of the federal states
- the intolerance shown towards any kind of political opposition
- the reduction of the *Reichstag* to complete impotence.

Clearly, *Gleichschaltung* decisively affected political traditions which had been key features of Imperial Germany 1871–1918. Thus, it is reasonable to view the events of 1933–4 as a 'political revolution', since the Nazis had turned their backs quite categorically on the federal and constitutional values which had even influenced an authoritarian regime like Imperial Germany.

Arguments against

There were elements of continuity. At the time of Hindenburg's death, major forces within Germany were still independent of the Nazi regime; namely, the army, big business and the civil service. One might even include the Christian Churches, although they did not carry the same degree of political weight.

Hitler's willingness to enter into political partnership with these representatives of the old Germany had encouraged Röhm and the SA to demand a 'second revolution'. The elimination of the power of the SA in the Night of the Long

Knives suggests that Hitler's claim for a 'national revolution' had just been an attractive slogan.

In reality, this 'revolution' was strictly limited in scope. It involved political compromise and had not introduced any fundamental social or economic change. In this sense, one could suggest that the early years of the Nazi regime were merely a continuation of the socio-economic forces which had dominated Germany since 1871.

Certainly, this would seem to be a fair assessment of the situation until late 1934. However, the true revolutionary extent of the regime can only be fully assessed by considering the developments in Germany throughout the entire period of the Third Reich. These will be the key points of the next few chapters.

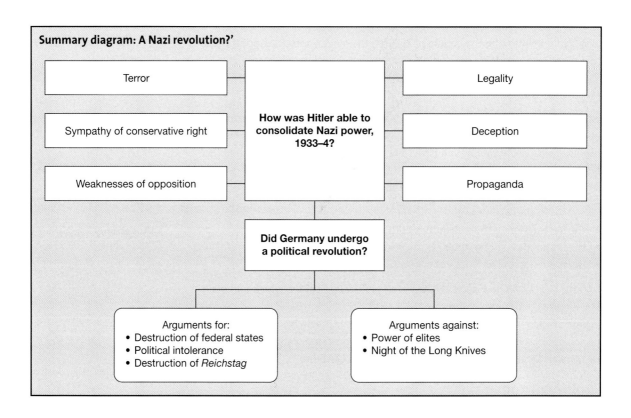

Summary diagram: A Nazi revolution?'

Terror

Sympathy of conservative right

Weaknesses of opposition

How was Hitler able to consolidate Nazi power, 1933–4?

Legality

Deception

Propaganda

Did Germany undergo a political revolution?

Arguments for:
- Destruction of federal states
- Political intolerance
- Destruction of *Reichstag*

Arguments against:
- Power of elites
- Night of the Long Knives

Chapter summary

When Hitler was legally appointed as chancellor, he did not have dictatorial powers. Yet, it took the Nazis just two months to impose a dictatorship by the Enabling Law. Hitler then effectively extended his powers in 1933–4 by 'co-ordinating' many aspects of German life. By the end of 1933 the trade unions, all other political parties and the federal states had been brought under Nazi control; although, in the short term, key forces such as the military, bureaucratic and economic elites initially escaped the process. Even so, the ongoing clash of the army leadership and the SA could have led to a German civil war. In the end, Hitler's bloody order to destroy his own stormtroopers secured his personal leadership and stabilised the dictatorship.

 Refresher questions

Use these questions to remind yourself of the key material covered in this chapter.

1 What were the main political strengths and constraints of Hitler?

2 How did the Nazis exploit the *Reichstag* fire?

3 Explain the significance of: a) the *Reichstag* election result of 5 March 1933, b) the Day of Potsdam and c) the Enabling Law.

4 What was the aim of *Gleichschaltung*?

5 How extensive was the process of co-ordination by the end of 1933?

6 When and why did the political conflict between the SA and the army come to a head?

7 Who gained and who lost from the Night of the Long Knives?

8 How significant was the Night of the Long Knives?

9 In what ways did the Nazis successfully consolidate their power between 1933 and 1934?

10 How far could Nazism be seen as a revolutionary dictatorship?

 Question practice

ESSAY QUESTIONS

1 Assess the reasons for Hitler's order to purge the SA in the Night of the Long Knives.

2 How successful was the Nazi policy of *Gleichschaltung*?

3 To what extent did the Nazis use the law to consolidate their hold on power in the years 1933–4?

4 Which of the following was of greater importance for the creation of the Nazi dictatorship in 1933–4? i) The use of violence and terror. ii) The sympathy of the conservative elites. Explain your answer with reference to both i) and ii).

CHAPTER 5

The Nazi dictatorship

It is all too easy to assume, in the wake of the Nazi consolidation of power, that the Third Reich was a tightly structured, well-organised dictatorship. Yet, in reality, it became a very complex system of political forces which changed over time. The following main areas need to be considered:

★ The role of Hitler
★ The party and the state
★ The 'police state'
★ Propaganda and censorship

★ The German Army
★ The economic recovery
★ The Four-Year Plan and the industrial elites
★ Conclusion: the nature of the dictatorship

Key dates

1933	March	Creation of the Ministry of Popular Enlightenment and Propaganda under Goebbels	1934 1935	Sept.	The New Plan introduced Mass arrests by *Gestapo* of socialists and communists
		Appointment of Schacht as president of the *Reichsbank*	1936	June	Appointment of Himmler as chief of the German police
	July 14	All political opposition to NSDAP declared illegal		Oct.	Four-Year Plan established under Göring
1934	June 30	Night of the Long Knives; purge of SA	1937	Nov.	Resignation of Schacht as minister of economics
	Aug. 2	Death of Hindenburg: Hitler merged posts of chancellor and president to become *Führer*	1938	Feb.	Forced resignation of Field Marshal Blomberg and General Fritsch. Purge of army leadership
	Aug. 20	Oath of loyalty taken by the German Army and civil service	1939	Sept.	Creation of RSHA (Reich Security Office)

 ## 1 The role of Hitler

▶ *What was the role of Hitler in Nazi Germany?*

In theory, Hitler's power was unlimited. Nazi Germany was a one-party state and Hitler was undisputed leader of that party. In addition, after the death of Hindenburg in August 1934, the 'Law Concerning the Head of State of the German Reich' combined the posts of president and chancellor. Constitutionally, Hitler was also commander-in-chief of all the armed services.

'Führer power'

If one studies contemporary documents, such as this extract from a leading Nazi theorist, E. Huber, it is clear that Hitler's personal dictatorship was portrayed in more than purely legal terms:

SOURCE A

From E. Huber, *Verfassungsrecht der Grossdeutschen Reiches*, Hamburg, 1939, p. 142. Quoted in J. Noakes and G. Pridham, editors, *Nazism 1919–45*, volume 2, Liverpool University Press, 2000, p. 198.

If we wish to define political power in the völkisch *Reich correctly, we must not speak of 'state power' but of '*Führer *power'. For it is not the state as an impersonal entity which is the source of political power, but rather political power is given to the* Führer *as the executor of the nation's common will.*

What was the nature and theory of Hitler's power as described in Source A?

Huber's grandiose theoretical claims for '*Führer* power' could not mask basic practical problems. First, there was no all-embracing constitution in the Third Reich. The government and law of Nazi Germany emerged over time in a haphazard fashion. Secondly, there was no way one individual could ever be in control of all aspects of government. Thus, Hitler was still dependent upon sympathetic subordinates to put policy decisions into effect. And thirdly, Hitler's own personality and attitude towards government were mixed and not conducive to strong and effective leadership.

SOURCE B

Adolf Hitler ist der Sieg!

'Adolf Hitler is victory'. A 1943 poster of Adolf Hitler.

What kind of image of Hitler is portrayed in Source B?

Hitler's character

Hitler certainly appeared as the charismatic and dynamic leader. His magnetic command of an audience enabled him to play on mass suggestion; he portrayed himself as the ordinary man with the vision, willpower and determination to transform the country. However, this was an image perpetuated by the propaganda machine and, once in government, Hitler's true character revealed itself, as is shown in the memoirs of one of his retinue:

SOURCE C

From F. Wiedemann, *Der Mann der Feldherr werden wollte*, Kettwig, 1965, p. 69. Quoted in J. Noakes and G. Pridham, editors, *Nazism 1919–45*, volume 2, Liverpool University Press, 2000, p. 207.

Hitler normally appeared shortly before lunch … When Hitler stayed at Obersalzberg it was even worse. There he never left his room before 2.00p.m. He spent most afternoons taking a walk, in the evening straight after dinner, there were films … He disliked the study of documents. I have sometimes secured decisions from him without his ever asking to see the relevant files. He took the view that many things sorted themselves out on their own if one did not interfere … He let people tell him the things he wanted to hear, everything else he rejected. One still sometimes hears the view that Hitler would have done the right thing if people surrounding him had not kept him wrongly informed. Hitler refused to let himself be informed … How can one tell someone the truth who immediately gets angry when the facts do not suit him?

Hitler liked to cultivate the image of himself as an artist, but really he was quite lazy. This was accentuated further by Hitler's lifestyle: his unusual sleeping hours; his long periods of absence from Berlin when he stayed in the Bavarian Alps; his tendency to become immersed in pet projects such as architectural plans. Furthermore, as he got older he became neurotic and moody, as was demonstrated in his obsession with his health and medical symptoms, both real and imagined.

Hitler was not well educated and had no experience that prepared him for any role in government or administration. As cynics say, Hitler's first real job was his appointment as chancellor. He followed no real working routine; he loathed paperwork and disliked the formality of committees in which issues were discussed. He casually believed that mere willpower was the solution to most problems.

Hitler's leadership

Surprisingly, Hitler was not even very decisive when it came to making a choice. Although he was presented to the world as the all-powerful dictator, he seldom showed any inclination to co-ordinate the government of Nazi Germany. For example, the role of the cabinet declined quite markedly after 1934. In 1933 the

? According to Source C, in what ways does Hitler appear to be a 'poor leader'?

cabinet met 72 times, but only four times in 1936 and the last official cabinet meeting was held in February 1938. Consequently, rivalry between the various factions of the party and state was rife and decision-making became, more often than not, the result of the *Führer*'s whim or an informal conversation rather than rational clear-cut chains of command.

Despite everything, Hitler still played a decisive role in the development of the Third Reich, as will be further discussed on pages 188–9. In his own research, Ian Kershaw has outlined an interpretation of Hitler's style of rule as one of 'charismatic domination' and suggests that:

- Hitler was crucial because he was still responsible for the overall Nazi dream.
- He had no real effective opposition to his aims.
- Although the government structure was chaotic, Hitler did not get lost in the detail of the day-to-day government.
- He generated an environment in which his followers carried out his presumed intentions. In this way, others willingly took the responsibility 'to work towards the *Führer*'.

SOURCE D

From a speech by Werner Willikens, state secretary in the Prussian Agricultural Ministry, in February 1934, quoted in Ian Kershaw, *Hitler, 1889–36: Hubris*, Allen Lane, 1998, p. 529.

Everyone with opportunity to observe it knows that the Führer *can only with great difficulty order from above everything that he intends to carry out sooner or later. On the contrary, up till now everyone with a post in the new Germany has worked best when he has, so to speak, worked towards the* Führer. *Very often and in many spheres it has been the case – in previous years as well – that individuals have simply waited for orders and instructions. Unfortunately, the same will be true in the future; but in fact it is the duty of everyone to try to work towards the* Führer *along the lines he would wish.*

In Source D, what insight does Willikens give into Hitler's style of government?

Summary diagram: The role of Hitler

Führer power	Hitler's character
In theory versus constitutional realities	Image versus reality

Leadership
- Decline of cabinet government
- Poor co-ordination of government
- 'Charismatic domination'

2 The party and the state

▶ *Why was the relationship between the party and the state so unclear?*

▶ *Who lost out: the party or the state?*

KEY TERMS

Totalitarian A system of government in which all power is centralised and does not allow any rival authorities.

Dualism A system of government in which two forces coexist, for example the Nazi Party and the German state.

March converts Those who joined the NSDAP immediately after the consolidation of power in January–March 1933.

By July 1933 Germany had become a one-party state, in which the Nazi Party claimed sole political authority. Nazi **totalitarian** claims, reinforced by a powerful propaganda machine, deceived many people at the time into thinking that Nazism was a clear and well-ordered system of government. The reality was very different. Fundamentally, this was because the exact relationship between the structure of the party on the one hand and the apparatus of the German state on the other was never clarified satisfactorily. It meant that there was much confusion between the two forces in Nazi government, and this clash has been given the term **dualism**.

The revolutionary elements within the party wanted party control of the civil service in order to smash the traditional organs of government and to create a new kind of Germany. However, there seem to have been three reasons why the Nazi leadership did not do this:

- Many recognised that the bureaucracy of the German state was well established and staffed by educated and effective people. Initially, therefore, there was no drastic purge of the state apparatus. The 'Law for the Restoration of the Professional Civil Service' of April 1933 only called for the removal of Jews and well-recognised opponents of the regime (see pages 157 and 217).
- Another factor which emerged during 1933 after the Nazi consolidation of power was a vast increase in party membership. It increased three-fold from 1933 to 1935 as people jumped on the bandwagon. The so-called '**March converts**' tended to dilute the influence of the earlier Nazis, further weakening the radical cutting edge of the party apparatus within the regime.
- Finally, Hitler remained unclear on the issue of the party and the state. The 'Law to Ensure the Unity of Party and State' issued in December 1933 proclaimed that the party 'is inseparably linked with the state', but the explanation was so vague as to be meaningless. Two months later, Hitler declared that the party's principal responsibilities were to implement government measures and to organise propaganda and indoctrination. Yet, in September 1934, he told the party congress that 'it is not the state which commands us but rather we who command the state', and a year later he specifically declared that the party would assume responsibility for those tasks which the state failed to fulfil. Hitler's ambiguity on this issue is partially explained by the political unrest of these years and by the need to placate numerous interest groups, and it was not really ever resolved.

Dualism: state institutions

In the German state the term 'civil servant' was a very broad one; it ranged from officials in the ministries to judges and even teachers. Generally, the state bureaucracy was unsympathetic to Weimar democracy, but was largely committed to the institutions of the state. However, in 1934 civil servants, the same as the army, were forced to make a new oath of loyalty to Hitler. Only five per cent of the civil servants dissented and were purged and, as time passed, more and more joined the party until it became compulsory in 1939 (see Figure 5.1).

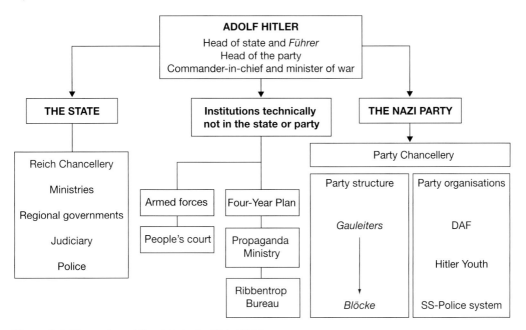

Figure 5.1 The party and the state in the Third Reich.

Reich Chancellery

The Reich Chancellery was responsible for co-ordinating government and, as the role of the cabinet declined from 1934, the Chancellery became increasingly important. Its head was **Hans Heinrich Lammers** and he played a pivotal role because he:

- drew up all government legislation
- became the vital link between Hitler and all other organisations, so he in effect controlled all the flow of information.

But even as a very efficient bureaucrat Lammers found it impossible to co-ordinate effectively the growing number of organisations.

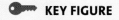 **KEY FIGURE**

Hans Heinrich Lammers (1879–1962)

Civil servant who joined the NSDAP in 1932. As head of the Reich Chancellery 1933–45, he gave legal advice and served as a crucial link between Hitler and the bureaucracy.

Ribbentrop Bureau
The office created by
the Nazi Joachim von
Ribbentrop, who ran his own
personal 'bureau' to oversee
foreign affairs.

High treason The crime
of betraying one's country,
especially by attempting to
overthrow the leader or
government.

Nacht und Nebel 'Night
and fog'. Name given
to a decree by Hitler in
December 1941 to seize
any person thought to be
dangerous. They should
vanish into *Nacht und Nebel*.

Government ministries

Ministries, such as transport, education and economics, were run by leading
civil servants. They were generally very conservative, most notably the
Foreign Office. They were under pressure in the late 1930s from growing Nazi
institutions: for example, the Economics Ministry was affected by the Four-Year
Plan (see pages 182–4) and the Foreign Office lost its position of supreme control
to the so-called **Ribbentrop Bureau**. Very significantly, the aristocrat Neurath
was replaced as foreign minister in 1938 by the Nazi Joachim von Ribbentrop.
More Nazi officials were then brought in.

Courts and judges

In the 1920s the judiciary was hostile to the Weimar Republic. It had been ultra-
conservative and in notorious cases it had been biased against the left and in
favour of the right (see page 39). So, on one level the judiciary was reasonably
content to work with the regime. Still, like the rest of the civil service, judges and
lawyers were 'co-ordinated' and obliged to join the Nazi Lawyers' Association
and make the oath. Yet, very few were replaced and, more surprisingly, the
justice minister until 1941, Franz Gürtner, was not a Nazi.

The judiciary was not immune from Nazi interference and over the years it felt
the ever-increasing power of the Nazi organisations. First of all, the structure of
new courts enabled the Nazis to get round the established system of justice:

- In 1933 Special Courts were set up to try political offences without a jury.
- In 1934 the People's Court was established to try cases of **high treason** with
  a jury composed specifically of Nazi Party members (7000 out of the 16,000
  cases resulted in a death sentence from 1934 to 1945).
- Eventually, in 1939, anyone qualifying to become a judge had to make 'a
  serious study of National Socialism and its ideological foundations'.

Furthermore, all legal authorities became subordinated to the arbitrary power
of the SS-Police system, which increasingly behaved above the law (see
pages 161–5). The decree ***Nacht und Nebel*** (night and fog) of 1941 gave the
SS-Police system the right to imprison without question any person thought to
be dangerous. In that way, although the traditional role of the judiciary in the
state continued to function, it was severely subverted.

Regional state governments

By early 1934 *Gleichschaltung* had destroyed the federal principle of government
(see page 142). The Nazi Reich governors existed only 'to execute the will of the
supreme leadership of the *Reich*', who more often than not were the local party
Gauleiters with full powers (although their role within the party structure was
certainly not clear – see page 177).

Dualism: party institutions

The role and shape of the Nazi Party were determined by its background and composition. Its organisation had been created and had evolved in order to *gain* political power and it had proved remarkably well designed for this purpose. However, the party had to find a new role from 1933 but it was by no means a unified structure and not really geared to the task of government. The party's problems were caused by the following:

- Up to 1933 it had developed out of the need to attract support from different sections of society and it consisted of a mass of specialist organisations, such as the Hitler Youth (see pages 200–2), the SA and the National Socialist Teachers' League. Once in power, such groups were keen to uphold and advance their own particular interests.
- The party became increasingly splintered. Various other organisations of dubious political position were created and some institutions were caught between the state and the party. For example, Goebbels' propaganda machine was a newly formed ministry (see pages 166–73) and the Four-Year Plan Office was added in response to the economic crisis of 1936 (see pages 182–4).
- The actual membership and administrative structure of the party was established on the basis of the *Führerprinzip* in a major hierarchy, but it did not really work in terms of effective government. The system led to the dominating role of the *Gauleiters* in the regions, who believed that their only allegiance was to Hitler. As a result, they endeavoured to preserve their own interests and tended to resist the authorities of both the state and the party (see Figure 5.2 below).

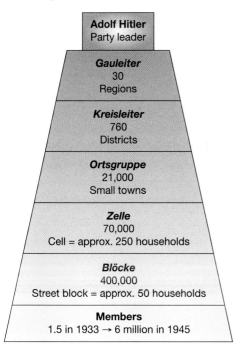

Adolf Hitler
Party leader

Gauleiter
30
Regions

Kreisleiter
760
Districts

Ortsgruppe
21,000
Small towns

Zelle
70,000
Cell = approx. 250 households

Blöcke
400,000
Street block = approx. 50 households

Members
1.5 in 1933 → 6 million in 1945

Figure 5.2 Nazi Party structure and leadership.

Rudolf Hess (1894–1987)

An early party member and long-standing secretary to Hitler, he was deputy leader of the party 1933–41. He was absolutely loyal to Hitler. His real power was limited, but he helped with Bormann to develop a more influential party bureaucracy. However, he became increasingly mentally unstable and flew to Scotland on his own initiative to negotiate peace in 1941. He was interned and sentenced to life at the Nuremberg trials.

Martin Bormann (1900–45)

Gauleiter of Thuringia and chief-of-staff to Hess. Improved the influence of the party's bureaucracy. Head of the party chancellery from 1941 and Hitler's secretary from 1943. Died in the ruins of Berlin in 1945.

In one way, the position of the party certainly did improve over the years. This was mainly because **Rudolf Hess**, deputy *Führer*, was granted special powers and developed a party bureaucracy in the mid-1930s. In 1935 he was given the right to vet the appointment and promotion of all civil servants, and to oversee the drafting of all legislation. By 1939 it had become compulsory for all civil servants to be party members. In this way, the foundations were laid for increasing party supervision.

The other key figure in the changing fortunes of the party was **Martin Bormann**, a skilled and hard-working administrator with great personal ambition. Working alongside Hess, he correctly analysed the problems confronting the party and created two new departments with the deliberate aim of strengthening the party's position (and thereby his own):

- The Department for Internal Party Affairs, which had the task of exerting discipline within the party structure.
- The Department for Affairs of State, which aimed to secure party supremacy over the state.

The trend of strengthening the party continued in the war years and Bormann was then put in charge of the party chancellery. Thereafter, by constant meddling, by sheer perseverance and by maintaining good personal relations with Hitler, Bormann effectively advanced the party's fortunes. By 1943, when he officially became Hitler's secretary, and thus secured direct access to the *Führer*, Bormann had constructed an immensely strong power base for himself.

Conclusion

The Nazi Party became more than merely an organisation geared to seizing power. It strengthened its position in relation to the traditional apparatus of the state. Undoubtedly, it was one of the key power blocs within Nazi Germany, and its influence continued to be felt until the very end. However:

- The party bureaucracy had to compete strenuously for influence over the established state institutions, and the latter were never destroyed, even if they were significantly constrained.
- The internal divisions and rivalries within the party itself were never overcome.
- The independence of the *Gauleiters* was one of the main obstacles to control.

Consequently, the Nazi Party never became an all-pervasive dominating instrument. The next section examines a number of other power blocs.

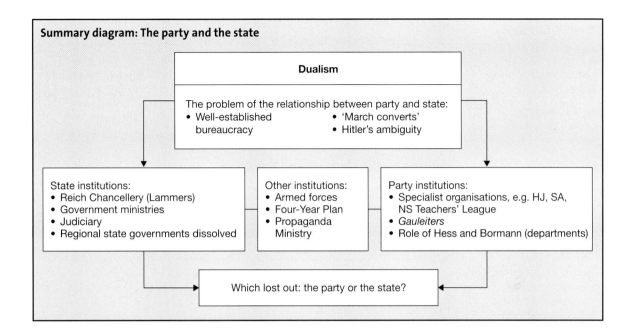

Summary diagram: The party and the state

Dualism

The problem of the relationship between party and state:
- Well-established bureaucracy
- 'March converts'
- Hitler's ambiguity

State institutions:
- Reich Chancellery (Lammers)
- Government ministries
- Judiciary
- Regional state governments dissolved

Other institutions:
- Armed forces
- Four-Year Plan
- Propaganda Ministry

Party institutions:
- Specialist organisations, e.g. HJ, SA, NS Teachers' League
- *Gauleiters*
- Role of Hess and Bormann (departments)

Which lost out: the party or the state?

3 The 'police state'

▶ *How did the SS emerge and how powerful did it become?*

▶ *Did the* Gestapo *really control the people?*

Amid all the confusion of the state and party structure an organisation emerged which became the mainstay of the Third Reich: the SS. The SS developed an identity and structure of its own which kept it separate from the state and yet, through its dominance of police matters, linked it with the state.

The emergence of Himmler and the SS

The SS had been formed in 1925 as an elite bodyguard for Hitler, but it remained a relatively minor section of the SA, with only 250 members, until Himmler became its leader in 1929 (see page 245). By 1933 the SS numbered 52,000, and it had established a reputation for blind obedience and total commitment to the Nazi cause.

Himmler had also created in 1931 a special security service, the **SD** (*Sicherheitsdienst*), to act as the party's own internal security police. In 1933–4 he assumed control of all the police in the *Länder*, including the *Gestapo* in Prussia. Thus, Hitler turned to Himmler's SS to carry out the purge of June 1934 (see pages 146–8). The loyalty and brutal efficiency of the SS on the Night of the Long Knives had their rewards, for it now became an independent organisation

KEY TERM

SD *Sicherheitsdienst*. Security service.

within the party. In 1936 all police powers were unified under Himmler's control as '*Reichsführer* SS and chief of all German police', including the *Gestapo*. In 1939 all party and state police organisations involving police and security matters were amalgamated into the **RSHA**, overseen by Himmler, but actually co-ordinated by his deputy, Heydrich (see page 220).

The SS-Police system which had been created served four main functions: policing; intelligence; treatment of opponents; military action of **Waffen SS**.

Policing by the *Gestapo* and the *Kripo*

The **Kripo** was responsible for the maintenance of general law and order, for example dealing with **asocials** and thieves. In 1936 the *Kripo* was linked with the *Gestapo*, which was the key policing organisation for waging war against the political and social enemies of the state. It had a reputation for brutality and it could arrest and detain anyone without trial, although its thoroughness and effectiveness have been questioned (see pages 164–5).

Intelligence gathering

Along with the *Gestapo* and the *Kripo*, the SD was responsible for all intelligence and security and was controlled by its leader, Heydrich, but still linked to the SS (see Figure 5.3). It made very effective use of informers, who were often Nazi sympathisers in the workplace or **block wardens**. In this way, informers operating at a local level were easily able to pass information to the authorities – and worst of all to denounce possible opponents.

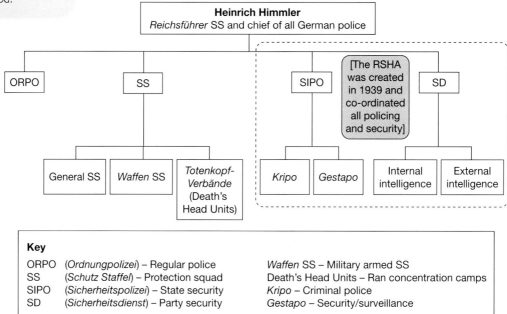

Figure 5.3 The SS-Police system in 1939.

Treatment of opponents

Within a few weeks of Hitler's coming to power, camps were created to deal with political opponents, mainly socialists and communists. Yet, by early 1934 many of the detainees in these early 'wild camps' had in fact been released. Instead, a more formalised system evolved from the prototype concentration camp of Dachau, near Munich, which was then followed by Sachsenhausen, Buchenwald and Lichtenburg (for women).

The commandant of Dachau was Theodore Eicke, who imposed a strict system of rules, routines and punishments carried out by SS guards, known as the Death's Head Units. On a daily basis, prisoners had to sleep on wooden planks (without blankets), attend lengthy parades for registration, and work a twelve-hour day of often physically demanding quarry work with minimal rations. Refusing to work was punishable by death, and even criticising the regime would result in two weeks of solitary confinement in tiny cells.

These early concentration camps were brutal, but they were not like the extermination camps of the war years. And the regime did not try to keep them secret – in fact, it publicised their existence as a deterrent. Up until 1936 the number of prisoners was no more than 6000, but after that it increased dramatically as the authorities started to round up anyone who did not conform – asocials, homosexuals, beggars, gypsies. By 1939 the number of inmates had grown to 21,000. During the war years the concentration camp system expanded enormously, with horrific consequences (see pages 241–8).

The *Waffen* SS

Up to 1938 the *Waffen* SS consisted of about 14,000 soldiers in three units; it was racially pure, fanatically loyal and committed to Nazi ideology. Its influence grew rapidly as a consequence of the weakening of the German Army in the Blomberg–Fritsch crisis (see pages 174–6) and also by the more anti-Semitic policies (see pages 218–21).

The SS state

It is important to keep in perspective the extent of the influence of the SS in its early years. Yet, the takeover of territories from 1938 to 1941 and the creation of the **'New Order'** marked the start of a significant expansion of the power of the SS and Himmler himself.

As *Reichsführer* SS, Himmler controlled a massive police apparatus answerable only to Hitler. The SS system grew into a key power bloc in the Third Reich. It became, in the words of E. Kogon in the 1950s, a 'state within a state'. It was a huge organisation, which numbered 250,000 in 1939 and had begun to eclipse other interest groups in terms of influence. As German troops gained control over more and more areas of Europe, the power of the SS was inevitably enhanced:

 **KEY TERM**

'New Order' A phrase given by the Nazis to the economic, political and racial integration of Europe under the Third Reich.

- *Security.* All responsibilities of policing and intelligence expanded as the number of occupied lands increased. The job of internal security became much greater and SS officers were granted the authority to crush opposition.
- *Military.* The *Waffen* SS increased from three divisions in 1939 to 35 in 1945, which developed into a 'second army': committed, brutal and militarily highly rated. By 1944 the *Waffen* SS was so powerful that it rivalled the position of the German Army.
- *Economy.* The SS became responsible for the creation of the 'New Order' in the occupied lands of eastern Europe. Such a scheme provided opportunities for plunder and economic exploitation on a massive scale, which members of the SS capitalised to the full. By the end of the war, the SS had created a massive commercial organisation of over 150 firms, which used slave labour to extract raw materials and to manufacture textiles, armaments and household goods.
- *Ideology and race.* The racial policy of extermination and resettlement was pursued with vigour, and the system of concentration camps was widely established and run by the SS Death's Head Units. The various 'inferior' races were even used for their economic value such as slave labour.

The SS was not immune to the rivalries and arguments which typified government in Nazi Germany. Disagreements often arose, particularly with local *Gauleiters* and the governors of the occupied territories. However, the SS state under Himmler not only preserved the Nazi regime through its brutal, repressive and arbitrary policies of law enforcement, it also gradually extended its influence. In this way, it evolved over time to become the key power group in the Third Reich.

The power of the *Gestapo*

Although it has been generally accepted that the SS developed into the key power in the Third Reich, its influence over people's everyday lives has been questioned. Traditionally, the *Gestapo* was seen as representing the all-knowing police state.

This view was actually cultivated by the *Gestapo* itself, by the Allied propagandists during the war and by many post-war films. This interpretation was largely upheld in academic circles, most notably in the standard work *The History of the Gestapo* by Jacques Delarue in 1962. He entitled one chapter 'The *Gestapo* is Everywhere' and then wrote: 'Never before, in no other land and at no other time, had an organisation attained such a comprehensive penetration [of society], possessed such power and reached such a degree of "completeness" in its ability to arouse terror and horror, as well as in its actual effectiveness.'

However, many local studies of Germany have led to an influential reinterpretation. The German historians K.M. Mallman and G. Paul, and the US historian R. Gellately, have drawn attention to the limits of the *Gestapo*'s policing by revealing that:

- The manpower of the *Gestapo* was limited: only 40,000 agents for the whole of Germany. Large cities, like Frankfurt or Hamburg, with about half a million people, were policed by just about 40–50 agents.
- Most *Gestapo* work was actually prompted by public informers: between 50 and 80 per cent in different areas. Much information and many denunciations were mere gossip, which generated enormous amounts of paperwork for limited return.
- The *Gestapo* had relatively few 'top agents', so it coped by over-relying on the work of the *Kripo*.

It should be noted that the police apparatus of the **GDR** from 1949 was much more extensive than the *Gestapo*.

More recently, the US historian Eric Johnson has tried to put the latest **revisionist** views into perspective through his case study of the Rhineland. He accepts the limitations of the *Gestapo*, and argues that it did not impose a climate of terror on ordinary Germans. Instead, it concentrated on surveillance and repression of specific enemies: the political left, Jews and, to a lesser extent, religious groups and asocials. Controversially, he claims that the Nazis and the German population formed a grim 'pact': the population turned a blind eye to the *Gestapo*'s persecution and, in return, the Nazis overlooked minor transgressions of the law by ordinary Germans.

 **KEY TERMS**

GDR German Democratic Republic. (DDR, Deutsche Demokratische Republik.) Communist East Germany, 1949–90.

Revisionist In general terms, it is the aim to modify or change something. In this context, it refers specifically to a historian who challenges a well-established interpretation.

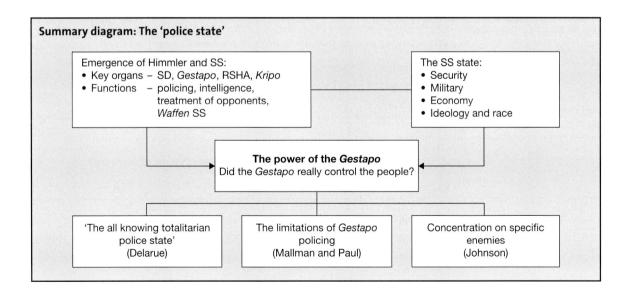

Summary diagram: The 'police state'

Emergence of Himmler and SS:
- Key organs – SD, *Gestapo*, RSHA, *Kripo*
- Functions – policing, intelligence, treatment of opponents, *Waffen* SS

The SS state:
- Security
- Military
- Economy
- Ideology and race

The power of the *Gestapo*
Did the *Gestapo* really control the people?

'The all knowing totalitarian police state'
(Delarue)

The limitations of *Gestapo* policing
(Mallman and Paul)

Concentration on specific enemies
(Johnson)

Propaganda and censorship

▶ *In what ways did Nazi propaganda use the media and German culture?*

▶ *How effective was Nazi propaganda and censorship?*

Goebbels declared at his very first press conference on the creation of the Ministry of Popular Enlightenment and Propaganda:

SOURCE E

? According to Goebbels in Source E, how did he intend to use and shape propaganda?

From a speech by Goebbels on 15 March 1933, quoted in J. Noakes and G. Pridham, editors, *Nazism 1919–45*, volume 2, Liverpool University Press, 2000, p. 381.

The most important tasks of this Ministry must be the following: first, all propaganda ventures and all institutions of public information belonging to the Reich and the states must be centralized in one hand. Furthermore, it must be our task to instil into these propaganda facilities a modern feeling and bring them up to date. We must not allow technology to run ahead of the Reich but rather the Reich must keep pace with technology. Only the latest thing is good enough. We are living in an age when policies must have mass support ... the leaders of today must be modern princes of the people, they must be able to understand the people but need not follow them slavishly. It is their duty to tell the masses what they want and put it across to the masses in such a way that they understand it too.

Considerable resources were directed towards the development of the propaganda machine in order to achieve the following aims:

- to glorify the regime
- to spread the Nazi ideology and values (and by implication to censor the unacceptable)
- to win over the people and to integrate the nation's diverse elements into the *Volksgemeinschaft*.

All the means of public communication were brought under state control.

Radio

Goebbels (and Hitler) had always recognised the effectiveness of the spoken word over the written and they had already begun to use new technology during the election campaigns of 1932–3. Up until this time, German broadcasting had been organised by regional states. Once in power, Goebbels efficiently brought all broadcasting under Nazi control by the creation of the Reich Radio Company. Furthermore, he arranged the dismissal of thirteen per cent of the staff on political and racial grounds, and replaced them with his own men. He told his broadcasters: 'I am placing a major responsibility in your hands, for you have in

Josef Goebbels

1897	Born in the Rhineland and slightly disabled
1926	Sided with Hitler against Strasser in the party conflict
	Appointed by Hitler as *Gauleiter* of Berlin
1930	Put in charge of Nazi propaganda
1933–45	Minister of public enlightenment and propaganda
1938	An affair with the actress Lída Baarová undermined his position
	Issued the orders for the anti-Semitic attacks of *Kristallnacht* (see page 219)
1943	Called for 'total war' to rouse the nation after the defeat at Stalingrad
1945	Died in a suicide pact with his wife after poisoning their children

Goebbels was a man from a humble background with many talents who became one of the few intellectuals in the Nazi leadership. He gained a doctorate from Heidelberg University in German and linguistics. However, he suffered from a strong inferiority complex over his physical limitations and he became an embittered and committed anti-Semite.

As propaganda chief of the party, Goebbels played a crucial role in exploiting every possible method to sell the Nazi image in the 1930–3 elections. He developed public relations techniques that were ahead of their time. Unscrupulous and amoral in his methods, he was mainly responsible for advancing the idea of Nazi totalitarianism, censoring all non-Nazi culture and media, and promoting all the main ideological ideas of Nazism. Goebbels was also a skilled, hypnotic orator, second only to Hitler.

Goebbels remained a central figure until the collapse of the regime, although other leading Nazis, such as Göring and Ribbentrop, distrusted him. His rivals exploited his many love affairs to undermine his political position and he became politically isolated in the years 1938–42. But with his personal leadership and his organisational skills he played an important part in the final two years of the Second World War in making the nation ready for 'total war' by:

- organising help for people in the bombed cities
- giving the orders to put down the July Bomb Plot (see page 258)
- maintaining civilian morale, for example by visiting bombed cities (unlike Hitler)
- taking the responsibility to mobilise the last efforts to resist the Allied advance.

your hands the most modern instrument in existence for influencing the masses. By this instrument you are the creators of public opinion.'

Yet, control of broadcasting was of little propaganda value unless the people had the means to receive it. In 1932 fewer than 25 per cent of German households owned a wireless (radio), although that was quite a high figure compared to the rest of the world. Consequently, the Nazi government arranged the production of a cheap set, the People's Receiver (*Volksempfänger*). Radio was a new and dynamic medium and access increased markedly. By 1939, 70 per cent of German homes had a radio – the highest national figure in the world – and it became a medium of mass communication controlled completely by the regime.

Broadcasting was also directed at public places. The installation of loudspeakers in restaurants and cafés, factories and offices made them all into venues for collective listening. 'Radio wardens' were even appointed, whose duty it was to co-ordinate the listening process.

Press

Control of the press was not so easily achieved by Goebbels. Germany had over 4700 daily newspapers in 1933 – a result of the strong regional identities which still existed in a state that had only been unified in 1871. All were owned privately, and traditionally owed no loyalty to central government; their loyalty was to their regional publishing company.

Various measures were taken to achieve Nazi control:

- The Nazi publishing house, Eher Verlag, bought up numerous newspapers, so that by 1939 it controlled two-thirds of the German press.
- The various news agencies were merged into one, the state-controlled DNB, which vetted news material before it got to journalists.
- Goebbels introduced a daily press conference at the Propaganda Ministry to provide guidance on editorial policy.
- The so-called Editors' Law of October 1933 made newspaper content the sole responsibility of the editor, who had to satisfy the requirements of the Propaganda Ministry or face the appropriate consequences. As a cynic implied, 'There was no need for censorship because the editor's most important function was that of censor.'

To a large extent, the Nazis succeeded in muzzling the press so that even the internationally renowned *Frankfurter Zeitung* was forced to close in 1943, whereas the circulation of the party's official newspaper, *Völkisher Beobachter*, continued to grow after 1933, reaching 1.7 million by 1944. However, the price of that success was the evolution of bland and sterile journalism, which undoubtedly contributed to a ten per cent decline in newspaper circulation before 1939.

The Berlin Olympics

The 1936 Olympic Games were awarded to Berlin in 1931, well before Hitler and the Nazis had come to power. Yet, despite Hitler's initial doubts, Goebbels was determined to exploit them as a propaganda 'gold-mine'. Initially, he saw the games as a means to present Nazi propaganda aims, but with several important caveats:

- They were to glorify the regime not only for the German people, but also for millions of people across the world, who would see Nazi Germany as a success.
- They were trying to spread Nazi ideological themes, without causing international upset. So, for example, many anti-Jewish posters were removed and newspapers were made to play down their virulent messages.

Everything was done to present a positive image of the 'new Germany'. Over 42 million *Reichsmarks* were spent on the 130-hectare (325-acre) Olympics sports complex and the gigantic Olympic stadium was built of natural stone in the classical style, the original modernist plan having been rejected. It could seat 110,000 spectators and at the time it was the world's largest stadium. The new Berlin Olympic Village was also a prototype for future games, with excellent facilities.

Not surprisingly, the Nazi government was meticulous in overseeing all the media preparations:

- *Radio.* Twenty transmitting vans were put at the disposal of the foreign media along with 300 microphones. Radio broadcasts at the Olympics were given in 28 different languages.
- *Film.* The Nazis promoted and financed filming by the director Leni Riefenstahl. She brought 33 camera operators to the Olympics and shot over a million feet of film. It took her eighteen months to edit the material into a four-hour film, *Olympia*, which was released in two parts beginning in April 1938.
- *Television.* Television was in its early stages, but the games prompted a significant technical development. Broadcasts of the games were made and seen by 150,000 people in 28 public television rooms in Berlin, although the image quality was variable.

The Nazi ideal of the tall, athletic, blue-eyed Aryan race was further emphasised through the image of the athlete Siegfried Eifrig lighting the torch at the start of the games in the Olympic stadium.

On the sports front, Germany successfully finished top of the medal table, gaining 89 medals with the Americans coming in second with 56. However, the Nazi dream was marred by the success of the black American athlete Jesse Owens, who won four gold medals in the 100 metres, 200 metres, long jump and four-by-four 100-metre relay.

Overall, the Berlin Olympics were a major success for the Nazis, who gained praise for their excellent management and impressive spectacle, as was recognised by the US correspondent William Shirer: 'I'm afraid the Nazis have succeeded with their propaganda. First, the Nazis have run the games on a lavish scale never before experienced, and this has appealed to the athletes. Second, the Nazis have put up a very good front for the general visitors, especially the big businessmen.'

Nazi ritual

One final aspect of the Goebbels propaganda machine was the deliberate attempt to create a new kind of social ritual. The *Heil Hitler* greeting, the Nazi salute, the **Horst Wessel** anthem and the preponderance of militaristic uniforms were all intended to strengthen the individual's identity with the regime. This was further encouraged by the establishment of a series of public festivals to commemorate historic days in the Nazi calendar (see Table 5.1, overleaf).

KEY TERM

Horst Wessel A song written by a young Nazi stormtrooper who was killed in a fight with communists in 1930. The song became a Nazi marching song and later virtually became an alternative national anthem.

Table 5.1 Significant days in the Nazi calendar

Date	Event
30 January	The seizure of power (1933)
24 February	Party Foundation Day (1925)
16 March	Heroes' Remembrance Day (war dead)
20 April	Hitler's birthday
1 May	National Day of Labour
Second Sunday in May	Mothering Sunday
21 June	Summer solstice
Second Sunday of July	German culture
September	Nuremberg party rally
October	Harvest festival
9 November	The Munich *putsch* (1923)
Winter solstice	Pagan festival to counter Christmas

Culture

Nazi culture was no longer to be promoted merely as 'art for art's sake'. Rather, it was to serve the purpose of moulding public opinion, and, with this in mind, the Reich Chamber of Culture was supervised by the Propaganda Ministry. Germany's cultural life during the Third Reich was simply to be another means of achieving censorship and indoctrination, although Goebbels expressed it in more pompous language: 'What we are aiming for is more than a revolt. Our historic mission is to transform the very spirit itself to the extent that people and things are brought into a new relationship with one another.'

Culture was therefore 'co-ordinated' (see pages 141–4) by means of the Reich Chamber of Culture, established in 1933, which made provision for seven sub-chambers: fine arts, music, the theatre, the press, radio, literature and films. In this way, just as anyone in the media had no option but to toe the party line, so all those involved in cultural activities had to be accountable for their creativity. Nazi culture was dominated by a number of key themes reflecting the usual ideological prejudices:

- anti-Semitism
- militarism and the glorification of war
- nationalism and the supremacy of the Aryan race
- the cult of the *Führer* and the power of absolutism
- **anti-modernism** and the theme of 'Blood and Soil'
- neo-paganism and a rejection of traditional Christian values.

Music

The world of music managed to cope reasonably well in the Nazi environment, partly because of its less obvious political overtones. Also, Germany's rich classical tradition from the works of Bach to Beethoven was proudly exploited by the regime. However, Mahler and Mendelssohn, both great Jewish composers,

 **KEY TERM**

Anti-modernism Strand of opinion which rejects, objects to or is highly critical of changes to society and culture brought about by technological advancement.

were banned, as were most modern musical trends. The new wave of modern classical composers, Schoenberg and Hindemith, were disparaged for their atonal music. Also the new 'genres' of jazz and dance-band were respectively labelled 'negroid' and 'decadent'.

Literature

Over 2500 of Germany's writers left their homeland during the years 1933–45. This fact alone is a reflection of how sadly German writers and dramatists viewed the new cultural atmosphere. Among those who left were:

- Thomas Mann, the author and Nobel Prize winner, who was a democrat and an old-fashioned liberal.
- Bertolt Brecht, the prestigious modern playwright, who was a communist.
- Erich Maria Remarque, the author of *All Quiet on the Western Front*, who was a pacifist.

Their place was taken by a lesser literary group, who either sympathised with the regime or accepted the limitations. It is difficult to identify a single book, play or poem written during the Third Reich, and officially blessed by the regime, which has stood the test of time.

Actors, like the musicians, tended to content themselves with productions of the classics – Schiller, Goethe (and Shakespeare) – in the knowledge that such plays were politically acceptable and in the best traditions of German theatre.

Visual arts

The visual arts were also effectively limited by the Nazi constraints. Modern schools of art were held in total contempt and Weimar's rich cultural awakening was rejected as degenerate and symbolic of the moral and political decline of Germany under a system of parliamentary democracy. Thus, the following were severely censored:

- 'New functionalist' artists, like Georg Grosz and Otto Dix, as their paintings had strong political and social messages (see page 77).
- The Bauhaus style started by Walter Gropius with its emphasis on the close relationship between art and technology (see page 77).

The modern styles of art were resented by Nazism so much that in July 1937 two contrasting art exhibitions were launched, entitled 'Degenerate Art' and 'Great German Art'. The first one was deliberately held up to be mocked and many of the pieces were destroyed; the second one glorified all the major Nazi themes of *Volksgemeinschaft* and celebrated classic styles and traditional nineteenth-century **German romanticism**. Most admired were:

- the sculptor Arno Breker
- the architect Albert Speer, who drew up many of the great plans for rebuilding the German cities and oversaw the 1936 Berlin Olympics stadium
- the artists Adolf Ziegler and Hermann Hoyer.

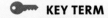

KEY TERM

German romanticism
German classicism in art, literature and music.

Cinema

Only in the field of film can it be said that the Nazi regime made a genuine cultural contribution. Germany's cinematic reputation had been established in the 1920s and a degree of continuity was maintained, as many of the major film studios were in the hands of nationalist sympathisers. However, Jewish film actors and directors such as Fritz Lang were removed and then decided to leave Germany. Perhaps the most famous German *émigrée* was the actress Marlene Dietrich, who swiftly established a new career in Hollywood.

Goebbels recognised the importance of expanding the film industry, not only as a means of propaganda, but also as an entertainment form; this explains why, out of 1097 feature films produced between 1933 and 1945, only 96 were specifically at the request of the Propaganda Ministry. The films can be divided into three types:

- Overt propaganda, for example *The Eternal Jew* (*Ewige Jude*), a tasteless, racist film that portrayed Jews as rats, and *Hitlerjunge Queux*, based on the story of a Nazi murdered by communists.
- Pure escapism, for example *The Adventures of Baron von Münchhausen*, a comedy based on an old German legend which gives the baron the powers of immortality.
- Emotive nationalism, for example *Olympia*, Leni Riefenstahl's docu-drama of the Berlin Olympics, *Triumph of the Will*, her film about the 1934 Nuremberg rally, and *Kolberg*, an epic produced in the last year of the war, which played on the national opposition to Napoleon. These last two films are still held in high regard by film buffs for their use of subtle cinematic techniques, despite the clear underlying political messages.

Conclusion

Control of the press and radio was Goebbels' prime objective, but he gradually also took control of film, music, literature and art. However, despite this, it is difficult for historians to assess the real effectiveness of Nazi propaganda. This clearly has implications for evaluating true public opinion at the time, which is considered on pages 221–8.

Historians initially assumed rather too readily that Nazi propaganda was successful because it was easy to see the way Goebbels exploited the means for propaganda: photographs, party rallies, sport and festivals. This view was underlined by R. Herzstein's book in the 1960s, *The War that Hitler Won*. However, more recent research from local studies of oral history has raised serious doubts about its real effectiveness and tended to show that the degree of success of propaganda varied according to different purposes. Very generally, it is felt that propaganda succeeded in the sense that it:

- cultivated the 'Hitler myth' of him as an all-powerful leader
- strengthened the Nazi regime after Germany's political crisis, 1929–33

- appealed effectively to reinforce established family values and German nationalism.

On the other hand, propaganda failed more markedly in its attempt:

- to denounce the Christian Churches
- to seduce the working classes away from their established identity through the ideal of *Volksgemeinschaft*
- to develop a distinctive Nazi culture.

Such points give backing to the view that the propaganda machine was of secondary importance compared to the power and influence of the SS-Police system (see pages 161–5) in upholding the Third Reich.

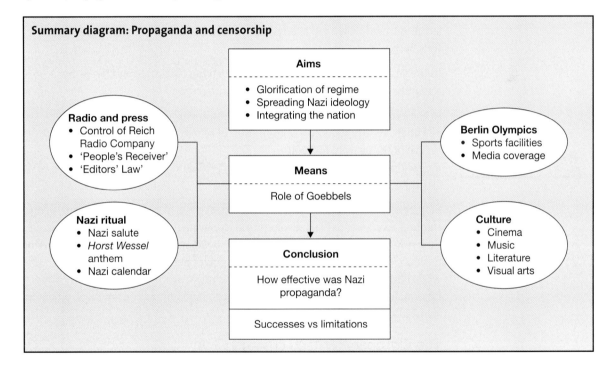

Summary diagram: Propaganda and censorship

Aims
- Glorification of regime
- Spreading Nazi ideology
- Integrating the nation

Radio and press
- Control of Reich Radio Company
- 'People's Receiver'
- 'Editors' Law'

Nazi ritual
- Nazi salute
- *Horst Wessel* anthem
- Nazi calendar

Means
Role of Goebbels

Conclusion
How effective was Nazi propaganda?

Successes vs limitations

Berlin Olympics
- Sports facilities
- Media coverage

Culture
- Cinema
- Music
- Literature
- Visual arts

5 The German Army

▶ *To what extent did the German Army co-operate with the Nazi regime?*

Despite its suspicion of Nazism, the army accepted the Nazi accession to power and co-operated in the manoeuvrings which led to the Night of the Long Knives (see pages 144–8). Moreover, the generals were confident that they had gained the upper hand when Hitler agreed to the destruction of his own SA. Ironically, they believed that now the radical element within Nazism had been removed they could make the Nazi state work for them.

Co-operation

The army succeeded only in preserving its influence in the short term by a compromise which was fatal in the long term. This is most clearly shown by the new oath of loyalty demanded by Hitler of all soldiers, and accepted by Field Marshal von Blomberg, the defence minister, and General von Fritsch, the commander-in-chief of the army, on 20 August 1934:

> I swear by God this sacred oath: that I will render unconditional obedience to the Führer of the German Reich and people, Adolf Hitler, the Supreme Commander of the Armed Forces, and will be ready as a brave soldier to risk my life at any time for this oath.

For a German soldier, bound by discipline and obedience, such words marked a commitment which made any future resistance an act of the most serious treachery.

In the years 1934–7 the relationship between the Nazi state and the army remained cordial. The generals were encouraged by:

- the expansion of the rearmament programme from 1935
- Hitler's reintroduction of conscription in March 1935, thereby increasing the size of the army to 550,000
- the diplomatic successes over the Saar (1935) and the Rhineland (1936) (see page 231).

Blomberg even issued a number of military decrees in an attempt to adjust army training according to Nazi ideology and to elevate the *Führer*. Yet, Blomberg and the army leaders deceived themselves into believing that the army's independent position was being preserved. In fact, the power of the SS was growing fast, while Hitler had little respect for the conservative attitudes held by many army officers. It was merely political realism which held him back from involvement in army affairs until 1938.

The Blomberg–Fritsch crisis 1937–8

The balance between the army and Hitler changed in the winter of 1937–8 after the so-called Hossbach conference meeting on 5 November 1937. In this meeting Hitler outlined to Germany's chiefs of the armed forces his foreign policy aims for military expansion. Blomberg and **Fritsch**, in particular, were both seriously concerned by Hitler's talk of war and conquest, especially bearing in mind Germany's state of military unpreparedness. Their doubts further convinced Hitler that the army leadership was spineless, and in February 1938 both men were forced out of office after revelations about their private lives. Blomberg had just married for the second time, with Hitler as principal witness, but it subsequently became known that his wife had a criminal record for theft and prostitution. Fritsch was accused of homosexual offences on evidence conveniently produced by Himmler.

KEY FIGURE

Werner von Fritsch (1880–1939)

Commander-in-chief of the army 1934–8, but hostile to growing power of the SS. Forced to resign in 1938, yet acquitted of homosexual accusations. Killed in the Battle of Warsaw in September 1939.

This infamous episode provided Hitler with the perfect opportunity to subordinate the army. He abolished the post of defence minister and took the title commander-in-chief and minister of war himself. Day-to-day leadership of all armed forces was given to the High Command, the *Oberkommando der* **Wehrmacht** (OKW), headed by a loyal and subservient General Keitel. The new commander-in-chief of the army was General Brauchitsch, another willing supporter of the regime. Also, a further sixteen generals were retired and 44 transferred from office. At the same time, Foreign Minister Neurath was replaced by the Nazi Ribbentrop. In the words of E. Feuchtwanger: 'It was a crisis of the regime not unlike the Night of the Long Knives in 1934, although this time there was no bloodshed. Again Hitler was the undisputed winner and the national-conservative elites who had helped him into the saddle, suffered a further loss of influence' (see Figure 5.4).

🔑 **KEY TERM**

Wehrmacht The name of the combined armed forces 1935–45. During 1921–35 the term *Reichswehr* had referred simply to the German Army. In 1935 the German armed forces were reorganised and given the name *Wehrmacht*. It consisted of the army, the navy and the air force.

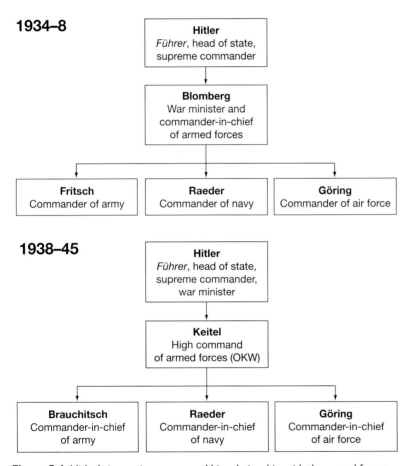

1934–8

Hitler
Führer, head of state, supreme commander

Blomberg
War minister and commander-in-chief of armed forces

Fritsch	Raeder	Göring
Commander of army	Commander of navy	Commander of air force

1938–45

Hitler
Führer, head of state, supreme commander, war minister

Keitel
High command of armed forces (OKW)

Brauchitsch	Raeder	Göring
Commander-in-chief of army	Commander-in-chief of navy	Commander-in-chief of air force

Figure 5.4 Hitler's increasing power and his relationship with the armed forces.

From 1938 the army's ability to shape political developments in Germany was drastically reduced. At first, Hitler had correctly recognised the need to work with the army leadership, but by early 1938 he was strong enough to mould it

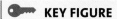

KEY FIGURE

**Ludwig Beck
(1880–1944)**

Chief of staff of the army 1935–8. Tried to organise joint action against Hitler's war plans in 1938, but failed. Resigned and became increasingly involved in the resistance. Shot in the July Bomb Plot.

more closely to his requirements. The army was not without power, but it had been tamed to serve its new master. It still remained the one institution with the technical means of striking successfully at the regime. For example, in the summer of 1938 a plan was drawn up by General **Beck** and other generals to arrest Hitler if a full-scale European war broke out over the Czech crisis (see page 227). It came to nothing because the peaceful surrender by Anglo-French appeasers in September cut the ground from beneath the plotters' feet.

Conclusion

Generally, historians have not been sympathetic to the role played by the German Army. It is difficult to avoid the conclusion that the army leadership played a naïve and inept political game. Conditioned by their traditions of obedience, loyalty and patriotism, and encouraged by the authoritarian position of the Third Reich, the army became a vital pillar of the Nazi regime in the early years. Even when its own power to influence events had been drastically reduced in 1938 and the full implications of Nazi rule became apparent during the war, the army's leaders could not escape from their political and moral dilemma. From 1938 to 1942 Nazi diplomatic and military policy was so successful that it effectively ruined the plans of any doubting officers.

Even before the war began in 1939, resistance was not only unpatriotic, but actually treasonable. However, by early 1943, when the military situation had changed dramatically, a growing number of generals come to believe that the war could not be won and opposition started to grow (see pages 257–9).

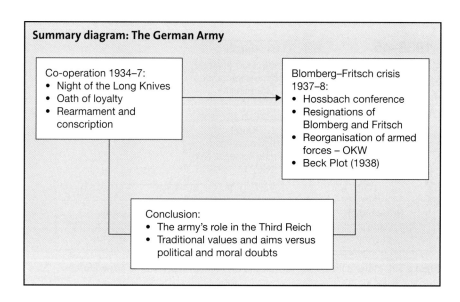

Summary diagram: The German Army

Co-operation 1934–7:
- Night of the Long Knives
- Oath of loyalty
- Rearmament and conscription

Blomberg–Fritsch crisis 1937–8:
- Hossbach conference
- Resignations of Blomberg and Fritsch
- Reorganisation of armed forces – OKW
- Beck Plot (1938)

Conclusion:
- The army's role in the Third Reich
- Traditional values and aims versus political and moral doubts

The economic recovery

▶ *How did Schacht's policies stimulate the economic recovery?*

The sheer scale of the world depression from 1929 meant that Germany had undoubtedly suffered in a particularly severe way (see pages 98–100). Yet, in the years before 1933 Hitler had been careful not to become tied down to the details of an economic policy. He even told his cabinet in February 1933 to 'avoid all detailed statements concerning an economic programme of the government'. Nevertheless, Hitler was also politically astute enough to realise that the survival and stability of the dictatorship depended on bringing Germany out of depression.

Schacht's economic strategy

In the early years, Nazi economic policy was under the control of Hjalmar Schacht, president of the *Reichsbank* (1933–9) and minister of economics (1934–7). This showed the need of the Nazi leadership to work with the powerful forces of the economic elites. Schacht was already a respected international financier because of his leading role in the creation of the new currency in the wake of the 1923 hyperinflation (see page 181).

It is certainly true that the economic depression reached its low point in the winter of 1932–3 and that afterwards the trade cycle began to improve. This undoubtedly worked to the political and economic advantage of the Nazis. Nevertheless, there was no single, easy 'quick fix' solution. The heart of economic recovery lay in the major revival of public investment led, for the most part, by the state itself, which embarked on a large-scale increase in its own spending in an effort to stimulate demand and raise national income. So, under Schacht's guidance and influence, deficit financing was adopted through a range of economic measures.

Banking and the control of capital

Initially, because the German banking system had been so fundamentally weakened, the state increasingly assumed greater responsibility for the control of capital within the economy. It then proceeded to set interest rates at a lower level and to reschedule the large-scale debts of local authorities.

Assistance for farming and small businesses

Particular financial benefits were given to groups such as farmers and small businesses. This not only stimulated economic growth but also rewarded some of the most sympathetic supporters of the Nazis in the 1930–3 elections. Some of the measures included:

- tariffs on imported produce in order to protect German farmers
- subsidies from the Reich Food Estate, as part of a nationally planned agricultural system

- more security of land ownership to small farmers through the Reich Entailed Farm Law: debts were reduced by tax concessions and lower interest rates
- allowances to encourage the rehiring of domestic servants
- the allocation of grants for house repairs.

State investment: public works

Of the greatest significance was the direct spending by the state on a range of investment projects. In June 1933 the 'Law to Reduce Unemployment' was renewed and expanded (from a scheme which had originally been started by Papen). The voluntary Labour Service was started specifically to employ 18–25-year-olds. Also, the RAD (*Reicharbeitsdienst*, Reich Labour Service) was established when in 1935 compulsory military conscription was introduced. The RAD required young men to serve six months of unpaid work – mainly in military construction projects – before joining the forces for their military service.

For a long time many historians assumed that rearmament was the main focus of investment, but the figures for public expenditure show that this was initially spread among rearmament, construction and transportation. The investment in the first three years was directed towards work creation schemes such as:

- reforestation
- land reclamation
- motorisation: the policy of developing the vehicle industry and the building of improved roads, for example the *Autobahnen* (motorways)
- building: especially the expansion of the housing sector and public buildings.

The cumulative effect of these policies was to triple public investment between 1933 and 1936 and to increase government expenditure by nearly 70 per cent over the same period (see Tables 5.2 and 5.3). By early 1936 the economic recovery was well advanced and then emphasis began to turn even more towards rearmament.

Table 5.2 Public investment and expenditure in billions of *Reichsmark* (RM) 1928–36

	1928	1932	1933	1934	1935	1936
Total public investment	6.6	2.2	2.5	4.6	6.4	8.1
Total government expenditure	11.7	8.6	9.4	12.8	13.9	15.8

Table 5.3 Public expenditure by category in billions of *Reichsmark* (RM) 1928–36

Category	1928	1932	1933	1934	1935	1936
Construction	2.7	0.9	1.7	3.5	4.9	5.4
Rearmament	0.7	0.7	1.8	3.0	5.4	10.2
Transportation	2.6	0.8	1.3	1.8	2.1	2.4

As a result of these strategies, there was a dramatic growth in jobs. From the registered peak of nearly 6 million unemployed in January 1932, the official figure for 1936 showed that it had declined to 1.6 million (see Table 5.4). For those many Germans who had been desperately out of work, the Nazi economic policy was to be welcomed. Even in other democratic countries scarred by mass unemployment, observers abroad admired Germany's achievement of job creation.

Table 5.4 Unemployment and production in Germany 1928–36

	1928	1929	1930	1931	1932	1933	1934	1935	1936
Unemployment (millions)	1.4	1.8	3.1	4.5	5.6	4.8	2.7	2.2	1.6
Industrial production (1928 = 100)	100	100	87	70	58	66	83	96	107

Yet, even in 1936, the government public deficit certainly did not run out of control, since Schacht maintained taxes at a relatively high level and encouraged private savings in state savings banks. Of course, it must be remembered that

In what ways do you think that the photograph in Source F could be seen as propaganda?

SOURCE F

The first *autobahn* was initiated by the mayor of Cologne, K. Adenauer; the stretch from Cologne to Bonn was opened in 1932. A further 3000 km of motorway roads were developed in 1930s. They served as an economic stimulus, but were also politically used as a propagandist tool. Their military value has been doubted.

all this took place as the world economy began to recover and Schacht was aided by the natural upturn in the business cycle after its low-point in winter 1932. Nevertheless, it is difficult to believe that such a marked turnaround in investment and employment could have been achieved without Nazi economic policy.

The balance of payments problem

Germany made an impressive economic recovery between 1933 and 1936, but two underlying worries remained:

- the fear that a rapid increase in demand would rekindle inflation
- the fear that a rapid increase in demand would lead to the emergence of a balance of trade deficit.

In fact, the problem of inflation never actually materialised, partly because there was a lack of demand in the economy, but also because the regime established strict controls over prices and wages. This had been helped by the abolition of the trade unions in May 1933 (see pages 142–3). On the other hand, what was to be a recurring balance of payments problem emerged for the first time in the summer of 1934. This was a consequence of Germany's importing more raw materials while failing to increase its exports. Its gold and foreign currency reserves were also low.

The balance of payments problem was not merely an economic issue, for it carried with it large-scale political implications. If Germany was so short of foreign currency (essential to buy foreign goods), which sector of the economy was to have priority in spending the money? The early economics minister, Schmitt, wanted to try to reduce unemployment further by manufacturing more consumer goods for public consumption, for example textiles. However, powerful voices in the armed forces and big business were already demanding more resources for major programmes, for example rearmament.

Hitler could not ignore such pressure, especially as this economic problem coincided with the political dilemma over the SA (see pages 144–8). Consequently, Schmitt's policy was rejected and he was removed, thereby allowing Schacht to combine the offices of minister of economics and president of the *Reichsbank*.

Schacht's 'New Plan'

In July, Schacht was given dictatorial powers over the economy, which he then used to introduce the 'New Plan' of September 1934. This provided for a comprehensive control by the government of all aspects of trade, tariffs, capital and currency exchange in an attempt to prevent excessive imports. From that time, the government decided which imports were to be allowed or prohibited. For example, imports of raw cotton and wool were substantially cut, whereas metals were permitted in order to satisfy the demands of heavy industry.

Hjalmar Schacht

1877	Born in North Schleswig, Germany
1923	Set up the new currency, *Rentenmark* (see page 53), and made president of the *Reichsbank* 1923–30
1933	Reappointed as president of the *Reichsbank*
1934	Appointed as minister of economics. Drew up and oversaw the 'New Plan' to control all capital and trade
1937	Increasingly lost influence and resigned as minister of economics
1939	Resigned as president of the *Reichsbank*
1944–5	Arrested after the 20 July Bomb Plot (see page 258) and held in Ravensbrück concentration camp
1945–6	Charged at the Nuremberg trials, but acquitted
1950–63	Private financial consultant to the governments of many countries
1970	Died

Schacht was an economic genius. He built his reputation on the way he stabilised the German economy through the creation of the new currency, the *Rentenmark*, in 1923. He served as president of the *Reichsbank* to all the Weimar governments 1923–30, but he was a strong nationalist and eventually resigned over the Young Plan (see page 101).

Schacht was increasingly persuaded by Hitler's political programme. From 1930 his influence went through three clear stages:

- He played a vital role in encouraging big business to finance the rise of the Nazis and he backed Hitler's appointment.
- In the years 1933–6 Schacht dominated the Nazi economy and it was he who shaped Germany's recovery by deficit financing and the 'New Plan' of 1934.
- However, he disagreed with the emphasis on rearmament in the Four-Year Plan crisis and his power waned.

Schacht resigned his major economic posts before the end of the war and became increasingly disaffected with the Nazi regime. He made connections with the anti-Nazi resistance, yet he survived a concentration camp and Allied war trials. Even in his eighties he remained a well-respected financial advisor to many developing countries.

The economic priorities were set by a series of measures:

- *Bilateral trade treaties.* Schacht tried to promote trade and save foreign exchange by signing **bilateral trade treaties**, especially with the countries of south-east Europe, for example Romania and Yugoslavia. These often took the form of straightforward barter agreements (thus avoiding the necessity of formal currency exchange). In this way, Germany began to exert a powerful economic influence over the **Balkans** long before it obtained military and political control.
- *The* Reichsmark *currency.* Germany agreed to purchase raw materials from all countries it traded with on the condition that *Reichsmarks* could only be used to buy back German goods (at one time it is estimated that the German *Reichsmark* had 237 different values depending on the country and the circumstances!).
- *Mefo bills.* Mefo were special government money bills (like a credit note) designed by Schacht. They were issued by the *Reichsbank* and guaranteed by the government as payment for goods and were then held for up to five years earning four per cent interest a year. The main purpose of Mefo bills was that they successfully disguised government spending.

KEY TERMS

Bilateral trade treaty
A trade agreement between two countries or parties.

Balkans A region taking its name from the Balkan mountains in south-east Europe. It covers mainly Albania, Bulgaria, Greece, Romania and Yugoslavia (Bosnia, Croatia, Macedonia Montenegro and Serbia).

Schacht was never a member of the Nazi Party, but he was drawn into the Nazi movement and the regime. His proven economic skills earned him respect both in and outside the party and it was he who laid the foundations for economic recovery. By mid-1936:

- unemployment had fallen to 1.5 million
- industrial production had increased by 60 per cent since 1933
- GNP had grown over the same period by 40 per cent.

However, such successes disguised fundamental structural weaknesses which came to a head in the second half of 1936 over the future direction of the German economy.

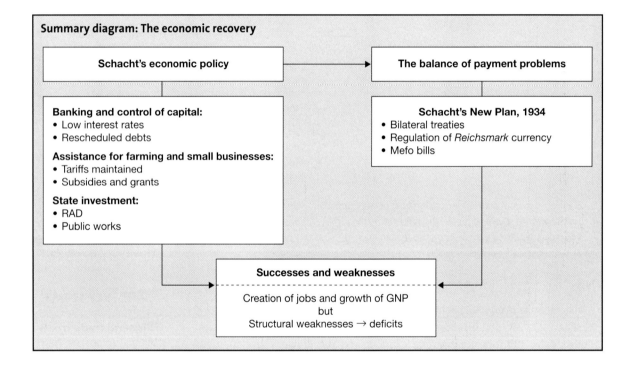

Summary diagram: The economic recovery

Schacht's economic policy → The balance of payment problems

Banking and control of capital:
- Low interest rates
- Rescheduled debts

Assistance for farming and small businesses:
- Tariffs maintained
- Subsidies and grants

State investment:
- RAD
- Public works

Schacht's New Plan, 1934
- Bilateral treaties
- Regulation of *Reichsmark* currency
- Mefo bills

Successes and weaknesses

Creation of jobs and growth of GNP
but
Structural weaknesses → deficits

7 The Four-Year Plan and the industrial elites

▶ *What was the purpose of the Four-Year Plan and why was its implementation so significant for the Nazi dictatorship?*

In many respects, as Schacht was only too aware, he had merely hidden the balance of payments problem by a series of clever financial tricks. Despite his sympathy for deficit financing, Schacht believed that a combination of a budget deficit and a balance of payments deficit could not be maintained indefinitely. In early 1936 it became clear to him that, as the import demands for rearmament and consumption of goods increased, the German balance of payments would go deeply into the red. He therefore suggested a reduction in arms expenditure in order to increase the production of industrial goods which at least could be exported so as to earn foreign exchange. Such a solution had its commercial supporters, especially among those with interests in exporting, for example textiles, coal, iron and steel, and tool-making. However, it was unacceptable to the armed forces and to the Nazi leadership, as it implied that it would be at the expense of rearmament. By the mid-1930s, then, this debate was popularly summed up by the question: should the economy concentrate on producing **'guns or butter'**.

The aims and objectives of the plan

Most significantly, Hitler expressed his position in a secret memorandum presented to Göring in August 1936. This has been seen as one of the most significant documents of Nazi history, as it provides a clear insight into Hitler's war aims and the development of the Nazi economy. He concluded by writing:

> *There has been time enough in four years to find out what we cannot do. Now we have to carry out what we can do. I thus set the following tasks.*
>
> (i) *The German armed forces must be operational within four years*
> (ii) *The German economy must be fit for war within four years.*

The politico-economic crisis of 1936 was resolved by the introduction of the Four-Year Plan – essentially the implementation of the August memorandum – under the control of Hermann Göring who, in October of that year, was appointed 'Director of the Four-Year Plan'. Its aims were clearly to expand rearmament and **autarky**. In order to achieve this, the plan highlighted a number of objectives:

- To regulate imports and exports, so as to prioritise strategic sectors, for example chemicals and metals at the expense of agricultural imports.
- To control the key sectors of the labour force, so as to prevent price inflation, for example the creation of a Reich price commissioner and increased work direction by DAF (see pages 194–5).
- To increase the production of raw materials, so as to reduce the financial cost of importing vital goods, for example steel, iron and aluminium.
- To develop *ersatz* (substitute) products, for example oil (from coal) and artificial rubber (buna).
- To increase agricultural production, so as to avoid imported foodstuffs, for example grants for fertilisers and machinery.

 **KEY TERMS**

'Guns or butter'
A phrase used to highlight the controversial economic choice between rearmament and consumer goods.

Autarky The aim for self-sufficiency in the production of food and raw materials, especially when at war.

The effects of the Four-Year Plan

The decision to implement the Four-Year Plan marked an important turning point in the Nazi regime. Nazi control over the German economy became much tighter, as Schacht described in his own book written in 1949:

SOURCE G

From H. Schacht, *Account Settled*, Weidenfeld & Nicolson, 1949, pp. 98–9.

On December 17th 1936, Göring informed a meeting of big industrialists that it was no longer a question of producing economically, but simply of producing. And as far as getting hold of foreign exchange was concerned it was quite immaterial whether the provisions of the law were complied with or not … Göring's policy of recklessly exploiting Germany's economic substance necessarily brought me into more and more acute conflict with him, and for his part he exploited his powers, with Hitler and the party behind him, to counter my activity as Minister of Economics to an ever-increasing extent.

> **?** In what ways does Schacht criticise the Four-Year Plan in Source G?

Schacht had no real respect for Göring, who had no economic expertise and who deliberately and increasingly ignored Schacht's advice. Schacht recognised that his influence was on the wane and eventually, in November 1937, he resigned. He was replaced by the weak Walther Funk, although from this time Göring became the real economic dictator.

The success of the plan was mixed over the years (see Table 5.5). On the one hand, production of a number of key materials, such as aluminium and explosives, had expanded greatly, or at least at a reasonable rate. On the other hand, it fell a long way short of the targets in the vital commodities of rubber and oil, while arms production never reached the levels desired by the armed forces and Hitler. All in all, the Four-Year Plan had succeeded in the sense that Germany's reliance on imports had not increased. However, this still meant that when war did break out Germany was dependent on foreign supplies for one-third of its raw materials.

Table 5.5 The Four-Year Plan launched in 1936

Commodity (in thousands of tons)	Four-Year Plan target	Actual output for 1936	Actual output for 1938	Actual output for 1942
Oil	13,830	1,790	2,340	6,260
Aluminium	273	98	166	260
Rubber (buna)	120	0.7	5	96
Explosives	223	18	45	300
Steel	24,000	19,216	22,656	20,480
Hard coal	213,000	158,400	186,186	166,059

The power and influence of the industrial elites

The position of the business community began to improve from 1933. However, it would be wrong to see business as a uniform interest group; different sectors were affected in different ways. Small business was squeezed out by the power of the industrial elites, whose support was more crucial in the creation of new jobs. The building and the giant coal and steel industries initially prospered most, while consumer goods' production remained relatively depressed. So, in the first few years of Nazi rule, big business was able to exert a strong influence, particularly through the leadership of Schacht. It maintained a privileged position in its own sphere, just as the army generals did in the military field (see also pages 173–6).

The Four-Year Plan in 1936 marked an important development. Schacht and the leaders of traditional heavy industry had urged for a reduction of rearmament and an increased emphasis on consumer goods and exports. However, this was a fatal error of political judgement which weakened Schacht's influence and brought an end to the supremacy of heavy industry. Instead, Göring was now in control and the only groups with real influence were in the electrics and chemicals sectors because of their crucial role in rearmament:

- In the chemicals industry IG Farben led the way with its development of synthetic substitutes for products such as rubber and oil.
- In the armaments and transport sector Daimler-Benz was crucial for the production of trucks and aircraft.
- The electrical industry was dominated by Siemens.

Most telling of all was the less influential position of the so-called 'Ruhr barons' of coal and iron and steel. When they refused to co-operate, Göring nationalised the iron-ore deposits and created a new state firm, the Reichswerke Hermann Göring, to exploit them.

From 1936 the divisions in big business meant that the needs of the economy were determined by political decisions, especially by foreign and military policy. Private property always remained in private hands, but the free market and business independence gave way to state regulation. On the whole, the industrial elites accepted the controls of the political leadership, fearing that resistance to state interference would weaken their situation further. This was because the material benefits were on the whole just too attractive. Profits generally continued to grow until the last phase of the war, so this was reason enough to work with the regime, although the industrial elites were never directly in charge of policy. From 1936 this was clearly determined by the Nazi leadership. In a mocking simile, the historian R. Grunberger writes: 'German business can be likened to the conductor of a runaway bus, who has no control over the actions of the driver, but keeps collecting the passengers' fares right up to the final crash.'

A war economy in peacetime?

Not surprisingly, the nature of the Nazi economy in the 1930s has been the focus of controversy because it was closely linked with the regime's leadership and the onset of war in 1939.

B.H. Klein: limited war preparations

Klein in the 1950s argued that Germany's economic mobilisation for war was initially 'quite modest'. He claimed that Nazi economic policy was deliberately connected with the military strategy of **Blitzkrieg**. In his view, Hitler and the armed forces recognised Germany's precarious position over the production of raw materials, and consequently developed the strategy of short wars. This would avoid the economic strain of 'total war' and also had the political advantage of not reducing the production of consumer goods excessively. In that way, Germany seemed to have both 'guns and butter'. Klein argued that pre-1939 civilian consumption remained comfortable. Indeed, he claimed, it was not until after the defeat at Stalingrad in 1943 (see pages 233–4) that a 'total war economy' began in earnest.

Tim Mason: overheating pressures

In contrast, the Marxist historian Mason in the 1970s has argued that the Nazi economy was in fact under increasing strain from 1937. He believes that Hitler's war aims were clearly driving the pace of rearmament to such an extent that the economy was put under tremendous pressures and it was in danger of expanding too quickly and overheating. He particularly points out economic indicators that:

- There were growing shortages of raw materials, food and consumer goods.
- There were labour shortages, especially of skilled workers, which increased wages.
- The balance of trade was going further into the red and becoming difficult to finance.
- The government expenditure and deficit were expanding.

Most significantly, Mason argues that all these pressures were contributing to significant social discontent among the working class. He goes so far as to suggest that by 1939 the situation was so serious that Hitler embarked on the war as the only way out of Germany's domestic economic dilemma.

Richard Overy: a massive economic mobilisation

Overy, writing in the 1990s, has rejected the traditional opinions. This is because, although an economic historian, he has been influenced by the work of diplomatic historians, who see Hitler stumbling unintentionally into a major European war in September 1939. Overy has argued that Hitler had always envisaged a great conflict for world power and that this necessitated the transformation of the economy to the demands of total war. However, his preparations for this kind of war were not intended to be finished until 1943. The war with Poland in 1939 was meant to be a local war which Hitler wrongly believed would not involve Britain and France. The premature outbreak of continental conflict inevitably found the German economy only partially mobilised.

Overy, therefore, believes that the underlying principles of Nazi economic policy were abundantly clear from 1936. The German economy had been unashamedly directed towards war preparation, so that two-thirds of all German investment went into war-related projects:

- Full employment was achieved, but over a quarter of the workforce was involved in rearmament.
- Levels of government expenditure more than doubled in the same period, with the result that the government debt increased accordingly.
- In the last full year of peace seventeen per cent of Germany's GNP went on military expenditure (compared to eight per cent in Britain and one per cent in the USA).

According to such a view, the German economy by 1939 was already dominated by the preparations for war, although not reaching the full-scale mobilisation required of total war, since that was not envisaged until about 1943. In a thought-provoking conclusion, Overy suggested: 'If war had been postponed until 1943–5 as Hitler had hoped, then Germany would have been much better prepared … The German economy in 1939 was still a long way short of being fully mobilised, but it was certainly on more of a war footing than Britain or France.'

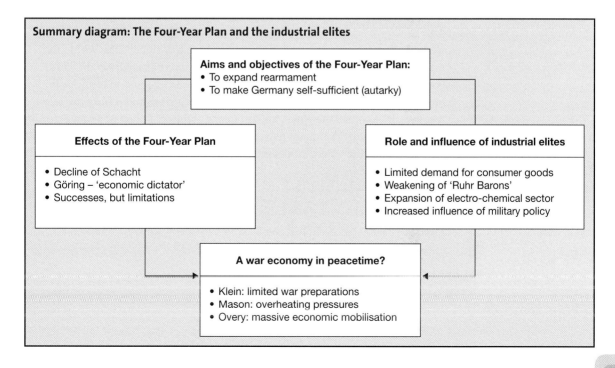

Summary diagram: The Four-Year Plan and the industrial elites

Aims and objectives of the Four-Year Plan:
- To expand rearmament
- To make Germany self-sufficient (autarky)

Effects of the Four-Year Plan
- Decline of Schacht
- Göring – 'economic dictator'
- Successes, but limitations

Role and influence of industrial elites
- Limited demand for consumer goods
- Weakening of 'Ruhr Barons'
- Expansion of electro-chemical sector
- Increased influence of military policy

A war economy in peacetime?
- Klein: limited war preparations
- Mason: overheating pressures
- Overy: massive economic mobilisation

8 Conclusion: the nature of the dictatorship

► *Who ran the Third Reich?*

In the early years, Hitler and the Nazis were heavily dependent on the sympathy of the army and the industrial elites; consequently, they did not attempt to control them directly as they feared alienating them. Indeed, the destruction of the SA in 1934 was driven by the need to satisfy those traditional vested interests, and was a blow to radical Nazis. At this stage the SS-Police system was relatively limited. The rearmament programme and the early moves in foreign policy acted as a powerful focus of common interest: profits for industry and the restoration of prestige for the army.

All this changed during 1936–8. Hitler's personal political position became stronger and was supported by the emerging power of Himmler's SS-Police system. Hitler was therefore less restricted by the need for political compromise and he could pursue his aims more vigorously. Moreover, the economic crisis of 1936 led to the introduction of the Four-Year Plan under Göring and the decline of Schacht. This development represented a major shift in the balance of political power away from big business as a whole, although the regime was strongly supported by the electrochemicals sector because of its links with arms production. Although the army had sided with the Nazi leadership in 1936, it was severely weakened two years later by the purge of major generals after Blomberg and Fritsch (see pages 174–5) had expressed their doubts about the direction of Hitler's foreign policy.

By 1938, therefore, big business, the army and the traditional elites within the state bureaucracy had been reduced to the role of junior partners in the Third Reich's power structure. The weakening of their positions was to continue in subsequent years, although at first the army gained great kudos from military victories. In contrast, the power and influence of the SS-Police system was to grow to make it the dominant power bloc – so much so that some historians have spoken of the emergence of the 'SS state'.

Internal Nazi tensions

Nazi propaganda successfully cultivated the 'Hitler myth' of him as an all-powerful leader, which helped to strengthen the Nazi regime. However, many structuralist historians have also highlighted a lack of planning and organisation on Hitler's part, which led to internal tensions; it is now generally appreciated that divisions and rivalries were rife in the government of the Third Reich. The leading Nazis headed their own institutional empires and their aims and interests often brought them into conflict with each other. For example, the economy from 1936 was in the hands of major wrangling leaders and their offices:

- Göring as the director of the Four-Year Plan
- Schacht as president of the *Reichsbank*
- Funk as minister of economics
- Ley in charge of DAF.

On top of this, there were personality clashes which led to personal rivalries and ambitions at the expense of efficient government. Most notably, Bormann and Himmler despised each other, and Göring and Goebbels were barely on speaking terms. In a telling phrase, the historian J. Noakes writes: 'Perhaps, the most outstanding characteristic of the political system of the Third Reich was its lack of formal structure.'

Despite all this talk of individual and institutional confrontation, it is difficult to ignore the importance of Hitler. He created the party and headed a regime built on the principle of authoritarian leadership. It is impossible to pinpoint any major domestic development which was contrary to Hitler's wishes. In I. Kershaw's words, 'Hitler's personalized form of rule invited radical initiatives from below and offered such initiatives backing, so long as they were in line with his broadly defined goals.' It was mainly his personality and ideology which led to a dramatic radicalisation of policy in key spheres, such as:

- politically, by the creation of a one-party state brutally upheld by the SS-Police system
- socially, by an increasingly radical racial policy to reshape society
- in foreign policy, by the drive towards a German world hegemony.

It is hard to envisage all these developments without Hitler at the helm. It is also surely telling that the SS-Police system eventually emerged as the dominant power bloc – and its guiding principle from the start had been unquestioning obedience to the will of the *Führer*.

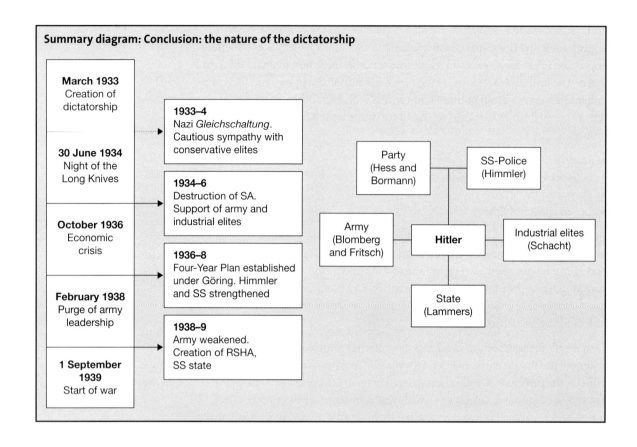

Summary diagram: Conclusion: the nature of the dictatorship

March 1933
Creation of dictatorship

30 June 1934
Night of the Long Knives

October 1936
Economic crisis

February 1938
Purge of army leadership

1 September 1939
Start of war

1933–4
Nazi *Gleichschaltung*. Cautious sympathy with conservative elites

1934–6
Destruction of SA. Support of army and industrial elites

1936–8
Four-Year Plan established under Göring. Himmler and SS strengthened

1938–9
Army weakened. Creation of RSHA, SS state

Party (Hess and Bormann)

SS-Police (Himmler)

Army (Blomberg and Fritsch)

Hitler

Industrial elites (Schacht)

State (Lammers)

Chapter summary

Despite the propagandist image of the Nazi regime as an all-powerful dictatorship, the reality was rather more complex. It was not effectively organised; instead, it continued to be a collection of overlapping competing powers. The traditional elites were moulded over time to satisfy Nazi political objectives but an unstable dualism prevailed between the institutions of the party and the state. Rivalries and divisions persisted – although it is true that eventually the party strengthened its position in relation to the traditional apparatus of the state. The SS-Police system extended its influence and became the key power group in the Third Reich. As for Hitler, his position was unique and through his personal leadership style he was able to direct events by ensuring that others were 'working towards the *Führer*'.

Refresher questions

Use these questions to remind yourself of the key material covered in this chapter.

1 What were Hitler's strengths and weaknesses as a political leader?

2 How did Goebbels intend to create mass support for the Nazis?

3 In what ways did the Nazis shape German culture?

4 How effective were Nazi propaganda and censorship?

5 Why was the relationship between the party and the state unclear?

6 How did the institutions of the Nazi Party and the state develop in the Third Reich?

7 Which lost out: the party or the state?

8 How did the SS-Police system emerge to become so powerful in the Third Reich?

9 Did the *Gestapo* really control the people?

10 To what extent did the German Army co-operate with the Nazi regime?

11 Why was the Blomberg–Fritsch crisis so significant?

12 How did Schacht's policies stimulate Germany's economic recovery?

13 How did Schacht try to resolve the balance of payments problem?

14 What were the main aims of the Four-Year Plan and why was it so significant politically and economically?

15 Was the Third Reich an efficient dictatorship?

Question practice

ESSAY QUESTIONS

1 How far did Germany's economy recover in the years 1933–9.

2 Assess the reasons why Hitler was able to extend his power over the conservative elites in the years 1933–9.

3 'The government of the Nazi regime was chaotic in the years 1933–9.' To what extent do you agree with this statement?

4 Which of the following was of greater importance for the development of the Nazi dictatorship?
i) The use of propaganda. ii) The creation of the SS-Police system. Explain your answer with reference to both i) and ii).

CHAPTER 6

Nazi society 1933–9

This chapter introduces the concept of the *Volksgemeinschaft*. It considers Nazi aims and policies and their impact on many aspects of German society. It finishes by assessing the degree of change and the level of success of the *Volksgemeinschaft* in the peacetime years. The main points are considered through the following sections:

★ The Nazi *Volksgemeinschaft*

★ Social groups

★ Education and youth

★ Religion

★ Women and the family

★ Outsiders

★ Nazi anti-Semitism

★ Conclusion: the impact of the Nazi *Volksgemeinschaft*

Key dates

1933	April 1	First official boycott of Jewish shops and professions	1934		Creation of the Confessional Church
	May	Creation of DAF (German Labour Front)	1935	Sept.	Nuremberg Race Laws introduced
	July	Concordat signed with the papacy	1937		Papal encyclical *Mit Brennender Sorge* issued
1934	May	Reich Ministry of Education created; control of education taken away from *Länder*	1938	Nov. 9–10	*Kristallnacht*: anti-Jewish pogrom
			1939		Creation of the Reich Central Office for Jewish Emigration

The Nazi *Volksgemeinschaft*

▶ *What purpose did the Nazis have in promoting the idea of the Volksgemeinschaft?*

When Nazi ideology developed in the 1920s it was based on three key elements: racism, nationalism and authoritarianism (see pages 90–4). However, Hitler always claimed that National Socialism was more than just a political ideology; it aimed to transform German society. It rejected the values of communism, liberal democracy and Christianity, and in their place upheld the concept of the *Volksgemeinschaft*.

The *Volksgemeinschaft* was probably the vaguest element of Nazi ideology, so it is difficult to define precisely. Historians are divided between those who see it as a 'pseudo-ideology' built on image alone, and those who see it as a more concrete movement with genuine support. The essential purpose of the *Volksgemeinschaft* was to overcome the old German divisions of class, religion and politics, and to bring about a new collective national identity by encouraging people to work together.

This new social mentality aimed to bring together the disparate elements and to create a German society built on the Nazi ideas of race and struggle. It aimed to unite traditional German values with the new ideology – although there were some clear ideological, biological and asocial groups who were 'outsiders' and did not conform to the Nazi dream (see page 213). The ideal German image was that of the classic peasant working on the soil in the rural community; this was exemplified in the Nazi concept of 'Blood and Soil' (***Blut und Boden***) and by upholding the traditional roles of the two sexes.

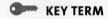 **KEY TERM**

Blut und Boden 'Blood and Soil'. Nationalist and racist romanticism which glorified the rural role of the peasantry.

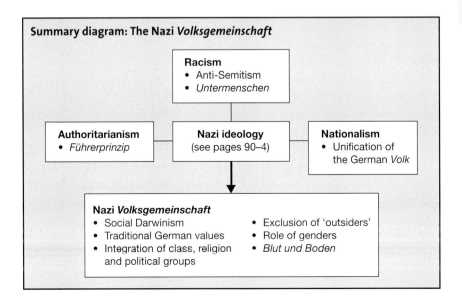

Summary diagram: The Nazi *Volksgemeinschaft*

② Social groups

▶ *Which classes lost out and which gained?*

Before the onset of war in 1939 it seemed to many Germans as if the revival of the economy had pulled their country out of the quagmire. However, in material terms, the effects varied considerably from one class to another.

Industrial workers

The working class was by far the largest social group, representing 46.3 per cent of German society (see Table 3.7 on page 117). The Nazi regime could not assume that the workers would be won over to the promised ideas of the *Volksgemeinschaft*. Under Weimar, many workers had belonged to independent trade unions and had generally voted for the SPD and KPD.

At first, the Nazi regime wanted to establish its authority and closed down all the trade unions (see pages 142–3). As a result, workers lost the right of industrial bargaining. Consequently, management and the government controlled pay increases and were able to limit workers' freedom of movement.

DAF (German Labour Front)

In the place of the unions, from May 1933, the only available option to workers was to join the German Labour Front (DAF, *Deutsche Arbeitsfront*). Led by **Robert Ley**, DAF became the largest Nazi organisation in the Third Reich with a membership that increased from 5 million in 1933 to 22 million in 1939. It was not compulsory to join, but advisable to do so if you wanted to make the best of things. It became responsible for virtually all areas of work such as:

- Setting working hours and wages.
- Dealing harshly with any sign of disobedience, strikes or absenteeism.
- Running training schemes for apprenticeships.
- Setting stable rents for housing.
- Supervising working conditions through the DAF subsection called the Beauty of Labour (SdA, *Schönheit der Arbeit*). The SdA aimed to provide cleaner working environments, meals, exercise and even smoking-free rooms.
- Organising recreational facilities through the Strength through Joy (KdF, *Kraft durch Freude*). It provided very real opportunities to millions of workers: cultural visits, education, sports facilities and holiday travel. By 1939 it had over 7000 paid employees and 135,000 voluntary workers, organised in every factory and workshop employing more than twenty people. Official statistics showed that the number of people going on KdF holidays had grown from 2.3 million in 1934 to 10.3 million in 1938.

 **KEY FIGURE**

Robert Ley (1890–1945)

Trained as a chemist and worked for IG Farben. Made leader of DAF 1933–45, but became an alcoholic and lost the support of other leading Nazis during the war.

Wages and conditions

Assessing the material effects of the Nazi regime on the workers is a highly complicated issue, mainly because there are so many variables, such as age, occupation and geographical location. The obvious and most significant benefit for industrial workers was the creation of employment. For the many millions who had suffered from the distress of mass unemployment, the creation of jobs was accepted gratefully. Indeed, by the late 1930s Germany had achieved full employment and there was a growing shortage of workers.

Yet, to put that major benefit into context, it is important to bear in mind a number of key factors:

- Average workers' real wages only rose above 1929 levels in 1938. Also, workers were forced to pay extensive contributions for DAF, insurance and tax.
- The generalised picture disguises the fact that the biggest gains were clearly made by the workers associated with the boom in the rearmament industries, whereas those in consumer goods struggled to maintain their real incomes.
- Working hours increased over time. The average working week was officially increased from 43 hours in 1933 to 47 hours in 1939. As military demands grew, there was pressure on many workers to do more overtime.
- The fall in unemployment figures from the statistics was caused in part by the removal of women and Jewish workers (albeit only one per cent of the working population) and the introduction of male conscription to the army and RAD, Reich Labour Service (see page 178). However, although there is considerable evidence suggesting that workers' discontent was increasing, there was little willingness for industrial action.

Peasants and small farmers

The farming community had been attracted to the Nazis by the promise of financial aid, as it had suffered from a series of economic problems from the mid-1920s. Moreover, peasants felt increasingly that they were losing out to the growing urban society of industrial Germany (see page 62).

The Nazi ideology of 'Blood and Soil' portrayed the peasantry as racially the purest element of the *Volk*; the providers of Germany's food and symbols of traditional German values. Hitler and Himmler were very much influenced by **Richard Darré**'s thinking, particularly his two key aims:

- to restore the role and values of the countryside and to reverse the drive towards urbanisation by promoting the concept of 'Blood and Soil'
- to support the expansionist policy of *Lebensraum* and to create a German racial aristocracy based on selective breeding.

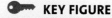 **KEY FIGURE**

Richard Darré (1895–1953)

Influential adviser on racial and agricultural ideas. In 1933 he became Reich peasant leader, minister of agriculture and food, and leader of the Central Office for Race and Settlement (RuSHA). But his vision of a rural utopia conflicted with the economic demands of war production and in 1942 he was forced to resign all offices.

It was under Darré's initiative that the Nazi regime introduced the following measures in agriculture:

- Many farm debts and mortgages were written off and small farmers were given low interest rates and a range of tax allowances.
- The government maintained extensive tariffs to reduce imports.
- The Reich Entailed Farm Law of 1933 gave security of tenure to the occupiers of medium-sized farms between 7.5 and 125 hectares, and forbade the division of farms, in order to promote efficient agriculture.
- The Reich Food Estate, established in 1933, supervised every aspect of agricultural production and distribution, especially food prices and working wages (although its bureaucratic meddling became the focus of resentment, when, for example, it stipulated that each hen had to lay 65 eggs per year).

Impact

The economic realities meant that in practice the impact of Nazi agricultural policy was rather mixed. At first, all farmers benefited from an increase in prices between 1933 and 1936 and so farmers' incomes did improve markedly, although they only recovered to 1928 levels in 1938. However, it seems that by 1936–7 any benefits were giving way to growing peasant disillusionment. This was for several reasons:

- Agricultural production increased by twenty per cent from 1928 to 1938, but a significant drift of people to the towns continued – three per cent of the population. Wages were higher there, and agriculture just did not have the economic power to compete with other sectors of the economy.
- The positive aspects of the Reich Food Estate were accepted, but the regulations became increasingly resented by the peasantry.
- The Reich Entailed Farm Law also caused resentment and family discontent. In trying to solve the problem of excessive subdivision by passing on farms to just one child, farmers faced the very real dilemma of not being able to provide a future for their remaining children.

With the onset of the war in 1939 pressures on the peasantry developed in many ways. Men were increasingly conscripted to the military fronts, so increasing the shortage of agricultural labour.

Landowners

The landed classes had been initially suspicious of radical social change. They resented the political interference of the party, but above all they feared that the Nazis would redistribute the large landed estates. However, they soon learned to live quite comfortably with the Nazi regime and in the years before 1939 their economic interests were not really threatened. Indeed, German victories in the early years of the war offered the chance of acquiring more cheap land. The real blow for the landowners actually came in 1945 when the occupation of eastern

Germany by the USSR resulted in the nationalisation of land. The traditional social and economic supremacy of the German landowners was broken.

Mittelstand

Another social class that expected to benefit from the Nazi regime was the *Mittelstand* (see page 49). Its problems were in many ways comparable to those of the peasantry. It had suffered from the decline in commerce in Germany since the First World War and it struggled to compete with the increasing power of big business and trade unions.

Research has shown that in the elections 1930–3 the *Mittelstand* had voted for Nazism in greater proportion than the rest of German society and the Nazi regime was keen to take sympathetic measures to maintain that support:

- Money from the confiscation of Jewish businesses was used to offer low interest rate loans.
- The Law to Protect Retail Trade (1933) banned the opening of new department stores and taxed existing ones, many of which were owned by Jews.
- Many new trading regulations were imposed to protect small craftsmen.

However, despite the Nazis' attempt to implement electoral promises made before 1933, the *Mittelstand* continued the decline that had started with Germany's industrialisation. The costs of small businesses meant that they could not compete with the lower costs of the large department stores. The problem was made worse because the Nazis needed big business to bring about rearmament.

The average age of the *Mittelstand* was rising. In 1933, twenty per cent of the owners of small businesses were under 30 years old and fourteen per cent over 60. By 1939 the corresponding figures were ten per cent under 30 and nineteen per cent over 60. In addition, from 1936 to 1939 it is reckoned that the number of traditional skilled craftsmen declined by ten per cent; the *Mittelstand* was being squeezed out.

Business

With the commercial recovery came general benefits for business; this is also considered on page 185. From 1933 the position of the business community was helped by the upturn in world trade, Schacht's economic stimulus and the Nazi destruction of the free trade unions. As a result, despite an increasing range of government controls, the financial gains were impressive. The value of German industry steadily increased, as shown by the following:

- The share price index (the list of the prices of shares) increased from 41 points in 1932 to 106 in 1940.

- Annual dividends (profits returned to investors) grew from an average 2.83 per cent to 6.6 per cent over the same period.
- Average management salaries increased from RM3700 in 1934 to RM5420 in 1938.
- The annexations of lands from 1938 (see pages 231–4) provided enormous opportunities for taking over foreign property, land and companies.

However, it would be wrong to see business as a uniform interest group; different sectors were affected in different ways. Small business was squeezed out more by the power of big business; and consumer goods' production remained relatively depressed.

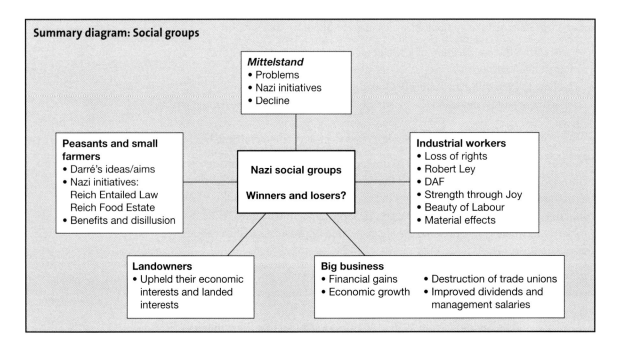

Summary diagram: Social groups

Mittelstand
- Problems
- Nazi initiatives
- Decline

Peasants and small farmers
- Darré's ideas/aims
- Nazi initiatives:
  Reich Entailed Law
  Reich Food Estate
- Benefits and disillusion

Nazi social groups

Winners and losers?

Industrial workers
- Loss of rights
- Robert Ley
- DAF
- Strength through Joy
- Beauty of Labour
- Material effects

Landowners
- Upheld their economic interests and landed interests

Big business
- Financial gains
- Economic growth
- Destruction of trade unions
- Improved dividends and management salaries

③ Education and youth

▶ *In what ways did the Nazis try to indoctrinate young people?*

▶ *How successful were the aims of Nazi education?*

In Nazi Germany, education became merely a tool for the consolidation of the Nazi system. Hitler expressed his views chillingly in 1933:

> *When an opponent declares, 'I will not come over to your side', I calmly say, 'Your child belongs to us already ... What are you? You will pass on. Your descendants, however, now stand in the new camp. In a short time they will know nothing else but this new community.'*

Education in the Third Reich was therefore intended to **indoctrinate** its youth so completely in the principles and ethos of National Socialism that the long-term survival of the 'New Order' would never be brought into question. A National Socialist Teachers' League official wrote pompously in 1937:

> German youth must no longer – as in the Liberal era in the cause of so-called objectivity – be confronted with the choice of whether it wishes to grow up in a spirit of materialism or idealism, of racism or internationalism, of religion or godlessness, but it must be consciously shaped according to the principles which are recognised as correct and which have shown themselves to be correct: according to the principles of the ideology of National Socialism.

This was to be achieved not only through the traditional structure of the educational system, but also by the development of various Nazi youth movements.

Schools

The actual organisation of the state educational system was not fundamentally altered, although by a law of 1934 control was taken from the regional states and centralised under the Reich Ministry of Education, Culture and Science, led by Reich Minister Bernhard Rust. The ministry was then able to adapt the existing system to suit Nazi purposes.

First, the teaching profession was 'reconditioned'. Politically unreliable individuals were removed, Jewish teachers were banned, and many female teachers were encouraged to conform to Nazi values by returning to the home (see pages 207–10). Special training courses were arranged for those teachers who remained unconvinced by the new requirements. The National Socialist Teachers' League (NSLB, *Nationalsozialistische Lehrerbund*) was established and its influence and interference continued to grow. By 1937 it included 97 per cent of all teachers and two-thirds of the profession had been on special month-long courses on Nazi ideology and the changes to the curriculum.

Secondly, the curricula and syllabuses were adapted. To fit the Nazi Aryan ideal, much greater emphasis was placed on physical education. Fifteen per cent of school time was given over to it, and games teachers assumed an increased status and importance in the school hierarchy. On the academic front, Religious Studies was dropped to downgrade the importance of Christianity, whereas German, Biology and History became the focus of special attention:

* German language and literature were studied to create 'a consciousness of being German', and to inculcate a martial and nationalistic spirit. Among the list of suggested reading for fourteen-year-old pupils was *The Battle of Tannenberg*, which included the following extract: 'A Russian soldier tried to bar the infiltrator's way, but Otto's bayonet slid gratingly between the Russian's ribs, so that he collapsed groaning. There it lay before him, simple and distinguished, his dream's desire, the Iron Cross.'

 **KEY TERM**

Indoctrination Inculcating and imposing a set of ideas.

Population policy
In 1933–45 the Nazi government aimed to increase the birth rate.

- Biology became the means by which to deliver Nazi racial theory: ethnic classification, **population policy** and racial genetics were all integrated into the syllabus.
- History, not surprisingly, was also given a special place in the Nazi curriculum, so that the glories of German nationalism could be emphasised.

One final innovation was the creation of various types of elite schools. They were intended to prepare the best of Germany's youth for future political leadership. They were modelled on the principles of the Hitler Youth, and focused on physical training, paramilitary activities and political education. The 21 *Napolas* (National Political Educational Institutions) and the ten Adolf Hitler Schools were both for boys of secondary school age, and the three *Ordensburgen* for boys of college age.

Hitler Youth

The responsibility for developing a new outlook lay with the youth movements. There was already a long and well-established tradition of youth organisations in Germany before 1933, but at that time the Hitler Youth (HJ, *Hitler Jugend*) represented only one per cent of the total.

SOURCE A

❓ In what ways could the poster in Source A be seen as effective propaganda for the Nazis?

'Youth serve the *Führer*! All 10-year-olds join the Hitler Youth!' A Nazi propaganda poster of 1940.

The term 'Hitler Youth' in fact embraced a range of youth groups under the control of its leader **Baldur von Schirach**. In the next six years the structure and membership of the HJ grew remarkably (see Table 6.1), although this was partly because parents were pressured to enrol their children and, by 1939, membership became compulsory. By then all other youth organisations had been abolished.

In all four youth groups shown in Table 6.2, there was a great stress on political indoctrination, emphasising the life and achievements of the *Führer*, German patriotism, athletics and camping. In addition, the sexes were moulded for their future roles in Nazi society. Boys engaged in endless physical and military-type activities, for example target shooting, and girls were prepared for their domestic and maternal tasks, for example cooking.

KEY FIGURE

Baldur von Schirach (1907–74)

Youth leader of the German Reich 1933–9 and *Gauleiter* of Vienna 1940–5. His loyalty and charm allowed him to remain influential with Hitler; he even wrote poetry to the *Führer*! But his effeminate nature alienated other leading Nazis.

Table 6.1 Hitler Youth movements. The percentages indicate the percentage of the total youth population aged ten to eighteen years who were members

Year	Number	Percentage
1932	200,000	1.5
1934	3,500,000	46.5
1936	5,400,000	62.8
1938	7,100,000	77.2

Table 6.2 Youth groups

Youth group	Organisation
Boys 10–14 years old	German Young People (DJ, *Deutsche Jungvolk*)
Boys 14–18 years old	Hitler Youth (HJ, *Hitler Jugend*)
Girls 10–14 years old	League of Young Girls (JM, *Jungmädel*)
Girls 14–18 years old	League of German Girls (BDM, *Bund Deutscher Mädel*)

Successes and failures

It is difficult to assess the 'success' of any educational system. It depends on the criteria chosen and the 'evidence' is open to conflicting interpretations. Therefore, conclusions must be tentative.

Teaching

The teaching profession certainly felt its status to be under threat, despite its initial sympathy for the regime. Thirty-two per cent were members of the party in 1936: a figure markedly higher than the figure of seventeen per cent of the Reich civil service as a whole. The anti-academic ethos and the crude indoctrination alienated many, while the party's backing of the HJ and its activities caused much resentment. Not surprisingly, standards in traditional academic subjects had fallen by the early years of the war. This was particularly the case in the various elite schools, where physical development dominated. By 1938 recruitment of teachers had declined and there were 8000 vacancies, with only 2500 graduating from teacher training colleges. In higher education, the number of students had halved even before the war.

Youth conformity

The impact of the HJ seems to have been very mixed. In some respects, the emphasis on teamwork and extracurricular activities was welcomed by many youngsters, especially when compared to the limited provision available in many European countries. The provision for sports, camping and music genuinely excited many of the youth, and for those from poorer backgrounds the HJ really offered opportunities. Most significantly, the HJ successfully conveyed to many youngsters an atmosphere of fun and a sense of belonging to the new Germany, as expressed by a young member of the Hitler Youth, Heinrich Metelmann:

SOURCE B

In what ways does Metelmann in Source B help to explain the appeal of the Hitler Youth?

From Heinrich Metelmann, 'Life in the Third Reich', in *New Perspective*, volume 2, number 3, March 1998.

The structural system of that youth organisation was based on the military. Our group consisted of about 150–200 boys, subdivided into three troops – just like a company of soldiers. We met together, marched and played together in close comradeship until the age of 18 … Every company had a Heim *[home; often a barn or cellar] which we decorated in a nationalist/militarist style. Swastika flags, and other Nazi emblems had places of honour, as well as decorated pictures of our* Führer *… But when we had our close togetherness there, we felt happy on our own. We were sure and proud that we were the future of Germany, come what may.*

The HJ suffered from its over-rapid expansion and the leadership was inadequate. By the late 1930s it became more difficult to run the movement effectively and, as a result, the increasing Nazi emphasis on military drill and discipline was certainly resented by many adolescents who saw it as too regimented. Recent research suggests that sizeable pockets of the adolescent population had not been won over by 1939 and that alienation and dissent increased quite markedly. The regime even established a special youth section of the secret police and a youth concentration camp was set up at Neuwied.

A number of youth groups developed that deliberately exhibited codes of behaviour at odds with the expected social values of Nazism. 'Swing Youth' was one such craze among mainly middle-class youngsters who took up the music and imagery associated with the dance-bands of Britain and the USA. The ***Edelweiss Piraten*** was a general name given to a host of working-class youths who formed gangs, such as the 'Roving Dudes' and 'Navajos'. Their members had been alienated by the military emphasis and discipline of the Hitler Youth. They met up and organised their own hikes and camps which then came into conflict with the official ones. In several instances during the war, 'Pirates' became involved in more active resistance (see page 227).

KEY TERM

Edelweiss Piraten Edelweiss Pirates. The name given to a loose collection of youth groups who did not conform. Edelweiss is a white alpine flower which served as a symbol of opposition.

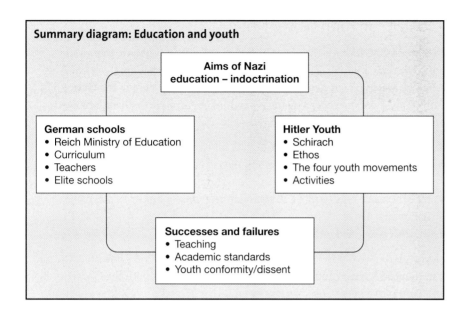

Summary diagram: Education and youth

Aims of Nazi education – indoctrination

German schools
- Reich Ministry of Education
- Curriculum
- Teachers
- Elite schools

Hitler Youth
- Schirach
- Ethos
- The four youth movements
- Activities

Successes and failures
- Teaching
- Academic standards
- Youth conformity/dissent

 # Religion

▶ *Did Nazi religious policy succeed in its aims?*

The rise of Nazism posed fundamental political and ethical problems for the Christian Churches, while Nazism could not ignore these well-established and powerful institutions.

In his rise to power, Hitler avoided direct attacks on the Churches, and number 24 of the party's 25-points programme spoke in favour of 'positive Christianity', which was closely linked to Nazi racial and nationalist views. However, there can be little doubt that Nazism was a fundamentally anti-Christian philosophy. Where Christianity taught love, forgiveness and neighbourly respect, Nazism glorified strength, violence and war. Moreover, Christianity was regarded as the product of an inferior race – Jesus was a Hebrew – and therefore, it could not be reconciled with Nazi *völkisch* thought. Some leading Nazis, such as Himmler and his deputy, Heydrich, openly revealed their contempt for Christianity. Hitler was more cautious, although what were probably his true feelings were revealed in a private conversation in 1933:

> *Neither of the denominations – Catholic or Protestant, they are both the same – has any future left … That won't stop me stamping out Christianity in Germany root and branch. One is either a Christian or a German. You can't be both.*

The German Faith Movement

In place of Christianity, the Nazis aimed to cultivate a **teutonic paganism**, which became known as the German Faith Movement. Although a clear Nazi religious ideology was never fully outlined, the development of the German Faith Movement, promoted by the Nazi thinker Alfred Rosenberg, revolved around four main themes:

- the propagation of the 'Blood and Soil' ideology
- the replacement of Christian ceremonies – marriage and baptism – by pagan equivalents
- the wholesale rejection of Christian ethics – closely linked to racial and nationalist views
- the **cult of** Hitler's **personality**.

However, the Nazi government knew that religion was a very delicate issue and it initially adopted a cautious conciliatory stance towards both the Churches to lull them into a false sense of security while the Nazi dictatorship was being established.

Conciliation and conflict 1933–5

In his very first speech as chancellor, Hitler paid tribute to the Churches as being integral to the well-being of the nation. Members of the SA were even encouraged to attend Protestant Church services. This was done to give weight to the idea that the Nazi state could accommodate Protestantism. The 'Day of Potsdam' (see page 139) further gave the impression of a unity between the Protestant Church and the state.

Likewise, the Catholic Church responded sympathetically to the overtures of the Nazis. Catholic bishops, in particular, were frightened of the possibility of a repeat of the so-called ***Kulturkampf*** in the late nineteenth century. They were concerned to safeguard the position of the Church under the Nazis so, in July 1933, a **Concordat** was signed between the papacy and the regime (represented by Vice-Chancellor Papen, who was a Catholic). In the agreement it was decided that:

- the Nazis would guarantee the Catholic Church religious freedom
- the Nazis would not interfere with the Catholic Church's property and legal rights
- the Nazis would accept the Catholic Church's control over its own education
- in return, the Catholic Church would not interfere in politics and would give diplomatic recognition to the Nazi government.

In the short term the Concordat seemed to be a significant success. However, the courting of both of the Churches by the Nazis was insincere and by the end of 1933 Nazi interference in religious affairs was already causing resentment and disillusionment in both Catholic and Protestant Churches.

The Nazi regime hoped that the Protestant Churches would gradually be 'co-ordinated' through the influence of the group known as the German Christians (*Deutsche Christen*). This group hoped to reconcile their Protestant ideas with Nazi nationalist and racial thinking by finding common ground. So, a new Church constitution was formulated in July 1933 with the Nazi sympathiser Ludwig Müller as the first Reich Bishop – an interesting application of the *Führerprinzip*.

Such Nazi policies alienated many Protestant pastors, and there soon developed an opposition group, the Confessional Church (*Bekennende Kirche*), which upheld orthodox Protestantism and rejected Nazi distortions. Led by Pastor **Niemöller**, by 1934 the Confessional Church gained the support of about 7000 pastors out of 17,000. They claimed to represent the true Protestant Churches of Germany.

Churches and the state

By 1935 it was clear that the Nazi leadership had achieved only limited success in controlling the Churches. It was torn between a policy of total suppression, which would alienate large numbers of Germans, and a policy of limited persecution, which would allow the Churches too much independence. In fact, although the ultimate objective was never in doubt, Nazi tactics degenerated into a kind of war of attrition against the Churches.

In order to destabilise the Churches, the Ministry of Church Affairs, led by **Hanns Kerrl**, was established. He adopted a policy of undermining both the Protestant and Catholic Churches by a series of anti-religious measures, including:

- the closure of Church schools
- the undermining of Catholic youth groups
- personal campaigns to discredit and harass the clergy, for example monasteries were accused of sexual and financial malpractices
- the confiscation of Church funds
- a campaign to remove crucifixes from schools
- the arrest of more and more pastors and priests.

The Churches were undoubtedly weakened by the approach, but it also stimulated individual declarations of opposition from both Protestants and Catholics:

- Niemöller delivered a sermon in which he said that 'we must obey God rather than man'; he was interned from 1937 and was held until the end of the war.
- The pope, **Pius XI**, eventually criticised the Nazi system but did not go so far as condemning Nazism in his encyclical, or public letter, of 1937 entitled *With Burning Concern* (*Mit Brennender Sorge*).

Clearly, the conflict between the Churches and the state was set to continue.

 **KEY FIGURES**

Martin Niemöller (1892–1984)

A nationalist and conservative U-boat commander, who became a Protestant pastor. He soon had doubts about the Nazi regime and was a co-founder of the Confessional Church in 1934. His critical sermons led to his arrest in 1937 and he was held in Sachsenhausen and Dachau concentration camps until the end of the war.

Hanns Kerrl (1887–1941)

Minister of Church affairs 1935–41. Increasingly marginalised by the more extreme Nazis. Died of natural causes in 1941 and not replaced.

Pius XI (1857–1939)

Accepted the dissolution of the Catholic ZP and agreed to the Concordat of July 1933. He issued the encyclical *With Burning Concern* (*Mit Brennender Sorge*) in 1937 and he was also preparing a further encyclical condemning anti-Semitism just before he died.

The outbreak of war initially brought about a more cautious policy, as the regime wished to avoid unnecessary tensions. However, following the military victories of 1939–40 the persecution intensified, as a result of pressure applied by anti-Christian enthusiasts, such as Bormann and Heydrich and the SS hierarchy. Monasteries were closed, Church property was attacked and Church activities were severely restricted. Even so, religion was such a politically sensitive issue that Hitler did not allow subordination of the Churches to give way to wholesale suppression within Germany.

Conclusions

The Nazis achieved only limited success in their religious policy. The German Faith Movement was clearly a failure. Neo-paganism never achieved support on any large scale. The 1939 official census recorded only five per cent of the population as members, although it shows the direction that might have been taken if the likes of Himmler had won the war.

Many individual Christians made brave stands against the Nazis. This made the dictatorship wary of launching a fundamental assault on religion, so German loyalty to Christianity survived in the long term despite Nazism. The historian J.R.C. Wright says: 'The Churches were severely handicapped but not destroyed. Hitler's programme needed time: he was himself destroyed before it had taken root.'

Both the Catholic and Protestant Churches failed to provide effective opposition to Nazism. Neither was 'co-ordinated' so both enjoyed a measure of independence. Both could have provided the focus for active resistance. Instead, they preferred, as institutions, to adopt a pragmatic policy towards Nazism. They stood up for their own religious practices and traditions with shows of dissent, but generally denunciations of the regime were left to individuals.

The reasons for the Churches' reluctance to show opposition to the regime lay in their conservatism:

- They distrusted the politics of the left, which seemed to threaten the existing order of society. The most extreme form of communism rejected the existence of religion itself and the Catholic Church saw Nazism as a bulwark against 'Godless communism'.
- There was a nationalist sympathy for Nazism, especially after the problems of 1918–33. For many Church leaders it was too easy to believe that Hitler's 'national renewal' was simply a return to the glorious days before 1914. This was particularly true of the Lutheran Protestant Church, which had been the state Church in Prussia under Imperial Germany.
- Both Churches rightly feared the power of the Nazi state. They believed that any gestures of heroic resistance were more than likely to have bloody consequences. In such a situation, their emphasis on pastoral and spiritual comfort was perhaps the most practical and realistic policy for them.

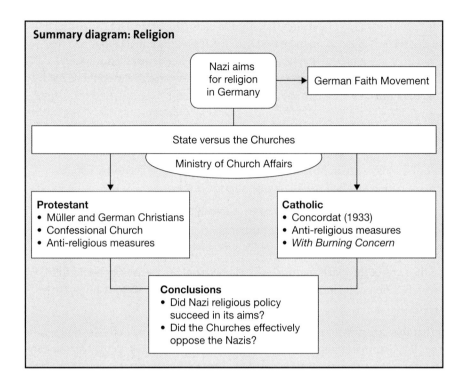

Summary diagram: Religion

5 Women and the family

► *What was the ideal role of women in Nazi society?*
► *How successful was Nazi policy on women and the family?*

The first quarter of the twentieth century witnessed two important social changes in German family life:

- Germany's population growth had decelerated markedly, which is not to say that the actual population had declined. In 1900 there had been over 2 million live births per annum, whereas by 1933 the figure was below a million.
- Over the same period female employment expanded by at least a third, far outstripping the percentage increase in population.

Both of these trends had been partially brought about by long-term changes in social behaviour common to many industrialised countries. It was recognised that the use of contraception to limit family size would improve the standard of living and give better-educated women the opportunity to have a vocation as well as children. However, Germany's recent past history exaggerated these developments. Economic mobilisation during the First World War had driven women into the factories, while the post-war difficulties caused by the inflation had encouraged them to stay on working out of economic necessity. In addition, the war had left a surplus of 1.8 million marriageable women, as well as many wives with invalided husbands. Finally, the changing balance of the economy in the 1920s had led to an increased demand for non-manual labour and the growth of mass-production techniques requiring more unskilled workers. These factors tended to favour the employment of women, who could be paid less than men.

The Nazi view of women

The ideology of National Socialism was in stark contrast to the above social trends. Nazism fundamentally opposed social and economic female emancipation and had the following aims for women:

- To have more children and to take responsibility for bringing them up.
- To care for the house and their husbands.
- To stop paid employment except for specialist vocations, such as midwifery.

In the view of the Nazis, nature had ordained that the two sexes should fulfil entirely different roles, and it was simply the task of the state to maintain this distinction.

What this amounted to was that 'a woman's place was to be in the home' (see the 'Ten Commandments' for choosing a spouse, below). Or, as the Nazi slogan presented it, women were to be devoted to the three German Ks: 'Kinder, Küche, Kirche' ('Children, Kitchen and Church'). Such dogma was upheld by the party, even before 1933 – there was not a single female Nazi deputy in the *Reichstag*, and a party regulation of 1921 excluded women from all senior positions within its structure.

Nazi views on women tied in with their concern about the demographic trends. A growing population was viewed as a sign of national strength and status – a reflection of Germany's aspiration to the status of an international power. How could they demand nationalist expansionism in eastern Europe, if the number of Germans was in fact levelling out? It was therefore considered essential to increase the population substantially and, to this end, women were portrayed as primarily the mothers of the next generation – an image that suited Nazi anti-feminism.

Nazi Ten Commandments for the choice of a spouse

1 Remember that you are German!

2 If you are genetically healthy, do not stay single.

3 Keep your body pure.

4 Keep your mind and spirit pure.

5 Marry only for love.

6 As a German, choose only a spouse of similar or related blood.

7 In choosing a spouse, ask about his forebears.

8 Health is essential to physical beauty.

9 Don't look for a playmate but for a companion in marriage.

10 You should want to have as many children as possible.

Female employment

Initially, attempts to reduce the number of women in work seem to have been quite successful. Between 1933 and 1936 married women were in turn debarred from jobs in medicine, law and the higher ranks of the civil service. Moreover, the number of female teachers and university students was reduced considerably – only ten per cent of university students could be female. Such laws had a profound effect on professional middle-class women, although their actual number was small.

Nazi incentives

In other sectors of the economy, a mixture of party pressure and financial inducements was employed to cajole women out of the workplace and back into the home. From June 1933 interest-free loans of RM600 were made available to young women who withdrew from the labour market in order to get married. The effects of the depression also worked in favour of Nazi objectives. They not only drastically reduced the number of female workers (although proportionately far less than male workers), but also enabled the government to justify its campaign for women to give up work for the benefit of unemployed men. On these grounds, **labour exchanges** and employers were advised to discriminate positively in favour of men. As a result of all this, the percentage of women in employment fell from 37 to 31 per cent of the total from 1932 to 1937, although the policy was not entirely effective as the actual *number* of women employed in this period rose because employment overall was growing.

Nazi women's organisations

Women were quite specifically excluded from the Nazi machinery of government. The only employment opportunities available to them within the party were within the various Nazi women's organisations, such as the National Socialist Womanhood (NSF, *National Sozialistische Frauenschaft*) and the German Women's Enterprise (DFW, *Deutsches Frauenwerk*), led by **Gertrud Scholtz-Klink**. Yet, the NSF and DFW were regarded by the party as mere tools for the propagation of the **anti-feminist** ideology by means of cultural, educational and social programmes. And so, when a campaign started in the NSF for enhanced opportunities for women within the party, its organisers were officially discredited.

Effects

By 1937 Nazi ideological convictions were already threatened by the pressures of economic necessity. The introduction of conscription and the rearmament boom from the mid-1930s soon led to an increasing shortage of labour, as the Nazi economy continued to grow. The anti-feminist ideology could only be upheld if economic growth was slowed down and that, in turn, would restrict the rearmament programme. Of course, Hitler was not prepared to sanction this. Consequently, market forces inevitably began to exploit this readily available

KEY TERMS

Labour exchanges Local offices created by the state for finding employment. Many were created in several countries to counter mass unemployment.

Anti-feminist Opposing female advancement.

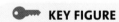

KEY FIGURE

Gertrud Scholtz-Klink (1902–99)

A nurse in Berlin who joined the NSDAP in 1929. Leader of the German Women's Enterprise (DFW, *Deutsches Frauenwerk*) 1934–45. Visited Britain in 1939 and portrayed as 'The perfect Nazi woman'. Remained committed to Nazism after the war and felt the benefits outweighed the bad.

pool of labour, and the relative decline in female employment was reversed. Between 1937 and 1939 the number of women workers rose from 5.7 million to 7.1 million, and the percentage of women as a percentage of the total workforce increased from 31 per cent to 33 per cent (see Table 6.3). At this point the government decided to end the marriage loan scheme (see below) for women who withdrew from the labour market.

Table 6.3 Women in regular manual and non-manual employment

	1932	1937	1939
Millions of women	4.8	5.7	7.1
Women as a percentage of the total	37	31	33
Note: the comparative figure for 1928 was 7.4 million.			

The contradictions between theory and practice of female employment were exacerbated further with the onset of war. So, although the trend of female employment continued to increase, the Nazi regime did not fully exploit the valuable resource of women as munitions workers. Whereas British women were required to play a major role on the home front, German women remained underemployed right to the end of the war. This was due to:

- Germany's poor economic mobilisation
- the unconvincing appeal for women to do war work in arms factories
- women's farming responsibilities.

Marriage and family

The Nazi state was obsessed not only with a desire to increase Germany's population (quantitative), but also with a 'qualitative' improvement.

> **SOURCE C**
>
> **From a Nazi pamphlet of October 1934, quoted in J. Noakes and G. Pridham, editors, *Nazism 1919–45*, volume 2, Liverpool University Press, 2000, p. 455.**
>
> *To be a mother means giving life to healthy children, bringing to fruition all the physical, mental and spiritual faculties of these children and creating a home for them which represents a place where nationalist and racialist culture is nurtured. It means realising in the community of the family a part of the ideal* Volksgemeinschaft *and giving to the nation, in the form of grown-up children, people who are physically and mentally developed to the fullest extent, who are aware of their responsibility to the nation and race who will lead their nation onwards and upwards.*

According to Source C, what was the Nazi view of a woman's role in the *Volksgemeinschaft*?

The Nazi regime therefore promptly introduced a series of measures:

- Marriage loans. The loan was worth just over half a year's earnings and a quarter of it was converted into a straight gift for each child that was born. (The scheme was introduced in June 1933, but progressively reduced from 1937.)

- Family allowances were improved dramatically, particularly for low-income families.
- Income tax was reduced in proportion to the number of children, and those families with six or more did not pay any.
- Maternity benefits were improved.
- The anti-abortion law introduced under the Weimar Republic was enforced much more strictly.
- Contraceptive advice and facilities were restricted.

Inevitably, these incentives and laws were backed up by an extensive propaganda campaign, which glorified motherhood and the large family. There were also rewards: the Honour Cross of the German Mother in bronze, silver and gold, awarded for four, six and eight children, respectively. Such glorification reached its climax in the coining of the Nazi slogan 'I have donated a child to the *Führer*' (as contemporary humourists soon pointed out, this was presumably because of Hitler's personal unwillingness or inability to father children of his own).

Table 6.4 Social trends in Nazi Germany 1933–9

Year	Marriages per 1000 inhabitants	Divorces per 10,000 existing marriages	Births per 1000 inhabitants
1933	9.7	29.7	14.7
1936	9.1	32.6	19.0
1939	11.1	38.3	20.3

The statistics in Table 6.4 show several trends:

- From 1933 the birth rate increased significantly, reaching a peak in 1939 (although thereafter it again slowly declined).
- The divorce rate continued to increase.
- The figure of marriages was fairly consistent (apart from the blip in 1939, probably connected to the onset of the war).

The real problem for the historian is deciding whether Nazi population policy was actually *responsible* for the demographic trends. Interpreting population statistics is difficult because it involves so many different factors: social, economic and even psychological. Also, it is extremely hard to assess the *relative* significance of Nazi population policy over such a short period, when its background was the effects of the depression.

Lebensborn

In connection with the aim of improving 'racial standards', the Nazis established an extraordinary organisation of social engineering called **Lebensborn**. Initially set up by Himmler and the SS in 1935, the programme provided homes for the increasing number of unmarried mothers as long as their illegitimate children met Nazi racial criteria. Eventually, ten 'homes' were created (and a further 25 abroad from 1939), all with very good maternity facilities. Later, the institution

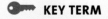 **KEY TERM**

Lebensborn Literally, the 'spring' or 'fountain of life'. Founded by Himmler and overseen by the SS to promote doctrines of racial purity.

also made the necessary arrangements for girls to be impregnated by members of the SS in organised brothels. It is reckoned that by the end of the regime about 11,000 children were born under these circumstances.

Conclusion

Feminist historians have been highly critical of Nazi population and family policies that reduced the status of women. One historian in the 1980s, Gisela Bock, viewed Nazi thinking on women as a kind of secondary racism in which they were the victims of a sexist–racist male regime that reduced them to the status of mere objects. Such an interpretation would have been denied by the Nazis, who viewed women as 'different', rather than inferior. Interestingly, some modern-day non-feminist historians have tried to explain the positive features of Nazi policy for women. Improved welfare services made life easier for women in many ways, especially in more isolated rural areas. Also, with husbands away during the war, they were protected from having to combine paid work with bringing up a family and running the household.

Despite these different perspectives, Nazi policy objectives for women and the family could not be squared with the social realities of twentieth-century Germany. With the changing population trend and the increasing employment of women, Nazi views on women and the family were idealistic but impractical. Consequently, Nazi policy towards women and the family was contradictory and incoherent.

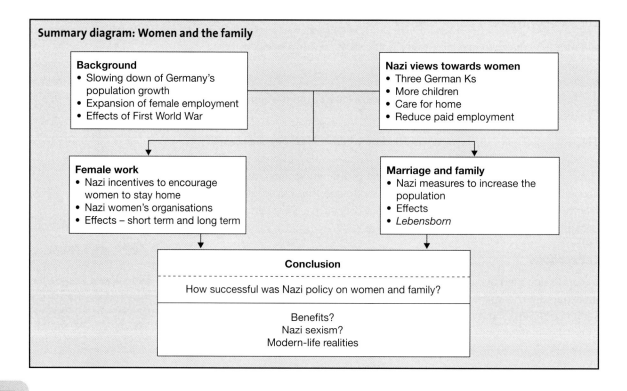

Outsiders

▶ *Who were the outsiders in the* Volksgemeinschaft?

Despite the Nazi vision of an all-embracing society, certain people were not allowed to be part of the *Volksgemeinschaft* in the Third Reich. Those who did not conform to the expected criteria were to be discriminated against and persecuted: they were definitely treated as 'outsiders'.

Ideological opponents

This term could most obviously be applied to the socialists and communists. Their leaders were sent to early concentration camps in 1933 and more were arrested by the *Gestapo* in the purge of 1935 (see page 227). However, increasingly it became a broader term to cover anyone who did not 'ideologically conform' to the regime. As the years went on, a broader range of political, religious and ethical opponents was identified and more were imprisoned, for example Pastor Niemöller (see page 205).

The 'biologically inferior' (*Untermenschen*)

The term **Untermenschen** covered all the races, according to the Nazis, who were seen as 'inferior' or subhuman, such as Gypsies, Slavs and Jews (see below). It also included mentally and physically disabled people.

The Nazis were strong supporters of **eugenics**, which had evolved from nineteenth-century Social Darwinism (see page 90) and had gained support from some scientists. Nazi ideology aspired to a pure Aryan race in which any 'inferior blood' – as found in other races and the mentally and physically unsound – should be removed.

As early as July 1933 the Nazis proclaimed 'The Law for the Prevention of Hereditarily Diseased Offspring', which allowed for the compulsory sterilisation of those with hereditary conditions like schizophrenia, Huntington's chorea, hereditary blindness or deafness. It also targeted those with existing conditions such as epilepsy or severe physical deformity which made them mentally or physically unfit.

SOURCE D

From the Law for the Prevention of Hereditarily Diseased Offspring, 14 July 1933, quoted in J. Noakes and G. Pridham, editors, *Nazism 1919–45*, volume 2, Liverpool University Press, 2000, p. 457.

Anyone who has a hereditary illness can be rendered sterile by a surgical operation, if according to the experience of medical science, there is a strong probability that his/her offspring will suffer from serious hereditary defects of a physical or mental nature …

> **KEY TERMS**
>
> **Untermenschen**
> Subhumans. Covered all races who, according to the Nazis, were 'inferior', or subhuman. Included Jews, Slavs and Gypsies (Sinti and Roma).
>
> **Eugenics** The scientific programme for the genetic improvement of the race.

According to Source D, what were the Nazi reasons for the sterilisation law?

It is not only the decline in population but also the deteriorating genetic make-up of our people which are causes of serious concern. Whereas the hereditary healthy families have for the most part adopted a policy of having only one or two children, countless numbers of inferiors and those suffering from hereditary ailments are reproducing unrestrainedly while their sick and asocial offspring are a burden on the community.

In twelve years 350,000 people were sterilised under this law, either voluntarily or as the result of judgments from one of the 220 hereditary health courts.

In addition, the 'Law for the Protection of the Hereditary Health of the German Nation' was passed in October 1935, which forbade the marriage of anyone suffering from mental disability or with a hereditary disease.

These policies went much further from 1938 when Hitler initiated the idea of using **euthanasia** for children with severe disabilities (such as Down's syndrome and cerebral palsy) by presenting it as a 'mercy death'. In order to counter any public outrage to their plans, the government launched a propaganda campaign which focused on the cost of caring for psychiatric patients at the expense of ordinary German citizens.

No specific law permitted the euthanasia of such patients, but many were killed in asylums under the name of **Operation T-4**. From September 1939 all public, private or religious institutions caring for mental patients had to submit details of their inmates' conditions to the T-4 offices in Berlin, where a panel of doctors selected those who should die. Initially, the patients were transferred to 'killing wards' where they were killed through drug overdose or gradual starvation, but, given the large numbers of victims, it soon became clear that carbon monoxide gassing would be more efficient. About 70,000 were gassed in 1940–1, but, following public rumours and Catholic opposition, the operation was stopped (see pages 227 and 255). Nevertheless, child euthanasia and the killing of mentally and physically disabled patients by other methods still continued until 1945.

Asocials

The term was used very broadly to cover anyone whose behaviour was not viewed as acceptable. These social outcasts included alcoholics, prostitutes, criminals, tramps and the workshy: indeed, anyone who did not, could not or would not perform their duties to the national community.

Those asocials who were 'orderly' but avoided work were rounded up and organised into a compulsory labour force; and those who were judged as 'disorderly' were imprisoned and sometimes sterilised or experimented on.

Homosexual men were also classed as asocials. They were seen as breaking the laws of nature and undermining traditional Nazi family values. In 1936 the Reich Central Office for the Combating of Homosexuality and Abortion was

KEY TERMS

Euthanasia The practice of putting an end to the lives of people suffering from incurable illnesses.

Operation T-4 The collation of information about mentally and physically ill patients in offices in Tiergartenstrasse No. 4, Berlin, as part of the euthanasia programme.

established. Between 10,000 and 15,000 homosexuals were imprisoned and
those sent to camps were forced to wear pink triangles. Provided they were
discreet, lesbians were not persecuted as much as men, as they were not seen as
a threat to society in the same way.

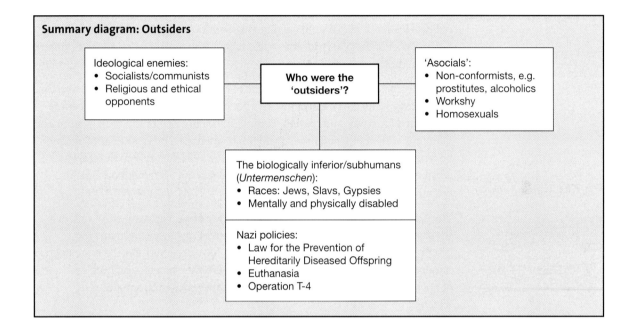

Summary diagram: Outsiders

Ideological enemies:
• Socialists/communists
• Religious and ethical opponents

Who were the 'outsiders'?

'Asocials':
• Non-conformists, e.g. prostitutes, alcoholics
• Workshy
• Homosexuals

The biologically inferior/subhumans (*Untermenschen*):
• Races: Jews, Slavs, Gypsies
• Mentally and physically disabled

Nazi policies:
• Law for the Prevention of Hereditarily Diseased Offspring
• Euthanasia
• Operation T-4

 # 7 Nazi anti-Semitism

▶ *How and why did Nazi anti-Semitism change over time?*

At the very centre of Nazi social policy was the issue of race and, specifically,
anti-Semitism. Hitler's obsessive hatred of the Jews was perhaps the most
dominant and consistent theme of his political career. The translation of such
ideas into actual policy was to lead to racial laws, government-inspired violence
and the execution of the **genocide** policy that culminated in what became
known as the **Holocaust**.

The context

The emergence of right-wing racist *völkisch* nationalism was clearly apparent
before 1914 (see pages 33–5). Its attractions expanded in the aftermath of
the First World War: the self-deception of the 'stab in the back' myth; the
humiliation of the Versailles Treaty; and the political and economic weaknesses
of the Weimar Republic. So, by the early 1920s, there were about 70 relatively
small right-wing racist parties, such as the Nazi Party.

 **KEY TERMS**

Genocide
The extermination of a whole race.

Holocaust Term to describe mass slaughter – in this context it refers to the extermination of the Jews.

In that environment Hitler was able to exploit hostility towards the Jews and turn it into a radical ideology of hatred. He was the product, not the creator, of a society that was permeated by such prejudices. Yet, it would be inaccurate to dismiss Hitler as just another anti-Semite. Hitler's hatred of Jews was obsessive and vindictive, and it shaped much of his political philosophy. Without his personal commitment to attack the Jews and without his charismatic skills as a political leader, it seems unlikely that anti-Semitism could have become such an integral part of the Nazi movement. He was able to mobilise and stir the support of the leading anti-Semitic Nazis.

It is all too easy to highlight the rhetoric of Nazi anti-Semitism as the reason for the success of the party. Certainly, 37.3 per cent of the population may seem to have voted for Hitler and his anti-Semitic stance in 1932, but the vast majority of Germans were motivated more by unemployment, the collapse of agricultural prices and the fear of communism. Indeed, in a 1934 survey into the reasons why people joined the Nazis, over 60 per cent did not even mention anti-Semitism.

KEY TERM

Gradualism Changing by degrees; progressing slowly.

The Nazi approach to anti-Semitism was **gradualist**. The early moves against Jews gave no suggestion of the end result. Indeed, for some Germans the discriminatory legislation was no more than Jews deserved. For the more liberal minded, who found such action offensive, there was the practical problem of how to show opposition and to offer resistance. Once the apparatus of dictatorship was well established by the end of 1934, the futility of opposition was apparent to most people. Feelings of hopelessness were soon replaced by those of fear. To show sympathy for, or to protect Jews, was to risk one's own freedom or one's own life. It was an unenviable dilemma.

Legal discrimination

Many radical Nazis were keen to take immediate measures against Jewish people and their businesses, but the party's leadership was worried that these could get out of hand. Those concerns were confirmed when a one-day national boycott was organised for 1 April 1933. Jewish-owned shops, cafés and businesses were picketed by the SA, who stood outside urging people not to enter. However, the boycott was not universally accepted by the German people and it caused a great deal of bad publicity abroad.

The Nazi leaders developed their anti-Semitism in a more subtle way. Once the Nazi regime had established the legal basis for its dictatorship, it was legally possible to initiate an anti-Jewish policy, most significantly by the creation of the Nuremberg Laws in September 1935. This clearly stood in contrast to the extensive civil rights that Jews had enjoyed in Weimar Germany. The discrimination against Jewish people got worse as an ongoing range of laws was introduced (see Table 6.5). In this way, all the rights of Jews were gradually removed even before the onset of the war.

Table 6.5 Major Nazi anti-Jewish laws 1933–9

Year	Date	Law
1933	7 April	Law for the Restoration of the Professional Civil Service. Jews excluded from the government's civil service
1935	15 September	The Nuremberg Race Laws: 1 Reich Citizenship Act. 'A citizen of the Reich is a subject who is only of German or kindred blood.' Jews lost their citizenship in Germany 2 Law for the Protection of German Blood and German Honour. Marriages and extramarital relations between Jews and German citizens forbidden
1938	26 April	Decree for the registration of Jewish property
	5 July	Decree prohibiting Jewish doctors practising medicine
	12 November	Decree to exclude Jews from German Economic Life (arising from inter-ministerial meeting chaired by Göring)
	15 November	Law excluding Jewish pupils from schools and universities
	28 November	Law restricting the freedom of movement of Jews, for example public swimming pools, theatres
	3 December	Law for the compulsory closure and sale of all Jewish businesses
1939	1 September	Decree for the introduction of curfew for Jews

Propaganda and indoctrination

Nazism also set out to cultivate the message of anti-Semitism; in effect to change people's attitudes so that they hated the Jews. Goebbels was a particularly committed anti-Semite and he used his propagandist skills to indoctrinate the German people. All aspects of culture associated with the Jews were censored. Even more forceful was the full range of propaganda methods used to advance the anti-Semitic message, such as:

- posters and signs, for example 'Jews are not wanted here'
- newspapers, for example *Der Angriff*, which was founded by Goebbels, and *Der Stürmer*, edited by the *Gauleiter* Julius Streicher, which was overtly anti-Semitic with a seedy range of articles devoted to pornography and violence
- cinema, for example *The Eternal Jew* and *Süss the Jew* (see page 172).

A particular aspect of anti-Semitic indoctrination was the emphasis placed on influencing German youth. The message was obviously put across by the Hitler Youth, but all schools also conformed to the new revised curriculum, which focused on reinforcing Nazi racism, for example through studying negative portrayals of Jews in literature and history, and even presenting anti-Semitic mathematical problems such as '… calculate the number of Jews in Germany'.

SOURCE E

? According to Source E, how were the Jews portrayed in Nazi Germany?

Poster for the anti-Semitic film *The Eternal Jew*. The caption reads: 'A Documentary about World Jewry'.

Terror and violence

In the early years of the regime, the SA, as the radical left wing of the Nazis, took advantage of their power at local level to use violence against Jews, for example damage to property, intimidation and physical attacks. However, after the Night of the Long Knives in June 1934 (see page 146), anti-Semitic violence became more sporadic for two probable reasons. First, in 1936 the anti-Semitic campaign was suspended because of the Berlin Olympics and the need to avoid international alienation. Secondly, conservative forces still had a restraining influence, for example Schacht had continued to express worries about the implications of anti-Semitic action for the economy. However, his dismissal in

September 1937, along with other conservatives (see pages 174–6), cleared the way for the development of a more extreme anti-Semitic policy. In 1938–9 the violence and intimidation of two major events showed that there was a more radical mood against the Jews, even before the start of the Second World War.

The *Anschluss*

The takeover of Austria (the *Anschluss*) in March 1938 (see page 231) was received with euphoric support by the vast majority in both countries, but it resulted in violence and humiliation for the 190,000 Austrian Jewish population, on a scale not seen in Germany.

At first, Jewish properties and businesses were looted, particularly in Vienna, and some Jews were made to publicly wash buildings and pavements. Thousands were also arrested. More systematically, later in that summer, Jewish houses and businesses were sold off at low prices and officially '**Aryanised**'.

 **KEY TERM**

Aryanise To remove all non-Aryans from office, business and property.

The events in Austria encouraged Göring to believe that there were benefits to adopting a similar, although more orderly, approach throughout Germany. On 26 April 1938 he issued a 'Decree for the Registration of Jewish Property', which demanded that all Jewish property worth more than RM5000 be valued and registered with the state. This was a step towards confiscating all Jewish property and excluding the Jews from German economic life.

Kristallnacht

On 9–10 November 1938 there was a sudden violent pogrom against the Jews, which became known as the 'Night of Crystal Glass' (*Kristallnacht*) because of all the windows which were smashed in the process. The pogrom was prompted by an unforeseen incident: the assassination of Ernst von Rath, a German diplomat, by Herschel Grünspan, a Polish Jew, on 7 November in Paris. *Kristallnacht* started in Berlin and spread throughout Germany with dramatic effects: the destruction of numerous Jewish homes with 100 deaths; attacks on 10,000 Jewish shops and businesses; the burning down of 200 synagogues and the deportation of 20,000 Jewish people to concentration camps. Nevertheless, even leading Nazis were surprised and shocked by the extent of the damage in the pogrom and concerned about international criticism. It was officially portrayed as a 'spontaneous demonstration' of popular outrage, but in fact it was very much fuelled by local Nazis and co-ordinated by Goebbels. He had hoped that the anti-Semitic actions might also win Hitler's favour, and compensate for his disreputable affair with a Czech actress.

Significantly, Göring exploited *Kristallnacht* to chair an interministerial meeting on Jewish policy which agreed on the 'Decree to Exclude Jews from German Economic Life'. This resulted in various laws (see Table 6.5 on page 217) which formally extended the Aryanisation of Jewish-owned property and laid the basis for the segregation of Germans and Jews in every aspect of day-to-day living.

Forced emigration

From the start of the Nazi dictatorship some Jews had decided to leave Germany voluntarily. Many Jews with influence, high reputation or sufficient wealth could find the means to leave. The most popular destinations were Palestine, Britain and the USA, and among the most renowned *emigrés* were Albert Einstein, the scientist, and Kurt Weill, the composer. However, from 1938 a new dimension to anti-Semitism developed: forced emigration. As a result of the events in Austria in 1938, the Central Office for Jewish Emigration was established in Vienna, overseen by **Adolf Eichmann**. Jewish property was confiscated to finance the emigration of poor Jews. Within six months Eichmann had forced the emigration of 45,000 and the scheme was seen as such a success that, in January 1939, Göring was prompted to create the Reich Central Office for Jewish Emigration, run by **Heydrich** and Eichmann (see Table 6.6).

Table 6.6 The Jewish community in Germany 1933–45

Year	Jewish population	*Emigrés* per annum
1933	503,000	38,000
1939 (May)	234,000	78,000*
1945	20,000	N/A

* The cumulative figure of Jewish *emigrés* between 1933 and 1939 was 257,000.

It is therefore estimated that the Nazi persecution led to about half of the Jewish population leaving before the war. Technically, the Jews had voluntarily emigrated, but they were forced to leave behind all their belongings. Faced with that prospect, the other half stayed. Some assumed that this was just another phase in the history of European pogroms, and would pass. Others felt they were so rooted in Germany that they could not comprehend living elsewhere. Whatever the reason, the remainder decided to take their chances, rather than lose their homes and all their possessions.

Conclusion

Despite the number of anti-Semitic measures of 1933–9, it is difficult to claim that the Nazis had pursued a planned overall policy to deal with the 'Jewish question'. In many respects the measures were at first haphazard. However, one point is very clear – the year 1938 marked an undoubted **radicalisation** of Nazi anti-Semitism. The laws, the violence connected with *Kristallnacht* and the forced emigration came together, suggesting that the regime had reached a pivotal year, a fact confirmed by the tone of the speech in the *Reichstag* by Hitler on 30 January 1939: 'If the international Jewish financiers in and outside Europe should succeed in plunging the nations once more into a world war, then the result will not be the Bolshevising [making communist] of the earth, and thus the victory of Jewry, but the annihilation of the Jewish race in Europe.'

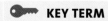 **KEY FIGURES**

Adolf Eichmann (1906–62)

Eichmann was an NSDAP member who was quickly chosen to join the SD of the SS in 1932. A central figure who was responsible for the deportation of millions of Jews to ghettos and camps. He took the notes at the infamous Wannsee Conference, 1942. Arrested and executed by the state of Israel in 1961.

Reinhard Heydrich (1904–42)

Undoubtedly talented, but his skills were marred by traits of selfishness, ambition and brutality. Made chief of secret police at the age of 32 and in 1939 appointed head of RSHA and the leader of the Central Office for Jewish Emigration. As Reich protector of Bohemia, he was assassinated in May 1942 by the Czech resistance in Prague.

KEY TERM

Radicalisation A policy of increasing severity.

It is difficult to truly assess how popular the anti-Semitic policies of 1933–9 were with non-Jewish Germans. Certainly there was much anti-Semitism, and it is likely that the initial commercial and social discrimination was generally well received. But attitudes in the aftermath of *Kristallnacht* are another matter. By then, open opposition from non-Jewish Germans would have been dangerous and there would have been serious consequences for any dissenters.

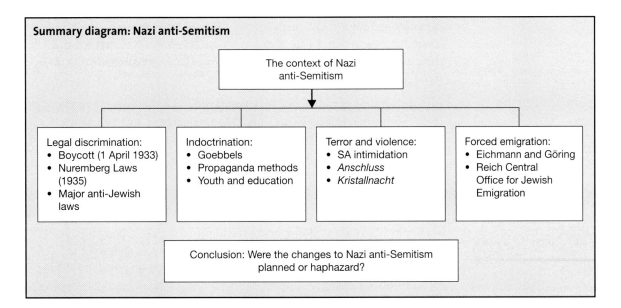

Summary diagram: Nazi anti-Semitism

The context of Nazi anti-Semitism

Legal discrimination:
- Boycott (1 April 1933)
- Nuremberg Laws (1935)
- Major anti-Jewish laws

Indoctrination:
- Goebbels
- Propaganda methods
- Youth and education

Terror and violence:
- SA intimidation
- *Anschluss*
- *Kristallnacht*

Forced emigration:
- Eichmann and Göring
- Reich Central Office for Jewish Emigration

Conclusion: Were the changes to Nazi anti-Semitism planned or haphazard?

8 Conclusion: the impact of the Nazi *Volksgemeinschaft*

▶ *How far did the Nazis succeed in creating a* Volksgemeinschaft?

▶ *How popular was the Nazi* Volksgemeinschaft?

In many ways, the Third Reich seemed to have had a dramatic impact on the daily life of the German people. Yet, how fundamental was the influence of the Nazi *Volksgemeinschaft* on German society?

Continuity or change?

Marxist historians have seen it as social reaction of the worst kind. This was because it reinforced the traditional class structure and strengthened the position of the conservative elites – especially the powerful interests of the military and big business – at the expense of more popular institutions, such as the trade unions.

In opposition, more liberal historians have believed that the Nazi *Volksgemeinschaft* brought about important changes in social values. Ralf Dahrendorf has suggested that Nazism resulted in a social revolution which caused the collapse of the social elites and the traditional loyalties and values which had dominated German life since the mid-nineteenth century. It had paved the way for the emergence of a liberal, democratic West Germany.

Alternatively, some historians feel that Nazism only led to 'a revolution of destruction'. They feel that many of the policies and effects were actually contradictory and that the social changes were very limited. In that sense, if there was any real transformation, it came from the destructive effects of the racial policies and the consequences of the war.

Although many Germans came to be convinced by Goebbels' propaganda that a new genuine Nazi *Volksgemeinschaft* was emerging, any real change is questionable. The reality was that the Third Reich lasted only twelve years – and the last six of those were spent fighting the bloodiest war in human history. Prevailing cultural traditions and social institutions, such as the family and the Churches, did not break down overnight. Therefore, it should be remembered that:

- Despite Nazi rhetorical support for the *Mittelstand* and the peasantry, both groups remained under social and economic pressure. In contrast, the traditional elites continued to dominate, with property and industry staying in private ownership.
- Women were supposed to stay at home and have more children, but really their role was set by the economic demands of the situation.
- The Christian Churches were expected to wither away. However, the Churches survived and enjoyed the support of the vast majority of the people.
- Nazi culture was meant to establish new roots in the *Volk*, but it exerted little more than a negative, censorious role.

If there was a 'revolutionary' core to Nazism, it is to be found in the obsessive nature and implementation of its racial policy, which resulted in the genocide of the war.

Popularity of the Nazi *Volksgemeinschaft*

Assessing the popularity of a regime is far from easy. It is hard enough in a modern-day democracy, like Britain or Germany, even when we have access to sophisticated methods of analysis. Trying to gauge the degree of consent and opposition to a totalitarian dictatorship is even more difficult. There was no black or white distinction between them, as is shown by the spectrum in Figure 6.1. Moreover, shades of opinion were not static – they changed over time.

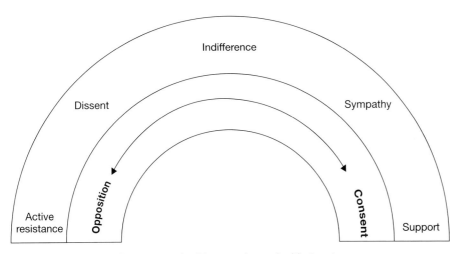

Indifference

Dissent

Sympathy

Opposition

Consent

Active resistance

Support

Figure 6.1 A suggested spectrum of public attitudes to the Nazi regime.

Support and sympathy

It is evident from the last two chapters that many groups of people had good reasons to back the Nazi regime. It is important to note the following key factors:

- The economic recovery, whether it was strong or weak, represented concrete gains for many German workers. Schacht's policies substantially reduced the pain of mass unemployment from the human crisis of 1930–3. Although industrial workers may have resented the longer hours and the relatively low wages, they benefited from the restoration of full employment by 1939.
- The restoration of political and economic stability was well received by many people, especially the middle classes, who were afraid of the threat of communism.
- Despite Nazi ideological objectives, many youngsters did enjoy the social and physical aspects of the Hitler Youth.
- The social benefits introduced through the Nazi welfare organisations, such as the KdF and SdA, had a broadly positive effect. Somehow the Nazi regime did succeed with its practical changes in making the people feel that the government recognised their problems and anxieties.
- Traditional family values – at the expense of women's rights – were not so unpopular, particularly in the rural areas.
- The diplomatic successes of 1935–9 (which soon gave way to the military victories of 1939–41) were seen as real achievements in foreign policy (see pages 231–4). For a nation that had lost the First World War and endured the 'shame' of the Versailles Treaty, Hitler was seen as an effective leader in contrast to the failings of Weimar.

These factors contributed greatly, at the very least, to the German people's acceptance or, even, support for the regime.

Shaped consent

Popular consent was also deliberately 'shaped' by the Nazi regime. Nazi control of all means of communication effectively enabled them to have power over all propaganda and censorship. As shown on pages 194–8, there were limitations to this control, but in the years before the war the propaganda machine was successful in the sense that:

- It cultivated the Hitler myth of him as an effective leader – of almost messianic qualities which glorified him as a 'saviour'.
- It portrayed the Nazi regime and its *Volksgemeinschaft* model as a stabilising force which promised harmony and security after the civil strife and conflicts of the Weimar years.
- It played on frustrated German nationalism.

For many, it was perhaps easier to believe the propaganda than to challenge it. Historians can question the true impact of the propaganda or marvel at the gullibility of those who were taken in. But to have lived in a society where only one point of view was disseminated must have blunted anyone's powers of judgement. Many people could push to one side their doubts about the regime because of its perceived successes and their memories of Weimar failures.

Terror and surveillance

Also, the Third Reich developed a regime built on terror and intimidation and backed by surveillance. Of course, the terror was not quite as pervasive as feared at the time (see pages 161–5); nevertheless, the brutality must not be underestimated. Civil rights and freedoms were lost and the courts were increasingly made to deliver judgments and sentences which upheld the regime. Any 'outsiders' were sent to camps or held in prison. Therefore, 'an atmosphere of fear' was created where people were coerced into submission. In this way, not only the potential opposition but also the non-committed and the indifferent were made aware of the dangers. Those individuals who were prepared to question must have known that their actions were futile gestures which would end in personal sacrifice. As the leading historian in this area, P. Hüttenberger, has written: '… the leadership of the Third Reich largely succeeded in producing such a degree of conformity, indeed readiness to collaborate, that its plans, especially preparation for war, were not endangered from within'.

Opposition before the war: non-conformity, dissent and resistance

The Third Reich may have had Nazi totalitarian aspirations, yet it fell a long way short of winning 'the hearts and minds' of the entire German population. Nevertheless, the real threat posed by opponents was fairly limited. Active resistance to undermine the Nazi state could only have come from the elites, and the disillusioned elements did not act together until the late 1930s. Even then, the conservative opposition did not enjoy a sufficiently strong or broad base of support.

A new generation of historians from the 1970s started to question the nature of the opposition by a completely new historical methodology. Mommsen adopted new research techniques to examine people's attitudes and beliefs at the grassroots of society through oral history. This was initiated by the so-called Bavaria Project led by Hüttenberger and then developed by English historians, Mason and Kershaw. The study of opposition to the Nazis has thus been broadened from the narrow area of active resistance to include anyone who did not conform to Nazi expectations.

Not surprisingly, such a methodology has its critics. Many see it as trying to play down active resistance and to exaggerate the importance of mere passive behaviour, which had little real effect on the regime. However, some historians, in an attempt to give clearer definition to the subtle differences of opposition, have proposed 'models' of resistance similar to the methods of social scientists. The models shown in Figure 6.2 are merely the suggestions of two historians who have tried to categorise opposition. None of the models should be seen as providing all the answers to the problems raised. They are starting points for discussion and analysis.

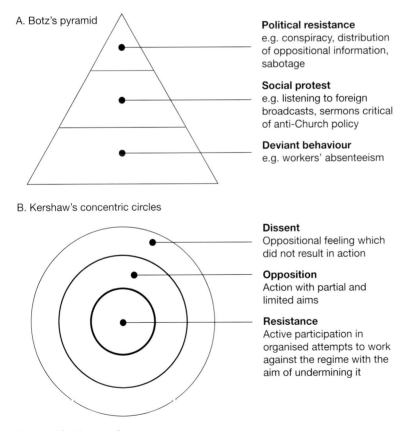

Figure 6.2 Models of opposition.

Much depends on the particular meanings applied to specific words. More significantly, there are dangers in the drawing of clear-cut boundary lines; what emerges from all the research is that any one individual's behaviour was rarely clear-cut. More often than not, most people exhibited a broad mixture of attitudes, variously shaped by religious, financial, moral or personal influences. It was quite feasible for a Catholic priest, for example, to show opposition in the following ways:

- protest publicly over the Nazi euthanasia policy
- deliberately carry on traditional Catholic customs within the community.

Yet, the priest could at the same time:

- still be generally supportive of Nazi foreign/military policy
- sympathise with the more authoritarian nature of Nazi government.

It should also be borne in mind that attitudes were rarely static; circumstances changed over time. Indeed, some of the most important figures in the active resistance among the conservative elites had initially supported the Nazi regime (see pages 255–61).

Conclusion

All the recent evidence suggests that the position of public opinion was a lot more 'fluid' than assumed previously. It is difficult to give a straight and clear answer to the question of how many people opposed or supported the regime. Nevertheless, a provisional assessment can be made of the state of play. It may now be possible to identify the range of dissent, but the underlying trend suggests that the regime enjoyed increasing popular support from its consolidation during the peace years – a position that was to be maintained until the winter of 1942–3.

Opposition: non-conformity, dissent and resistance

Army (see pages 173–6)

Conditioned by their traditions of obedience, loyalty and patriotism, many army officers initially worked with the Third Reich. However, the leading generals Blomberg and Fritsch, who were critical of Hitler's ambitions, were removed in February 1938.

General Beck was particularly opposed to Hitler from the start. After his resignation in August 1938 he drew up plans to arrest Hitler over the Czech crisis, but this failed because of the peaceful surrender by Anglo-French appeasers in September. The following diplomatic successes and early military victories further allayed the doubts of many generals.

Churches (see pages 203–7)

The creation of the Confessing Church by Protestants was a significant gesture of resistance to the Nazi dictatorship; and by 1939 there were increasing concerns in the Catholic Church on ethical differences regarding sterilisation and euthanasia.

There were also brave individual Christian clerics, like Niemöller, who were openly critical in their sermons, and others did not conform. This made the dictatorship wary of launching a fundamental assault on religion in the years of peace. However, both the Catholic and Protestant Churches failed to provide effective opposition to Nazism and concentrated on protecting their own positions.

Youth (see page 202)

Despite Nazi indoctrination, sizeable pockets of the adolescent population had not been won over. There were a number of youth subcultures exhibiting behaviour which challenged the expected social values of Nazism. Groups such as the 'Swing Youth' were born out of the popularity of American jazz, but were seen by the Nazis to be unpatriotic. Other groups such as the *Edelweiss Piraten* were more explicitly critical of Nazi society, particularly of the Hitler Youth, which they boycotted and ridiculed. However, in peacetime the alternative youth groups were merely non-conformist, it was not until the war that youth opposition turned into active resistance.

Conservative elites

There were critics in the government, the civil service and the judiciary. The conservative non-Nazi Konstantin von Neurath remained as foreign minister until 1938 and he maintained connections with the group of diplomats, like Ulrich von Hassell, who had reservations about the regime. Surprisingly, a crucial centre of opposition was *Abwehr*, the German Military Intelligence Office. The deputy leader, Hans Oster, established an extensive network of opponents, including Beck and even Schacht. The main problem confronting these conservatives was staging any kind of resistance in the face of Hitler's successes and his popularity with the ordinary German people.

Workers

All other political parties were banned in 1933, but those of the left wing were the focus of real persecution: in the wake of the *Reichstag* fire many communists were thrown into the early camps; and in 1935 there were mass arrests of socialists and communists by the *Gestapo*, who were becoming increasingly repressive.

Consequently, communists and social democrats went underground: the SPD was reformed in Prague and later Paris; while the KPD also established an office in Prague and maintained its connections with Moscow. Both groups arranged for the publication and distribution of newspapers and anti-Nazi pamphlets and they also established cells within Germany, especially in many of the large cities. As for ordinary workers, there were some strikes and other industrial action – such as work-to-rule – held in the early years, 1933–5. However, the key obstacle continued to be the lack of any co-ordinated opposition.

Assassination attempts

- Maurice Bavaud, a Catholic theological student. On 9 November 1938 in Munich he planned to shoot Hitler at a parade but abandoned the idea when he stood too far away. Later arrested and executed.
- Georg Elser, a socialist cabinet-maker. On 8 November 1939 in Munich he planned to blow up Hitler during a speech. The bomb exploded killing seven, but Hitler had left a few minutes before. Arrested and executed.

Chapter summary

In the *Volksgemeinschaft* the Nazis had an ambitious purpose to change German society. Yet, its actual impact over such a short period has been questioned. Evidence suggests that Hitler enjoyed considerable support before the war – indeed, any opposition revealed itself as mere non-conformity, rather than active resistance. However, the *Volksgemeinschaft* failed to create an alternative new Nazi culture, or to challenge the Christian Churches with the new religion of the German Faith Movement. Likewise, it is debatable whether Nazi ideology on the youth and the role of women had a real long-term impact on the people. In fact, those Nazi policies created real practical problems for the regime. Furthermore, even the initial benefits for the working class, peasantry and *Mittelstand* were offset by the increasing economic realities of the late 1930s.

If there was a revolutionary core to Nazi *Volksgemeinschaft*, it can be seen in the shift of Nazi racial policy from gradualism to radicalism in its treatment of 'outsiders', such as the *Untermenschen*, the asocials, the Jews and people with mental and physical disabilities. The consequences of these policies can be seen in Chapter 7.

 Refresher questions

Use these questions to remind yourself of the key material covered in this chapter.

1 How did the Nazis aim to transform German society?

2 What was the overall impact of full employment on the working classes?

3 How was education used to indoctrinate Nazi values?

4 To what extent did the Hitler Youth succeed in making youngsters conform?

5 How did the relationship between the Churches and the Nazi state change over time?

6 What were the main features of the German Faith Movement?

7 How successful was Nazi policy for women?

8 What was the impact of Nazi policy on population and the family?

9 Who were the outsiders in the *Volksgemeinschaft* (people's community)?

10 In what ways could Nazi anti-Semitism be seen as gradualist during the Third Reich?

11 Why was Nazi anti-Semitism radicalised in 1938?

12 To what extent did the German people support the regime?

Question practice

ESSAY QUESTIONS

1 Assess the consequences of Nazi religious policies.

2 To what extent did the German people have more benefits than drawbacks from Nazi social and economic policies?

3 Which of the following had a greater impact on changes in German society? i) Nazi policies on education and youth. ii) Nazi policies on women and the family. Explain your answer with reference to both i) and ii).

4 How successful was Hitler in making anti-Semitism a powerful feature of German society up to 1939?

5 'Nazism had not produced a social revolution in Nazi Germany by the start of the war.' To what extent do you agree?

CHAPTER 7

The impact of war 1939–45

Although there is a brief overview of military operations, the main aim of this chapter is to consider the impact of the war. This picks up and focuses on a range of issues raised in previous chapters: the direction of the economy, the actual effect on the people on the home front, racial policy and resistance. These issues are considered through the following sections:

★ The war

★ The Nazi war economy

★ The racial war

★ The home front

★ Resistance and repression

★ Germany's defeat

The key debate on *page 262* of this chapter asks the question: Where did the responsibility lie for the Nazi racial war?

Key dates

1939	Sept. 1	German invasion of Poland
	Dec.	Hitler's war economy decrees
1941	June 22	German invasion of USSR: Operation Barbarossa
	Aug.	Bishop Galen's sermons against euthanasia
	Dec.	Rationalisation Decree
1942	Jan.	Wannsee Conference: 'Final Solution' to exterminate the Jewish people
	Feb.	Appointment of Albert Speer as minister of armaments
	Nov.	German defeat at El Alamein
1942–3		White Rose student group; distribution of anti-Nazi leaflets

1942–4		Transportation of Jews to death camps
1943	Jan.	German surrender at Stalingrad
	Feb. 18	Goebbels' speech rallying the people for a 'total war'
	July 24	Hamburg firestorm
1944	July 20	Stauffenberg Bomb Plot, which failed to overthrow the regime
	Nov.	Execution of twelve Edelweiss Pirates in Cologne
1945	May 7–8	German surrender: occupation and division of Germany

The war

> ▶ *Why was Germany so successful initially?*
>
> ▶ *When and why did the military balance turn against Germany?*

In *Mein Kampf* Hitler openly stated his ambitions for foreign policy (see page 92). Indeed, some historians believe that Hitler had a clearly defined set of objectives, which amounted to a stage-by-stage plan:

- The destruction of the Treaty of Versailles and the restoration of Germany's pre-1914 boundaries.
- The union of all German-speaking peoples such as those in Austria, western Poland, the borders of Czechoslovakia (the Sudetenland) and provinces in Hungary and Romania.
- The creation of *Lebensraum*: the establishment of a Nazi racial empire by expanding into eastern Europe at the expense of the Slavic peoples, particularly in Poland and Russia.

In the years 1935–8 Germany rapidly made some key gains which changed the continental balance of power:

- The Treaty of Versailles was challenged by the creation of an air force and by the introduction of a conscripted army of 555,000 (March 1935).
- The Rhineland was remilitarised (March 1936).
- The *Anschluss* ('union') with Austria took place (March 1938).
- The Munich agreement ceded the German-speaking Sudetenland to Germany (September 1938).

However, once Nazi Germany had militarily occupied the non-German lands of Czechoslovakia in March 1939, Britain and France found it difficult to tolerate further German expansionism and immediately guaranteed to uphold the independence of Poland. Thus, when the German armed forces attacked Poland on 1 September 1939 Britain and France were obliged to declare war.

Although Germany found itself committed to a major war in the autumn of 1939, which Hitler had not expected to wage until the mid-1940s, Germany was not militarily destined to fail from the start. The string of victories from September 1939 to November 1941 bears witness to the military power exerted by the Nazi war-machine and suggests that Germany did not have to go down the road to total collapse. Even though in early 1943 Germany faced serious military reverses, its eventual defeat was not inevitable.

Initial victories

Without direct help, Poland was crushingly defeated within weeks by German *Blitzkrieg* tactics. This gave the Germans access to valuable raw materials; they also received aid from the USSR under the terms of the **Nazi–Soviet Pact**.

 **KEY TERM**

Nazi–Soviet Pact
A non-aggression pact of 1939 between the USSR and Germany that opened the way for the invasion of Poland by both countries.

Hitler was keen to maintain the military momentum and to invade France straight away, but the German attack was postponed, mainly because of the lukewarm attitude of senior army generals.

Phoney war

The German attack on the Western Front did not finally take place until May 1940, thus prolonging the Anglo-French '**phoney war**' for eight months. Hitler aimed to remove the threat posed by the Western democracies before turning east again. To that end, Germany needed to destroy France and to make Britain accept German aspirations on the continent. It was hoped to force Britain, under the pressure of military circumstances, into a deal with Germany.

The Low Countries and France

The German defeat of the Low Countries and France within six weeks was a dramatic triumph. Diffident generals were relieved and German popular opinion was triumphant. Hitler ruled from Paris to Warsaw, while the Third Reich was bordered by the three 'friendly' powers of Spain, Italy and the USSR. It was assumed by many that the war was as good as over.

The Battle of Britain

Britain could have settled with Germany; however, the prime minister, Winston Churchill, refused to consider negotiations. The implications of this stubbornness for Germany were clear-cut: Germany needed to secure air superiority to invade Britain and disable its military and strategic potential. Thus, Germany's failure to win the **Battle of Britain** in 1940 was significant. Even more so was Hitler's decision to switch the military focus, and to prepare for the invasion of the USSR before neutralising Britain.

Operation Barbarossa

The German decision to invade the USSR on 22 June 1941 can only be explained by Hitler's belief that *Blitzkrieg* tactics could succeed in bringing a quick victory against the USSR, as they had against Poland and France. At first all went well. Vast tracts of Russian territory were occupied and thousands of prisoners were taken, and by November 1941 German troops were only miles from Moscow and Leningrad.

Reasons for success

The German military advance was successful in the years 1939–41 for the following reasons:

- France and Britain failed to take the initiative and Poland was left to fight alone.
- Germany's *Blitzkrieg* strategy of rapid advances overwhelmed all of its enemies in the first two years.

KEY TERMS

Phoney war Used to describe the war period from September 1939 to May 1940 because there was no real aggressive activity on the Western Front.

Battle of Britain Name given to the air battle fought over the skies of southern England in July to October 1940.

- The French defensive strategy was based on the **Maginot Line** and it proved to be powerless in the face of German *Blitzkrieg* tactics. As a result, the French political and military leadership lost the will to resist.
- Germany's expansion (from 1938) allowed it to exploit all the labour and resources of those countries for its own purposes.
- The USSR was taken by surprise by the German attack and was not really prepared.

However, despite Germany's successes, the military advance halted in December 1941. Hitler's gamble to break the USSR had failed and Germany was now faced with the prospect of a long war on two fronts.

The 'turn of the tide'

December 1941 was significant in another sense, too, as the Japanese attack on the US naval base at **Pearl Harbor** 'globalised' the conflict, as Hitler aligned Germany with Japan and declared war on the USA. This move was prompted by

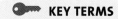

KEY TERMS

Maginot Line Extensive defence fortifications built on the Franco-German frontier by the French governments in the 1930s.

Pearl Harbor A US military base in the Pacific.

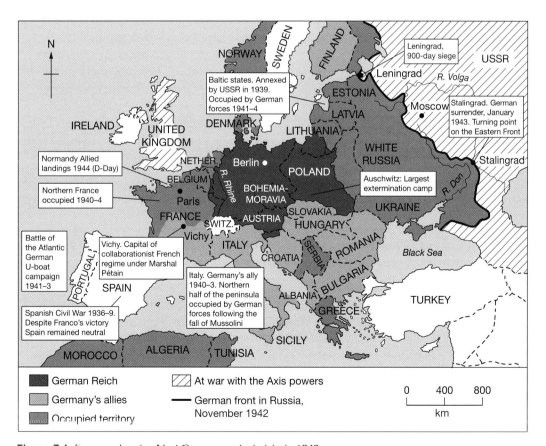

Figure 7.1 Europe, showing Nazi Germany at its height in 1942.

KEY TERMS

Battle of the Atlantic
The naval struggle between the Allied convoys and the German U-boats in the northern Atlantic Ocean.

'Turn of the tide' Used to describe the Allied military victories in the winter of 1942–3, when the British won at El Alamein in North Africa and the Soviets forced the surrender of 300,000 German troops at Stalingrad.

Final Solution
A euphemism used by the Nazi leadership to describe the extermination of the Jews from 1941, although in the earlier years the term had been used more loosely before there was any real overall plan.

Unconditional surrender
Roosevelt and Churchill's statement in 1943 that the Allies would not accept a negotiated peace.

the USA's involvement in the **Battle of the Atlantic** even before Pearl Harbor. However, it did not fit easily with Germany's existing strategy and above all it turned the industrial capacity of the world's greatest power against it. It is tempting, therefore, to suggest that by late 1941 Hitler had lost his military and diplomatic intuition. Events were now starting to run out of the *Führer*'s control.

Although it appears that December 1941 was a vital turning point for German fortunes in the war, this was not so apparent at the time. Throughout 1942 German forces pushed deep into the Caucasian oilfields with the objective of capturing Stalingrad, while the Afrika Korps drove the British back across North Africa into Egypt. It was the eventual failure of these two offensives that enabled contemporaries to see the winter of 1942–3 as the **'turn of the tide'**. The British victory at El Alamein eventually led to the ejection of German forces from North Africa, and the encirclement and surrender of 300,000 troops at Stalingrad marked the beginning of the Soviet counter-offensive. These two defeats showed that the German armies were no longer invincible.

Defeat

From 1943 Germany's strategy was defensive. Hitler was determined to protect 'Fortress Europe' from Allied invasion, but he was driven by his belief in German invincibility and his own ideological prejudices about race and communism. For example, in spite of all the military difficulties, the creation of the new racial order continued: there was no postponement of the **Final Solution**. However, Allied military co-ordination continued to work well. By late 1943 Anglo-American forces had linked up in Africa and had established a hold on southern Italy, while Soviet forces had reconquered much of Ukraine after the great tank victory at the Battle of Kursk. The war had also begun to have an impact on Germany itself. The massive bombing raids caused destruction and dislocation, although their exact strategic value has been questioned over the years (see pages 239–40 and 252–4). It was becoming clear that the war could not be won by Germany and that it faced total devastation unless the Allied demand for **unconditional surrender** was accepted.

Such military failures triggered the attempted assassination of Hitler in July 1944 (see pages 258–9). However, his survival meant that the war would have to be fought to the bitter end. Strong German resistance forced the Western Allies to fight extremely hard in the battle for Normandy in 1944, while in the east the Soviet advance progressed through eastern Europe in the face of desperate defensive measures. It was not until 30 April 1945, when Soviet soldiers had advanced to within a mile of the Chancellery in Berlin, that Hitler killed himself. Only then was the German nation freed from the *Führer*'s command, and Germany surrendered on 7–8 May.

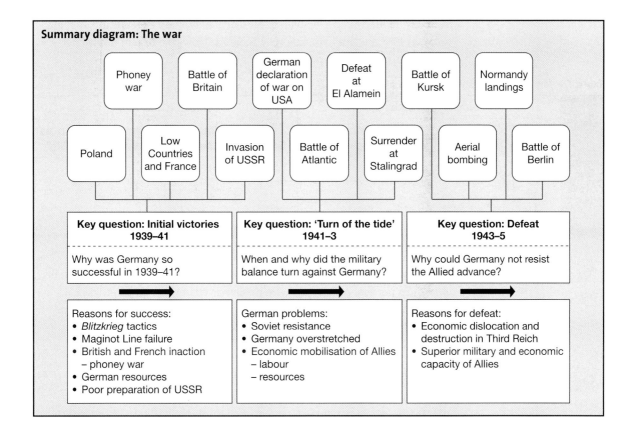

Summary diagram: The war

| Phoney war | Battle of Britain | German declaration of war on USA | Defeat at El Alamein | Battle of Kursk | Normandy landings |

| Poland | Low Countries and France | Invasion of USSR | Battle of Atlantic | Surrender at Stalingrad | Aerial bombing | Battle of Berlin |

Key question: Initial victories 1939–41	**Key question: 'Turn of the tide' 1941–3**	**Key question: Defeat 1943–5**
Why was Germany so successful in 1939–41?	When and why did the military balance turn against Germany?	Why could Germany not resist the Allied advance?

Reasons for success:
• *Blitzkrieg* tactics
• Maginot Line failure
• British and French inaction – phoney war
• German resources
• Poor preparation of USSR
	German problems:
	• Soviet resistance
	• Germany overstretched
	• Economic mobilisation of Allies
	  – labour
	  – resources
		Reasons for defeat:
		• Economic dislocation and destruction in Third Reich
		• Superior military and economic capacity of Allies

 # The Nazi war economy

▶ *How effectively did the Nazis mobilise the German economy to meet the demands of war?*

The string of military successes achieved by the German armed forces with their use of the *Blitzkrieg* strategy up to December 1941 won Hitler and the regime valuable popular support. Moreover, it gave the impression of an economy that had not been overstrained by the demands of war. Such a view, however attractive, does not actually square with either Nazi intentions or the economic statistics.

The expansion of the Nazi economy

First, Hitler was determined to avoid the problems faced by Germany in the First World War and to fight the coming war with an economy thoroughly prepared for a major and perhaps extended conflict. To this end, he issued a series of war economy decrees in December 1939 outlining vast programmes for every possible aspect of war production, for example submarines and aircraft. These plans suggest that the Nazis went well beyond the demands of *Blitzkrieg* and a limited war.

Secondly, in real and percentage terms, German military expenditure doubled between 1939 and 1941, as shown by Table 7.1. However, Britain trebled its expenditure in the same period.

Table 7.1 Military expenditure of Germany and Britain 1937–41

Year	Germany (RM billions)			Britain (£ billions)		
	GNP	Military expenditure	Military expenditure as a percentage of GNP	GNP	Military expenditure	Military expenditure as a percentage of GNP
1937	93	11.7	13	4.6	0.3	7
1938	105	17.2	17	4.8	0.4	8
1939	130	30.0	23	5.0	1.1	22
1940	141	53.0	38	6.0	3.2	53
1941	152	71.0	47	6.8	4.1	60

Thirdly, food rationing in certain items was introduced from the very start of the war and the German labour force was rapidly mobilised so that, by the summer of 1941, 55 per cent of the workforce was involved in war-related projects: a figure which then only crept up to a high point of 61 per cent by 1944. In this light, it is hardly surprising that the first two years of war also witnessed a twenty per cent decline in civilian consumption of goods.

The limitations of economic mobilisation

Despite the intent of wholesale mobilisation, the actual results, in terms of armaments production, remained disappointingly low. Admittedly, there was a marked increase in the number of submarines, but surprisingly, Germany's air force had only increased from 8290 aircraft in 1939 to 10,780 in 1941 while in Britain over the same period the number of aircraft had trebled to 20,100. Likewise, Hitler was astonished to learn when drawing up plans for the invasion of the USSR that the Germans' armoured strength totalled only 3500 tanks, which was just 800 more than for the invasion of the West and fewer than the USSR put into the field.

It seems that despite the Nazi image of German order and purposefulness, the actual mobilisation of the German economy was marred by inefficiency and poor co-ordination. The pressures resulting from the premature outbreak of war created problems, since many of the major projects were not due to be ready until 1942–3. So, at first, there was undoubtedly confusion between the short-term needs and long-term plans of the Nazi leadership.

Nevertheless, this should not have been an impossible barrier if only a clear and authoritative central control had been established over the economy. Instead, a host of different agencies all continued to function in their own way and often in a fashion which put them at odds with each other. Although there was a Ministry of Armaments under **Fritz Todt**, it existed alongside three other competing governmental ministries: those of Economics, Finance and Labour. In addition, there was political infighting between the leading Nazi figures –

KEY FIGURE

Fritz Todt (1891–1942)

Although a Nazi, Todt was more of an engineer and technician than a politician. He was responsible for the construction of motorways from 1933 and in 1940 he was appointed minister of armaments, which caused increasing clashes with Göring and the *Wehrmacht*. He died in a plane crash.

for example, the *Gauleiters* tried to control their local areas at the expense of the overall plans of the state and the party – and also considerable financial corruption.

There were a number of groups responsible for armaments: the Office of the Four-Year Plan, the SS bodies and the different branches of the *Wehrmacht*. The armed forces, in particular, were determined to have their way over the development of munitions with the very best specifications possible and, as a result, the drive for quality was pursued at the expense of quantity. The consequence of all this was that after two years of war, and with the armed forces advancing into the USSR, Germany's economic mobilisation for total war had not achieved the expected levels of armaments production.

Total war 1942–5

By the end of 1941 Germany was at war with Britain, the USSR and the USA and yet its armaments production remained inferior to that of Britain. Preparations for a new approach had begun in the autumn of 1941 and Hitler had issued a 'Rationalisation Decree' to Todt in December of that year, which was intended to eliminate the waste of labour and materials.

The death of Todt and his replacement by **Albert Speer** as minister of armaments in February 1942 marked a real turning point. Speer had previously been the *Führer*'s personal architect and he enjoyed excellent relations with Hitler. He now used the *Führer*'s authority to cut through the mass of interests and to implement his programme of 'industrial self-responsibility' to provide mass production. The controls and constraints previously placed on business, in order to fit in with Nazi wishes, were relaxed. In their place a Central Planning Board was established in April 1942, which was in turn supported by a number of committees, each representing one vital sector of the economy. This gave the industrialists a considerable degree of freedom, while ensuring that Speer as the director of Central Planning was able to maintain overall control of the war economy. Speer also encouraged industrialists and engineers to join his ministerial team. At the same time, wherever possible, he excluded military personnel from the production process.

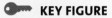

KEY FIGURE

Albert Speer (1905–81)

Close friend of Hitler who became the *Führer*'s personal architect. Appointed minister of armaments in 1942 and skilfully managed the war economy, with a significant increase in arms production 1942–4. Sentenced to 20 years at the Nuremberg trials.

SOURCE A

From the Decree to Create the Central Planning Board, 22 April 1942, quoted in J. Noakes and G. Pridham, editors, *Nazism 1919–45*, volume 1, Liverpool University Press, 1988, p. 229.

A Central Planning Board shall be established with the framework of the Four Year Plan. Its sphere of activity embraces the whole economy and includes the power to decide whether existing schemes should be continued or new arrangements introduced, the apportionment of existing raw materials, the distribution of coal and energy to manufacture plants and the coordination of transport.

According to Source A, what were the key powers of the Central Planning Board?

Speer was what would now be called a 'technocrat', in that he simply co-ordinated and rationalised the process of war production to more effectively exploit the potential of Germany's resources and labour force. Speer was able to exert influence because of his friendship with Hitler and he used his personal skills to charm or blackmail other authorities. In this way, he took a whole range of other personal initiatives to improve production, such as:

- employing more women in the arms factories
- making more effective use of forced labour
- preventing skilled workers from being lost to military conscription.

The successes and limitations of Speer's economic rationalisation

In a famous speech in February 1943, after the German army surrendered at Stalingrad, Goebbels invited the crowd to support 'total war'. However, the transformation of the Nazi economy really pre-dated Goebbels' propagandist appeal and was down to the work of Speer. As a result of Speer's first six months in power:

- ammunition production increased by 97 per cent
- tank production rose by 25 per cent
- total arms production increased by 59 per cent.

By the second half of 1944, when German war production peaked, there had been more than a three-fold increase since early 1942 (see Tables 7.2 and 7.3).

Table 7.2 Number of German, British, US and USSR tanks produced 1940–5

Year	Germany	Britain	USA	USSR
1940	1,600	1,400	300	2,800
1941	3,800	4,800	4,100	6,400
1942	6,300	8,600	25,000	24,700
1943	12,100	7,500	29,500	24,000
1944	19,000	4,600	17,600	29,000
1945	3,900	N/A	12,000	15,400

Table 7.3 Number of German, British, US and USSR aircraft produced 1940–5

Year	Germany	Britain	USA	USSR
1940	10,200	15,000	6,100	7,000
1941	11,000	20,100	19,400	12,500
1942	14,200	23,600	47,800	26,000
1943	25,200	26,200	85,900	37,000
1944	39,600	26,500	96,300	40,000
1945	N/A	12,100	46,000	35,000

Yet, despite Speer's economic successes, Germany probably had the capacity to produce even more and could have achieved a level of output close to that of the USSR or the USA. He was not always able to counter the power of the party *Gauleiters* at a local level and the SS remained a law unto themselves, especially in the conquered lands. Indeed, although territories occupied by the Third Reich were well and truly plundered, they were not exploited with real economic efficiency.

Foreign labour

It is important to note that foreign workers became an increasingly growing element of the labour force in the Nazi war economy. Indeed, by 1944, 6.5 million foreign workers made up nearly 25 per cent of the whole force. Some of them were volunteers in occupied territories, but the great majority were forced labour, including prisoners of war. They were mainly of the following nationalities:

- French: 1.1 million
- Poles: 1.4 million
- Russians: 2.1 million
- Czechs: 0.3 million.

There was a hierarchy of nationality and race, ranging from workers from France and Belgium at the top to the slave labourers from the so-called *Untermenschen*, or Slavic countries. Racially, the Jews were the most exploited and seen as generally expendable.

Despite the Nazi racial contempt for the foreign workers, with the turning point of 1942 and the push for total mobilisation, they became key to the war effort. **Fritz Sauckel** was tasked with co-ordinating millions of forced labour workers, as able-bodied German workers were drafted to the fronts. Both large and small companies exploited foreign labour, with the type of work ranging from mining to farming.

Living conditions for these workers varied: the worst were confined to forced labour camps sleeping in draughty wooden barracks with meagre food rations. They were defenceless against air raids as they were barred from the shelters. Women were particularly vulnerable, as they were often victims of sexual harassment.

The recruitment of foreign labour did not solve Germany's economic problems. Because of their appalling treatment and poor diet, it was not surprising that the foreign workers were not very productive.

 **KEY FIGURE**

Fritz Sauckel (1894–1946)

Gauleiter of Thuringia. General-plenipotentiary for mobilising labour 1942–5. He was responsible for the exploitation and death of millions of forced labour workers. Found guilty of war crimes at the Nuremberg trials and hanged.

Economic effects of Allied bombing

The question of whether Allied bombing of Germany inhibited or undermined the Nazi economy is not a simple one. Certainly, at first in 1940–2, the effects of bombing were very limited, as Allied aircraft only had the technology to launch little more than nuisance raids.

KEY TERM

Blanket bombing
The military policy of dropping large numbers of bombs to cause devastation of an area.

With hindsight, the deliberate use of **blanket bombing** by the Allies in 1942–5 has been condemned by some on moral grounds and its effectiveness questioned (see Table 7.4). It has been seen as a very blunt instrument, as bomb targeting was so inaccurate; indeed, critics have pointed to Speer's production figures as proof that the strategy had failed to break the German war economy. However, it is probably more accurate to say that the effects of bombing prevented Germany from increasing its levels of arms production even further. The results of Allied bombing caused industrial destruction and breakdown in communications. Also, Germany was forced to divert significant available resources towards the construction of anti-aircraft installations and underground industrial sites.

German arms production peaked in August 1944 at a level well below its full potential (see also page 239). And in the last nine months of the war the Allies had free rein to bomb Germany with limited resistance.

In the end, the Nazi economy had proved incapable of rising to the demands of total war and the cost of that failure was all too clearly to be seen in the ruins of 1945.

Table 7.4 Major Allied air raids

Date	Target
December 1940	First night raid on the German city of Mannheim
May 1942	First thousand-bomber raid on Cologne
March 1943	Raids on Ruhr industrial area
May 1943	'Bouncing bomb' raid on German dams
July 1943	Massive raid on the seaport of Hamburg, creating firestorm
November 1943	Sixteen raids on Berlin with 9000 bombers
March 1944	Raid on Nuremberg. Heavy RAF losses because of improved German air-defences
February 1945	Huge raid on the defenceless historic city of Dresden

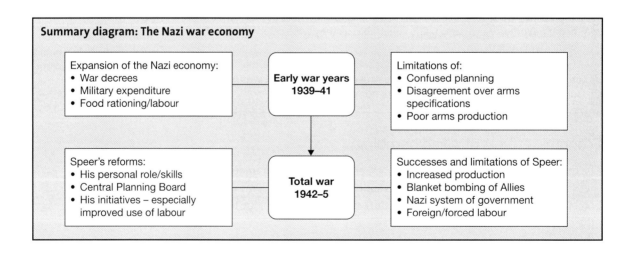

3 The racial war

▶ *How did Nazi racism degenerate into genocide?*

It is clear that the year before the war marked an undoubted radicalisation in Nazi anti-Semitism (see pages 218–21). However, at the time it would have been hard to imagine that the Holocaust was possible. Who, in 1939, could have predicted the scenario of the next six years (see Table 7.5)? It is an event in modern European history which even now seems almost beyond comprehension. For those who lived in occupied Europe it was easier and more comfortable to dismiss the rumours as gross and macabre exaggerations – the result of wartime gossip and Allied propaganda. Yet, the unbelievable did happen and it required not only the actions of a 'criminal' minority but also the passive acceptance of the 'innocent' majority. For Germans the moral dimension has made historical debate particularly delicate.

Table 7.5 The Nazi racial war 1939–45

	Date	Action
1939	September	German invasion of Poland. Action units (**SS *Einsatzgruppen***) moved in
1940	April	First 'sealed' ghetto established in Łódź
1941	June	SS *Einsatzgruppen* moved into the USSR behind the advancing armies to round up and kill Jews
1941	1 September	All Jews forced to wear the Yellow Star of David
1941	October	First deportations of Jews from certain German provinces
1942	20 January	Wannsee Conference. Various government and party agencies agreed on the 'Final Solution' to the Jewish problem
	Spring	Extermination facilities set up at Auschwitz, Sobibór and Treblinka
1942–4		Transportation of Jews from all over German-occupied Europe to death camps began
1943	February	Destruction of Warsaw Ghetto
		The start of sending Germany's Gypsies to Auschwitz
1945	27 January	Liberation of Auschwitz by Soviet troops

Impact of Nazi racial policy in Poland

The onset of the continental war changed circumstances for Poland dramatically, and Germany's rapid victory in autumn 1939 left its citizens in a disastrous situation. Hitler was set on a 'harsh racial struggle' which had serious consequences for the Poles and the 3 million Polish Jews.

From the start of occupation, Nazi policies in Poland were brutal. In addition to the advancing German troops, SS *Einsatzgruppen* were sent in to destroy all the elements of resistance and to 'render harmless' the Polish leadership. About 16,000 Poles were summarily executed in mass shootings in the autumn.

 **KEY TERM**

SS *Einsatzgruppen*
SS Special Action Units. First used during the invasion of Poland. After the invasion of the USSR four units were launched in eastern Europe. They were responsible for rounding up local Jews and murdering them in mass shootings.

Politically, the country was divided into three areas, with draconian effects (see Figure 7.2):

- Warthegau. These were the territories annexed and incorporated into the Reich. They were to be 'Germanised', with Poles arbitrarily deported and ethnic Germans imported into the area. Nazi legislation discriminated against all aspects of Polish life, and schools and churches were closed.
- 'General Government'. This was the area not annexed by the Reich, but controlled by Germany. Its population was exploited and the Poles were reduced to a slave labour pool. Many were sent by force to work as labourers in Germany in factories and farms.
- The occupied Soviet area. This was the area initially controlled by the USSR in the period after the Nazi–Soviet Pact until the German invasion of Russia.

Figure 7.2 Occupied Poland.

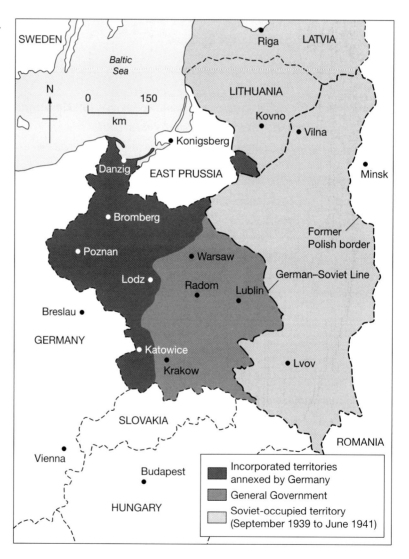

Polish Jews

Violent persecution of Polish Jews started immediately. The army encouraged its soldiers in the degrading, humiliating and arbitrary torturing of Jews, and there were many cases of mass shootings. However, at this stage, this did not yet amount to their systematic murder.

It soon became clear to the Nazis that the problem of what to do with the estimated 3 million Jewish people was not easily resolved. Initial plans to 'resettle' large numbers of people in the Lublin reservation in the south-west corner of the General Government were initiated, but this placed a great strain on food supplies and the transportation system. There was also conflict between some of the leading Nazis: **Hans Frank**, the governor general, in particular, stood firm against the forced deportation of so many to his region. All plans were soon abandoned in early 1940.

In the years 1939–41 the Nazi leadership was reduced to pursuing a policy of 'ghettoisation'. This is not to suggest that it was a planned policy, but rather more a pragmatic approach to the racial problem which they had created for themselves. The Jewish **ghettos** were established in cities such as Łódź, Warsaw, Krakow and Lublin. They were initially set up as temporary holding bays while the Nazis decided what to do with the Jews but, because of the failure of the Lublin reservation plan, they lasted much longer. Jewish councils – called *Judenrat* – were created, on the pretext of maintaining 'an orderly community life', but in fact they were used as a means of control by the German authorities. From spring 1940, these ghettos became sealed, with the penalty of death for anyone caught trying to escape. Because of the heavy concentration of people, the situations in the ghettos deteriorated and the population ended up living in appalling conditions:

- *Food.* Food supplies were much reduced, which resulted in deaths through malnutrition.
- *Disease.* Poor sanitation and cramped living conditions led to diseases such as tuberculosis and typhus.
- *Heating.* Limited access to heating fuel caused hardship and deaths during the cold Polish winters.

In the first two years of the war, about half a million Polish Jews died.

 **KEY FIGURE**

Hans Frank (1900–46)
Trained as a lawyer and was one of the earliest members of the NSDAP. Became governor general of the General Government of Poland 1939–45 and oversaw the creation of many of the ghettos. He was found guilty of war crimes at the Nuremberg trials and hanged.

KEY TERM

Ghetto A term used to describe the historic area lived in by the Jews in a city.

Plans for a Jewish resettlement in Madagascar?

The beginning of a general European war made the emigration of Jews to independent countries more difficult. Because of this, during 1939–40, various plans for a 'resettlement' were considered by the Nazis. Most interesting was the suggestion of using Madagascar, a French colony, as a solution, and this was met with much enthusiasm from Hitler and other leading Nazis. The plan could be seen as quite callous and calculating, since it was anticipated that many of the Jews would fail to survive the journey or the punishing living conditions on the island. In the end, the plans came to nothing because Germany failed to defeat Britain by autumn 1940 and to take control of the high seas.

The invasion of Russia

The invasion of Russia in June 1941 marked a decisive development in the racial war. As with the attack on Poland, SS *Einsatzgruppen* moved in behind the advancing armies. These four special Action Units, A, B, C and D, were responsible for rounding up local Jews and Communist Party officials. They were then murdered in their thousands in a series of mass shootings in the Baltic states, western Russia and the Ukraine. Most infamously, 30,000 men, women and children were slaughtered in just two days in a ravine at Babi Yar near Kiev. It is estimated that, by the end of 1941, 600,000 Russian Jews had been killed. The massacring represented a major escalation of Nazi racial action. Yet, it is not entirely clear how this mass killing then progressed to the racial extermination in the gas chambers of the Holocaust.

The Final Solution

The actual decision-making process surrounding the Final Solution remains unclear. All the available evidence has been closely scrutinised and analysed, causing much controversy and debate among historians. Written sources are hard to come by, either because they never existed or because they were destroyed in 1945 – either deliberately or by accident. Where there is written evidence, much of the language is deliberately euphemistic and open to interpretation. Added to that, no written order for the killing of the Jews from Hitler has ever been found. However, among all this uncertainty there is also hard evidence. In January 1944 Himmler publicly stated in a speech to army officers that Hitler had given him 'a *Führer* order' to give priority to 'the total solution of the Jewish question'. This was further supported by the trial testimonies of Eichmann and R. Höss, the commandant of Auschwitz. For some historians, such as R. Hilberg and C. Browning, the initial rapid German military advance and the bloody massacre of the Russian Jews meant that July was the vital turning point. Indeed, Browning talks of the month's 'euphoria of victory' and he highlights below Göring's memorandum of 31 July:

SOURCE B

From Göring's memorandum of 31 July 1941 to Heydrich, quoted in the Harry S. Truman Library, 'The War Crimes Trials at Nuremberg'.

As supplement to the task dated 24 January 1939, namely to solve the Jewish question by emigration and evacuation, in a way which is the most favourable in connection with the conditions prevailing at present, I herewith commission you with all preparations with regard to organisation, the material side and financial viewpoints for bringing about a final solution of the Jewish question within the territories in Europe under German influence …

I furthermore commission you to submit to me as soon as possible a draft showing the administrative material and financial measures already taken for the execution of the intended final solution of the Jewish question.

? How significant is Source B as evidence of plans to proceed with the Final Solution?

Heinrich Himmler

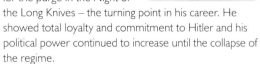

1900	Born in Munich and studied agriculture at technical college
1923	Joined the Nazi Party and took part in the Beer Hall *putsch*
1929	Appointed leader of the SS
1934	Arranged the purge of the SA on 30 June
1936	Given responsibility of '*Reichsführer* SS and Chief of all German Police'
1939	Made commissar of the Strengthening of the German Nationhood
	Formed the RSHA
1943	Appointed minister of interior (replacing Frick)
1945	Arrested by British forces, but killed himself before trial

Himmler was in many respects a nondescript, unremarkable character who before 1929 achieved little in his work or in the party. Yet, with a reputation for an organised, obsessive, hard-working style, he quickly converted the small group of 250 SS troops into a major elite force.

Until 1934 Himmler and the SS were very much in the shade of Röhm and the SA. Himmler was responsible for the purge in the Night of the Long Knives – the turning point in his career. He showed total loyalty and commitment to Hitler and his political power continued to increase until the collapse of the regime.

Himmler became the leader of the brutally efficient SS machine, which really held the Third Reich together. He was responsible for:

- the development of surveillance, which created a system of control and repression
- the pursuit of the creation of a German master-race and the development of elite institutions like *Ordensburgen* and the *Lebensborn*
- the extermination of Jews and Gypsies in concentration camps
- the exploitation of all the occupied lands for slave labour and arms production
- the development of the *Waffen* SS as an elite military force that matched the might of the German Army by the end of the war.

There is still no further hard evidence of an overall genocide plan at that time. Rather, the majority of historians, such as P. Burrin and Kershaw, view the crucial period as a little later – between mid-September and mid-October. This interpretation also fits in with the growing military concerns of not winning the war with Russia within four months, combined with the increasing chaos of dealing with so many Jewish people in eastern Europe. Although the evidence is limited, it clearly supports this view:

- With the support of Hitler, Eichmann actually began the process of transporting German Jews eastwards in October, to 'resettle' them.
- Furthermore, Eichmann, in his testimony in 1960 in Israel, claimed to remember Heydrich telling him two or three months after the invasion of Russia that 'the *Führer* had ordered the physical extermination of the Jews'.
- There were also various local initiatives at that time to use vans to gas the Jews at Belzec and Łódź.
- The first practice gassings using Zyklon B took place in Auschwitz in September.
- Heydrich was starting to make plans for the Wannsee Conference.

The Wannsee Conference

The Wannsee Conference, in west Berlin on 20 January 1942, is often portrayed as the 'decisive' meeting for the Final Solution. But it should be borne in mind that the meeting was initially planned for early December, with the original invitations being sent out on 29 November, strongly suggesting that the decision for systematic extermination had been made in the previous month.

Moreover, the meeting, chaired by Heydrich and organised by Eichmann, did not discuss any fundamental new decisions on the Jewish question. It was more about co-ordinating the logistics, clarifying German law, and securing the agreement of the various agencies of police, finance, labour and transport (railways). All those who attended at Wannsee understood that the purpose of their gathering was to put Hitler's wishes into effect.

The meeting, which lasted a mere 90 minutes, outlined the grim details of the plan to gas to death Europe's 11 million Jews.

Extermination

In the course of 1942 a number of camps in Poland were developed into mass extermination centres, most notably Auschwitz, Sobibór and Treblinka. Most of the Polish Jews were cleared from their ghettos and then transported by train in appalling conditions to their deaths in the gas chambers. It is believed that, of the original 3 million Polish Jews, only 4000 survived the war. In 1942–4 Jews from all over Europe were deported to face a similar fate, so that by 1945 it is estimated that 6 million European Jews had been murdered altogether in the Holocaust.

Conclusion

Hitler's authority was such that it encouraged initiatives from below as long as they were seen to be in line with his overall ideological vision, and clearly Hitler had often spoken in violent and vengeful terms about the Jews from an early stage in his political career. What is important to understand is how the Nazis' ideological hatred of the Jews developed into the systematic plan for the mass extermination of the race.

It now seems that the initial arrangements for the implementation of the 'Final Solution' were haphazard and makeshift. Hitler and the Nazi leadership did not have any clear systematic programme for dealing with the Jewish question until 1941.

Probably around autumn 1941 it was decided by the top Nazi leadership to launch an extermination policy, and this was endorsed at the Wannsee Conference in January 1942 by a broad range of representatives of key agencies. If these points are accepted, then it might be that the 'Final Solution' could be viewed as a pragmatic (practical) response to the confusion and chaos of war in 1941–2 rather than the culmination of long-term ideological intent (see key debate on pages 262–6).

SOURCE C

Jewish men are forced to work as labourers under the Nazi regime. They are guarded by German soldiers.

Gypsies

In addition to Jews, Gypsies (Sinti and Roma) were subject to racial persecution and became victims of Nazi genocide. Gypsies had been viewed as 'outsiders' throughout European history for several reasons:

- Their religion was indeterminate and they had their own Romany customs and dialect.
- They were non-white – because they had originated from India in the late medieval period.
- Their 'traveller' lifestyle, with no regular employment, was resented.

Even before the Nazi dictatorship and during Weimar's liberal years, there was official hostility towards Gypsies and, in 1929, 'The Central Office for the Fight Against the Gypsies' was established.

> How does the photo in Source C convey the treatment of the Jewish people in concentration camps?

By 1933 it is believed that the number of Gypsies in Germany was about 25,000–30,000, and they, too, were beginning to suffer from the gradualist policy of Nazi discrimination:

- Gypsies were defined exactly like the Jews as 'infallibly of alien blood' according to the Nuremberg Laws of 1935.
- Himmler issued, in 1938, a directive titled 'The Struggle Against the Gypsy Plague', which ordered the registration of Gypsies in racial terms.
- Immediately after the outbreak of the war, Gypsies were deported from Germany to Poland – and their movements were severely controlled in working camps. Notoriously, in January 1940, the first case of mass murder through gassing was committed by the Nazis against Gypsy children at Buchenwald.

As with the Jews, the Gypsies during the war were the focus of ever-increasing repression and violence but there was no real, systematic Nazi policy of extermination until the end of 1942. In the first months of 1943 Germany's Gypsies were sent to Auschwitz camp and over 1943–4 a large proportion of the Gypsy population from south-eastern Europe was exterminated: a figure between 225,000 and nearly 500,000.

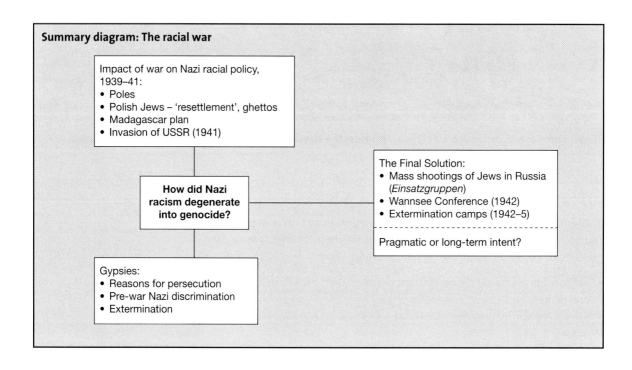

Summary diagram: The racial war

Impact of war on Nazi racial policy, 1939–41:
- Poles
- Polish Jews – 'resettlement', ghettos
- Madagascar plan
- Invasion of USSR (1941)

How did Nazi racism degenerate into genocide?

The Final Solution:
- Mass shootings of Jews in Russia (*Einsatzgruppen*)
- Wannsee Conference (1942)
- Extermination camps (1942–5)

Pragmatic or long-term intent?

Gypsies:
- Reasons for persecution
- Pre-war Nazi discrimination
- Extermination

The home front

▶ *What was the impact of the war on the German people?*

The declaration of war in September 1939 was not met with the patriotic frenzy of August 1914. Rather, the mass of people seemed to be resigned and apprehensive. However, the German strategy of *Blitzkrieg* was incredibly successful and the victories of 1939–40 gave the impression of military and economic strength. Most of the people's doubts were, therefore, dispelled. On Hitler's return journey from France back to Berlin he was met by ecstatic crowds, the images of which were cleverly recorded in the newsreels.

Living standards

Despite the economic priorities for the military build-up, the Nazi economy was not really ready for a major war in 1939 (see pages 235–7). As a result, from the earliest days, the Nazis had to prioritise and introduce the rationing of food, clothes, and basics like soap and toilet paper. Still, the German population continued to be adequately fed – even up until early 1944 – with rations about ten per cent above the minimum calorific standard. However, the diet was very boring and restricted to such staples as bread and potatoes. In the final twelve months of the war food rationing led to real shortages (and real hunger by 1945).

Not surprisingly, the trade in consumer goods struggled from the very start. In the first two years furniture and clothing sales fell by 40 and 25 per cent, respectively. Coal was reserved for industrial production, which meant that there was less available for domestic heating. In the final months of the war the situation worsened dramatically, for example:

- clothes were in very short supply
- boots and shoes were also hard to find, because of the shortage of leather, leading to an increase in the use of wooden clogs
- small luxuries, like magazines and sweets, were also stopped.

Despite every attempt to make the ration system fair for all, the high demand for the above goods meant that the black market flourished.

Workers

The demand for labour had remained critical from the mid-1930s, so there was never a shortage of work. Workers in high-demand war industries were exempt from conscription but non-essential workers had to enlist for military service.

In order to maintain productivity, the bonus and overtime payments, which had initially been stopped, were reintroduced. However, workers were not able to feel any real benefit because of the government's increases in income taxes as well as the imposition of higher taxes on beer, tobacco, cinemas and travel.

From 1942 the demand for labour was extended when Speer directed the economy to focus on fighting a 'total war' (see pages 237–8). This created pressures:

- Working hours were increased from 52 hours in 1940 to 60 hours in 1944.
- Skilled labour became in seriously short supply.
- Millions of foreign workers were mobilised to work (see page 239).
- Non-essential businesses were closed in 1943 and all workers aged to 16–65 had to register for vital work (which caused great resentment with the *Mittelstand*).

As circumstances from 1944 became more desperate there was a total ban on holidays, all bonuses were stopped, and rewards were limited to just an increase in rations.

Peasantry

With the onset of the war in 1939 pressures on the peasantry developed in many ways. Young men were increasingly conscripted to the military fronts, which caused a growing shortage of agricultural labour. This necessitated the use of cheap forced labour from peasants from eastern Europe, for example Poles and Czechs, despite this conflicting with the Nazi view that these labourers were not racially acceptable. Although the rural communities complained of hardship because of the shortage of farm machinery and animal food supplies, they were largely self-sufficient and did not suffer the same adversity and levels of bombing of those in the cities.

Women

In the early war years, the conscription of women to essential work was used sparingly. Indeed, because of the decline of consumer industries, the number of female workers actually decreased. Also, there was less incentive for women to work since families of conscripted soldiers received benefits.

Speer's aim to mobilise the economy for total war called for an increase in the conscription of women workers. However, Hitler wished to retain the traditional roles of women in order to maintain civilian morale. As a result, conscription for women aged 17–45 to work was introduced from 1943, but there were many exemptions, which limited the impact.

The Nazis were caught in the contradictions of their own ideology between the theory and practice of female employment. They were motivated by military expansionism which needed to employ women effectively, so, in the final two to three years of the Nazi state, more and more women ended up in work. Only in the last desperate twelve months of the war were women up to age of 50 conscripted, with many of them taking up auxiliary roles within the armed forces. By 1945 women comprised nearly 60 per cent of the workforce, but this only came about because of the decline in male workers.

With the unfolding of the war, greater pressure was put on women; with so many men away, they had to take on more responsibilities both in and out of the home. In the cities, long hours in arms factories made life very arduous, especially if women had to combine this with running a household and bringing up children. In the countryside, German women experienced considerable hardship meeting the continual demands of running farms on their own. The shortage of agricultural labour had created major problems from the 1930s (see page 196), but once the young men were sent away for military service, it got worse. Yet, the government could not bring itself to renounce fully its anti-feminist stance. As an official in the NSF wrote, 'It has always been our chief article of faith that a woman's place is in the home – but since the whole of Germany is our home we must serve wherever we can best do so.'

Youth

The youth of Nazi Germany in the war was a very dislocated generation. The effects of evacuation, Allied bombing and family losses all combined to take their toll on them, emotionally and socially.

One main impact of the war on young people was the decline in education and academic standards, although this had already started in the late 1930s. Now, with the conscription of teachers to military service there was a marked decline in the number and quality of teaching staff. Formal exams ceased in 1943 and by the end of 1944 any teaching in schools had all but petered out.

There was a general move in emphasis from learning to drill and discipline. With compulsory membership of the HJ in 1939 (see pages 200–2), an even stronger focus on militarism was imposed on the youth. The age of military service was reduced to seventeen in 1943 and lowered again to sixteen in 1945. In addition, increasing numbers of teenagers were used for defence work such as manning anti-aircraft batteries. For young people there was no avoiding the increasing demands of war.

The German youth became increasingly polarised between those committed to the cause and the disaffected. Many of them were repelled by the regimentation and military training of the HJ and, as the war progressed, alienation set in. For a few, this disillusionment developed into the formation of counter-groups such as the Edelweiss Pirates (see page 202), but they remained a small minority.

Interestingly, a youth leader wrote in 1942 that 'the formation of cliques, i.e. groupings of young people outside the Hitler youth … has particularly increased during the war, to such a degree that a serious risk of the political, moral and criminal breakdown of youth must be said to exist'. The Nazi response became increasingly harsh. Various gangs were rounded up by the *Gestapo* and had their heads shaved. In some cases, young people were sent to camps – and most notoriously twelve Edelweiss Pirates were publicly hanged in Cologne.

Morale and propaganda

The onset of the war underlined the totalitarian nature of the Nazi regime. Although the leadership no longer needed to show any regard for international approval, within Germany the Nazis remained very aware of public opinion and the importance of keeping up the nation's morale.

The early Nazi military victories were very easy to exploit as propaganda for the war. However, it became increasingly difficult for Nazi propaganda and censorship to disguise the reality of the situation from the winter of 1942–3. The German defeat at El Alamein was a significant loss, but the German surrender at Stalingrad was a strategic disaster and a damaging blow to the confidence of the German people.

An SD report highlighted the deepening cynicism in the nation about the political and military situation after Stalingrad: 'A large section of the nation cannot imagine how the war will end and the telling of vulgar jokes against the state, even about the *Führer* himself, has increased considerably since Stalingrad.'

Effects of bombing

The military defeats abroad, although demoralising, were at a distance for the people in Germany, but the Anglo-American bombing had a much more direct impact by bringing the war into their very homes. Certainly, one of the aims of the Allies in hitting the great urban centres day and night was to weaken morale.

In purely human terms, it is estimated that as a result of the air raids:

- 400,000 Germans were killed plus 60,000 foreign workers and prisoners of war
- 500,000 people were disabled and severely injured
- 3.6 million homes were destroyed (twenty per cent of the total housing).

Most notably, on the night of 24 July 1943, a massive raid on Hamburg created a firestorm that killed 40,000 civilians. And, more controversially, the bombing of Dresden on 13–15 February 1945, just twelve weeks before the end of the war, saw 1300 heavy bombers drop over 3900 tons of high-explosive bombs and incendiary devices, killing 35,000 Germans and destroying 34 square kilometres (13 square miles) of the city.

The effects of the Allied bombing on German civilians (as opposed to the effects on industry, see pages 239–40) have been the subject of considerable discussion. Some historians have claimed that, despite the difficult circumstances faced by most Germans in the final two years of the war, there was no real sign of a decline of morale leading to the collapse of the regime itself. Indeed, in the face of Allied mass bombing many people came together against the enemy. H. Rumpf (1963) claims, 'Under the terrible blows of that terror from the skies the bonds grew closer and the spirit of solidarity stronger.' Nevertheless, morale was affected. Despite considerable efforts to counteract food shortages and repair the damage to housing, it became increasingly difficult for the government to withstand the cumulative effect of the sustained physical suffering and psychological trauma inflicted on the German people.

In response to these difficulties, Goebbels and his propaganda machine used all their skills. Hitler became more distant and instead Goebbels became the public face and voice of the Nazi regime. His famous speech on 18 February 1943 at the Berlin *Sportpalast* was in response to the surrender of Stalingrad – and a

SOURCE D

'One battle, one will, one goal: victory at any cost!' A propaganda poster from May 1942.

How does Goebbels' propaganda poster in Source D urge all German people to strive for total war?

clear statement of defiance, which rallied the people for 'total war'. He used the multimedia approach of the Propaganda Ministry to appeal to all their emotions. The people were urged to:

- strive their very hardest
- resist all Germany's enemies
- endure all suffering.

In addition, he specifically used cinema to distract people from the realities of the war through fantasy action films such as *The Adventures of Baron Münchausen* and grand patriotic epics such as *Kolberg*, based on a historic German battle against Napoleon (see page 172).

Despite Goebbels' efforts, from 1943 the reports from the SD began to show an escalation in grumbling and complaints, which illustrated the growing disaffection. People became increasingly resigned to the coming disaster. A.D. Welch writes in his conclusion on *The Third Reich: Politics and Propaganda* (2002): 'The debacle of Stalingrad undoubtedly affected the morale of the German people. It forced them to question Nazi war aims and led to a crisis of confidence in the regime amongst broad sections of the population.' By autumn 1944 there had developed a growing atmosphere of doom because of the fear of the **Red Army** and the failure of special weapons like the **V-1 and V-2**. As a consequence, there was a significant loss of faith in the Nazi regime, but it was never really threatened from within.

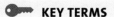 **KEY TERMS**

Red Army The name given to the Soviet Army created in 1917.

V-1 and V-2 The flying pilotless bombs and the long-range rocket developed by scientists in Germany. Used in air raids against Britain 1944–5.

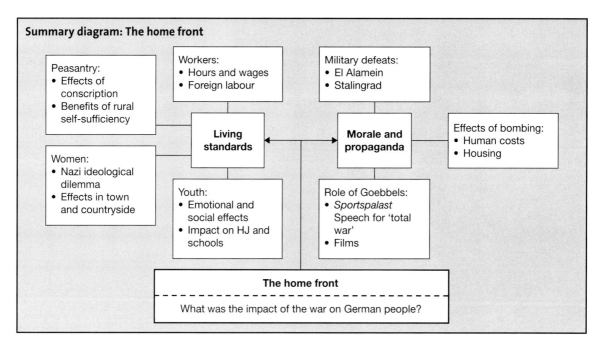

Summary diagram: The home front

Peasantry:
- Effects of conscription
- Benefits of rural self-sufficiency

Workers:
- Hours and wages
- Foreign labour

Military defeats:
- El Alamein
- Stalingrad

Women:
- Nazi ideological dilemma
- Effects in town and countryside

Living standards

Morale and propaganda

Effects of bombing:
- Human costs
- Housing

Youth:
- Emotional and social effects
- Impact on HJ and schools

Role of Goebbels:
- *Sportspalast* Speech for 'total war'
- Films

The home front

What was the impact of the war on German people?

5 Resistance and repression

▶ *Who resisted the Nazi regime and why did they fail?*

'Active resistance' failed to topple Nazism and in the end the Third Reich was only destroyed when Germany was militarily defeated by the Allies. Those who set out to subvert the regime – however gloriously and heroically they have been portrayed – made enormous personal sacrifices without making any real impression on the Nazi stranglehold of power. The real question is: why did they fail?

Communists

Over half of KPD members were interned during the first year of Nazi rule and, by 1935, the *Gestapo* had infiltrated the remains of the party, leading to a series of mass trials. Nevertheless, the communist movement was never entirely broken, but went underground. Small communist cells continued in many of the large German cities and they were particularly revived after the invasion of the USSR; examples of these were the Uhrig Group in Berlin and the Home Front in Hamburg. The most famous was the so-called ***Rote Kapelle*** (Red Orchestra), a spy network which successfully infiltrated the government and military through Arvid Harnack and the aristocratic sympathiser Schulz-Boysen. The cell transmitted vital information back to Moscow and produced pamphlets attacking the Nazi government. However, the Red Orchestra, along with many of the other cells, was destroyed by the *Gestapo* at the end of 1942.

The impact of the activities of German communists should not be overstated. They failed because:

KEY TERM

Rote Kapelle 'Red Orchestra'. Name given to the communist spy network which passed information to the USSR.

- they took their orders from Moscow and were tainted by their association with Stalin and his purges of the 1930s
- they were seriously compromised by the period of co-operation between the Nazi government and the USSR as a result of the Nazi–Soviet Pact 1939–41
- even when the USSR and Germany did end up at war with each other in June 1941 the resistance groups remained very isolated.

Communist active resistance to the Nazi state was limited. In the end, it really became more focused on self-preservation and preparation for the day when Nazism would be defeated and the Soviet 'liberation' could take place.

Christians

As Nazi persecution intensified from 1941, the evidence suggests that church attendance increased and many individual churchmen put their own freedom and lives at risk in order to uphold their beliefs or to give pastoral assistance. It has been estimated that 40 per cent of the Catholic clergy and over 50 per cent of the Protestant pastors were harassed by the Nazis. The most damning

Dietrich Bonhoeffer (1906–45)

Academic and pastor who joined the Confessional Church. In 1940 he was banned from preaching and then made contact with the active resistance movement.

Clemens von Galen (1878–1946)

Bishop of Münster 1933–46 who became known as 'The Lion of Münster'. Made cardinal in 1945 and beatified in 2005.

Alfred Delp (1900–45)

A German Jesuit priest and philosopher.

opposition came from individual clerics rather than the religious institutions, and of these the most famous were:

- **Dietrich Bonhoeffer**. From the very start he was a consistent opponent of Nazism. However, by 1940 he had moved from religious dissent to political resistance, which brought him into direct contact with the conservative elites in the Kreisau Circle (see pages 257–9). Over the next three years he helped Jews to emigrate and actively worked with the resistance movement until he was picked up by the *Gestapo* in 1943.
- Bishop **von Galen** of Münster. He was a conservative, nationalist, aristocrat and a strong anti-communist, yet in the 1930s he began to have doubts about Nazi policy and the excesses of the *Gestapo*. He delivered three sermons in 1941, which condemned the Nazi euthanasia policy (see page 214). His attacks proved so powerful with his congregations that the authorities recoiled from arresting him and actually stopped the programme.
- **Alfred Delp**. A member of the inner part of the Kreisau Circle. He was implicated in the Stauffenberg Plot and was executed in 1945.

Many individual Christians had doubts about Nazi ideology and their totalitarian aspirations. Indeed, a *Gauleiter* reported in June 1943:

> … the war with all its sorrow and anguish has driven some families into the arms of the priests and the Church … in their weekly reports, the party regional organisations have repeatedly emphasised that the Churches of both confessions – but especially the Catholic Church – are in today's fateful struggle one of the main pillars of negative influence upon public morale.

But the Churches posed no real active threat to the strength of the regime. They were mainly concerned with self-preservation and maintaining their property and wealth and their power as institutions. There was no public condemnation of the Nazi genocide of the Jews.

Students: the White Rose group

The White Rose student resistance movement is probably the most famous of the youth groups because it went well beyond mere dissent. It was led by the brother and sister Hans and Sophie Scholl. *The White Rose* (the symbol of peace) was the title given to a series of leaflets printed in 1942–3; these were distributed initially among the students of Munich University but, in time, to many towns in central Germany. The content of the leaflets was highly political and openly condemned the moral and spiritual values of the Nazi regime. One of the early leaflets bore the headline: 'Isn't every decent German today ashamed of his government?'

The group represented a brave gesture of defiance and self-sacrifice. However, from the start the group's security was weak and it was only a matter of time before the *Gestapo* closed in. In February 1943 the six leaders were arrested, tortured and swiftly executed. Sophie Scholl openly said to the court: 'What we wrote and said is in the minds of you all. You just don't say it aloud.'

Conservative elites

It might seem surprising that the most influential active resistance emerged from the ranks of Germany's upper classes, who dominated the civil service and, most particularly, the officer corps. After all, these were the very same conservative nationalists who had initially given sympathetic backing to the Nazi dictatorship. The army as an institution was not fully 'co-ordinated' (until summer 1944) and therefore it enjoyed a degree of freedom from Nazi control. Moreover, with its access to arms, the military had the real capacity to resist. For these reasons the development of the active resistance of the German elites formed around the army, although, like the other groups, it was to fail in its primary objective.

Kreisau Circle

There had been some opponents within the conservative elites from the late 1930s, for example Beck (see page 227) and Goerdeler (see below). In 1939–41 some army officers and foreign office officials became outraged by the criminality of the massacres and destruction on the Eastern Front. As a result, elements of an organised resistance began to emerge slowly from 1942, and they were brought together by the military setbacks of winter 1942–3.

> ### Key members of the Kreisau Circle
>
> - *Helmuth James Graf von Moltke* (1907–45). Great-nephew of Field Marshal Moltke, born at the family estates in Kreisau. A trained lawyer who refused to practise law in Nazi Germany, instead focusing on international law. A leading member of the Kreisau Circle. Arrested, tortured and executed.
> - *Carl Friedrich Goerdeler* (1884–1945). A conservative and monarchist member of the DNVP. He served as long-term mayor of Leipzig, but was forced to resign in 1937 and became a prominent opponent of Hitler. He was nominated by the Kreisau Circle to be the new chancellor if the Stauffenberg Plot succeeded.
> - *Ulrich von Hassell* (1881–1944). Lawyer and diplomat who served as ambassador to Rome until 1938. An active opponent from the late 1930s, who worked closely with Beck and Goerdeler. He was convicted of treason after the Stauffenberg Plot.
> - *Henning von Tresckow* (1901–44). Army officer, but quickly disillusioned with Nazism and an opponent even before the war. Appalled by the atrocities on the Eastern Front and personally tried to kill Hitler with a bomb attempt on his plane. Killed himself the day after the failure of the Stauffenberg Plot.
> - *Dietrich Bonhoeffer* (1906–45). Academic and pastor who joined the Confessional Church (see page 256). In 1940 he was banned from preaching and then made contact with the active resistance movement. Arrested by the *Gestapo* in 1943 and murdered in Flossenbürg concentration camp. An SS doctor wrote: 'in nearly 50 years as a doctor I never saw another man go to his death so possessed of the spirit of God'.

The so-called Kreisau Circle was a wide-ranging group of officers, aristocrats, academics and churchmen who met at the Kreisau estate of Helmuth von Moltke. Their meetings discussed plans for a new Germany after Hitler and, in August 1943, a programme was drawn up in the 'Basic Principles for the New Order'. These principles were conservative and strongly influenced by Christian values. They called for:

- the principle of law
- the upholding of freedoms and civil rights
- the democratic integration of Germany into an interdependent Europe.

But behind these high principles there were many shades of opinion within the group about political constitution and the economy. Indeed, there were pacifist elements in the group who were even opposed to killing Hitler.

Stauffenberg Plot

By 1944 the *Gestapo* was aware of the existence of the Kreisau Circle and Moltke was arrested early in the year. Nevertheless, remaining members of the Circle become supporters of the most daring act of resistance to Hitler's Germany: the Bomb Plot of 20 July 1944.

In this plot, a number of the civilian resistance figures approached dissident army officers, such as Beck and Tresckow, and schemed to assassinate Hitler and create a provisional government. In the words of Tresckow just before the attempt:

SOURCE E

From a letter by Tresckow to Stauffenberg in July 1944, quoted in J. Fest, *Plotting Hitler's Death*, Weidenfeld & Nicolson, 1994, p. 236.

The assassination must take place, whatever the cost. Even if it should fail, the attempt to seize power in Berlin must take place. The practical consequences are immaterial. The German resistance must prove to the world and to posterity that it dares to take the decisive step.

> Why does Tresckow claim in Source E that it was vital for the resistance to try to seize power?

The key figure in leading this plot was Colonel von Stauffenberg, who also came to believe that the assassination of Hitler was the only way to end the Nazi regime. He was an able and committed soldier who initially admired Hitler; however, his strong Catholic moral outlook raised increasing doubts about the regime by 1941. Initially he was on the fringes of the Kreisau Circle, but he gave the resistance group a real purpose from early 1944 when he drew up the plan – codenamed 'Operation Valkyrie' – to kill Hitler.

Stauffenberg took the personal responsibility to place the bomb in Hitler's briefing room at his headquarters in East Prussia on 20 July 1944. Unfortunately for the conspirators, the briefcase containing the bomb was moved a few metres away from the target just a minute before it exploded. Hitler consequently sustained only minor injuries. In the confused aftermath, the generals in Berlin crucially hesitated, thus enabling a group of Hitler's loyal soldiers to arrest the conspirators and re-establish order. About 5000 supporters of the resistance were killed in the aftermath, including Stauffenberg, Beck, Tresckow, Rommel, Moltke and Goerdeler.

Conclusion

The conservative elites proved incapable of fundamentally weakening the Nazi regime and in that sense their active resistance failed. Among the reasons for this are:

- They only recognised the need to resist the regime after the crucial developments of 1934 and 1938, by which time it was too well established.
- Because of the military oath (see page 174) the army was tied to the Nazi regime and its leader.
- Hitler's diplomatic and military successes in 1938–42 undoubtedly blinded the elites.
- Even after the 'turn of the tide' (see pages 233–4) and the growing knowledge of brutal actions, the majority of army generals did not work with the resistance.
- Planning and organisation of effective resistance was always fraught with difficulties. The long-term political aims of the conservative elites lacked clarity. Their practical plans were inhibited by the environment of suspicion of the police state.

In the end, the bad luck and confusion of the Bomb Plot of 20 July became a symbol of the doomed nature of the resistance of the elites.

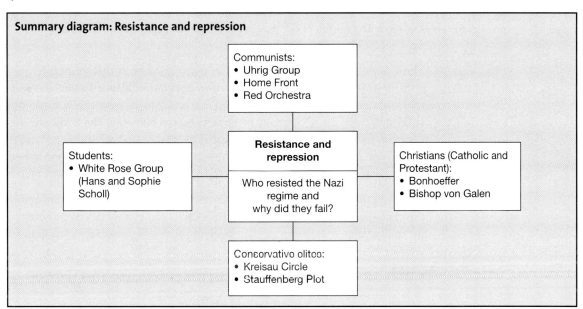

Summary diagram: Resistance and repression

Communists:
- Uhrig Group
- Home Front
- Red Orchestra

Resistance and repression

Who resisted the Nazi regime and why did they fail?

Students:
- White Rose Group (Hans and Sophie Scholl)

Christians (Catholic and Protestant):
- Bonhoeffer
- Bishop von Galen

Conservative elites:
- Kreisau Circle
- Stauffenberg Plot

6 Germany's defeat

▶ *Why did Germany lose the war?*

By May 1945 Germany lay in ruins. Nazi foreign policy had reached its destructive conclusion. Its ambitions had been extensive:

- To establish a 'greater Germany', which went well beyond Germany's 1914 frontiers.
- To destroy Soviet Russia.
- To create a new order based on the concept of Aryan racial supremacy.

The means to these ends had involved the acceptance of violence and bloodshed on a massive scale.

On a superficial level, Hitler's final failure in his ambitions could be explained by his strategic bungling. It should be stressed that Hitler had always believed (along with most generals going back to Imperial Germany) that a war on two fronts had to be avoided. To this end, he needed an alliance with Britain and/ or France – or at least their neutrality – so that he could be free to launch an unrestrained attack in the east. Consequently, when Germany failed to secure either British neutrality or a British surrender in 1940–1 before attacking the USSR, the foundations for defeat were laid.

Germany had become engaged in a conflict for which it was not fully prepared. As has been seen on pages 236–7, at the start of the war Germany did not exploit fully the available resources and manpower. The alliance with Mussolini's Italy was also of little gain. Indeed, Italian military weakness in the Balkans and North Africa proved costly, since it diverted German forces away from the main European fronts. Yet, Hitler was driven on ideologically to launch an attack on the USSR with another *Blitzkrieg*.

The failure to defeat the USSR before the onset of winter in 1941, combined with the entry of the USA into the war, now tipped the balance. Britain was still free to act as a launchpad for a Western Front and also, in the meantime, could strike into the heart of Germany by means of aerial bombing. The USSR could maintain the Eastern Front by relying on its geography and sacrificing its huge manpower. As Stalin recognised, the Allied victory could be summarised in his words: 'Britain gave the time; America the money; and Russia the blood.'

Hitler had militarily misjudged the antagonists, and now all the resources and the industrial capacity of the world's two political giants were directed towards the military defeat of Germany. The following economic factors counted against Germany:

- The Four-Year Plan. In 1936 it was meant to make the country 'fit for war within four years', but the German economy was not really ready for a long war in 1939. Its capacity was only strong enough to sustain a couple of short campaigns.

- Anglo-American bombing. German industry peaked in the production of weapons in summer 1944, yet the German armed forces could not fully benefit from this because of the detrimental effect of Allied air raids.
- Shortage of labour. From the start Germany was short of labour. Millions of workers were required to keep up the industrial and agricultural production, and the gaps were only partially filled by forced labourers and an increase in female employment.
- Germany was deeply in debt. The reserves in gold and foreign currencies were almost completely used up by 1939 and the Nazi state had run up a debt of roughly 42 billion *Reichsmarks*.
- The power of the US economy. The USA was just too powerful. In 1944 the ratio of Germany's fuel supply compared to the supply of the Western Allies was one to three. The USA sent massive support to the Allies, especially to the USSR, which received 13,000 tanks and 15,000 planes.
- Soviet resources. The Soviet economy had undergone a ruthless industrialisation programme in the 1930s under Stalin and, despite its limitations, Russia had vast resources of people and raw materials, for example oil, coal and iron.

These are all important contributory factors, but ultimately it was Hitler's strategic errors that led to Germany's defeat, not a lack of military preparedness or economic strains.

Such explanations might make historical analysis of Germany's defeat in the Second World War seem like a relatively straightforward exercise. However, before accepting such a simple view, it should be borne in mind that, even in 1942, Germany came very close indeed to capturing Stalingrad and to defeating Britain in Egypt. Such successes would have changed the course of the war and the final outcome might have been very different.

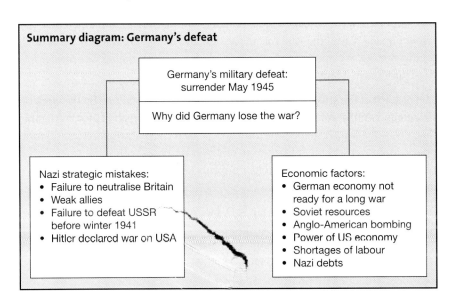

Summary diagram: Germany's defeat

Germany's military defeat: surrender May 1945

Why did Germany lose the war?

Nazi strategic mistakes:
- Failure to neutralise Britain
- Weak allies
- Failure to defeat USSR before winter 1941
- Hitler declared war on USA

Economic factors:
- German economy not ready for a long war
- Soviet resources
- Anglo-American bombing
- Power of US economy
- Shortages of labour
- Nazi debts

7 Key debate

▶ *Where did the responsibility lie for the Nazi racial war?*

Nazi Germany's racial war of 1939–45 remains one of the most fundamental controversies in history. Historians have raised important questions about the role and power of Hitler and all the other institutions in bringing about the genocide.

Nazism: a model of totalitarianism

In the 1950s historians saw the Nazi apparatus of terror and destruction as an example of totalitarianism. According to such interpretations there were no fundamental differences between the regimes of Fascist Italy, Nazi Germany and Soviet Russia. Indeed, Carl Friedrich's analysis went so far as to identify six major features common to totalitarian dictatorships:

- an official ideology
- a single mass party
- terroristic control by the police
- monopolistic control over the media
- a monopoly of arms
- central control of the economy.

The idea of Nazism as a form of totalitarianism held great weight in the 1950s, but this thinking was a product of the **Cold War**, when liberal Western historians rather too readily assumed close similarities between Hitler's Germany and Stalin's Russia.

 **KEY TERM**

Cold War The period of tension between the USA and the USSR, 1945–90, that did not result in open warfare.

Hitlerism: the strong dictator

Not surprisingly, the so-called 'intentionalist' approach has maintained that Hitler himself played the vital role in the directing of the Third Reich. As N. Rich tellingly wrote: 'The point cannot be stressed too strongly. Hitler was master in the Third Reich.' Many continue to concur.

The concept of the strong dictator has been most overtly outlined by the work of Hildebrand and Jäckel. In their view, Hitler took the responsibility for taking the 'big' decisions, which shaped the direction of Nazi Germany in foreign and race policy. Moreover, although there were other power bases within the party, Hitler preserved his own authority by tolerating only key Nazis who were personally loyal, for example Himmler.

Interestingly, although the historian K.D. Bracher remains in the same camp, he differs in focus of emphasis. He recognises that there was division and confusion in Hitler's regime. However, he believes that it was the result of a *deliberate* policy of 'divide and rule' on the part of Hitler. Moreover, he claimed that this strategy was successful in maintaining the *Führer*'s own political authority.

EXTRACT 1

From Sebastian Haffner, *The Meaning of Hitler*, Macmillan, 1979, pp. 43–4.

Hitler deliberately destroyed the State's ability to function in favour of his personal omnipotence and irreplaceability, and he did so from the start … [He] brought about a state of affairs in which the most various autonomous authorities were ranged alongside and against each other, without defined boundaries, in competition and overlapping – and only he was at the head of them … absolute rule was not possible in an intact state organism but only amid chaos. That was why, from the outset, he replaced the State by chaos – and one has to hand it to him that, while he was alive, he knew how to control it.

According to Haffner in Extract 1, how did Hitler set out from the start to establish total authority?

As a result, for intentionalist historians, Hitler is therefore the key to our understanding of the Final Solution. Indeed, for those upholding the most extreme position, such as G. Fleming and L. Dawidowicz, Hitler is seen as having been committed to the extermination of the Jews from an early stage in his political career. This commitment was followed by a consistent gradualist policy which led systematically from the persecution of 1933 to the gates of Auschwitz. In the simplest explanation, they suggest that the Holocaust happened because Hitler willed it.

Indeed, P. Burrinin, writing in 1989, interestingly poses the question: 'If Hitler had died in the summer of 1941, would the Final Solution have taken place?' He concludes: 'Without him, the decisive thrust would probably have been absent.'

A polycracy: a chaotic power structure

In marked contrast, structuralist historians, such as Broszat and Mommsen, writing in the 1970s (see pages 130–1), have focused their analysis on the structure of the Third Reich. They believe that the Nazi regime really just evolved from the pressure of the circumstances and not from Hitler's dominant role. In fact, Hitler's personal weaknesses and limitations led to poor leadership. He was considered incapable of making effective decisions and, as a result, the government lacked clear direction. He was not able to keep the tensions in the economy and the state under control. Moreover, he was never able to manage the other powerful institutions. Structuralists have seen the Third Reich in its power system as a 'polycracy', which became an alliance of different overlapping power groups consisting of the Nazi Party itself, the SS-Police system and the army, big business and the higher levels of the state bureaucracy. Although they did not always agree, they were dependent on each other and prepared to work together as partners in power.

Finally, the leading Nazis exerted their own influence for their own objectives and frequently Hitler did not intervene. Indeed, Mommsen even goes as far as to describe Hitler as 'unwilling to take decisions, frequently uncertain, exclusively concerned with upholding his prestige and personal authority, influenced in the strongest fashion by his current entourage, in some respects a weak dictator'.

Historians of the 'structuralist' school, also called 'functionalist', emphasise the unsystematic nature of Nazi policies as unclear responses to a disorderly government. According to the structuralist interpretation, the moral responsibility for the 'Final Solution' extends beyond Hitler to include the whole apparatus of the regime. Most notably, K. Schleunes, writing in 1970, has suggested that there was no direct path because of the existence of rival policies and the lack of clear objectives. He describes the road to Auschwitz as a 'twisted one' and concludes that 'the Final Solution as it emerged in 1941 and 1942 was not the product of a grand design'. Instead, from 1941 it came to be implemented as a result of the chaotic nature of government within the regime. Various institutions and individuals were responsible for developing the improvised policy which would deal with the military and human situation in eastern Europe by the end of 1941.

Obviously, that approach has led to claims of abnegating of individuals' responsibility. But nearly all 'structuralist' historians have been keen to emphasise that this in no way reduces the guilt of Hitler, who was in total agreement with such a policy. For example, H. Mommsen concludes his analysis as follows: 'That the solution was put into effect is by no means to be ascribed to Hitler alone, but to the complexity of the decision-making process in the Third Reich, which brought about a progressive and cumulative radicalisation.'

Charismatic domination: working towards the *Führer*

Kershaw provides a synthesis of structuralist and intentionalist interpretations. In many ways, his methodology may well be defined as structuralist, and yet he insists that the extent and centrality of Hitler's authority is placed in the wider context, particularly of the German elites and the complicity of German society. He certainly does not portray Hitler as the weak dictator. This is because Hitler succeeded in generating an environment in which his followers carried out his presumed intentions and willingly took the responsibility 'to work towards the *Führer*' (see pages 155 and 189). As Kershaw says: 'Hitler's personalised form of rule invited initiatives from below and offered such initiatives backing, so long as they were in line with his broadly defined goals'.

EXTRACT 2

From Ian Kershaw, *Hitler's Role in the Final Solution*, Yad Vashem Studies, 2006, p. 38.

Hitler's 'prophecy' of January 30th 1939, which he was to invoke so frequently in the following years, has claim to be regarded as a key both to Hitler's mentality, and to the ways he provided 'directions for action' … It illustrates, in fact, how 'charismatic leadership' operated in the crucial area of genocidal policy, and how Nazi activists at different levels of the regime were adept in

According to Extract 2, how did Hitler's personalised form of rule pave the way for the 'Final Solution'?

knowing how to 'work towards the Führer' without having to wait for a precise Führer order. It seems unlikely that Hitler ever gave one single, explicit order for the 'Final Solution'. Within the unchanging framework of his prophecy, he needed to do no more than provide requisite authorisation at the appropriate time to Himmler and Heydrich to go ahead with the various escalatory stages in the murder of Europe's Jews.

The Germans: ordinary people

Some historians have taken the structuralist interpretation a lot further and have adopted a more 'bottom-up' approach to explaining Nazi Germany. They go as far as claiming that the Nazi leadership had little to do with starting the Holocaust and that the real initiative came from other groups. Götz Aly, writing in 1999, for example, has focused on the role of the German Army in instigating genocidal crimes (as opposed to the SS). He also highlighted the involvement of the broader government bureaucracy, 'a planning intelligentsia' and even the financial banking sector in driving anti-Semitic policy.

Even more controversially, the American historian Daniel Goldhagen has suggested in his book, *Hitler's Willing Executioners* (1996), that the Holocaust was 'intended' by the ordinary German people because so many were prepared to participate in the Third Reich's darkest deed. This is explained, according to Goldhagen, by the fact that within German culture there had developed a violent variant of anti-Semitism in the Nazi years which was set on eliminating the Jews. Such a view resurrected the old argument of 'collective national guilt and shame':

EXTRACT 3

From Daniel Goldhagen, *Hitler's Willing Executioners*, Little, Brown, 1996, pp. 416–18.

The men and women … who peopled the institutions of genocidal killing … were overwhelmingly and most importantly Germans … this was above all a German enterprise; the decisions, plans, organisational resources, and the majority of its executors were German. Comprehension and explanation of the perpetration of the Holocaust therefore requires an explanation of the Germans' drive to kill Jews. Because what can be said about the German cannot be said about any other nationality or about all of the other nationalities – namely no German, no Holocaust – the focus here is appropriately on the German perpetrators.

How convincing is Goldhagen's interpretation in Extract 3?

In his very broad conceptual overview of Nazism, M. Burleigh has also distanced himself from the structuralist interpretation of chaotic government. Although in his book, *The Third Reich: A New History* (2001), he still portrays Hitler as a messianic leader who guided the movement, he also emphasises that the Holocaust was the direct result of the ideology of the *Volksgemeinschaft* utopia.

In his interpretation he replaces the term 'class' with 'race', and shows how the Nazi policies on eugenics and euthanasia, the action against asocials and homosexuals, and the introduction of forced labour all combined to create an ideological justification for the racial war. By interpreting Nazism as a 'political religion', the Final Solution can be seen as a result of the 'moral force and consensual climate' of Germany.

Chapter summary

Despite the increasing military difficulties from 1942, the German resistance made no more impact than a few brave gestures. It was divided because of ineffective leadership. Still, there was a marked increase in dissent from 1943 in the wake of shortages and bombings, although the Nazi regime was never seriously threatened from within. In any case, all shades of opposition were dealt with brutally. In the end, it was only the Allies' military occupation which ultimately destroyed the Third Reich in 1945. The war economy was not effectively mobilised at first, and even Speer's reforms did not solve the fundamental problems of labour and resource shortages. The Nazi racial war was the result of ideology and 1930s' policies, but the Final Solution was not really premeditated: it was more a pragmatic response to the pressures and the desire of key forces to satisfy Hitler's vision.

 ## Refresher questions

Use these questions to remind yourself of the key material covered in this chapter.

1 Why was Germany so militarily successful in 1939–41?

2 When and why did the military balance turn against Germany?

3 How effectively did the German economy expand in the early years of the war?

4 To what extent did the Nazis fail to mobilise the economy to the demands of 'total war'?

5 When and how did Nazi anti-Semitism degenerate into genocide?

6 Why were Gypsies persecuted?

7 How did the war affect people's living and working conditions?

8 Why did the war put particular pressure on German women?

9 How did the war change German people's attitudes to the regime?

10 Why was active communist resistance to the Nazi state so limited?

11 To what extent did the resistance of Christians and the students achieve anything?

12 Why did 'active resistance' fail to undermine the Third Reich?

13 Was military bungling the main reason for Germany losing the war?

Question practice

ESSAY QUESTIONS

1 Assess the reasons for the failings of the Nazi economy in the years 1939–45.

2 To what extent was German civilian morale on the home front weakened in the years 1939–45?

3 Which of the following had a greater influence in destabilising the Nazi regime during the war?
   i) The German opposition. ii) Public morale. Explain your answer with reference to both i) and ii).

4 To what extent do you agree the view that economic factors explain Germany's military defeat in the
   Second World War?

INTERPRETATION QUESTION

1 Read the interpretation and then answer the question that follows. 'The Final Solution as it emerged was
   not the product of a grand design.' (From K. Schleunes, *The Twisted Road to Auschwitz*, 1970.) Evaluate the
   strengths and limitations of this interpretation, making reference to other interpretations that you have
   studied.

CHAPTER 8

Defeat and occupation

Britain, the USSR and the USA had forged a 'Grand Alliance' in 1941 due to military pressures. Once it became clear after 1943 that Germany could lose the war, decisions had to be made about what type of country Germany should become politically, militarily and economically.

The purpose of this chapter is to examine how the early post-war plans led to the Allied occupation of Germany and how Cold War divisions ultimately led to the creation of two Germanys. It does this through the following sections:

★ Germany in 1945: 'zero hour'

★ Allied plans for post-war Germany

★ The Allies and the Nazi legacy

★ Democratisation and decentralisation

★ Allied occupation: the Soviet zone

★ Allied occupation: the Western zones

★ The division of Germany

★ Conclusion: the creation of two Germanys

The key debate on *page 305* of this chapter asks the question: Why was divided Germany the focus of the Cold War in 1945–9?

Key dates

1945	Feb. 4–11	Yalta Conference of Roosevelt, Stalin and Churchill
	May 7–8	Surrender of German forces to Allies
	July 17–Aug. 2	Potsdam Conference of Truman, Stalin and Churchill (later Attlee)
	Nov. 20	Nuremberg trials began
1946	April 21–22	Formation of SED by merging East German SPD and KPD
1947	Jan. 1	Formation of Bizone between USA and Britain

1947	June 5	George Marshall announced the Marshall Plan or ERP
1948	June 18	Currency reform in Western zones
	June 24	Berlin blockade started
1949	Jan. 25–28	First SED party conference. Supremacy of SED in Soviet zone
	May 12	Berlin blockade ended
	May 23	Foundation in West Germany of FRG (Federal Republic of Germany)
	Oct. 7	Foundation in East Germany of GDR (German Democratic Republic)

Germany in 1945: 'zero hour'

▶ *What were the immediate problems faced by the occupying Allied forces?*

▶ *Why was there disagreement between the Allied leaders over Germany's future and what was finally agreed at Yalta?*

In the weeks before the capital fell to the Soviets, a typical Berliner's joke began to circulate: 'Enjoy the war while you can! The peace is going to be terrible.'

It is no exaggeration to say that the German state had ceased to exist by May 1945. A number of Nazi leaders had killed themselves while others had fled or been captured and arrested. As a result, the central government had broken down in the final week of April. In its place, Germany, and the city of Berlin, had both been divided by the Allies into four zones; and each one of the **occupying powers** had its own military commander giving orders and guidelines for the local economy and administration (see page 272). But, in the short term, the most telling problem facing Germany that spring was the social and economic crisis.

Population displacement

At the end of the war it is estimated that one in two Germans was on the move. These people consisted of:

- Roughly 12 million German refugees fleeing from the east after the changes to the frontiers, known as **expellees**.
- Ten million of the so-called 'displaced persons' who had been in forced labour or had been prisoners in the various Nazi camps.
- Families that had been torn apart by the war who were looking for each other.
- Over 11 million German soldiers who had been taken as prisoners of war. Of these, 7.7 million were soon released from camps in the west, whereas the 3.3 million in the USSR were captives until the 1950s and, of these, one-third perished.

Urban destruction and shortages of food and fuel

The occupying powers faced the serious problem of not only feeding all these people, but also finding them accommodation. Twenty per cent of housing had been completely destroyed and a further 30 per cent badly damaged. Cities like Cologne, Hamburg and Berlin had been reduced to rubble, leading to acute housing shortages and forcing people to accept temporary accommodation or to escape to the countryside. By the winter of 1945 the average calorie consumption had dropped from the recommended 2000 per person per day to 950–1150; the people also faced severe fuel shortages.

KEY TERMS

Occupying powers The four Allies: the USA, the USSR, Britain and France.

Expellees Ethnic Germans who either fled their homes in central and eastern Europe, or were forcibly expelled following the Second World War.

Economic dislocation

While the economy had not completely disintegrated, it was very badly dislocated. Industrial capacity had obviously declined dramatically, but the extent of its destruction was exaggerated at the time. Moreover, the infrastructure of bridges and railways and utilities, like gas and water, had broken down during the end of the war. Also, the state had massive debts, so Germany once again faced the problem of rising inflation leading to a major black market for the supply of food and other goods.

 **KEY TERM**

Stunde Null 'Zero hour'. A term used in German society to describe Germany's collapse in the months after 1945.

Not surprisingly, many Germans after the war saw the desperate situation as **Stunde Null**, the zero hour. However, in a way, this term for 1945 is misleading, as there were still major continuities in Germany:

- an efficient civil service
- long-standing local government authorities
- a well-established banking system (despite the currency problems)
- an industrial base and potential for productivity.

Despite the immense social pressures, especially on the women of Germany, the fundamentals of the social fabric were not completely destroyed. There was no social breakdown, and the Allies restored law and order quite quickly; the entrepreneurial middle class still aspired; Christianity had survived Nazism, and the Churches were once again free to practise their faiths (although the situation in the Soviet zone was later to make this more difficult). All these factors point to the key question of whether the Germany which emerged from 1945 was truly 'new', or largely rooted in its past.

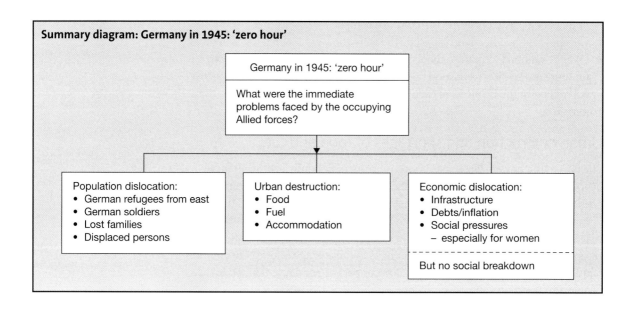

Summary diagram: Germany in 1945: 'zero hour'

Germany in 1945: 'zero hour'

What were the immediate problems faced by the occupying Allied forces?

Population dislocation:
- German refugees from east
- German soldiers
- Lost families
- Displaced persons

Urban destruction:
- Food
- Fuel
- Accommodation

Economic dislocation:
- Infrastructure
- Debts/inflation
- Social pressures
  - especially for women

But no social breakdown

2 Allied plans for post-war Germany

▶ *What were the early aims of the Grand Alliance?*

▶ *Why was there disagreement between the Allied leaders over Germany's future during the war conferences?*

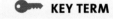 **🔑 KEY TERM**

Grand Alliance A term initially used by Churchill to describe the alliance of Britain, the USA and the USSR 1941–5.

The **Grand Alliance** of the USSR, the USA and Britain was forged out of the pressures of their military situation in the latter half of 1941. Neither the USA nor the USSR had even joined the war voluntarily; both had been attacked without warning. Therefore, the 'Big Three' of Stalin, Roosevelt and Churchill were brought together initially through the simple necessity of the military survival of their nations.

Teheran 1943

Roosevelt and Churchill had agreed in January 1943 that they would demand the unconditional surrender of Germany, and the first summit of the 'Big Three' took place in Teheran, Iran, in December of that year. While the main aim of the meeting was to determine military strategy for the final phase of the war, it soon became clear that there were serious disagreements about territorial changes in Europe after Hitler's defeat, and self-interest and mutual mistrust stood in the way of compromise.

At the heart of the discussions lay the issue of the borders between Poland and Germany. The USSR wanted to keep its territorial gains from the Nazi–Soviet Pact of 1939 (see pages 231 and 242). The Western Allies, to keep Stalin on board, largely agreed to his demands. More difficult was the issue of the extent of compensating Poland with German territories in the west. A line along the two German rivers Oder and Neisse was finally taken as a provisional basis for further negotiations at the next meetings.

Roosevelt suggested that Germany be divided into smaller states as a means to eliminate the German threat once and for all. While plans were proposed, no agreements were found, and they were given to a special commission for further negotiation. The most notorious plan was one drawn up by the US secretary of state, Henry Morgenthau, in 1944. It suggested not only dividing up Germany, but also turning it into a backward, purely agrarian territory, demolishing all existing industry. The plan was acknowledged and seriously considered, but later was to be overruled for practical reasons.

Yalta Conference, February 1945

The next meeting took place at Yalta in the Crimea. By then Germany was on the verge of defeat and it became clear that the power of Churchill and Britain was in decline and the other two superpowers could increasingly shape events by themselves. The Soviet Red Army had advanced steadily into Germany whereas the Western Allies had struggled to make their expected rapid progress, not reaching the Rhine until February. Moreover, the Soviet 'liberation' of states in eastern Europe was not viewed favourably by many and it was to become the focus of discussion. Roosevelt and Churchill have been subsequently criticised for allowing Stalin to establish a substantial sphere of influence in the east and the Baltic states.

The Yalta agreement

While some compromises were made at Yalta, many decisions remained postponed or open to debate. The Western Allies relied on terms like 'democratic' or 'free elections' without specifying their exact meaning, which they later found to be to their own cost. Nevertheless, the 'Big Three' agreed that:

- The USSR would keep most of the eastern Polish territory it demanded and parts of north-east Prussia, while Poland would in return receive German territory on its western border, although the exact frontier of the Polish–German border was again postponed (see Figure 8.1, page 275).
- Germany was tentatively divided up into four occupied zones. The administration of each zone would lie in the hands of the respective occupying power: the USA, USSR, Britain and France, whereas decisions concerning the whole of Germany would be taken unanimously by the four high commanders in the **Allied Control Council** (ACC). Similarly, the capital, Berlin, would be divided into four zones to be ruled by the ACC.
- The Allies would set up a commission to look into reparations.

Yalta was intended only to be an initial understanding before a peace settlement, and yet Stalin was put in an increasingly powerful negotiating position.

Potsdam Conference, 17 July to 2 August 1945

A couple of months after the meeting at Yalta, Germany capitulated and yet the relationship between the Soviet Union and the Western Allies deteriorated markedly. The increasing disagreements between the Allies over the future of Germany and Europe bedevilled the first few months of peace. Finally, the leaders of the Allies met from 17 July to 2 August, in the noble residence of Cecilienhof at Potsdam, near Berlin, but with significant changes to the line-up.

Truman

Roosevelt had died on 12 April leaving his inexperienced successor, Harry S. Truman, with an unfinished war and an unclear situation as to Europe's future. Truman was at first prepared to continue with American policies along the lines mapped out by Roosevelt, but he was distinctly less trustful towards Stalin because of their contrasting views of democracy. These were highlighted by

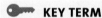
KEY TERM

Allied Control Council
The name given to the military occupation governing body of the four Allied occupation zones.

the Red Army's occupation of eastern Europe, which was unsympathetic to democratic ideals. In addition, the president was waiting for his scientists to bring him news of some new weapon tests in the desert of New Mexico, which might change his whole standing in Potsdam and the Pacific (see page 275).

Churchill

Churchill was even less optimistic and increasingly antagonistic towards Stalin. He judged Stalin's promises for democratic elections in the east European states as a deceptive manoeuvre and urged the Americans to prevent the further spread of Soviet influence in Europe, and in particular in Germany. However, Britain's position as a world power was already beginning to wane, and its status was demeaned further by the defeat of the war leader Churchill at the general election in the middle of the summit. He was replaced by the less well-known Labour politicians, Prime Minister Clement Attlee and Foreign Minister Ernest Bevin.

Stalin

Stalin's interests at Potsdam were above all concerned with reparations and security. The USSR had lost at least 20 million people and the country's industry and infrastructure in the west had been badly damaged. In the first year after the war, compared with the year previously, agrarian production had been reduced by 40 per cent and steel production by 50 per cent. Stalin needed the reparations to rebuild his country and for economic reasons he was against a division of Germany at that time. He wanted to have access to the industrial areas along the Rhine and Ruhr.

The Potsdam agreement

At the end of the meetings they agreed on just a 'Protocol of Proceedings' (a diplomatic statement) and not a peace settlement. It stated that occupied Germany was to be built on the principle of the **four Ds** of de-Nazification, demilitarisation, decentralisation and democratisation. Yet, it proved to be difficult for them to define these terms more precisely. The main points of agreement were:

- occupation zones
- the German–Polish border
- reparations
- armed forces.

Occupation zones

Germany would be divided into four zones of occupation. Although the French were absent from the Potsdam Conference, it was agreed that France should be allocated a zone of occupation along with Britain, the USA and the Soviet Union. Each occupying power was to administer its zone independently. However, at the same time, it was assumed that the Allies would soon negotiate a final

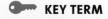

KEY TERM

Four Ds De-Nazification, to eliminate Nazi influence; demilitarisation, to destroy German armed forces; democratisation, to re-establish democratic institutions in Germany; and decentralisation, to break down the centralised Nazi political structure and restore local/regional government.

settlement for the whole of Germany. In the meantime Germany was to be treated as one economic unit and all issues concerning the country were to be decided by all the four powers unanimously.

The German–Polish border

This issue caused great disagreement when Stalin demanded that it be confirmed further west at the line of the rivers Oder and Neisse. Churchill had no sympathy and refused to accept this concession, pointing out that the question of the borders could only be settled at a final comprehensive peace conference. The Americans agreed with Churchill and this decision was also postponed. However, in practice, the Polish administration of those lands and the 'peaceful resettlement' (expulsion) of millions of Germans tacitly were accepted by the Western Allies. The shift of Poland to the west became quickly a *fait accompli* and there was no chance of renegotiation with Stalin without risking a direct confrontation. The Oder–Neisse line was to become an issue of great grievance for many Germans.

Reparations

The USSR demanded reparations of $20 billion, a sum which in the eyes of the Western Allies was so exorbitant that it would make it impossible for the German economy to support its population. (Although, interestingly, the Americans had estimated that Soviet damages amounted to $35.7 billion.) In the end an agreement was reached by which each power was to take reparations from its own occupying zone. In addition, the USSR was to receive a quarter of the reparations from the Western zones partially in exchange for the supply of raw materials and agricultural goods.

Armed forces

All German military forces were disbanded, and they were prevented from having any independent military presence under Allied occupation.

Consequences of Potsdam

Allied differences over Germany had crystallised in the twelve months leading up to Potsdam in July 1945. The Allies had become estranged and it is telling that Potsdam was just a protocol, not a peace treaty. Indeed, Potsdam left more questions open about Germany and Europe than it answered. For example:

- Within which borders should the German state be defined?
- Was Germany to stay as one state after the time of the occupation?
- Was there to be a central government at some stage again, or had the Allies already accepted a division into spheres of influence that would become permanent?

Areas under Polish control
Areas under Soviet control
···· Oder–Neisse line
Areas under British control
Areas under French control
Areas under US control

Figure 8.1 How Germany was divided by the Allies.

The Potsdam protocol therefore reflected the grim realities of power politics. Germany had imploded, but the vacuum was quickly filled with the international rivalry of the superpowers over the issues of:

- Ideology: communism versus democracy and capitalism.
- Security: the power of the Red Army in land forces versus the American development of the **atomic bomb**.
- Economy: American desire to maintain its world trade role versus the Soviet aim to recover from the enormous economic losses of the war.

As a result, from 1945 to 1949, when it came to the development of a post-Nazi Germany, all relevant critical decisions were really subject to the context of the emerging Cold War.

KEY TERM

Atomic bomb Western scientists developed atomic/nuclear weapons as part of the Manhattan Project 1942–5. The first bomb was tested in New Mexico in July 1945 and the next two were dropped on Hiroshima and Nagasaki in Japan in August 1945.

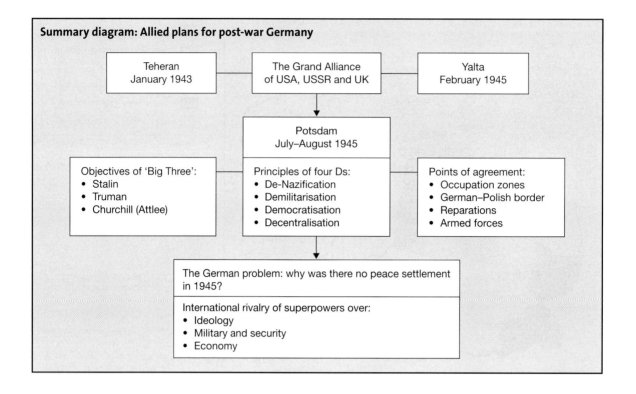

Summary diagram: Allied plans for post-war Germany

```
┌─────────────────┐   ┌──────────────────────┐   ┌─────────────────┐
│    Teheran      │───│   The Grand Alliance  │───│     Yalta       │
│  January 1943   │   │  of USA, USSR and UK  │   │  February 1945  │
└─────────────────┘   └──────────────────────┘   └─────────────────┘
                                 │
                                 ▼
                      ┌──────────────────────┐
                      │       Potsdam         │
                      │   July–August 1945    │
                      └──────────────────────┘

┌──────────────────────┐  ┌──────────────────────┐  ┌──────────────────────┐
│ Objectives of 'Big   │  │ Principles of four Ds:│  │ Points of agreement:  │
│ Three':              │  │ • De-Nazification     │  │ • Occupation zones    │
│ • Stalin             │  │ • Demilitarisation    │  │ • German–Polish border│
│ • Truman             │  │ • Democratisation     │  │ • Reparations         │
│ • Churchill (Attlee) │  │ • Decentralisation    │  │ • Armed forces        │
└──────────────────────┘  └──────────────────────┘  └──────────────────────┘
                                 │
                                 ▼
           ┌──────────────────────────────────────────────────────┐
           │ The German problem: why was there no peace settlement │
           │ in 1945?                                              │
           ├──────────────────────────────────────────────────────┤
           │ International rivalry of superpowers over:            │
           │ • Ideology                                            │
           │ • Military and security                               │
           │ • Economy                                             │
           └──────────────────────────────────────────────────────┘
```

③ The Allies and the Nazi legacy

▶ *Were the Nuremberg trials an effective way to address the Nazi war crimes?*

▶ *How far was de-Nazification a success?*

At the end of the war, when concentration camps were liberated, the pictures of horror that were broadcast to the world shocked and outraged the public. Yet, the motivation of the victors when they set up the International Military Tribunal at Nuremberg was one of punishment of the Nazi leaders, rather than revenge.

SOURCE A

? According to Source A, what were the aims of the Allies in the declaration?

From the Berlin declaration of 5 June 1945, quoted in Armin Grünbacher, *The Making of German Democracy, West Germany During the Adenauer Era, 1945–65*, Manchester University Press, 2010, p. 5.

Article 11

a) The principal Nazi leaders as specified by the Allied representatives, and all persons from time to time named or designated by rank, office or employment by the Allied Representatives as being suspected of having committed, ordered

> *or abetted war crimes or analogous offences, will be apprehended and surrendered to the Allied Representatives …*
>
> *c) The German authorities and people will comply with any instructions given by the Allied Representatives for the apprehension and surrender of such persons.*

This military tribunal was a completely new concept and there were no real existing international laws. This fact has caused a lot of controversy on the validity of these trials with legal and historical experts to this day.

The court, made up of judges from the four Allies, was to conduct individual trials of the Nazis on four counts:

- war crimes
- crimes against peace
- crimes against humanity, for example the mass murder of Jews
- conspiring to commit the crimes in the first three counts.

The trials started on 20 November 1945 and sessions stretched over 218 days. Twenty-two of the leading members of the Nazi regime were indicted. (Hitler, Himmler and Goebbels had all killed themselves before the trials.)

The prosecution lawyers of the four Allies presented 2360 documents and questioned 240 witnesses for the prosecution. The necessity to translate all the procedures into the different languages represented only one of the many difficulties of the trials. It became clear that it would be impossible to conduct such trials against the mass of the party members somehow involved in crimes.

While twelve leaders were sentenced to death, only ten were actually executed. Three life sentences and four sentences of up to twenty years' imprisonment were passed on the rest. Only three people were acquitted: von Papen, Schacht and Fritzsche. The NSDAP with all its organisations was condemned as criminal and forbidden. (The fate of many Nazis can be found by referring to this book's profiles and key figures in the text.)

In the following years similar trials were conducted against leading lawyers, doctors and industrialists at Nuremberg. Thousands of trials were to follow after those infamous cases and hundreds of death sentences were passed. Yet, it should also be remembered that many Nazis responsible for war crimes were not brought to trial and were able to hide their past, and even able to carry on pursuing their careers.

From their start the Nuremberg trials were controversial. On the one hand, some have claimed that the trials did not go far enough, on the other hand many critics have seen the process as **show trials** or 'kangaroo courts' on two counts:

 **KEY TERM**

Show trial A trial held for show with a predetermined judgment.

- That questionable evidence was produced to prove the legal guilt of particular individuals in a court.
- That the victors' justice applied two different sets of morals, as the Allies refused to be judged by the same international standards of justice with respect to Allied war actions, for example the use of the atomic bomb by the Americans, the behaviour of the Soviet troops in Poland and Germany, and the British mass bombing of Dresden.

Nevertheless, despite all the difficulties, the trials succeeded in revealing the cruelties of the Nazi leaders and bringing them to a kind of justice. Even in Germany, the principle of the trials was mostly acknowledged and accepted. Rather, it was the broader process of de-Nazification and re-education which caused upset within Germany.

De-Nazification

One of the foremost aims agreed at the meeting at Potsdam was to erase Nazism and re-educate the German population towards democracy. Yet, there were practical problems in how to implement this aim:

- The Nazi Party was declared illegal in Germany and the vast majority of the 6.5 million members in 1945 threw away their membership cards in the hope of distancing themselves from the regime.
- Germany had been destroyed and the Allies needed German experts, such as engineers, to overcome the most urgent problems in their zones.
- The skilled labour shortage led to another major point. The Allies would need to find experts who had not been involved in Nazism. That was almost impossible because of the dualism between the German state and the party (see pages 156–61). The so-called 'educated middle classes' had been essential for the regime and obviously non-loyal elements had largely been purged from the state in the 1930s. Therefore, the original US plan to dismiss all Nazis from their offices was bound to lead to chaos.

In the very first few weeks of the creation of the British and American zones, thousands of Germans were forced to visit the opened concentration camps in their neighbourhoods to confront the horrible truth they had ignored for so long, and make them face up to their guilt. Although this action was accepted by many Germans, it caused much resentment from others because of the way the Allies seemed to be blaming the entire German population collectively.

Then, from the summer of 1945, the Allies embarked on screening more rigorously for Nazis. All ex-members of the NSDAP were banned from leading positions in private and public service, and thousands of officials and suspects were automatically arrested and held in internment camps. By late 1946 nearly a quarter of a million Germans were being held. However, it was clear early on that the directives were contradictory or applied differently between the zones. Nearly half of the internees had been in the American zone, much higher than in the British and French zones.

In an attempt to formalise the situation, the Western Allies, prompted by the US military governor, General **Lucius Clay**, decided that all German adult citizens should fill in a detailed questionnaire comprising 131 questions (although this was not applied by the Soviet authorities). This resulted in their categorisation into five groups:

I. Major offenders.
II. Offenders incriminated.
III. Less incriminated offenders.
IV. 'Fellow-travellers' – sympathisers.
V. Exonerated persons.

The people who were categorised in the first three classes had to appear in front of a court for further interrogation and possible punishments that included fines, imprisonment or the death penalty. Rather than face such penalties, many Germans downplayed their involvement in the National Socialist regime.

It soon became clear that the process of de-Nazification varied markedly between the Western Allies (see Tables 8.1 and 8.2).

Table 8.1 Percentage distribution of de-Nazified persons by category in the three Western zones of occupation

Zone	Category of Nazi				
	I & II	**III**	**IV**	**V**	**Not pursued**
US	2.5	11.2	51.1	1.9	33.3
British	(Not available)	1.3	10.9	58.4	29.3
French	0.1	2.5	44.7	0.5	52.2

Table 8.2 Nazi criminals before military courts

Zone	Number sentenced	Death penalty
US	1517	324
British	1085	240
French	2107	104

US zone

The Americans had an almost missionary zeal. So, although they did not really want to destroy the capitalist structure, they felt it was necessary to purge German society of the Nazi 'evil'. As an example, all of those who were party members before 1937 were dismissed from office. As a result, it was the Americans who were seen to judge the most sternly.

British zone

The British took a more pragmatic approach than the Americans to the whole procedure. They tended to work on a case-by-case basis and the questionnaire was not so thoroughly pursued. Indeed, they soon allowed ex-party members to return to their positions and, as a result, ex-Nazis were often permitted to

KEY FIGURE

Lucius Clay (1898–1978)
US officer who became military governor of the US occupation zone in Germany 1947–9. Orchestrated the Berlin airlift when the USSR blockaded the Western sectors of the city.

assume leadership roles in the zone, something which US policies prohibited. Also, students forbidden to enrol in universities in the US zone because of Nazi connections were allowed to enrol in universities in the British zone.

French zone

The French zone was relatively small and French manpower was limited. Also, de-Nazification was a relatively low priority compared with French concerns about defence and security.

Soviet zone

The Soviets took a very different approach to the problem of de-Nazification. They blamed the capitalist system for the development of Nazism, so accordingly the most efficient means to prevent another fascist state was to develop new social and economic conditions. Therefore, the Soviet approach was sharp and decisive, with immediate mass internments in some former Nazi concentration camps that resulted in the deaths of many inmates due to their terrible conditions. Yet, there was no overall 'Nazi hunt' (the US questionnaire system was not applied). As a result, by early 1948:

- A number of 'war criminals' had been executed (the figure is not exactly clear) and leading Nazi functionaries had been imprisoned and punished.
- Nazi property had been confiscated and redistributed by the Soviet authorities (see pages 290–1).
- 450,000 ex-Nazi Party members had been dismissed from office, including teachers, lawyers and so on.

However, the Soviets needed experienced and skilled Germans, especially engineers and doctors, so many were later reappointed. So, perhaps not surprisingly, de-Nazification served more as a calculating tool for the Soviets to get rid of opposition to the new form of society, rather than as a serious attempt to bring all the Nazi criminals to justice. Moreover, many Germans felt that by aligning themselves to the new anti-fascist state, they could be freed from the taint of any previous Nazi past and subsequent guilt.

Conclusion

De-Nazification by all of the Allies did not succeed as planned. They had certainly secured the destruction of the Nazi state, yet in the end, for various reasons, the purge was limited and the real change of values was questionable.

Justice

The process was undermined by too many examples of injustice. Too many of the small fry were caught and punished, whereas the big fish got away. For example, Germans could produce testimonies of their innocence from character references that became known as *Persilscheine*, named after a well-known washing powder. These documents were in great demand by many Germans and were increasingly traded on the black market or signed in exchange for all kinds of favours among the population. There were many loopholes, even for hardline Nazis, while many of those Nazis who were imprisoned were given amnesties from 1951.

The size of the task

The Allies created a task which grew out of hand and they simply did not have the staff to pursue it. The problems in Germany were immense from the start, and the questionnaire system generated enormous amounts of paperwork. Ironically, the massive task of evaluating all those questionnaires and passing judgements was increasingly passed to local German authorities.

Differences between the zones

It became clear very soon that the zones were not in agreement and the different approaches between the Allies undermined their initial aim. This problem was not just a practical one; it also reflected the conflicting domestic political interests of the Allies.

German attitudes

German opposition to de-Nazification increased because of the introduction of questionnaires and the inconsistencies of the whole process. In addition, Germans were more interested in the reconstruction for the future (rather than looking at the past).

Cold War

In 1947–8 the Allies' interests moved away from de-Nazification and towards the Cold War. The Western Allies became more concerned about 'containing' Soviet influence by making western Germany a strong bulwark against it.

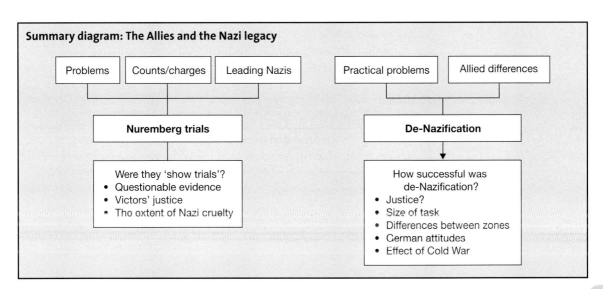

Democratisation and decentralisation

▶ Did the Allies really try to decentralise?

▶ How did democratisation affect German politics in the Western zones?

At Potsdam the Allies had outlined the treatment of occupied Germany built on the principle of the four Ds (see page 273). De-Nazification had been applied with mixed success, whereas demilitarisation was thoroughly applied at first: no armed forces were permitted and the manufacture of all arms was banned (see page 341 for the issue of remilitarisation in the 1950s). The two principles of decentralisation and democratisation 'as rapidly as is consistent with military security' were at the heart of what kind of Germany would emerge.

Decentralisation

On one issue the Allies did agree: namely that Prussia was seen as the symbol of militarism, nationalism and power politics and it could not remain a political unit. Admittedly, some of it became part of Poland (see map on page 275), but Prussia itself was dissolved for good, with the aim of decentralisation. However, the Allies had very different views of how to achieve political decentralisation in the rest of Germany.

Soviet zone

Certainly, the Soviet zone had accepted the principle and, by the end of 1945, had created five *Länder* as states. Yet, these proved to be of less political importance than first thought. The Soviets distrusted the idea of a genuinely federal structure and so established at the same time a range of centralised authorities responsible for transport, housing and so on. Consequently, the regional authorities were controlled and directed by the communists, and in 1952 they were dissolved.

US zone

The Americans were the strongest supporters of German decentralisation, as a result of their own federal government system. Under the influence of the military governor, Clay, the foundations of the administrative structure for three *Länder* had been established in his zone and as early as May 1946 the first free federal state elections were held.

SOURCE B

From a speech by General Clay on 6 September 1946, quoted in *Akten zur Vorgeschichte der Bundesrepublik Deutschland 1945–1949*, volume 1, September 1945–December 1946, Walter Vogel and Christoph Weisz, editors, R. Oldenbourg Verlag, 1976, pp. 125–7.

Our policy calls for the decentralization of governmental authority in the Länder … within the next two and a half months … We propose the election of representative assemblies in January of next year and … a free press and radio at the earliest date. You have complete freedom of religious worship …

We believe in the operation of Germany as an economic unit. We support the establishment of central administrative machinery for finance, industry, transport, communications, and foreign trade [and] administrative agencies … for food and agriculture and labor …

These administrative machines do not exist … The securing of this coordination is your job, not ours.

> From studying Source B, identify the organisational aims for the US zone.

British zone

At first, the British doubted the Germans' ability to build up a genuine democracy and were wary of giving them political freedom and powers. They preferred to keep close control over their zone through their own centralised administration and although they took in German experts, at first their input was limited. However, it seems that the growing financial costs of the occupation pushed the British towards encouraging decentralisation and they started to pass back political responsibility to the Germans. In May 1947 free elections for federal state parliaments were held.

French zone

France continued to remain the strongest supporter of the lasting dismemberment of Germany because of its own security and financial interests. Consequently, it blocked any attempt by the other two Western powers in the ACC for a more co-ordinated, centralised administration of Germany. The French zone was therefore held under tight rule and economically cut off from the others. France even stubbornly resisted the re-establishing of democratic parties and it was not until March 1947 that *Länder* elections were permitted in its zone.

Conclusion

The Allies believed that decentralisation would be achieved by restructuring the German regions, to reflect some of its old historical territories (see also the federal structure in Weimar Germany, pages 15–16). Yet, for the first two years, the process was implemented in different ways at different paces by all four of the occupying powers. By 1947 a clear contrast lay between the Soviet zone, with its centralised authorities, and the three Western zones, which had established the nine newly created federal *Länder*, albeit still under strict Allied control (see Figures 8.1 and 9.1 on pages 275 and 312, respectively).

The re-emergence of German political life

Alongside the issue of decentralisation was the necessary one of democratisation. If Nazism was to be wholly extinguished the Allies wanted it to be replaced with genuine democratic political parties, and it did not take long for political party life to be revived. As early as 10 June 1945 the Soviets permitted the re-establishment of non-fascist, democratic parties and the formation of free unions. Within the next few months the Western Allies also agreed to 'license' the formation of democratic parties, mainly because the Allies wanted to control political developments in their zones. As a result, by the end of 1945 the essence of party politics had been re-established through the creation of four major parties: the SPD, the CDU, the LDPD and the KPD.

SOURCE C

From the Military Government Gazette – Germany, British Zone of Control, 1945, quoted in Armin Grünbacher, *The Making of German Democracy, West Germany during the Adenauer Era, 1945–65*, Manchester University Press, 2010, p. 22.

Ordinance No. 12 Formation of Political Parties

Article 6. Penalties

(12) Any person:

a) who takes part in political activities … which have as their objective or tend towards:

> *(i) undermining of the authority of the Military Government, or*

> *(ii) creation or dissension between the Allied Powers, or*

> *(iii) glorification of or the preparation for war or militarisation, or*

> *(iv) restoration of the Nazi regime or the establishment of any similar regime, or*

> *(v) introduction of discrimination against any person or group of persons on the grounds of race, colour, nationality or religious beliefs …*

Shall upon conviction by a Military Government court suffer such punishment (including death) as the court may determine.

> **?** Why was it necessary for the British to pass the decree in Source C?

The Social Democrats (SPD)

It was not difficult for the SPD to re-establish itself, as it enjoyed a large and traditionally loyal mass electorate of workers and it was simply able to revive and rebuild the old organisational structures that pre-dated 1933. Its first national party leader was Dr **Kurt Schumacher**, and his main problem in 1945–6 was to fight off the demands from left-wing members of the party to merge with the communists to create one united socialist party. He was able to prevent the parties merging in the Western zones, but not in the Soviet zone, where the SED was created (see pages 288–9).

The post-war SPD has been described as a 'moralist' party, although its programme was shaped very much by its history and by a rather dated outlook:

- It wanted to improve living conditions for the working class, but within the context of parliamentary democracy.
- It was in theory an anti-capitalist party and regarded itself as Marxist. It was committed to working for a socialist economy by transferring natural resources and key industries to the state.
- It remained deeply opposed to the communists and refused any political compromise, which reflected their bitter hostility from the Weimar years.
- It viewed positively the possibility of a neutral socialist Germany located between the capitalist economies of the West and the Soviet dictatorship of the East.

The Christian Democrats (CDU)

At first, it seemed difficult for the conservative forces to re-emerge as a viable political influence because of their regional and religious differences. However, in the creation of the CDU on 16 December 1945, its founders astutely recognised the need for a unified Christian conservative party, although its various organisations were only officially merged into a national party in 1950.

Thus, this new party only partly played on its traditional roots from the pre-Hitler era. It appealed to the following: Catholics, from the old ZP (Centre Party) whose geographical base was in the Rhineland and the south; and Protestants, from the DVP and DNVP, whose strength was in the north.

In using the word 'union', the CDU stressed its desire to unite all Christian Democrats, Protestant and Catholic alike, and to appeal to the broadly conservative middle classes. In Bavaria, an independent sister party to the CDU was launched, the CSU (Christian Social Union), which was more conservative and focused predominantly on Bavarian interests.

An astute French journalist described the establishment of the CDU as: 'socialist and radical in Berlin, clerical and conservative in Cologne, capitalist and reactionary in Hamburg and counter-revolutionary and separatist in Munich'. However, the CDU had more to offer than its appeal to political unity, as it was strongly built on Christian social ideas and the Christian trade union movement. Its Ahlen programme of 1947 adopted radical social policies, which demanded the public ownership of key industries and a greater influence for the workers' unions in political decisions.

KEY FIGURE

Kurt Schumacher (1895–1952)

A lifetime socialist who became chairman of the SPD from 1946 and leader of the opposition in the first *Bundestag*. A strong opponent of Adenauer, but he was also vehemently against communism and the creation of the SED in the Soviet zone. Despite his early death he is seen as one of the founding fathers of post-war democracy.

Liberal parties (LDPD and FDP)

At first, the liberal parties had tried to establish one German Liberal Democratic Party (LDPD) across the zones. But the leader of the party in the east, Wilhelm Külz, had to concede so much to the supremacy of the SED (see page 289) that the membership from the Western zones formed the FDP (Free Democratic Party) in 1948. It stressed the right of private property and upheld the advantages of a free market in its programme. The new party was initially led by Theodor Heuss, who later became the first president of West Germany.

The Communists (KPD)

The KPD still enjoyed quite substantial grassroots support and its aim was to unify the working classes of the whole of Germany under its leadership. The Communists enjoyed the full political backing of the Soviets in their zone and they played a crucial role in the merger of the KPD and SPD to create the SED (see pages 288–9). In the Western zones, it really had only a limited chance to gain real political power once it came to be seen as a tool of the Soviets. In the first elections of 1949 it gained about five per cent of the vote.

Table 8.3 The major parties licensed by the Allies by the end of 1945

Party	Major leaders	Background and aims
KPD (German Communist Party)	Walter Ulbricht (see page 356) and Wilhelm Pieck	Banned under the Nazis and had only survived underground. Resurrected by Moscow exiles in spring 1945 and enjoyed substantial grassroots support. Aimed to unify the working classes from the whole of Germany under its leadership. They led the way in the merger of the SPD and the KPD in the Soviet zone by creating the SED in 1946
SPD (Social Democratic Party of Germany)	Kurt Schumacher, national party leader (see page 285), and Otto Grotewohl, party leader in the Soviet zone	Once licensed, it was easy for the SPD to re-establish itself. Its programme was shaped very much by its history. In theory, it was still an anti-capitalist party and regarded itself as Marxist working for a socialist economy. Yet, the vast majority were deeply opposed to the Communists and refused any political compromise
CDU (Christian Democratic Union)	Konrad Adenauer, leader of the party in the British zone (see page 317), and Jakob Kaiser, co-founder and leader of the party in the Soviet zone	A new party, which grew out of the old ZP, DVP and DNVP from the Weimar years. It portrayed itself as a Christian conservative party aiming to unify Germany's regional and religious differences
LDPD (Liberal Democratic Party of Germany)	Wilhelm Külz, leader of the party in the Soviet zone and Theodor Heuss, based in the French zone	The liberal parties had been weak and divided in the Weimar years. In 1945 the LDPD was established across the zones, but differences soon emerged and in 1948 Heuss created the Free Democratic Party (FDP)

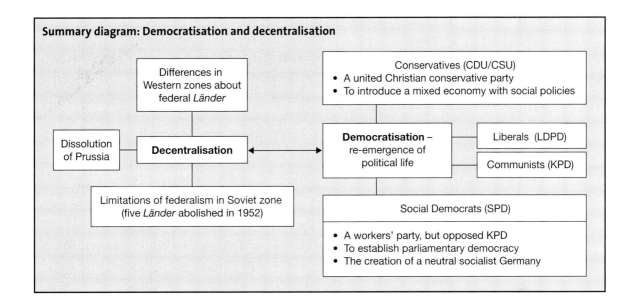

Summary diagram: Democratisation and decentralisation

Differences in Western zones about federal *Länder*

Dissolution of Prussia

Decentralisation

Limitations of federalism in Soviet zone (five *Länder* abolished in 1952)

Conservatives (CDU/CSU)
- A united Christian conservative party
- To introduce a mixed economy with social policies

Democratisation – re-emergence of political life

Liberals (LDPD)

Communists (KPD)

Social Democrats (SPD)

- A workers' party, but opposed KPD
- To establish parliamentary democracy
- The creation of a neutral socialist Germany

 # 5 Allied occupation: the Soviet zone

▶ *How did the SED become the dominant political party in the Soviet zone?*

▶ *What were the effects of Soviet socio-economic policies in the years 1945–9?*

Even before the Red Army had launched the Battle for Berlin, the Soviets had started to plan the reorganisation of their zone. As early as April 1945 they flew in a small group of exiled German communists under the leadership of Walter Ulbricht, who had been working in Moscow (see page 356).

The new political powers in eastern Germany

Ulbricht and his supporters had been trained by the Soviets as advisors to the Red Army. They had already developed detailed plans to gain political power in Germany in order to achieve social and economic changes. The Soviet Military Administration, **SMAD**, which was established in the Soviet zone, was initially prepared to follow their advice to win over the co-operation of the German population. The aims of the 'Ulbricht group' were as follows:

- to destroy the remnants of Nazism
- to create a unified working-class party under the leadership of the KPD

 **KEY TERM**

SMAD The Soviet Military Administration in Germany. The name given to the Soviet authorities that supervised the occupation in the Soviet zone. It was renamed the Soviet High Commission in October 1949.

- to occupy the key power positions in local administration, such as the chief of police
- to arrange for the appointment of respected non-communist representatives, such as mayors.

However, in installing communists as their deputies they managed to create an illusion of democracy while at the same time keeping everything under their direction. As Ulbricht said, 'it has to appear to be democratic, but we must keep everything under our control'.

Somewhat surprisingly, SMAD did allow the re-establishment of non-fascist, democratic parties and the formation of free unions, leading to the re-creation of the KPD, SPD, CDU and LDPD within a month in the Soviet zone (see Table 8.3, page 286). Yet, what looked like the rebirth of German democracy soon turned out to be a sham. Under Stalin's personal pressure, the four parties were forced to create a united front called the 'Block of Anti-Fascist Parties' (*Antifas*). The parties theoretically had organisational independence, but in fact their co-operation was forced over all important decisions because of harassment from the SMAD, with its single-minded support of Ulbricht and the KPD.

The creation of the SED

It was soon clear that the communists were not winning sufficient popularity to secure a mass political base. The elections in Austria and Hungary were catastrophic for the communists there, while in the Soviet zone the membership of the democratic parties was increasing, mainly because the KPD was seen as blindly serving Soviet interests. As a result, in the winter of 1945–6, Soviet pressure increased to bring about a political merger of the KPD and its rival, the SPD.

From the start, the issue of the merger was highly controversial within the SPD. The leader of the SPD in the Western zones, Kurt Schumacher, was a committed anti-communist and warned strongly against the plan. Moreover, many of the grassroots of the SPD in the Soviet zone were wary and wanted a genuine conference of the whole party. Finally, the pressure which the SMAD put on the SPD – in the main by threats, arrests and censorship – achieved success. At a conference on 22 April 1946, the SPD from the Soviet zone, led by Otto Grotewohl, and the KPD merged to create the new Socialist Unified Party, the **SED**. However, this merger was not entirely democratic. Ballots on this issue for the members of the SPD had been forbidden by SMAD in their zone – and the one held in the Western sector of Berlin had shown that 72 per cent of the SPD members there rejected the idea.

The establishment of the SED was undoubtedly a crucial development:

- The SED enjoyed the backing of SMAD, who hoped its creation would set the communists on the path to political success.

 **KEY TERM**

SED *Sozialistische Einheitspartei.* Socialist Unity Party of Germany. The new party created in April 1946 by the merger of the KPD and SPD in the Soviet zone.

- The SPD had lost its long-established status as the strongest political party across the whole of Germany.
- The SED put up a new hurdle for the chances of future political co-operation in the Eastern and Western zones.

However, despite all the pressure put on other parties, the SED still could not gain an overall majority of votes in the state elections in October 1946 (see Table 8.4).

Table 8.4 State elections in the Soviet zone, October 1946, as a percentage of vote

SED	CDU	LDPD	Peasants' League
47.5	27.3	21.6	3.5

The new SED party with its compromise programme had therefore failed to convince with its claim to offer 'a special independent German path to socialism'. Moreover, the development of the Cold War and the rising tensions between the Soviet Union and most communist parties in the '**Eastern bloc**' resulted in Moscow taking a much harder stance on the issue of loyal party discipline. Over the next few years the SED was regularly purged and forced to conform to Soviet policies. This process culminated, at the SED party conference of January 1949, in adopting a party structure after the Soviet model in Russia, proclaiming 'a party of a new type' committed to **democratic centralism**. In the words of Berghahn: 'The Soviet Zone of Occupation had effectively become a copy of the Stalinist dictatorship' (see pages 353–7).

Economic and social changes

In 1945 the Soviet zone of occupied Germany had several advantages and disadvantages. On the one hand:

- the territory benefited from large areas of agricultural land, although of mixed quality
- it had areas of well-developed light industry, such as textiles, chemicals and optics, in Saxony and Thuringia
- it was less war-damaged than the Western zones, with the main exceptions of Dresden and Berlin.

On the other hand:

- it lacked raw materials compared to the Ruhr area in the British zone; its only natural resource were potash and brown coal, which were of much lower energy value
- it had lost important provinces to Poland: Silesia, an industrial area with coal and iron reserves; the important port of Danzig and the agricultural land of Prussia
- it was suffering from a major influx of refugees from the east and starvation was even worse than in the Western zones

 **KEY TERMS**

Eastern bloc A label given to the countries controlled by the USSR in eastern Europe from 1945: Poland, Czechoslovakia, Hungary, Romania, Bulgaria, Albania and the GDR.

Democratic centralism Based on the idea from Marxist–Leninist theory of the decision-making practice and discipline of the Communist Party. Any decisions made at the centre should be passed down and accepted as policy below, and free expression from the lower ranks of the party should be passed up to the Central Committee for scrutiny to maintain discipline and control.

- the transportation infrastructure had been seriously dislocated; railways had been destroyed and roads from east to west Germany were blocked by border checkpoints
- it had no effective currency.

These features were to be exacerbated by the two major aims of Soviet economic and social policies: the pursuit of reparations in order to rebuild the USSR, and the application of a socialist economic policy in order to transform the socio-economic structures. Also, because in the eyes of the Soviets the Nazi state had been rooted in a capitalist society, it was seen as quite justified in destroying old Nazi capitalist power structures.

Nationalisation of industry and commerce

Despite the difficult conditions in the Soviet zone, the Russians significantly dismantled much of the industry, often using German female labour. The Soviets sent 1400 industrial plants from their zone to the USSR, with the result that by 1948 the overall industrial capacity in the Soviet zone had fallen dramatically. In effect, it meant that 213 firms were brought directly under Soviet financial control, known as **SAGs**. As these Soviet-owned companies produced about 30 per cent of the zone's industrial output, this represented a major loss and it also weakened all efforts at rebuilding it. The scale and impact of dismantling also had a human side, as many skilled workers and scientists were sent to the USSR to work.

Soviet economic policy was not just about compensation, it was at the heart of the Soviet socialists' aim to restructure Germany. Privately owned banks were dispossessed and replaced by state control as early as June 1945 and in the next year the process of nationalisation was started; private firms were expropriated and the state took control over them by creating **VEBs**. By 1948 only 39 per cent of industry and commerce remained in private hands – the rest was in the ownership of the SAGs and the VEBs.

Land reform

From 1945 to 1947 far-reaching land redistribution was carried out. More than 7000 estates of the *Junkers* were dispossessed (those with more than 100 hectares, equivalent to 250 acres). Altogether two-thirds of the land was redistributed to private smallholders, refugees and expellees from eastern Europe who all generally saw the process very positively. However, the results in terms of efficiency and production were disappointing, and by the early 1950s it was decided to implement **collectivisation**.

KEY TERMS

SAGs *Sowjetische Aktiengesellschaft*. Soviet state-controlled companies set up in January 1946 as part of reparations for the USSR.

VEBs *Volkeigener Betrieb*. People-owned companies in the GDR. Factories owned on behalf of the people and managed by the state, which controlled production targets and all worker discipline.

Collectivisation The policy of creating larger and more efficient agricultural units controlled by the state. It was initiated by Stalin in the USSR in the 1930s.

SOURCE D

'Junkerland in Bauernhand'. *Junker* lands in the hands of the peasants. An SED poster of 1947.

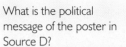

What is the political message of the poster in Source D?

The pace and thoroughness of the reforms in the Soviet zone show very clearly that in the years immediately after 1945 the Soviets had the will and the means to push through 'socialist' changes in the zone. The directives of the SMAD and the SED had made strong efforts to nationalise all means of production and to change the social structures of society there. Moreover, the creation of its own German Economic Commission, **DWK**, in June 1947 suggested that the Soviet zone had laid the basis for a planned state economy. These changes raised serious questions for the Western Allies, which are considered in the next section.

 **KEY TERM**

DWK *Deutsche Wirtschaftkommission.* German Economic Commission. Created in 1947 to administer the economy of the Soviet zone. It was very much in response to the creation of the German Economic Council in the Bizone.

Summary diagram: Allied occupation: the Soviet zone

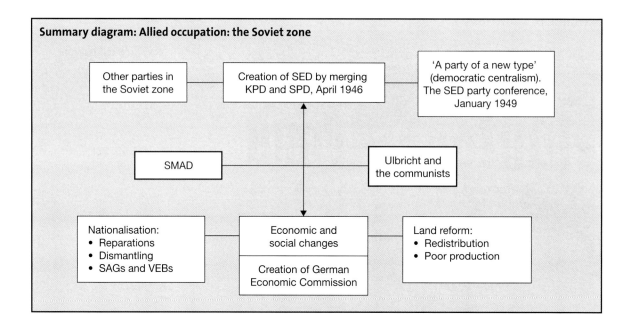

Allied occupation: the Western zones

▶ *How did the policies introduced by the Western Allies set out to solve Germany's problems in the post-war period?*

It soon became clear that there were no quick solutions to Germany's problems. Indeed, the practical problems were exacerbated by several harsh winters, especially the one of 1946–7. Yet, as has been seen, the Soviets had already set their own agenda, and so the immediate problem for the Western Allies was to make sure that the German population could survive the following winter and restart the economic life necessary to sustain the needs of the population.

Basic problems and basic solutions

The Western Allies were also confronted by having to cope with the structure of the system of the occupied zones:

- As each zone was administered individually, each occupying power had to take care of food, shelter, heating, medical services and so on. This situation proved particularly difficult for the British as their zone in the north and west of Germany included not only some of the most heavily industrialised areas with the densest population, but also many of the worst damaged cities.

- The French sought to extract as many resources as they could from Germany and the Saar territory was again under their control (see page 341).
- The Soviets continued to demand the payment of the additional reparations from the Western zones as laid down in Potsdam.

Increasingly, the British and Americans resorted to 'crisis management' in 1945–6 as the extent of Germany's problems emerged.

Housing

Almost a quarter of the housing in the three Western zones had been destroyed in the war. The remaining stock was put under extreme pressure, as it had to serve the requirements of the local inhabitants made homeless by the war, and provide shelter for the occupying forces and also the refugees from the East. Consequently, those people with undamaged houses had to take in refugees or bombed-out families, often leaving them with no more than one room at their disposal. Many families had to live in old bunkers or ruined houses without any sanitation or heating. To partially alleviate the housing problem, the British put up provisional shelters, 'Nissen-huts', which actually became more permanent accommodation, lasting for some years.

Fuel

House heating and industrial energy were major problems, as coal production had collapsed disastrously by mid-1945. The Western Allies were so concerned about the implications of the short supply that they made massive efforts together with German authorities to get the mines moving again. Although the real industrial recovery only came in the 1950s, the three-fold increase in coal production by early 1946 was crucial and prevented the fuel crisis getting even worse.

Food

The Germans had been used to food rationing since the beginning of the war but the rations fell dramatically from 1945, even though the Allies had tried to control the scarce resources. As a result, the level of malnourishment, along with the cold, led to illnesses like typhus, diphtheria and whooping cough, which took its toll on many Germans during the first two winters. It is no exaggeration to say that by 1947 Germany faced real famine. Every available patch of land was turned into a vegetable garden and in the Anglo-American zone the authorities were sometimes forced into limiting food distribution to a maximum of between 700 and 1200 calories per day for an average adult. Private aid initiatives also started across the world. In the USA and Canada, CARE (Cooperative for American Remittances to Europe) organised initiatives sending food and clothes, which were given to the German Red Cross, the Churches and other social organisations. Also significantly, these parcels became one of the first symbols of a newly growing bond between the Germans in the Western zones and their occupying powers.

Study Sources E and F.
Why would such stories be reported in the German press?

SOURCE E

From an article in the *Hamburger Freie Presse*, 10 April 1946, quoted in Armin Grünbacher, *The Making of German Democracy, West Germany During the Adenauer Era, 1945–65*, Manchester University Press, 2010, pp. 16–17.

At the world food conference in London the former American President Hoover indicated that a human needs a minimum daily intake of 2300 calories to sustain his vitality and capacity to work. In the British Zone of Occupation the daily calorific value of a normal ration is 1040 calories. In the American zone it is 1275 calories, in the French zone … 927 to 1144 calories. There is no detailed information from the Russian-occupied zone but it can be … assumed … that the calorific intake is not higher than in the western part of the Reich territory.

SOURCE F

From an article in the *Kriminalpolizeiliches Meldeblatt für Groß-Hamburg*, 15 August 1945, quoted in Armin Grünbacher, *The Making of German Democracy, West Germany During the Adenauer Era, 1945–65*, Manchester University Press, 2010, pp. 16–17.

On 11 August 1945 between 8 and 9 pm a number of boys aged between 10 and 13 years gained possession of bread in a rather original way. At the Bockmann bakery in Altona … they smashed a … big window with the help of a long stake they had wrapped in rags. They were able to spike six loaves of bread from inside the bakery onto the tip of the stake and get them out.

Conclusion

It is difficult to escape the conclusion that the extent of the problems the Allies in Germany had to face was grossly underestimated. Although the British and US authorities were initially moved by revenge and punishment, they soon came to recognise the reality of starvation and social dislocation. The early directive of non-fraternisation gradually gave way to pragmatic co-operation and indeed elements of trust began to grow on both sides. They worked very hard and actually coped remarkably well, which is not to say that millions of Germans did not still suffer from many traumatic experiences in those early years. It soon became clear that the Allies needed to go further than just providing human relief and had to find political and economic solutions.

Economic revival

German political life had revived in 1945 in the Western zones, but the process of decentralisation and democratisation had been cautious and slow (see pages 284–6). Moreover, political developments had been controlled very much by the Western Allies. As early as 1946 it became increasingly clear for the British and Americans that the fundamental economic problems in Germany could be managed much better if the occupying powers co-operated much more closely. This was for several reasons:

- The extent of the humanitarian crisis was getting worse because of the influx of the millions of expellees and refugees (see page 269).
- It made no real sense to dismantle the industry of the continent's strongest economy when Europe needed every bit of help to reconstruct.
- Britain, in particular, was so desperately indebted from the war that the government was increasingly keen to offload the financial costs of maintaining the old enemy.
- There was growing concern about the perceived threat of the Soviets, who had started to rebuild the economy in their zone along socialist lines, which did not conform to the concepts of a 'free-market economy'.

This political anxiety was reinforced by Churchill's **'iron curtain'** speech in March 1946 at Fulton, in the USA.

The Bizone

In the course of 1946 a series of talks among the Allies tried to determine a basis for economic co-operation. In reality they underlined the emerging differences between Britain and the USA, on the one hand, and the USSR and France on the other. Indeed, in May, General Clay even stopped the deliveries of industrial goods from the US zone to the Soviet zone, as the Soviets had failed to fulfil their part of the Potsdam agreement to send agricultural goods, which were needed in the industrial areas in the west. Moreover, two months later the Americans even suggested a merger with any of the zones – an offer accepted by the British, but rejected by the French and the Soviets. The frustration of the Americans came to a head in a speech in Stuttgart on 6 September by the US secretary of state, James Byrnes, which signalled a change in his country's policies on Germany. In effect, the speech was a cautiously worded offer to the Germans of co-operation and protection in rebuilding their state, as a member of the free democratic world rather than the old official US stance of control and punishment of the Germans.

KEY TERM

'Iron curtain' A term used by Churchill in 1946 to describe the border between Soviet-controlled countries and the West.

SOURCE G

From a speech by US Secretary of State J.F. Byrnes, 'Restatement of Policy on Germany' given in Stuttgart, 6 September 1946 (quoted in http://usa.usembassy.de/etexts/ga4-460906.htm).

The United States is firmly of the belief that Germany should be administered as an economic unit … The barriers between the four zones of Germany are far more difficult to surmount than those between normal independent states. The American Government … has formally announced that it is its intention to unify the economy of its own zone with any or all of the other zones … So far only the British Government has agreed to let its zone participate ... Of course, this policy of unification is not intended to exclude the governments not now willing to join … If complete unification cannot be secured, we shall do everything in our power to secure the maximum possible unification.

According to Source G, what were the USA's aims for Germany?

Bizone The name given to the two zones of Britain and the USA which were merged into a unified economic zone in January 1947.

BRD Bundesrepublik Deutschland. The Federal Republic of Germany (FRG) was formed on 23 May 1949.

Greek Civil War A conflict (1946–9) between communists and monarchists, which was backed by British troops until their withdrawal in February 1947.

Truman doctrine In March 1947 President Truman explained his decision to help the anti-communist forces in Greece. Truman's doctrine was to contain communism by sending money and equipment to any country facing communist influence.

Marshall Plan Also known as the European Recovery Programme (ERP). Proposed in 1947, it aimed to provide enough money (in the form of grants) to stabilise and strengthen Europe.

The change in direction was strongly supported by the British and so, on 1 January 1947, the British and the Americans agreed to merge their two zones into a unified economic one, the **Bizone**. This move was supposedly not intended to be a political union, yet during 1947 when inter-Allied conferences resulted in more disputes, Britain and the USA agreed to pass increased authority to the Germans in the Bizone. This action laid the basis for a form of German administrative government, which has led the historian Eschenburg to describe the Bizone as 'the germ cell of the **BRD**'. Most significantly, the Bizone created the German Economic Council, which had the power to pass laws on a range of economic matters such as taxation.

The Marshall Plan

From 1945 to 1946 the USA had pumped an immense amount of goods, raw materials and money into Europe, and by 1947 there were still real anxieties that the European market was continuing to decline. The US government was very concerned that this would destabilise many European countries, making them politically more susceptible to communist influence. Also it increasingly realised that it was impossible to bring about a lasting economic recovery in Europe without Germany, so Germany was seen as economically and politically vital.

Nevertheless, developments within Germany must be put very much in the context of the growing Cold War, and in 1947 several international events were highly significant:

- The revival of the **Greek Civil War** and the feared spread of communism.
- The declaration of the **Truman doctrine** on 12 March 1947, when the president proclaimed that it was the mission of the USA to help all free nations threatened by what he saw as communist aggression and to contain the spread of that ideology.
- The offer on 5 June 1947 from the new secretary of state, George Marshall, to seek Congress's agreement to provide enough money (in the form of grants) to stabilise and strengthen a European free market. This became known as the European Recovery Programme (ERP or **Marshall Plan**).

The Marshall Plan aimed to achieve a comprehensive economic recovery for Europe. It was therefore offered to all European states, including the four German zones, the USSR and the Soviet bloc. Stalin predictably forbade his satellites and the Soviet zone from taking up the offer. The Western zones welcomed it as a political necessity (including the French zone, although the Trizone of all three zones was not legally formed until April 1949).

The integration of the three zones into the ERP run by the OEEC (Organisation for European Economic Co-operation) took important decisions away from the occupying powers. This move marked another step in widening the gap between the east and the west of the country.

By 1951 Germany had been given $1.5 billion out of the $12.7 billion of the Marshall Plan. This investment was to prove to be the spark for economic recovery and paved the way for currency reform.

Currency reform: the creation of the *Deutsche Mark*

It was becoming increasingly clear that it was only possible to sustain hopes of economic revival by reforming the currency. The German currency, the *Reichsmark*, had been severely distorted by Nazi policies and the effects of the war, and so in the years after 1945 it was not the base for economic stability, because:

- The financing of the war had created inflation and there was far too much money in circulation for the few goods that were available.
- The inflation was hidden by the state-regulated economy of the Nazis, which continued as the Allies tried to control prices, wages, production and rations.
- The loss of real value of the German *Reichsmark* had led to a thriving black market based on barter, which was reckoned to amount to nearly one-half of economic activity in the Western zones.

These financial problems were seen as a main barrier to production and trade, and the quickest and most efficient solution was to introduce a new hard currency in which the Germans and their trading partners could trust again.

The introduction of a new currency had not only economic implications, but also profound political ones: it would be opposed by the Soviets, for instance, which would fundamentally divide Germany (see pages 298–302). Nevertheless, despite reservations, the German Economic Council decided to go ahead, very much backed by the Americans. Indeed, the new banknotes and coins were produced in the USA and sent to the *Bank Deutscher Länder* (later the Bundesbank) under the strictest secrecy in order to avoid financial disturbance and to present the Soviets as much as possible with a *fait accompli*.

The new *Deutsche Mark* (DM) was introduced on 20 June 1948 to all three of the Western zones and to the western sectors of the city of Berlin. They gave every German DM60 at a rate of one new DM for each *Reichsmark* of the old currency; they also revalued wages, pensions, rents and property at exactly the same level. However, savings in banks were exchanged at a different rate of 100 *Reichsmark* to DM6.50. At the same time, the markets in the Western zones were largely freed from state regulations by a law passed in the German Economic Council, so prices were set by supply and demand.

On one level the introduction of the DM was a really painful cut, since it was in effect a major devaluation. Small savers, as in 1923, lost out once again, whereas industrialists, shareowners and landowners were protected. Nevertheless, the new currency had a liberating effect because:

- The black market collapsed almost immediately and goods returned to the legal market.

- Hard work was encouraged and workers' absenteeism plummeted.
- It stimulated business to increase production and selling.
- It complemented the Marshall Plan and resurrected trade.

The currency reform was an undoubted success. It seemed almost immediately to liberate the economy, and the German people could almost see the effects in the streets. A US banker wrote: 'The spirit of the country changed overnight. The gray, hungry, dead-looking figures wandering about the streets in their everlasting search for food came to life.' In statistical terms, it is estimated that by the end of 1948 the index of industrial production had increased so much that there were inflationary pressures. Moreover, the political effects of the creation of the DM were profound indeed. The Soviets were taken completely by surprise and it prompted a major international crisis over Berlin.

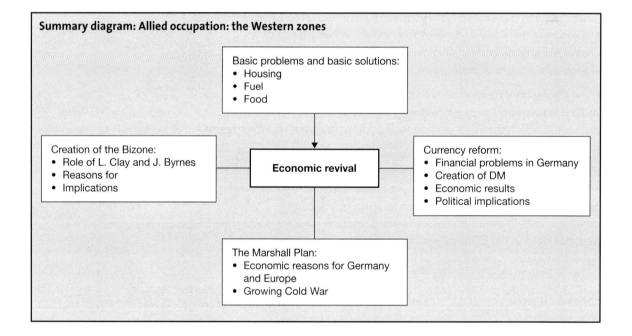

Summary diagram: Allied occupation: the Western zones

Basic problems and basic solutions:
- Housing
- Fuel
- Food

Creation of the Bizone:
- Role of L. Clay and J. Byrnes
- Reasons for
- Implications

Economic revival

Currency reform:
- Financial problems in Germany
- Creation of DM
- Economic results
- Political implications

The Marshall Plan:
- Economic reasons for Germany and Europe
- Growing Cold War

 # The division of Germany

▶ *What was the Soviet purpose of the Berlin blockade and what were its effects?*

In the short term, the decision of the Western Allies to push through the currency reform was the direct cause of the Berlin crisis in 1948–9. For the Soviets this measure was seen as a deliberate attempt by the Western Allies to undermine the Soviet zone and contrary to the unanimity of the ACC. Therefore, immediate plans were made for introducing their own new currency

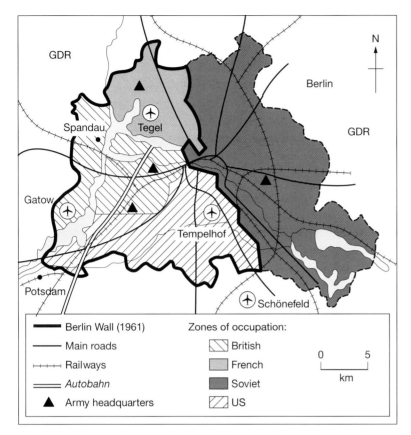

Figure 8.2 Berlin 1945–61. Like the rest of Germany, its old capital Berlin had been divided into four sectors by the Allied Powers in 1945 (see pages 274–5) and they agreed to co-ordinate the administration for Berlin and rule it together. Each sector was placed under the control of one power. As Berlin was in the east of Germany, the Western Allies could only reach it by passing through the Soviet zone and access was only possible to West Berlin by four roads, two railways and three air-corridors.

for the whole of the Soviet zone (including the western sectors of Berlin), known as the *Ostmark*. A more serious response to this Western action was the decision of the Soviet authorities from 24 June 1948 to block all access by road, rail and canal to West Berlin, as well as cutting water, power and food supplies from the Soviet zone. West Berlin had become an isolated island within the Soviet zone.

The Berlin airlift

The Soviets hoped by this blockade not only to pressurise the Western Allies into giving up their plans for the new currency, but also to make the three powers surrender the western sectors of Berlin. However, the vast majority of West Berliners wanted to stay part of the Western zones, and the Western Allies were determined not to lose control of their sectors. Therefore, the Berlin crisis really became the first major flashpoint of the Cold War. Stalin wanted to use the blockade to exert his influence over the whole of Berlin and to regain the political initiative over Germany. The Americans simply did not want to lose their presence in the city.

In desperation, the population of West Berlin found a strong advocate in General Clay, who started to organise an airlift which flew through the air-corridors across the Soviet zone to bring basic supplies into West Berlin. This action was quite legal according to the Potsdam agreement and in effect it meant that the supplies could only be stopped by the Soviets shooting down the British and US planes.

The Berlin airlift, as it became known, was essentially a logistical operation, and over eleven months:

- it carried out 279,000 flights, one every minute at its peak
- it provided 2.3 million tons of food and supplies (7000 tons daily to West Berlin)
- it supplied 1.5 million tons of coal.

The blockade ended on 12 May 1949 when the Soviets realised it was useless to carry on with it. There had been human costs, 76 aircrew lost their lives in 24 plane crashes, but the *Rosinenbomber* (raisin bombers), as the people affectionately called them, had allowed West Berlin to survive the winter. The commitment of the Western Allies was crucial for the morale of West Berliners, who gratefully joked: 'Better to be occupied by the Americans than liberated by the Soviets.' Even more significantly, the Berlin airlift reinforced the growing integration between the Germans in the Western zones with the Western occupied powers. Yet, the Berlin crisis had only been solved in the short term: there remained a serious long-term problem for the status of the city (see pages 387–9).

Two Germanys

The consequences of the dramatic months of the Berlin crisis were really the opposite of what the Soviets had hoped for. They lost a lot of credibility with the German population, while the blockade had brought the Western Allies and the majority of Germans together as friends rather than enemies. Berlin was officially divided, with West and East sectors creating their own mayors and administrations, while the whole of Germany itself was politically split (until 1990) by the creation of two new states:

- Federal Republic of Germany (FRG) on 23 May 1949 (BRD, Bundesrepublik Deutschland).
- German Democratic Republic (GDR) on 7 October 1949 (DDR, Deutsche Demokratische Republik).

The Berlin crisis was really just the occasion, not the fundamental cause of creating two Germanys in 1949. Indeed, from 1945 it seems that the chances of establishing a united Germany were unlikely. That is not to say that the political division cemented by 1949 had been inevitable, but the unfolding of events between 1945 and 1949 increasingly narrowed the chances of politically uniting Germany.

In particular, it is clear that several crucial economic decisions had really created the basis for separated political entities. On the one hand, the Western Allies decided to:

- stop paying reparations to the USSR in response to Soviet failure to fulfil their obligations, May 1946 (see page 295)
- create the Bizone, January 1947 (see pages 295–6)
- introduce the Marshall Plan, June 1947 (see page 296)
- create the DM, June 1948 (see page 297).

And on the other hand, the Soviets decided in their zone to:

- nationalise industry and land reform, 1945–6 (see page 290)
- establish a German Economic Conference, June 1947 (see page 291)
- create the *Ostmark* currency, June 1948 (see page 299).

The economic division of Germany was becoming ever more apparent by 1947 and when the Cold War inflamed the atmosphere, the development of political institutions was driven further forward, particularly by the Americans and British.

SOURCE H

What is the political message behind the caricature in Source H?

'The Ballast'. A cartoon by Kurt Poltiniak from 1949. This cartoon shows Federal Chancellor Adenauer and Federal President Heuss, influenced by the USA, throwing overboard the common interests of the whole of Germany in order to make the balloon (West Germany) rise.

The creation of the FRG

Political partition was obviously accelerating by the end of 1947. When a foreign ministers council failed in London in late 1947, the Americans and the British were prepared to start establishing a democratic West German state which amalgamated with the French zone. As a result, even a few days before the currency reform and the start of the Berlin crisis, a London Six Power Conference of the Western Allies and the Benelux states (Belgium, Netherlands and Luxembourg) met from 20 April to 6 June 1948. It agreed on the outline of a new federal state in West Germany to be set up by the *Länder*. The Parliamentary Council of 65 delegates provided the legal framework for the new state, which was officially called the *Grundgesetz* ('basic law'). It was ratified in May 1949 by the three occupying powers and the *Länder* parliaments from West Germany. On 23 May 1949 it became law. The new capital was to be Bonn, a small provincial town on the Rhine, a symbolic contrast to the old imperial Berlin.

The creation of the GDR

Although the Soviets pushed through the fundamental economic reforms in terms of land and property ownership as early as 1945, it is probably fair to say, in the words of M. Fulbrook, that the foundation of the GDR arose 'in response to, and lagging behind, developments in the West'. Indeed, while the authorities in the Western zones were carrying on their plans to establish a West German state during the 'Berlin crisis', the Soviets and the SED leadership were unwilling to go as far as creating an East German state. A new constitution was only drawn up at the end of May 1949 after the creation of the FRG, and it was only after the BRD elections and the formation of the first government under Adenauer that the SED created a provisional government and announced the creation of the GDR in the Soviet zone on 7 October 1949. The president of the new state was the communist Wilhelm Pieck and the prime minister was Otto Grotewohl, the ex-leader of the SPD from the Soviet zone. Two states had finally come into existence.

Table 8.5 Summary of the divided Germany

	West Germany	East Germany
German title	BRD, Bundesrepublik Deutschland	DDR, Deutsche Demokratische Republik
English title	FRG, Federal Republic of Germany	GDR, German Democratic Republic
Capital	Bonn	Berlin (East)
Date of creation	23 May 1949	7 October 1949
First leaders	Chancellor: Konrad Adenauer 1949–63	President: Wilhelm Pieck 1949–60
	President: Theodor Heuss 1949–59	Prime minister: Otto Grotewohl 1949–60
		SED party leader: Walter Ulbricht 1946–71
Status	Parliamentary democratic federal republic	In effect, one-party communist republic

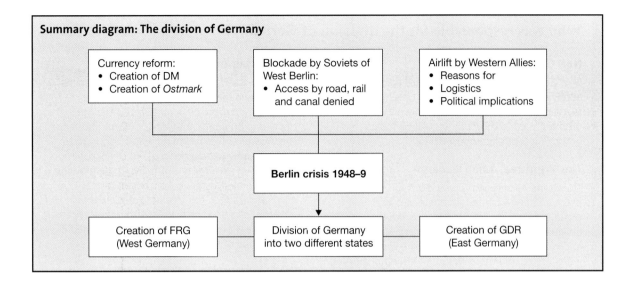

Summary diagram: The division of Germany

Currency reform:
- Creation of DM
- Creation of *Ostmark*

Blockade by Soviets of West Berlin:
- Access by road, rail and canal denied

Airlift by Western Allies:
- Reasons for
- Logistics
- Political implications

Berlin crisis 1948–9

Creation of FRG (West Germany)

Division of Germany into two different states

Creation of GDR (East Germany)

Conclusion: the creation of two Germanys

▶ *Who was responsible for the creation of two Germanys in 1949?*

Before Hitler's war of 1939 the division of Germany was totally unthinkable, so the primary responsibility for that division lay with those Germans who supported an unjustified war. Once defeated, the capacity of Germans to control events was lost and it meant that the Allies could exert their influence over future developments.

Yet, the emerging ideological gulf between the Western Allies and the Soviets (even before the end of the war) meant that Germany was split right in the middle. All attempts at co-operation gave way to growing confrontation, making the occupying powers increasingly set on stabilising and securing their respective zones of influence. Nevertheless, by 1947, in the changing international climate of the Cold War, it was the Americans and British who united to take the initiative to create a western German state. Moreover, even if the German people still had hopes for a united Germany after the war, it seems that the German political leaders were in fact moving towards increasing co-operation with their respective allies. The eventual division of Germany is summed up in the words of P. O'Dochartaigh: 'Ultimately, both chose to settle for half a cake baked to their own preferred recipe. The respective recipes had been supplied by the occupying forces.'

Who was responsible for the division of Germany?

Nazi Germany

Nazi Germany had been responsible for initiating and waging the war of 1939–45. It was Germany's failed policy of military expansionism that ultimately led to the victorious Allied forces occupying central Europe in 1945.

The 'Big Three' Allied leaders

The Grand Alliance was created out of extraordinary wartime circumstances with just the initial aims of national defence and the defeat of Nazi Germany. Despite the conferences at Yalta and Potsdam, the agreements of the 'Big Three' were limited and there was no permanent solution to the 'German problem'. This was because of ideological differences and the Allies' own vested economic and political interests.

Stalin and the Soviets

The Soviets wanted to exploit all the economic potential of Germany to pay for the cost of the war. Also, they were determined to secure their safety by creating a major buffer for the USSR in eastern Europe. This was achieved by the belt of satellite states such as Poland and Czechoslovakia.

Truman and US 'containment'

US perceptions (rightly or wrongly) of Soviet policies became more hostile in 1946–7. In declaring the Truman doctrine and the Marshall Plan, the president committed the USA to a global foreign policy of 'containment', which had serious implications for the zones in Germany. The USA would:

- aid the reconstruction of the West German economy (on the basis of capitalism)
- use its troops to actively defend western Germany from any threat of Soviet expansionism beyond the iron curtain.

Consequently, the American position had made the chance of restoring German unity very unlikely.

Zonal disagreements

From the start, the Allies were in a way 'victims' of their own misperceptions and this made co-operation more difficult because the ACC depended on unanimous decisions. Additionally, the Western Allies found it increasingly hard to agree on how to bear the costs of the occupation. By late 1946, in an attempt to avoid the growing chaos, the military governors began to act more and more in the interests of their own governments and the people within their zones. This move was most obviously demonstrated in the creation of the Bizone.

Post-war German politicians

Between 1945 and 1949 German political leaders were quite prepared to work with the Allies who shared their political and economic objectives, at the expense of German unity:

- Ulbricht and the SED leadership could only really envisage a united Germany under a communist model.
- In the Western zones, the CDU leaders Adenauer and Erhard became increasingly committed to a partial German state which was capitalist and pro-Western.

If the German political forces had really been committed to German unity they might have achieved a way forward. Instead, the famous conference of representatives of all German *Länder* in Munich in May 1947 failed even to find a common agenda.

Key debate

▶ *Why was divided Germany the focus of the Cold War in 1945–9?*

The division of Germany in the years 1945–9 had never been envisaged and yet it proved to be one of the most significant developments in twentieth-century history:

- It brought an end to the German national state created in 1871, which was not to be re-created until the reunification of 1990.
- It resulted in the joint control of central Europe by the USA and the USSR.
- It became the initial focus of the Cold War, which was to last for 40 years.

Traditional orthodox: Soviet ideology and aggression

From the division of Germany many historians from the West, such as H. Feis and W.H. McNeil in the 1950s and 1960s, upheld the prevailing view that it was a clear result of Stalin's aggressive and expansionist foreign policy. They argued that it was part of the Soviets' broad ambitions to create a major security buffer, which they had arguably achieved through the belt of satellite states such as Poland and Czechoslovakia. They also wanted to exploit all the economic potential of Germany and to secure the establishment of a Soviet-style socialist regime. A.M. Schlesinger claims:

EXTRACT I

From A.M. Schlesinger Jr, 'Foreign Affairs XLVI Foreign Affairs (Oct 1967)', quoted in E.P. Hoffmann and F.J. Fleron, editors, *The Conduct of Soviet Foreign Policy*, Walter de Gruyere, 1980, pp. 248–9.

… The fundamental explanation of the speed with which the Cold War escalated lies precisely in the fact that the Soviet Union was not a traditional national state. This is where the 'mirror image', invoked by some psychologists, falls down. For the Soviet Union was a phenomenon very different from America and Britain: it was a totalitarian state, endowed with an all-explanatory, all-consuming ideology, committed to the infallibility of government and party, still in a somewhat messianic mood, equating dissent with treason, and ruled by a dictator who, for all his extraordinary abilities, had his paranoid moments.

Marxism–Leninism gave the Russian leaders a view of the world according to which all societies were inexorably destined to proceed along appointed roads by appointed stages until they achieved the classless nirvana. Moreover, given the resistance of the capitalists to this development, the existence of any non-communist state was by definition a threat to the Soviet Union.

According to Schlesinger in Extract I what was the reason for the rapid escalation of the Cold War?

 KEY TERM

Marxism–Leninism
The political ideology of the USSR adopted under Stalin.

That perception has continued to be upheld by some more recent historians. In his book *Stalin's Drive to the West, 1938–45*, R.C. Raack still claimed that Stalin was set on spreading international Marxism and 'the Soviets were intending to annex land and to use German communists to take over all of Germany'.

Revisionist: US economic and military expansion

Of course, pro-Soviet historians had portrayed the stance of the USSR as necessary in defence against US imperialism, for example, B. Ponomaryov, *The Official History of the USSR* (1960). Yet, in the late 1960s and 1970s a number of Western historians, writing in the context of the unpopular Vietnam War, also turned the blame on the USA for the division of Europe and the world for its own global economic ambitions.

Leading historians, such as G. Kolko and W. LaFeber, have therefore argued that the insatiable demands of capitalism had resulted in the unlimited expansion of US economic influence overseas. For this reason, the USA could not tolerate Soviet interests in eastern Europe and Germany.

Post-revisionist views

In the 1980s the blame mentality of the previous 40 years gave way to a more balanced objective approach.

Scholars looked for multi-causal factors which led to the division of Europe. D. Yergin wrote: 'For how do you blame a single man – whether Stalin, Churchill or Truman – for so complicated a phenomenon, involving events in so many different countries and so many different levels. Of course, it was hard to restrict the impulse during the years when the antagonism was at its sharpest, but perhaps time has liberated us from the need to apportion blame in the course of explanation.'

Western zones took the lead to divide Germany

It has been long known that ACC effective policy making for the whole of Germany was vey difficult because the Allies depended on unanimous decisions. However, with the opening of British, US and French archives of the zones in the 1980s, sources revealed how far the military governors of the Western zones acted in the interests of their own governments and the German people under their control within their zones. Consequently, Rolf Steininger claimed that really it was the Western powers that had precipitated the real division of Germany. Eisenberg reiterates and develops this further.

EXTRACT 2

From C. Eisenberg, *Drawing the Line: The American Decision to Divide Germany, 1944–9*, Cambridge University Press, 1996, pp. 484–93.

Though long forgotten, the Americans and British had initiated all the formal steps towards separation. In violation of the quadripartite framework established at Yalta and Potsdam, they had opted to fuse their two zones economically (December 1946), to incorporate western Germany in the Marshall Plan (July 1947), to implement a separate currency reform (June 1948), and to convene a Parliamentary Council for the establishment of a West German state (September 1948). In each instance, there was some equivalent

According to Eisenberg, in Extract 2 in what ways was the USA responsible for the division of Germany?

move in the eastern zone. Yet, the pattern of US-British action and Soviet response was a consistent one …

The oppressive internal policies of the Soviet Union that were gradually imposed upon the population of East Germany were not the source of the post war schism. In the aftermath of victory, what produced that unwanted result was an ambitious American agenda … Had American officials been more flexible and sought a compromise solution in occupied Germany, it is possible that the Soviets would have blocked or overturned it. But this is something we cannot know since the United States selected a different course. In the wreckage of the Cold War, America has yet to acknowledge responsibility for the structures that it built.

Post-1989 views

The **fall of the Berlin Wall** and the collapse of the USSR completely changed the historical context. Moreover, historians for the first time had access to many more archives in the GDR and in the USSR and have questioned the nature of and extent of communist aims for Germany after 1945.

The role of Ulbricht and the SED

Quite controversially, W. Loth's analysis in his book *Stalin's Unwanted Child* (1998) claims that Stalin never wanted a separate state from the Soviet zone, or any socialist state in Germany at all. He wanted to secure or restore German unity and was ready to accept a neutral Germany, and even a Western-style democracy. In Stalin's defence, he highlights the crucial role of Ulbricht in the division of the country.

> **EXTRACT 3**
>
> **From W. Loth, *Stalin's Unwanted Child: The Soviet Union, The German Question and Founding of the GDR*, Macmillan, 1998, pp. 171–4.**
>
> *In the first decade after the war many hundreds of independent witnesses confirm that Stalin strove for a democratic post-war Germany – a Germany democratic according to Western standards … At no point could Stalin imagine that the occupation forces would remain in Germany permanently …*
>
> *Walter Ulbricht, however, must be regarded as the person mainly responsible for the real existing socialism in the GDR … The GDR is inconceivable without him … he was in fact a revolutionary in his own right – one driven by a mixture of ideological sense of mission and thirst for power … That he believed himself to be in agreement with Stalin, did not hinder him from actually pursuing his own course – by interpreting instructions from Moscow in his own way, by accepting stimulus from the SMAD in so far as it fitted into his concept, and by using the frequent vagueness of Moscow's signals in order to introduce his own influence.*

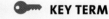

KEY TERM

Fall of the Berlin Wall
The symbolic turning point on 9 November 1989 for the breakdown of the GDR, which led to German reunification and the eventual collapse of the USSR (1991).

What reasons does Loth give in Extract 3 for holding Ulbricht, rather than Stalin, mainly responsible for the division of Germany?

Soviet aims and policies

In contrast, other historians who have examined records in Russia have reviewed the Soviet role in Germany's division. On the one hand, C. Kennedy-Pipes has emphasised that 'the dominant concern of the Soviet leadership was the security and survival of the new Soviet state'. She does not see ideology as being the basis of Soviet foreign policy; its major concern was to limit the revival of German power and to win US co-operation in that aim.

On the other hand, N. Naimark in his book *The Russians in Germany* (1997) has highlighted what he sees as the haziness of Soviet behaviour. He believes that the Soviets did not have 'specific long-range goals in mind' when occupying Germany. Indeed, he concludes that Soviet leaders were never able to square their divergent strategies '… the Sovietisation of the Eastern zone, the creation of unified Germany run by the SED, or the establishment of a demilitarised "neutral" Germany in the centre of Europe remained unreconciled during the period of the occupation'.

Chapter summary

The impact of Germany's military defeat was immense: politically, economically and socially. Moreover, Allied plans at Yalta and Potsdam were limited – and shaped by the differences between the superpowers. The four years 1945–9 which resulted in the division of Germany were totally unpredictable and were to set the tone for 40 years of German history (even world history).

The Nazi state was convincingly destroyed, yet there were clear limits to the de-Nazifying purge (especially in the Western zones). In its place a non-Nazi political life actually revived quickly, although different interpretations over decentralisation and democratisation soon emerged. Most significantly, there were profound differences in the social and economic aims in the zones in 1946–7. The Soviet zone pressed ahead with nationalisation and land reform, whereas the creation of the Bizone in the US and British zones offered a more liberal capitalist economic system. In the end, the move by the Western zones for currency reform and the creation of the *Deutsche Mark* resulted in the Soviets' blockade of Berlin, which impeded any chance of German unity and established two very different German states in 1949.

Refresher questions

Use these questions to remind yourself of the key material covered in this chapter.

1 Why do you think Germans saw 1945 as a 'zero hour'?

2 Why was there no peace settlement in Germany in 1945?

3 Were the Nuremberg trials more like 'show trials'?

4 How successful was de-Nazification?

5 How did the Allies differ over decentralisation?

6 How did democratisation affect German politics in the Western zones?

7 What were the aims of the 'Ulbricht group'?

8 How and why did the SED become the dominant political party in the Soviet zone?

9 Did the Soviets achieve their social and economic aims in their zone?

10 How well did the Western Allies cope with the problems in Germany after the war?

11 Why was the Bizone created?

12 What were the aims and effects of the Marshall Plan?

13 Was the currency reform a total success?

14 Was the Soviet decision to blockade Berlin a mistake?

15 Who was responsible for the division of Germany?

 Question practice

ESSAY QUESTIONS

1 How successful was the policy of the Four Ds in Germany between 1945 and 1949?

2 Assess the consequences for Germany of the currency reform.

3 Which of the following was more important for economic stability in post-war Germany? i) The Marshall Plan. ii) The creation of the *Deutsche Mark*. Explain your answer with reference to both i) and ii).

4 To what extent do you agree with the view that the 'Berlin blockade was responsible for the division of Germany in 1949'?

INTERPRETATION QUESTION

1 Read the interpretation and then answer the question that follows. '... the Americans and British had initiated all the formal steps towards separation.' (From C. Eisenberg, *Drawing the Line: The American Decision to Divide Germany, 1944–9*, 1994.) Evaluate the strengths and limitations of this interpretation about the division of Germany, making reference to other interpretations that you have studied.

West Germany 1949–63

From its very creation, the challenges were immense for West Germany, yet it made rapid progress because of its strong political leadership and the commitment of the people. The purpose of this chapter is to consider how successfully the new democratic state in West Germany, the FRG, developed in its early years. The main themes are:

★ The Bonn Republic

★ Party politics

★ The 'economic miracle'

★ West German society

★ Foreign relations

★ Adenauer's final years

Key dates

1949	May 23	Basic Law came into force; FRG set up
	Sept. 15	Konrad Adenauer elected chancellor following the first *Bundestag* election
	Nov.	Petersberg agreement
1951	April	Creation of the European Coal and Steel Community
1952	Aug. 21	Death of Schumacher
1952	May	European Defence Community treaty agreed (but later rejected by French parliament)
1954	Oct.	Paris Treaties signed and later approved
1955	May	FRG became a sovereign state
1955		FRG joined NATO
	Nov. 12	Basic Law amended by the *Bundestag* to create the *Bundeswehr* (Federal Army)
1957	March	Treaty of Rome signed creating the European Economic Community
	Sept. 15	Adenauer re-elected for his third term with a CDU/CSU overall majority
1959	Nov.	Godesberg programme of SPD confirmed
1961	Aug. 13	Berlin Wall started
1962	Oct.–Nov.	*Der Spiegel* affair
1963	Oct. 15	Resignation of Adenauer

1 The Bonn Republic

▶ *What did the fathers of the FRG constitution learn from the Weimar constitution?*

▶ *In what ways did the new constitution help to stabilise the development of democracy in the FRG?*

The new constitution

At the London Six Power Conference in 1948 (see page 302) it was decided to draft a new constitution for a West German state, which was then quickly implemented, with two caveats:

- First, the new constitution was to remain under the strict control of the Western occupying powers, as outlined by the **Occupation Statute**.
- Secondly, the new constitution was to be drawn up by a parliamentary council of 65 delegates from the *Länder*, not by an elected constituent assembly (as it had been in January 1919).

Clearly, the fathers of the new constitution were very much aware of the past – the failure of Weimar, the rise of the Nazis – and of the present emerging threat of communism. Their aim was to create a stable and strong democracy that could not be overthrown. In their eyes, the Weimar state had enabled Hitler to come to power and then undermine democracy while seemingly staying within the legal constitutional framework. Accordingly, the new framework was meant in many respects to be made safer and to fend off future threats from the right or left.

When the FRG was founded in May 1949, the new constitution was recognised as a provisional arrangement called the **Basic Law** (*Grundgesetz*). The preamble to the 'law' spoke to all people of German descent including those resident in former German territories under Polish or Soviet rule, as they too were entitled to FRG citizenship. A key point of the Basic Law was that it could be changed when all parts of Germany were reunited. It should be noted that the FRG claimed to be the only legal successor to the Weimar Republic and the Basic Law was seen to be fundamentally built on Weimar's constitutional framework (see pages 15–20). Both were federal, parliamentary, democratic and republican, but with several significant differences.

Rights

The new constitution placed special emphasis on human and civil rights. They were seen as even standing above constitutional laws, and were 'inalienable' (a term also used in the US constitution). In contrast, in Weimar those rights had only been listed within the constitutional framework and could be suspended or abolished by a two-thirds majority in parliament.

KEY TERMS

Occupation Statute
The roles and responsibilities drawn up by the USA, Britain and France in 1949 for the newly created FRG, which remained in place until it became a sovereign German state in 1955. (A sovereign state is one which has the full right to govern itself.)

Basic Law *Grundgesetz*. Technically, the document approved in May 1949 was *not* a constitution, as it was not permanent because the founding fathers wanted to have the flexibility to amend it if and when Germany became reunified. Thus, all the terms had the features of a constitution but it was called the Basic Law.

KEY TERMS

Federal president
Bundespräsident. The head of state.

Bundestag The 'federal assembly' or 'lower house' of the FRG parliament. It claimed to be the successor to the *Reichstag*.

The head of state

The powers of the **federal president** were dramatically diminished to mainly representative functions, his or her term in office was reduced from seven to five years, and he or she was only re-electable for one further term. The president was chosen by a special assembly made up of all the members of the **Bundestag**, and an equal number of members elected by the *Länder* parliaments. In contrast, in Weimar, the people had elected the president, who came to be seen as a 'substitute Kaiser' with far-reaching political powers (see page 69) such as influence over the appointment of the chancellor and the use of Article 48 to make law by decree (see pages 15 and 18).

Figure 9.1 West Germany was created as the FRG in May 1949. It was a democratic parliamentary republic, but with strong federal autonomy. The eleven federal states (*Länder*) elected their own provincial assemblies which sent representatives to the *Bundesrat*.

Parliament

The new constitution was like Weimar, with a two-tiered parliamentary structure made up of the *Bundestag* (the federal parliament) and the ***Bundesrat*** (the federal council). However, because the president's role could only be ceremonial, the chancellor had a clear line of authority, as he had to be elected by and solely responsible to the *Bundestag*. Moreover, unlike Weimar, where a *simple* vote of no confidence had regularly brought down a government and destabilised the political system, in the new constitution the *Bundestag* could only bring down the chancellor and his government by a so-called '*constructive* vote of no confidence'. This meant that the opposition not only required a majority supporting the vote of no confidence, but also had to be able to offer a stable positive majority for a new alternative government.

Electoral system

The new constitution upheld the **pluralism** of political parties as a necessity for a stable, functioning democracy. The constitution therefore prevented any abolition of them as had happened in Weimar. Also, the option for using direct votes on laws and other important issues (plebiscites or referendums) was not allowed by the new democracy. This was because the Third Reich had used such methods to manipulate the people.

Moreover, the electoral system was changed too. Weimar had been based on straightforward proportional representation (PR) (see page 17), which had led to many small parties in parliament, making it more difficult to form a coalition government. Instead, the rather complicated process introduced was the 'mixed-member PR', which allowed each voter to have two votes. Half the seats in the *Bundestag* would come from majority votes in the constituencies (first past the post); the other half from representatives nominated by the parties' lists (PR).

Additionally, in 1953 a five per cent hurdle was introduced for elections. So if any party won less than five per cent of the national vote, it was barred from parliament. In these ways the electoral system was geared to favour the larger parties at the expense of the smaller ones, in the hope of establishing more stable coalitions.

Supreme court and democratic rights

Although Weimar had created the idea of a supreme court, its judiciary had not been wholly sympathetic to democracy (see pages 17 and 39). The new constitution went much further to protect its values. A new agency was created with the right to investigate and prevent any anti-democratic activities from left or right in the FRG. Together with the FRG's new **constitution court**, these measures were intended to fend off possible threats to democracy.

 **KEY TERMS**

Bundesrat The 'federal council' or upper house of the German parliament. Its members were appointed by members of the *Länder* governments.

Pluralism The idea that *democratic* parties are an essential part of the constitution and cannot be abolished (Article 20). However, in the second paragraph of this article it states that if a party acts or aims against the constitution and is anti-democratic it can be banned.

Constitution court *Bundesverfassungsgericht*. The main task is to review judicial cases and rule whether they are unconstitutional.

Table 9.1 The Weimar and West German constitutions compared

	Weimar constitution	Basic Law of the FRG
Rights	• Possible to suspend by constitutional legislation	• Inalienable and standing above the constitution
Head of state	*Reichspräsident* • Extensive powers: to dissolve the *Reichstag*, to appoint and dismiss the government, to pass emergency decrees without parliamentary consent • Direct election by the people for seven years: re-election always possible	*Bundespräsident* • Mainly ceremonial functions • Very limited powers in the case of emergencies • Elected by parliament and special representatives for five years: only one re-election possible
Parliament	*Reichstag* • Able to bring down the chancellor's government by a simple vote of no confidence • Main legislative power (in normal times)	*Bundestag* • Approved the chancellor • Able to take control of the government through the 'constructive vote of no confidence' • Participated in the election of the head of state and federal court judges
	Reichsrat • Only able to delay bills passed in the *Reichstag*	*Bundesrat* • Participated in legislation in assenting acts • Participated in the election of the federal court judges
Government	National government (*Reichsregierung*) • Weak position: chancellor and ministers dependent on the president and the *Reichstag* • Chancellor quite easily removed from office by a simple vote of no confidence by the *Reichstag* or dismissed by the president	Federal government (*Bundesregierung*) • Strong position: chancellor solely responsible to the *Bundestag* • Chancellor only removed from office by a 'constructive vote of no confidence' in the *Bundestag* (to guarantee stability/continuity)
Electoral system	• Right of existence for political parties, not fixed in the constitution • Plebiscites and referendums allowed • Pure proportional representation system in *Reichstag* (leading to many parties in the *Reichstag* and making it more difficult to form a government)	• Party pluralism defined in the constitution as essential to democracy • Plebiscites and referendums not allowed • Mixed-member proportional representation with a five per cent hurdle in *Bundestag* elections (leading to fewer parties in the *Bundestag* and more stability)

In the 1950s various parties and organisations were judged as threatening to the democracy, and banned. These included:

- The right-wing Socialist Reich Party (SRP) in 1951.
- Eleven communist organisations, most notably the Free German Youth in 1950.
- The League of German Youth (an extreme right-wing group) in 1953.
- Most controversially, the Communist Party, which gained 2.2 per cent in the 1953 elections but no representatives, was banned after a long legal case in 1956.

Evaluation of the Basic Law

In many respects, the Basic Law successfully laid the basis for the FRG to create a stable democracy in the 1950s. Of course, it is easy to say that the Germans 'learned' from the mistakes of Weimar, but it should be remembered that the political and socio-economic environment was much more favourable in the 1950s. First, West Germany experienced real economic growth and, secondly, it overcame its diplomatic isolation and soon found major friends and allies. These factors allowed the FRG to evolve more easily than Weimar in the 1920s.

A few critics on the political extremes have pointed to aspects of the constitution which suggested that the FRG was not so genuinely democratic; for example, the five per cent rule, and the banning of left- and right-wing extremists. Nevertheless, despite everything, the foundations of the new constitution and its cautious flexibility did create an effective democracy and the FRG was set to survive. Its federal structure and constitutional court particularly allowed the democracy to mature in the long term, most significantly in the way it embraced the eastern *Länder* in the political reunification of 1990.

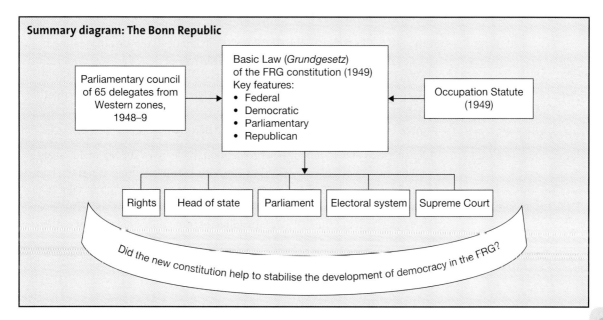

Summary diagram: The Bonn Republic

(2) Party politics

▶ *How did Adenauer and the CDU politically stabilise Germany in the 1950s?*

▶ *Why did the SPD remain in political isolation in the 1950s?*

At first sight, it was quite an achievement to draw up the new constitution and to make arrangements for the FRG's first *Bundestag* election within four years of 1945. Furthermore, it can be seen in Table 9.2 that the votes of the three major parties were a strong endorsement of the democratic process, which showed the German people's general acceptance of the new state.

Table 9.2 Results of the 1949 *Bundestag* election

Party	Percentage of vote	Number of seats
CDU/CSU	31.0	139
SPD	29.2	131
FDP	11.9	52
Communist	5.7	22
Others	22.2	65

The election results did not so easily provide the basis for creating an effective government. The fourth largest party was the Communist Party, which polled 5.7 per cent. Perhaps more significantly, the remaining 22.2 per cent of the vote for the first *Bundestag* was won by a diverse range of regional and splinter groups. All in all, eleven parties and two independent members got into parliament, some with distinctly right-wing leanings. In 1949 six of the parties gained less than five per cent of the votes, but still won seats before the hurdle was introduced in 1953.

Although the left wing of the CDU was sympathetic to the idea of creating a great coalition with the SPD, Adenauer, the leader of the CDU, was determined to form a small coalition with the FDP and one of the smaller parties. The reasoning behind this decision was the significant differences between the CDU and SPD over economic and foreign policy, over which Adenauer did not really want to compromise (see pages 318–19 and 321–2).

Adenauer was able to put together a coalition made up of 208 out of 402 seats, not a really comfortable majority, but one with a strong common working basis. On 15 September 1949 in the *Bundestag*, Adenauer was elected chancellor of the first government with a majority of just one: including his own vote! Theodor Heuss, the leader of the FDP, was invited to become the first president of the FRG.

Konrad Adenauer

1876	Born in Cologne and trained as a lawyer
1917–33	Elected mayor of Cologne, but removed from office by the Nazis
1945	Co-founder of the CDU
1948	Elected president of the Parliamentary Council which drew up the foundations for the FRG
1949	Elected to the German *Bundestag* and chosen as Germany's first federal chancellor
1949–63	Chancellor of Germany. Re-elected in 1953, 1957 and 1961. (In addition, he served as foreign minister 1951–5)
1955	FRG became a sovereign state and joined NATO
1962	*Der Spiegel* affair
1963	Resigned as chancellor at the age of 87
1967	Died at his villa near Bonn and was granted a state funeral

Adenauer joined the original ZP in Imperial Germany and his political framework was shaped by his strong Catholicism. His moral integrity was proved by his refusal to co-operate with the Nazis, despite suffering persecution. He was a strong-willed character and, as a strong anti-communist, he was determined to follow what he saw as the only possible course for West Germany: namely, to gain the trust of the occupying powers and to lead the country into a strong alliance with the West.

Although in 1949 Adenauer was already 73 years old, he won four elections for his party, the CDU, and stayed in his position of power for fourteen years. Together with Erhard, minister of finance, he instigated the success story of the 'economic miracle' and led West Germany into the European Economic Community (see page 339). By the mid-1950s his single-minded pro-Western course and his refusal to believe in the possibility of a reunited neutral and free Germany during the Cold War brought him disapproval from the opposition. He was criticised for being a 'chancellor of the Allies' and for sacrificing Germany's national interests. Nevertheless, he continued to block all possibilities for negotiations with the East on their terms.

In his final years in office this obstinate attitude and his rigid style of government brought him increasing criticism, even from within his own party. Unable to read the signs of change in national and international politics and not wanting to let go of his power, he was finally forced to resign in 1963.

Adenauer may have outstayed his time in office but it was under his leadership that the country recovered from the Nazi dictatorship, built Europe's strongest economy and gained a leading role in Europe. The 'old man' became the political father and most influential leader of the emerging young democracy of West Germany. At his death in 1967 his state funeral was attended by every international key figure.

Adenauer and the CDU 1949–63

With hindsight it is all too easy to assume that the story of the 'Adenauer era' was bound to unfold. Yet, many contemporaries had limited faith in Adenauer's government to survive. It was felt that the difficulties in creating the government could lead to disagreements within the coalition and the withdrawal of partners. Also, the new government faced a range of problems:

- *Economic*. Despite the liberating effects of currency reform (see pages 297–8), the fledgling economy still faced difficulties and in 1949–50 it suffered a recession. Unemployment rose to 2 million, about thirteen per cent, and prices continued to rise.

- *Social.* There was an urgent need to build millions of houses to make up for the bombing and to accommodate the millions of refugees and expellees from eastern Europe.
- *Political.* The FRG was still under the control of the Occupation Statute and did not have sovereignty. Only the Allies could approve many aspects of government, such as trade and internal security. However, from this delicate political power base Adenauer and his party were to dominate and stabilise the FRG until the mid-1960s. He personally was to win four *Bundestag* elections and his leadership was to shape post-war Germany, as can be seen from Table 9.3.

Adenauer's aim

Adenauer identified himself as a supporter of Western liberal democracy and Catholic conservatism; very much in contrast to the atheism and planned economy of the socialist movement. In political terms, the coalition of the CDU and CSU proved itself successful in uniting a broad majority of conservative Christian middle-class voters.

Adenauer's aims in the 1950s were shaped by four major issues:

- Western integration
- the 'German question'
- economic policy
- social aspects.

Western integration

Like many West Germans, Adenauer mistrusted and feared the Soviets and consequently looked for protection from the West. He wanted to gain the trust of the Western powers in order to revise the restrictions of the Occupation Statute as quickly as possible and to become a reliable ally and strong economic partner.

The 'German question'

On the 'German question', Adenauer believed that the reunification of the FRG and the GDR had to be on the terms of maintaining a Western capitalist-orientated state. He publicly assured the people that although reunification was close to his heart, he was determined not to make any concessions to communism and that he saw other priorities first. He believed that if the FRG could achieve a Western partnership, not only would it secure the state against communism, it would also attract East Germans to join West Germany through their own volition. In a way, this **'magnet theory'** was a success, as nearly 3 million refugees left East Germany for the West before the closing of the frontiers with the building of the Berlin Wall in 1961 (see pages 387–90).

Economic policy

The economic history of Germany, 1914–45, was traumatic. So Adenauer and his finance minister, Ludwig Erhard, were determined to create economic stability

KEY TERM

'Magnet theory' The idea that the attraction of a free and prosperous West Germany would sooner or later draw East Germany irresistibly towards it.

for the new state in the wake of depression, war and the spread of communism. Certainly, the onset of the **Korean War**, 1950–3, spurred the German economy out of recession and into boom. This boom was also shaped by the economic reforms initiated by Erhard's 'social market' policy (see page 323), which aimed to create a free market, but one limited by social regulation from the state. This 'economic miracle' sustained years of major growth until the recession of 1966–7, and provided the economic context for the development of the FRG.

Social aspects

Adenauer recognised the need for the CDU/CSU to give more than economic growth. Above all, it needed to provide a social policy that would overcome the hardships of the poor and refugees through new social legislation, industrial peace and a quick growth in living standards. In that way, it was hoped to create a degree of social unity that would counter the threat of communism and put the privations of the German people behind them.

CDU political domination

In the second election of 1953 the CDU/CSU increased their share of the vote to 45.2 per cent, which, because of the complicated distribution of the seats in parliament, gave them an absolute majority of one seat (although Adenauer maintained the coalition with the FDP).

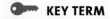 **KEY TERM**

Korean War The first armed confrontation of the Cold War in 1950–3. The FRG was not in a position to give military support, but the war did act as a major boon to the production of German goods.

Table 9.3 Bundestag elections

	August 1949	September 1953	September 1957	September 1961
Electorate (millions)	24.5	28.5	31.1	32.8
Turnout (%)	78.5	85.8	87.8	87.7
CDU/CSU				
Percentage	31.0	45.2	50.2	45.3
(seats)	(139)	(243)	(270)	(242)
SPD				
Percentage	29.2	28.8	31.8	36.2
(seats)	(131)	(151)	(169)	(190)
FDP				
Percentage	11.9	9.5	7.7	12.8
(seats)	(52)	(48)	(41)	(67)
KPD				
Percentage	5.7	2.2	–	–
(seats)	(15)	(0)		
Others				
Percentage	22.2	14.3	10.3	5.7
(seats)	(65)	(44)	(17)	(0)

SOURCE A

? How do you think the
poster in Source A was
meant to appeal to the
electorate? How could it
have added to the success
of the election?

Election poster for
the *Bundestag*. It
reads, 'With
Adenauer. For the
peace, freedom
and unity of
Germany choose
the CDU'.

In 1957 the successful election campaign with the leading slogan 'no
experiments' enabled Adenauer and the CDU/CSU to reach their high point,
which underlined the growing political stability:

- They gained an absolute majority of 50.2 per cent of the votes and the FDP
  did not join the government.
- Significantly, democratic participation improved markedly. In the first
  Bundestag election in 1949, 78.5 per cent of the electorate had gone to the
  polls, but by 1957 the issues raised in the election campaigns were met with
  more interest, which was to grow even further in the next two elections until
  the turnout reached 87.8 per cent.
- The small extremist splinter groups and parties in the first parliament, which
  seemed a possible danger to the new democracy, quickly disappeared; not
  only because of the introduction of the five per cent hurdle in 1953, but also
  because the big parties proved to be more inclusive and drew more voters
  from the extreme right and left.

Perhaps unsurprisingly, the success of the CDU is closely connected with the role of Adenauer and, indeed, the years 1949–63 have been called the 'Adenauer era'. In view of Germany's immediate past, the political domination of Adenauer and the CDU could have revoked old fears within the state and abroad. Yet the leadership of Adenauer proved to be very positive, not only in the eyes of most West Germans, but in those of the Western powers, too. Under the liberal-conservative governments in the 1950s the economy was stabilised, a balanced social security system established and the participation of the unions in industry enhanced and regulated. The early political and economic restrictions and control of the new state through the Western Allies were revised and turned into close co-operation and partnership.

Adenauer's early successes in the first half of the 1950s confirmed to his supporters that he had made the right decisions economically and politically by opting for a clear way West. He had also rejected temptations from the communists for a quick reunification process under the restricted conditions demanded by the Soviets. Even his opponents in the end had to admit grudgingly that their criticism and alternative ideas might have been misguided and impracticable in the context of the Cold War at the end of the 1950s.

SPD

When the SPD was reconstituted in the Western zones in 1945 it still held on to its old social democratic values. It considered itself to be a workers' party with its roots in Marxist ideology. In the light of the awful experiences of the Nazi state, the vast majority of the party were therefore committed to the nationalisation of the financial sector and key industries alongside the redistribution of large private property, as had happened in the Soviet zone.

The SPD argued that Erhard's social market economy plans were just liberal capitalism and therefore not in the interests of the majority, or were even a threat to the new democracy. The two different economic concepts became the key issue of the first election. The SPD's leader, Kurt Schumacher (see page 285), denounced Adenauer and Erhard's plans of fast-rising living standards and social security for everyone as unachievable and declared to the *Bundestag* that the 'CDU's promises were just a bag of lies'.

With regard to the 'German question' after 1945, the SPD saw itself as the only party which could serve the true interests of the whole of Germany. In 1946 it rejected a merger with the KPD, which it viewed as serving Stalin's interests rather than the development of a democratic and unified Germany.

The SPD was hostile to Adenauer's policy with the West (see the Petersberg agreement on page 339). They viewed *rapprochement* as a sell out which ruined any chance of negotiating with the Soviets to agree on a reunified, largely demilitarised and politically neutral Germany. In a heated debate about this issue, Schumacher mocked Adenauer as a 'chancellor of the Allies', for

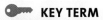

KEY TERM

Rapprochement
The re-establishing of cordial relations between two powers.

which he was suspended from parliament for twenty days. The charismatic Schumacher died unexpectedly in 1952 and was replaced by Erich Ollenhauer, a rather colourless character. The SPD, up against Adenauer, failed to engage the sympathies of more than one-third of the electorate, whereas the CDU went from strength to strength.

The limitations of the SPD are clear. Not only were people seeing an economic recovery with falling unemployment and modest pay rises, but also people began to fear communism after the Berlin blockade and the Korean War. Consequently, many people sympathised with Adenauer's view that a defenceless Germany was at risk from Soviet influence. While the SPD opposed German rearmament, the CDU focus on protection by the Western powers and integration with the West became increasingly attractive to a population already accepting of a divided Germany.

The SPD lost for a third time in 1957, and it seemed destined to remain a party of opposition. Then, in 1959, a new SPD programme was announced at its party conference at Bad Godesberg. Gone was the Marxist rhetoric and instead a new liberal economic course was outlined which still aimed to overcome social injustice. The necessities of Western integration and remilitarisation were also acknowledged. The Bad Godesberg programme engaged with a broader electorate that would embrace the middle classes, and over the following ten years the SPD managed to slowly increase its support and overtake the CDU/CSU in votes. However, it was not until 1969 that **Willy Brandt** became the first SPD chancellor since 1930.

KEY FIGURE

Willy Brandt (1913–92)

Mayor of West Berlin 1959–66, and the leader of the SPD 1964–87. He became the first SPD German chancellor since the war (1969–74) and focused on strengthening European integration, while launching *Ostpolitik* aimed at improving relations with eastern Europe.

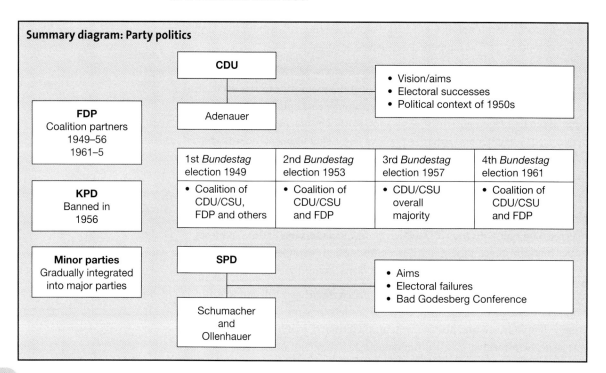

Summary diagram: Party politics

3 The 'economic miracle'

▶ *How strong was the West German economy by the mid-1960s?*

▶ *Why did the FRG become an 'economic giant'?*

Although the CDU had drawn up the so-called Ahlen programme in 1947 (see page 285), the party quickly drew back from its tentative ideas of nationalisation and instead came to propose a new form of economic liberalism. This idea was named the 'social market economy' and it was principally put into practice by one man, Ludwig Erhard, the minister of trade and industry 1949–63. He became the symbol of the 'economic miracle' in the 1950s (see page 327).

The 'social market economy'

The thinking behind the concept of the 'social market' had evolved among Erhard's colleagues at Nuremberg Business School even during the Nazi years. However, it was only as the director of the German Economic Council of the Bizone from 1948 that he began to put his principles into effect. He played a crucial role with the Western powers in preparing the currency reform and in ending state regulations, thereby opening the market for industrial and consumer goods and stimulating their production (see pages 297–8).

The aims of the social market economy lay in rising consumption and economic growth. However, Erhard did not support the theory of classical liberal economists who opposed state intervention. Instead, the 'social market economy' was attempting to construct a 'third way' between unrestrained capitalism and an over-regulated socialist economy. Its aim was to combine political and economic freedom with social justice and security. While private property should be protected, and enterprise and investment supported with as many financial incentives as possible, a strong state should also be able to intervene in the free market in order to defend the common interests of the individual.

The economic record: from recession to boom 1948–66

Erhard's implementation of the social market economy in 1948–9 did not immediately launch an economic take-off. Admittedly, the currency reform and the abolition of price controls liberated the economy, which made more consumer goods available. But the steep rise in prices was not matched by the rate of wage increases; this caused hardship for the poorer elements in society. In addition, the shortages of many resources, especially coal, which were required for rebuilding industry, led to a sharp increase in imports and a serious balance of payments deficit. The years 1949–50 were the time of the 'foundation crisis', when the German economy actually faced recession because there was not enough demand to sustain growth and also a lack of foreign currency for investment. With unemployment as high as 13.5 per cent and with prices still rising (the cost of petrol went up by 50 per cent), Erhard was under pressure from many quarters by 1950 to change his economic policy to a return to state controls. Yet, although it was not recognised at the time, the worst was over by 1951, as the economic stimulus of the Korean War had begun to take effect and exports, especially to the USA, rose steeply.

By 1952 the success of the economic recovery was clearly evident from the statistics.

Economic growth

Economic growth was high and carried on for nearly fifteen years until the first recession in 1966–7. Nowadays, in Britain an annual growth rate of 2.5–3.0 per cent would be very pleasing, yet the FRG had a rate which rose as high as twelve per cent in 1955 and an average annual growth rate of eight per cent during that time (see Table 9.4).

Table 9.4 Real growth of the West German economy

	1951	1953	1955	1957	1959	1961	1963	1965
Growth (%)	10.4	8.2	12.0	5.7	7.3	5.4	3.4	5.6

Gross national product

From 1950 to 1955 the gross national product (GNP) almost doubled, and by 1960 it nearly increased another 50 per cent. By the middle of the 1950s more coal was being mined in the FRG than in the whole of Germany in 1936. Most significantly, production went hand in hand with the massive growth of motorisation: bicycles, motor scooters and cars. This was symbolised by the dream of the man in the street to own a Volkswagen car, or 'Beetle'.

Table 9.5 West German industrial production

	1950	1955	1960	1965
Index of industrial production (100 = 1961)	36.5	64.4	90.7	118.3
Change on previous year (%)	–	15.5	11.8	5.4

Balance of trade

From its worrying deficit in 1950, the balance of trade quickly turned positive from 1952 because of Germany's rapid growth of exports. By 1954 the FRG had already become the third biggest trading power behind Britain and the USA, especially for tools, machines, cars, electronic and chemical products. It proudly sold its products with the label 'Made in Germany', which stood for good quality at reasonable prices: partly because the DM price was at first quite undervalued.

Table 9.6 Exports and imports in West Germany

	1950	1955	1960	1965
Exports (DM millions)	8,363	25,717	47,900	71,700
Imports (DM millions)	11,373	24,461	42,700	70,400

Employment

The economic expansion was reflected in the creation of jobs and the decline in unemployment. Unemployment went down to just 1 million (4.2 per cent) by 1955 and, within a few years, West Germany enjoyed a period of full employment which did not really end until the early 1970s. The creation of jobs even managed to satisfy the influx of another 3 million people who arrived from the GDR before 1961. By the early 1960s the shortage of workers had led to the recruitment and immigration of foreign labour from Italy and Turkey.

Agriculture

The one economic sector that enjoyed mixed fortunes was agriculture which, of course, had faced problems since the 1920s (see page 61). Although farmers continued to receive heavy subsidies the structure of the economy was changing and, as a consequence, the proportion of the workforce employed in farming was nearly halved – from 23 to 13 per cent – in the 1950s. Nevertheless, the rationalisation by more mechanisation still brought about a substantial increase in production – nearly 25 per cent over the same years.

Table 9.7 Unemployment in West Germany

	1950	1955	1960	1965
Number of unemployed (millions)	1.87	1.07	0.27	0.15
Working population unemployed (%)	8.1	4.2	1.0	0.5

The 'economic miracle'

At the time, Erhard did not like the use of the term 'economic miracle'. And, as the historian R. Overy acknowledged, Germany's recovery was not really a miracle 'in the sense that [it] defied explanation'.

In the long term the FRG inherited several advantages. It had access to extensive resources, such as coal and iron from the Ruhr region, and the country's population was well educated with a high level of technical skills. Moreover, in the medium term the Marshall Plan (see page 296) provided the economic context for recovery. The generous terms of this programme enabled the FRG to get off to a good start by building new factories and equipping them with modern machinery. This Marshall Aid provided a real stimulus to the German economy and an important boost to political morale in the emerging state. Nevertheless, over time, historians have considered its impact from a broader perspective. First, the amount of money should not be exaggerated, and it should be noted that Britain received twice as much aid as Germany. Secondly, Erhard's financial reforms (including the 'currency reform') are now generally seen as by far the most significant factor. As J. Singleton writes: 'In other words, it is policy that principally matters, rather than the amount of aid a country gets.'

The long boom from 1951 to 1966 can also be explained by several additional key factors which evolved in the 1950s.

SOURCE B

? What impression of Erhard does the cartoonist convey in Source B?

A caricature of Erhard drawn in 1959.

World trade

Ever since 1914, world trade had been seriously hampered by the effects of both world wars and the economic depression. After 1945 the USA used its influence to reduce tariffs globally. The Korean War led to a real growth in world trade in the early 1950s. Initially, the aid from the Marshall Plan was only meant to last three years, but was superseded by the **OEEC**, which helped to open up the European markets and speed up the reintegration of German trade into the world market. In western Europe specifically, German exports received another boost by the creation of the **ECSC** in 1951 and, more significantly, by the foundation of the **EEC**.

Refugees

At first, the number of refugees was seen as an imposing problem, but as industry began to grow again they became an advantage. The continued influx of refugees from the GDR provided a continuous supply of qualified, disciplined and highly motivated employees to the labour market who were easily satisfied with moderate incomes.

Industrial peace

The government was keen to establish more peaceful industrial relations by creating a sense of responsibility and ownership in the trade unions. The idea

KEY TERMS

OEEC Organisation for European Economic Co-operation, 1948–60. An inter-governmental organisation of west European countries, which was initially set up to administer the Marshall Aid, but was later used to open up the European markets.

ECSC The European Coal and Steel Community, created in 1951.

EEC The European Economic Community. Created by the Treaty of Rome in March 1957 and comprising six countries: FRG, France, Italy and the Benelux states.

Ludwig Erhard

1897	Born in Bavaria, the son of a draper
1928–42	Joined the Nuremberg Business School and later became its director. Removed from this position by the Nazis
1945–8	Held various posts as an economic consultant in the Western zones
1948	Appointed director of the Economic Council of the Bizone
	Oversaw the currency reform and the creation of the *Deutsche Mark*
1949	The CDU adopted Erhard's policy of a 'social market economy'
1949–63	Minister of economics in all four of Adenauer's governments
1957	Publication of his book, *Prosperity for All*
1963–6	Elected by the *Bundestag* as chancellor. Re-elected with an increased majority in 1965
1966	Resigned as chancellor following withdrawal of the FDP from the coalition
1977	Died

Erhard was not a born politician: he refused to join any Nazi organisations. Instead, he developed his economic expertise through academic study and with practical business experience. He concentrated on his teaching and on working out his theories of the liberal market. His apolitical background and economic ideas put him in a good position with the Western powers in the rebuilding of the ruined German economy.

When he was made director of economics for the Bizone his role proved to be vital in:

- implementing currency reform in the Western zones
- lifting most restrictions on control prices in the market
- reducing taxation.

The immediate effects of Erhard's reforms on the German economy were dramatic and quickly recognised. He developed his concept of the social market economy, which has been described as a 'free economy with a social conscience' and, in 1949, joined Adenauer's CDU. He then served the government as economics minister continuously from 1949 to 1963. In effect, he shaped the German economy and in that time oversaw its development into an economic giant.

By 1957 Erhard had become vice-chancellor and the public saw him as the 'crown prince'. Indeed, his popularity rivalled that of Adenauer, which soured their relationship. Adenauer saw Erhard as too weak and not politically refined enough for the highest post and his instincts seemed to have had some basis; although he became chancellor in 1963, after only three years in office Erhard stepped down when the country faced recession in 1966. Erhard still remained a member of the *Bundestag* and, when he died in 1977 at the age of 80, he was celebrated by his countrymen as 'the father of the economic miracle'.

of **co-determination** between employers and employees was shaped by two crucial laws: the Co-determination Law of 1951 and the Works' Constitution Law of 1952 (see pages 330–1). The number of strikes in West Germany fell dramatically and the country enjoyed real industrial peace for twenty years; both sides reaped the benefits.

Consumption demand

Demand expanded enormously and housing was the motor of economic recovery. Incentives, like special subsidised savings programmes to buy your own property, pushed up private demand. As confidence recovered, the demand for consumer goods, such as cars, televisions, refrigerators and vacuum cleaners, served as evidence of increasing prosperity (see pages 324 and 334).

 **KEY TERM**

Co-determination
The practice in which employees have a role in the management of a company.

Financial stability

In contrast to the financial problems of the years 1914–48, West German banking afterwards came to be seen as a symbol of financial correctness. Initially, the *Bank Deutscher Länder* was created in 1948 by the Western powers (see page 297) to establish the *Deutsche Mark*, but in 1957 it was restructured and officially became the federal bank, the *Bundesbank*. It was the central bank, but it operated independently from the government. It watched over the stability of the currency by controlling the money circulation and the interest rates, in order to prevent an overheating of the market and rising inflation.

Government expenditure

Although in 1952 the FRG signed an agreement in London to pay debts from the Marshall Plan credits and the Dawes Plan, it did not have to pay reparations and its defence costs were at first limited. (It was only allowed to form an army in 1955 when the FRG became a member of **NATO**.) Therefore, its government expenditure was more limited than other countries, like Britain for example, and Erhard was able to be more generous with social spending, which enhanced the stability of the young democracy (in comparison with Weimar).

Conclusion

There is little doubt that the economic record of the FRG in its early years was remarkable. Moreover, the years of growth, 1951–66, laid the long-term foundations that enabled the FRG to mature into an economic giant. However, although Erhard in his own book, *Prosperity for All* (1957), claimed economic success, critics have pointed out that the country became somewhat obsessed with financial progress and that the economic miracle was achieved at the expense of other factors. These factors are the focus of the section on social history on pages 329–37.

KEY TERM

NATO The Berlin blockade resulted in the emergence of a Western military alliance, NATO, the North Atlantic Treaty Organisation. NATO was formed in 1949 and included the USA, Canada, Britain, France and seven other countries. The FRG was invited to join in 1955.

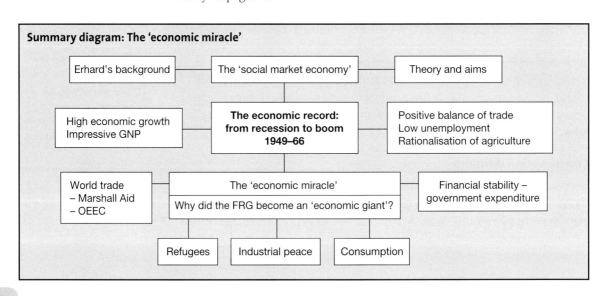

Summary diagram: The 'economic miracle'

Erhard's background — The 'social market economy' — Theory and aims

High economic growth / Impressive GNP — **The economic record: from recession to boom 1949–66** — Positive balance of trade / Low unemployment / Rationalisation of agriculture

World trade – Marshall Aid – OEEC — The 'economic miracle' / Why did the FRG become an 'economic giant'? — Financial stability – government expenditure

Refugees / Industrial peace / Consumption

West German society

> ▶ *What steps were taken by the German government to guarantee social peace after the war?*
>
> ▶ *How far was West German society changed in the twenty years after the war?*

Social policies

The success of Erhard's social market economy put West Germany on an upward course. The GNP grew in the 1950s at a yearly average of eight per cent and by 1956 full employment was almost achieved, despite the continuous influx of migrants from the GDR. The flourishing economy enabled the government to realise its promises to build up the welfare state and to integrate more effectively all social groups into society.

Social redress

The 'economic miracle' could not disguise the fact that many millions of the West German population were still in a dire situation in the aftermath of the war, and several pieces of legislation in 1950 provided relief for 4.5 million people: refugees, prisoners of war and disabled people.

Crucial for social harmony in the newly established state was the passing of the 'Equalisation of Burdens Law' of 1952. This law introduced a property levy on capital and real estate that had not been affected by the war to give something to those people who had suffered heavy losses. Through this legislation over DM143 billion was gradually redistributed in the next three decades. Although this did not fundamentally change the old social and economic structures of society, like a real redistribution of the property as demanded by the SPD would have done, it eased social tensions.

Also, in 1951, the so-called Law 131 (based on the Basic Law) restored the employment and pension rights of civil servants. This move was financially very expensive and quite controversial; however, it did reconcile millions of middle-class public employees to the emerging new state. It regulated pensions and, in many cases, reintegrated ex-civil servants and military into the new state administration to help its quick rebuilding. In this way, quite a few Nazi sympathisers (for example the secretary of state and Adenauer's right-hand man, Globke), who had been dismissed by the Allies at the end of the war, were generously re-employed in their old positions. Although Globke's appointment was later highly disputed, it served its purpose in fostering the reintegration of a relevant group of people within the new democratic state.

A key issue for Adenauer and Germany was the 'coming to terms with the past'. Adenauer knew that the policy of ***Wiedergutmachung***, of paying

 KEY TERM

Wiedergutmachung
Literally means making good again. The policy introduced by Adenauer of paying reparations, or restitution, to the victims of Nazism.

compensation to the survivors of Nazi brutality, would be vital for achieving the respect of West Germany among the international community. However, he had to balance the controversy of German collective guilt for the atrocities with the financial needs of the country still recovering from the war. To that end, Adenauer made a pivotal speech to the *Bundestag* concerning Israel in September 1951. He did not explicitly accept any moral responsibility for the crimes under National Socialism, and indeed he stated to his German audience that 'the vast majority of German people rejected the crimes that were perpetrated against the Jews and did not participate in them.' Instead, he expressed the moral obligation to atone and make some compensation towards the Jews as the crimes were 'committed in the name of the German people'. Thereby, the vast majority of people were exonerated of any crimes and there was no acceptance of any collective guilt. The speech further stated that any reparations would be 'within the limits to German capacity', as the country was still facing its own problems with caring for refugees and expellees. Talks between Israel and Germany began in March 1952 and were finalised six months later with an agreement which was signed in Luxembourg.

SOURCE C

From the German–Israeli compensation agreement signed on 10 September 1952, quoted in Armin Grünbacher, *The Making of German Democracy, West Germany During the Adenauer Era, 1945–65*, Manchester University Press, 2010, p. 310.

In consideration of the fact that unspeakable crimes have been committed against the Jewish people during the National Socialist terror regime … the Government of the FRG in its Bundestag *statement of 27 September 1951 has expressed its willingness to compensate for the material damage of these deeds within the limits of the German capacity. And that the State of Israel has taken the burden of resettling so many uprooted and destitute Jewish refugees from Germany and the formerly German-occupied territories and thus made a claim against the FRG … Germany will pay the State of Israel … DM 3,450 million.*

> ? What were the terms of the German–Israeli compensation agreement in Source C?

Integration of the trade unions

Trade unions had begun to be recognised during the occupation, with many of the FRG developments originating in the British zone. As a result, in the years from 1949, a new understanding emerged between labour, employers and government:

- First, pre-Nazi internal conflicts between the different unions were overcome when the system was simplified in 1949 by the creation of sixteen workers' unions – one per industry. Moreover, they were affiliated to one umbrella organisation, the **German Federation of Trade Unions**, and did not see themselves as separate organisations. Union activities were co-ordinated in the individual companies so that they worked together rather than in conflict with each other and, by doing so, they became much stronger in their negotiations with the government and employers' associations.

> **KEY TERM**
>
> **German Federation of Trade Unions**
> DGB (*Deutscher Gerwerkschaftsbund*). The civil service and unions of other professional sectors organised themselves into two large umbrella organisations (*Deutscher Beamtenbund* and *Deutsche Angestellten-Gewerkschaft*).

- Secondly, although the workers' unions and the SPD had wanted a complete restructuring of the economy and society, through, for example, a redistribution of property, nationalisation of key industries and a planned economy, Adenauer's government recognised the importance of achieving industrial peace. He therefore appeased the unions by introducing the Co-determination Law of 1951, which gave workers their own representatives on managerial boards in the coal, iron and steel industries.
- Thirdly, the principle of co-determination was extended by the Works' Constitution Law of 1952, which created a works council for all employees of companies with more than 500 workers.

In the most obvious way these initiatives were very successful, as West Germany had very few strikes compared to Britain and France and the industrial peace resulted in much improved conditions for the union members. Most significantly, the 1950s witnessed the development of a new approach from German trade unions which, to a large extent, agreed to abstain from party politics, despite their sympathy for the SPD. They overcame their initial doubts about the economic policies of Erhard and eventually warmed towards capitalism in the free social market. In the end, the unions started to act as critical partners rather than antagonists to the employers.

The welfare state

The SPD had campaigned for a completely new tax-based system aimed at thoroughly reforming the welfare state. However, the essence of the insurance system initiated by Bismarck and developed by Weimar was kept as the model by the government in the 1950s. In that way, the system of social security was reinstituted, but expanded for:

- Unemployment benefit: based on the 1927 legislation until 1969 (see page 60).
- Accident insurance.
- Sickness insurance: much improved by a law of 1957 which increased sick pay.
- Pensions: one of the most important achievements after the war was the reform of the pension insurance system in 1957. It raised a person's pension to 60 per cent of final-year earnings (Britain's was 29 per cent).
- Public assistance: for desperate cases.
- Family welfare: families were particularly supported by a whole range of measures: such as tax-based child allowances and, from 1954, by the introduction of child benefit.

Of course, house building played an important part in restoring the economy, but the emphasis clearly had a social dimension (see Table 9.8, overleaf). Throughout the 1950s the state supported and subsidised the public and private building sector in order to alleviate the shortage of housing and create affordable accommodation, especially for families. From 1949 to 1961 there were 6 million new flats built, and significantly half of the new accommodation was social housing or council homes.

Table 9.8 West Germany's social welfare budget 1950–70

Year	Budget (DM millions)	Percentage of GNP
1950	16.8	17.1
1960	62.8	20.7
1970	174.7	25.7

Further reforms were to be introduced in the 1960s, yet the policies and laws of the FRG government had laid the basis for a highly advanced welfare state. It compared very well in this field with other Western industrialised societies.

Education

From 1945 the Allies had aimed to reshape the German educational system as Nazi influence in that area had had such a devastating effect. They wanted educational reforms which would make Germany a democratic society. In the Soviet zone educational reform was introduced fundamentally and rapidly (see pages 376–80), yet it never really happened in the Western zones. The Western powers could not agree on a common educational policy; the USA strongly pushed for a US-style comprehensive school system, whereas the British were less directive and more pragmatic by simply issuing guidelines. Moreover, German regional authorities resisted the Allied proposals.

As a result, when responsibility for education passed on to the *Länder* in 1949, it meant that the traditional school system was not significantly changed, and the majority of Germans generally welcomed that. The primary schools were still maintained, as well as the selective system between grammar and vocational schools. German universities were retained as 'ivory towers': a preserve for the intellectual elite.

All in all, education remained very makeshift and practical problems prevailed because of:

- a lack of school buildings
- a shortage of appropriate teaching material (as most school books had been published by the Nazis)
- large classes (as a high proportion of qualified teachers had been killed in the war or removed as Nazis).

Too many new teachers were not properly qualified, and certainly had no in-service training for the changes and demands of the new West Germany. Educational authorities resorted to the curriculum and the teaching methods of the Weimar years. Therefore, in the early 1950s, there was no clear consensus on how to proceed with educational developments. The changes made by the *Länder* were limited to, for instance, the abolition of fees (1958) and the Düsseldorf agreement (1955), which covered the number of examination subjects, length of studies, holidays, the beginning of school years, A-level examination standards and so on. Some critics described the education policy as *Schulchaos* (school chaos).

The limitations of the FRG educational system in the 1950s can probably be put down to:

- the economic prosperity disguising the nature of Germany's educational weaknesses
- the conservative perspective of the FRG, which tended to look back beyond the Nazi era to the Weimar years
- the anti-communist suspicions of West Germans, who had no desire to mimic the reforms of the GDR
- most importantly, the inability of the *Länder* to overcome their differences for a more national educational policy.

However, eventually, in 1959 a draft of a report by the *Länder* for a new modern school system triggered fierce discussions among politicians and the public. This marked the beginning of expansion and changes to the educational system from the mid-1960s which would eventually lead to the age of student revolt.

Women

The contribution of women during the war and in the post-war occupation played an essential role in the survival and stability of German society. Women significantly outnumbered men after the war and, out of necessity, were able to take on new roles that they had been previously denied.

On one level, the legal one, it is clear that women's status in the 1950s was advanced in the FRG. Article 3 of the 1949 Basic Law gave women equal rights and superseded any old rules. The Law of Equality of the Sexes of 1957 went a step further towards female emancipation, giving wives the right to take up work even without the permission of their husbands and enabling them to keep control of their property after marriage.

In addition, in a period of full employment, a female workforce was seen as an advantage rather than a problem, particularly in the expanding service and administration sectors which offered new career opportunities to women. Also, the growth in new household gadgets gradually made the chores at home more manageable, thus making it easier for young women to combine work and family.

These developments cannot disguise the fact that the prevailing ethos of the 1950s and early 1960s was conservative, even patriarchal – a view which was very much promoted by the Catholic Church. The distinction was statistically clear:

- Working women in many cases could not expect equal pay for equal work.
- The average woman's wage was still about 40 per cent less than the average man's.
- In higher education the proportion of female students had only risen from nineteen per cent in 1950 to 30 per cent in 1968.

Moreover, despite the improvements in the system, social welfare was more geared to preserving the family rather than equality. The typical female role reflected by the married women of the three Ks (see page 208) prevailed widely until the mid-1960s and Eva Kolinsky writes: 'the expectations that a woman should marry, raise a family and build her life around the private sphere remained in force'. Real emancipation was still a long way off.

Social change

The 1950s and early 1960s were years of social stability as well as change.

A consumers' society?

Although the economy began to boom in the early 1950s, the income of industrial and office workers grew slowly at first and most people lived very modestly. Remembering the war and the recent years of privation, people saved every penny and were prepared to work hard and for long hours. Therefore, up to 1955 it should be noted that:

- Twenty per cent of households still lived on little more than the mere subsistence level.
- Over half of the population had no more than a one-bedroom flat to live in.
- Only eleven per cent of households owned a fridge.
- The average weekly working hours were 49 and over a third of the population had never been on a holiday in their life.

However, in the second half of the 1950s there was a marked rise in living standards for 'the man in the street' as unions became more self-confident in their demands for higher pay rises. The working week was reduced to 45 hours with the introduction of the five-day working week, and in 1965 it was reduced again to 40 hours, with increasingly longer holidays.

So, by 1962:

- 63 per cent of households owned a fridge
- 42 per cent owned a television
- 38 per cent owned a car
- 36 per cent owned a washing machine.

And, very significantly, the number of privately owned houses increased steeply thanks to special tax relief programmes.

With the rising living standards of the 1950s, a general mood of optimism and satisfaction prevailed. Social envy was not a major issue as many believed in progress and felt that they would soon have their share of the economic miracle, too. People who could afford it were not ashamed to show off their new wealth. However, by the mid-1960s this new prosperity was starting to show the signs of a rather complacent and smug consumerist society. It was this self-satisfaction which provoked a more critical and radical decade.

SOURCE D

From *Ratgeber 1950*, No. 9, 257, quoted in Christoph Kleßmann and Georg Wagner, editors, *Das gespaltene Land. Leben in Deutschland 1945–1990. Texte und Dokumente zur Sozialgeschichte [The Divided Land. Life in Germany 1945–1990. Texts and Documents on Social History]*, C.H. Beck, 1993, p. 186.

Along with whipped cream, ham rolls, chocolate and smoked eel, [come] worries over one's slender figure. Worries – that is actually something different from the deep sighs that … life that is too good, and which we should call 'pangs of conscience' about the fact that we have gone a little overboard in our joy over the good things that have returned.

But the coat is too tight, the ladies' suit jacket won't button anymore, the dress is straining at the seams, and the blazer – yes, you too, gentlemen … can no longer be expanded by moving buttons or taking out the seams.

What does Source D tell you about the changes in the FRG and the new worries that some people had?

SOURCE E

A poster produced by the German trade unions, DGB: 'On Saturdays, Daddy belongs to me.'

What messages are conveyed in the poster in Source E about the role of trade unions in protecting family life in the FRG?

'Home sweet home'?

In the early years of the FRG most people were simply happy with their newfound stability, although this view was soon followed by an urge to make up for the 'lost years' of chaos, hunger and destruction. The longing for private happiness and normality helped to form a society that concentrated on material achievements and family life. As a consequence, the great majority of the West German population was fed up with the ideology and militarism of the Nazi years and wanted to enjoy the freedom of individual choice again.

In a way, the popular suspicion of politics and ideology also led to the emergence of a **'without me'** (*ohne mich*) mentality. This belief became most clear in the controversy about the remilitarisation of the FRG, which many people did not want (see page 341). In the end, however, the faith in Adenauer's alliance with the West was stronger than the scepticism and fear. Despite all criticism, he remained the reliable father figure most West Germans were prepared to trust.

A 'Coca-Cola society'?

In many ways the influence of Germany's traditional culture and class divisions gradually declined. The modern mass media, especially the cinema and, by the late 1950s, the first televisions, began to spread new ideas and US culture, first introduced to West Germans through the occupying troops.

US mass culture began to exert a strong influence on young people in particular, who were soon attracted by the appeal of jeans, rock 'n' roll, chewing gum and Coca-Cola especially. This influence was regarded with a lot of scepticism by the older generations, as it was often coupled with youth protest. In 1956–8 there were a number of teenage riots by 'teddy boys' who rebelled against the old-fashioned family values and the strict working ethos of their parents.

A modern industrial society?

With a booming economy and developed technology, West Germany in the 1950s was turning into a modern industrial society undergoing all kinds of changes. Its population grew markedly from 47.5 million in 1951 to 58.6 million in 1965 (although the population growth was to decelerate from the mid-1960s).

Even more significant was the shift in the structure of the labour force (see Table 9.9). **Social mobility** grew as more and more people moved from the countryside to the cities. Despite real efforts by the government to improve the situation of farmers through subsidies and a new pension system, the number

Table 9.9 Number in millions employed by each economic sector in the FRG

Employment sector	1955	1970
Industry	10.2	12.4
Agriculture	4.3	2.3
Mining	0.6	0.5
Transport/commerce/banking	5.7	7.6

of people working in the agrarian sector declined drastically. The old-fashioned, hard lifestyle and low income of the countryside lost its attraction for many young people.

The lure of jobs in urban Germany was not to be found in the older heavy industries; rather, the search for employment was in the light, electronics and service industries. Most marked was the massive expansion of transport manufacture, which saw the growth of the number of cars from 2 million in 1950 to 12.1 million in 1965 along with the systematic expansion of the road network.

West German society presented contradictory images. Nearly all Germans were much better off and more secure and yet, the new wealth heightened financial inequalities, and the disparity in the distribution of wealth and income remained the same to a large extent in the 1960s as it had been after 1945. Thus, 1.7 per cent of all households still owned 35 per cent of private wealth, whereas 3.7 per cent of households only owned a mere 17 per cent of private wealth.

The modernising elements show that West Germany was no longer such a class-based society. The influence and status of the Prussian *Junkers* had gone and the Ruhr barons who had dominated heavy industry were in decline. So there was a kind of levelling effect within West German society, particularly in psychological terms. Ideological gaps grew smaller as the new materialism created a bond of new common values and workers gradually adopted the lifestyle of the middle classes. That is not to say that it was a classless society; instead, according to Mary Fulbrook, 'West Germans appeared rather homogenously middle class.'

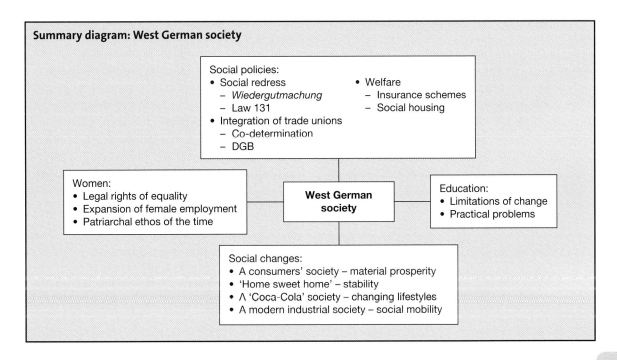

Summary diagram: West German society

Social policies:
- Social redress
  - *Wiedergutmachung*
  - Law 131
- Integration of trade unions
  - Co-determination
  - DGB

- Welfare
  - Insurance schemes
  - Social housing

Women:
- Legal rights of equality
- Expansion of female employment
- Patriarchal ethos of the time

West German society

Education:
- Limitations of change
- Practical problems

Social changes:
- A consumers' society – material prosperity
- 'Home sweet home' – stability
- Λ 'Coca-Cola' society – changing lifestyles
- A modern industrial society – social mobility

Foreign relations

> ▶ *What were Adenauer's foreign policy aims and how far were they*
> *achieved?*

The new West Germany was born out of the Cold War at a time of tensions and fears between the East and the West. By 1949 the Soviets had developed the atomic bomb and, in 1950, the outbreak of the Korean War seemed to confirm all the fears of 'the free Western world' about communist aggression. Divided Germany was therefore at the frontline of the Cold War and Adenauer was very much aware that maintaining the peace and freedom of the FRG was vital. Moreover, the FRG in the early 1950s remained politically impotent. The country was under the control of the Allied High Commission and it did not enjoy real sovereignty, as the Western powers had the ultimate authority. (The FRG was not even allowed to have a foreign office, which is why Adenauer acted as chancellor and foreign minister.)

In this situation, Adenauer's foreign policy was geared towards establishing sovereignty for the new state and exploiting the economic, political and military strength of the free Western world by fully integrating the FRG. His aims and visions went far beyond his own state. His aim was a united west Europe led and protected by the superpower USA. To reach this ideal, Adenauer saw that it was essential for the FRG to put to one side national interests and create a close network of multinational institutions. In Adenauer's plan the FRG was to play an active and vital part in this process: stability, reliability and close co-operation were to be the principles with which he hoped to win the trust of partners in the West.

Most significantly Adenauer, had a strong antipathy to communism. He mistrusted the Soviets and felt that only a policy of strength could really deter communist aggression. He was, therefore, opposed to attempts at reunifying Germany if it left the FRG neutralised, as it would be left largely defenceless and prey to communist influence. In his eyes, reunification could only be considered under Western conditions. As W. Carr writes of Adenauer: 'Above all a realist cast in the mould of Bismarck and Stresemann, Adenauer supposed that the temporary division of Germany was likely to be of long duration and that West Germany's only hope of recovery lay in full co-operation with the Western Powers.'

Eyes to the West: economic integration

The major hurdle that Adenauer had to overcome to achieve his aims was winning the trust of west European states, especially that of France. Indeed, the new state was also constrained by significant economic conditions, as well as the political ones, for example:

- The Occupation Statute of April 1949, which gave the occupying powers the right to supervise the country's trade.
- The International Ruhr Authority, which gave the right to France, Belgium, the Netherlands and Luxembourg to control the distribution of the area's resources, especially coal and steel.
- The status of the Saar, a mainly German-speaking area, but very rich in coal which, since 1947, had been virtually a puppet state controlled by France by means of a **customs union** (see pages 23 and 341).

Adenauer reckoned that economic co-operation was the best way to establish political trust.

The Petersberg agreement

As early as the autumn of 1949 the FRG government agreed to sign the Petersberg agreement with the Allied High Commission. Primarily, the purpose of this agreement was simply to allow the FRG to join the International Ruhr Authority. Indeed, Schumacher attacked Adenauer viciously as a 'chancellor of the Allies'. However, the chancellor actually gained a lot from this co-operation:

- the dismantling of industry by the Allies was radically limited
- the FRG gained the right to establish diplomatic relations with other states
- the FRG was allowed to join the **European Council** in 1950.

The European Coal and Steel Community (ECSC)

The results of the seeds sown by the Petersberg agreement soon began to grow. The mistrust of some French gave way to the insight that co-operation could bring economic advantages, as well as security. In 1950 the French foreign minister, **Robert Schuman**, suggested a **supranational** organisation to oversee German and French steel and coal production. His initiative became known as the Schuman Plan and led to the foundation of the ECSC in 1951 by its six members: the FRG, France, Italy and the Benelux states. They agreed on a common policy for prices, subsidies and investment and, most significantly, they lifted restrictions on imports and exports of coal and steel between member states.

The establishment of the ECSC supplanted the old International Ruhr Authority, which allowed the FRG to be treated as an equal partner in that area. Perhaps most significantly in the long term, the nature of the agreement laid the basis for Franco-German understanding after generations of hostility.

The European Economic Community (EEC)

The ECSC was an immediate success and production of coal and steel within the community increased by 44 per cent from 1952 to 1957. Not surprisingly, the six members began to take Western integration further and extensive negotiations culminated in the Treaty of Rome, which was signed in March 1957. This, in effect, created the EEC as a customs union between the six, which

KEY TERMS

Customs union
An association of independent nations, which create a free trade area and remove customs/tariffs between them; also they usually agree on a common tariff for countries outside the area.

European Council
An international organisation set up in May 1949 to promote co-operation between European countries on legal standards, human rights and democratic values. It pre-dated the creation of the EEC. Most famously, it established the European Court of Human Rights.

Supranational Beyond the authority of one national government, creating a project or policy by a group of nations, for example, EEC, World Trade Organisation.

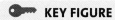

KEY FIGURE

Robert Schuman (1886–1963)
Schuman was briefly French premier 1947–8 and then foreign minister 1948–53. He was instrumental in developing post-war European institutions and a strong supporter of NATO. His 'Schuman Plan' laid down the basis of the ECSC and later the EEC.

set out to harmonise measures of trade and prices in areas such as agriculture and fisheries. By 1964, 85 per cent of West German agricultural produce came under EEC trade. This was the starting point of an ever closer union of the EEC members and the community's aims to:

- co-ordinate transportation systems
- develop general economic policies
- remove measures restricting free competition
- assure the mobility of labour and capital.

The EEC was colloquially known as the 'Common Market'. It proved to be a turning point for Europe and even more so for the FRG. As the country was the largest member of the EEC, Adenauer recognised that working within the union provided the chance for the FRG to exert political and economic influence.

Other economic agencies

In addition, West Germany readily joined a broad range of organisations to improve international economic co-operation and co-ordination:

- The General Agreement on Tariffs and Trade (GATT) was formed in 1948 by the United Nations with the main objective of reducing barriers to international trade. The FRG joined in 1951.
- The Organisation for European Economic Co-operation (OEEC) was created in 1948 to administer the Marshall Plan and to continue work on a joint recovery programme through economic co-operation. The Bizone was one of the original founding members.
- The International Monetary Fund (IMF) was created in 1945 to stabilise exchange rates and supervise the world's international payment system to prevent financial imbalance. The FRG joined in 1952.

All these points were not just economically important; they played a crucial part in the rehabilitation of Germany in the international community.

Eyes to the West: military and political integration

Economic co-operation was only one factor that helped Adenauer to speed up the acceptance of West Germany as a valued and trusted partner. The outbreak of the **Chinese Revolution** (1949) and the Korean War (1950) heightened the fear of communism and led to a change in attitudes between the USA and west European politicians. The USA particularly urged Europeans to make a greater effort to contribute to their own defence, especially the FRG. However, the idea of German rearmament was still regarded very warily by its neighbours, especially France. So, understandably, the early plans of French prime minister René Pleven were to create a **European Defence Community** (EDC) that was very much under French leadership and with a strictly limited German contingent.

KEY TERMS

Chinese Revolution
The civil war between the nationalists and the communists 1948–9 led to a communist revolution and the proclamation of the Chinese People's Republic on 1 October 1949, which was led by Mao Tse-tung.

European Defence Community A plan proposed by France's prime minister, Pleven, to form a pan-European defence force. The plan was signed in May 1952 by the FRG, but not ratified by the French parliament.

Adenauer quickly agreed to make the FRG a member of the EDC while at
the same time making the German contribution dependent on the return
of sovereignty to West Germany and the end of the Occupation Statute. Yet,
the agreement signed in 1952 creating the EDC caused some intense political
opposition. In Germany, although the treaty was ratified by the *Bundestag*,
there was serious resistance to German rearmament. This opposition came not
only from within the SPD, but also from elements within the CDU; a leading
government ex-minister, Gustav Heinemann, left the CDU in protest.

At first, the proposal was defeated by the French parliament and, to overcome
French doubts, Adenauer went straight back to the negotiating table. Within
a few months new terms were signed in the Paris Treaties of October 1954 to
settle openly all the major political and economic disputes between Germany
and France. This time they were signed by their respective parliaments, which
agreed on the areas considered below.

German sovereignty

The Occupation Statute was ended and the FRG became a fully sovereign state
in May 1955. The Western powers kept their rights and responsibilities over
West Berlin and the stationing of their troops in West Germany to guarantee
its security was assured. (Yet, at that time, the question remained of German
reunification and any future peace settlement, which had still not been agreed
by the Allies.)

West European Union

The EDC plan was put to one side and, instead, the West European Union
(WEU) of France, Britain and the Benelux states was expanded to include West
Germany and Italy. This action was a defensive pact, which allowed the FRG
to create its own national armed forces, the **Bundeswehr** (whereas the EDC
had originally suggested a European army, which would have caused political
problems).

NATO

The North Atlantic Treaty Organisation (NATO) had been formed in 1949 and
the FRG was allowed to become a full member in 1955.

The future of the Saar

Adenauer agreed to accept the autonomous status of the Saar and its close
economic connection with France. However, it was agreed to give the population
of the Saar a plebiscite. When it was held, a 68 per cent majority rejected the
terms for the Saar; instead, two-thirds of the Saar parliament pushed for
unifying with West Germany. Five years previously this could have been the
cause of a major political conflict. Yet, Franco-German relations had improved so
much that as a result of negotiations between the two capitals it was agreed to
accept the return of the Saar to the FRG in 1957 as the eleventh *Land*.

KEY TERM

Bundeswehr The name
given to the German Army
created in the FRG by the
Paris Treaties. It was ratified
by the *Bundestag* in 1955
and came into effect the
following year. It introduced
conscription for all men aged
over eighteen years.

Conclusion

By the mid-1950s the FRG was thoroughly integrated into the West, although Adenauer's triumph was not undisputed at home. The ratification of the Paris Treaties was harshly attacked by the political opposition because of the revival of remilitarisation, which seemed to quash the last chance of reunification. Stalin added fuel to this criticism when he tried to obstruct the process of integration by offering new negotiations for the reunification of Germany on seemingly generous terms in 1952 (see pages 343–4). When Adenauer and the Western powers rejected Stalin's offer, it confirmed the views of the opposition that he had sacrificed the national interest of reunification in return for Western integration.

Nevertheless, just ten years after the trauma of 1945, the position of the FRG had been transformed. Adenauer's achievement is particularly striking in comparison with Weimar Germany after 1918, as W. Carr has written: 'Seldom in history has a defeated power recovered so quickly. The FRG had become a fully integrated part of a Western military defence system and its freedom was guaranteed: it had gained back its political sovereignty; it was being accepted on an equal level with the other West European states.'

Adenauer's greatest personal triumph, and the culmination of his foreign policies, was achieved in 1963, when he signed the French–German treaty with the French president, Charles de Gaulle. This secured the basis for a lasting friendship and political co-operation between the two old national enemies. His unambiguous devotion to Western integration paid off in this respect – and even set the direction of FRG foreign policy until 1989.

Relations with the GDR and the USSR

Adenauer's firm commitment to the West and his own mistrust of communism meant that relations between the FRG and the USSR were difficult and strained. The FRG claimed to be the only rightful heir to the Weimar Republic and it saw itself as the only legal representative of the German nation. This claim implied that the GDR was not even accepted as a state:

- In the official language of the FRG, East Germany was referred to simply as the 'Soviet occupation zone'.
- There were no official international diplomatic relations between the FRG and the GDR.
- When the GDR signed a peace treaty with Poland in 1950 and accepted the Oder–Neisse frontier, this frontier was not recognised by the FRG.
- People generally spoke of the GDR in derogative language as *drüben* (over there) or *Ostzone* (the east zone).

Adenauer clearly only wanted to negotiate on the 'German question' from a position of strength. His strategy of the 'magnet theory' (see page 319) was based on the assumptions of developing an economically and politically strong FRG within the West to contrast with the failings of the communist system. It was believed that the peoples of eastern Europe, including the GDR, would be attracted to liberal democracy and join the West, which of course would facilitate the reunification of Germany. Indeed, the fact that there were 3 million refugees from the GDR flooding into the FRG during the 1950s confirmed that theory (see page 374).

The 'Stalin notes'

The question of German reunification has become the focus of much controversy over the events of March 1952, when the USSR sent a seemingly tempting offer to the Western powers (at the same time as negotiations about the EDC Treaty, see pages 340–1). These proposals have become known as the 'Stalin notes' and offered a negotiated settlement to the German question on the following terms:

- The signing of a final peace treaty for a united Germany with free democratic elections.
- The establishment of a united Germany with the Oder–Neisse line as the eastern frontier.
- The removal of all foreign troops from Germany, which was not allowed to join any military alliance and which had to stay neutral.
- The creation of a defensive army for the new state.

Stalin's offer was rejected by the Western powers, especially by the USA, as they were keen for the success of the EDC negotiations. It seems that Adenauer viewed the offer as a dangerous one, as it would make Germany a weak neutral state prey to communist power. Almost certainly he used all his influence to ensure that the offer did not make any more progress. It is interesting to note that Adenauer practically ignored the June 1953 uprising in the GDR (see pages 361–5), in which he was accused by the people there of abandoning them to their fate, rather than risking getting the West involved. The Soviet offer of reunification was renewed on several occasions in the years 1954–5 after Stalin's death. Yet, Adenauer did not budge from his position and there was no softening from the Western powers.

The negotiations with the USSR over the 'German question' between 1952 and 1955 have been the focus of much controversy over the years. Adenauer was blamed by his opponents for not seriously pursuing the negotiations and therefore missing a real chance to bring about German reunification. In contrast, his supporters have seen Stalin's offer as simply a bluff to prevent remilitarisation and to block Western interests before restoring communist influence over Germany.

The opening of the Soviet archives after 1990 shed some light on the matter. It suggests that the very first note from Stalin was more than likely a tempting offer motivated by an attempt to prevent the FRG from being absorbed into the Western military alliance. Once it had been rejected by the West, though, the later Soviet offers were motivated more by propaganda aimed at presenting the right image. With regard to Adenauer's responsibility, it is recognised that his foreign policy aims for Germany were rooted in the integration of the West, and his position coincided with that of the USA and Britain. Adenauer abhorred the idea of a weak, neutral state that could fall under communist influence, and he saw this offer not only as disadvantageous but also as dangerous and therefore used all his influence to make sure it would be rejected.

The Hallstein doctrine

By the summer of 1955, the relationship between the FRG and the East was at last clearer. Adenauer visited Moscow in September, when he was prepared to establish diplomatic relations with the USSR in exchange for 10,000 prisoners of war and 20,000 civilians still held in the Soviet Union since 1945. However, the two sides were strongly entrenched by that time.

On the one hand, the USSR had recently launched its 'two-state theory', which claimed that there were two sovereign German states, both representing the German nation. (This belief was directly in contrast to the claim of the FRG to be the only rightful representative of German interests.) Moreover, around the same time the USSR officially changed its policies over Germany by giving the GDR full sovereignty and by integrating the GDR into the **Warsaw Pact**.

On the other hand, on his return from Moscow, Adenauer stated that his own government would refuse to have diplomatic relations with any state that officially recognised the GDR (with the exception of the USSR). This policy became known as the **Hallstein** doctrine, named after the state secretary in the foreign office who was a close advisor of Adenauer. For ten years it was generally successful. In that time, it effectively discouraged many countries from recognising the GDR through offering extensive economic aid to countries in the developing world; only two countries – Yugoslavia (1957) and Cuba (1963) – were to break relations.

Therefore, there was no real chance to reunite Germany in the years 1952–5 or after. The competing forces were irreconcilable and so, although Stalin's death on 5 March 1953 did lead to a gentle thaw in the Cold War, the talks on German reunification drove them further apart in the later years. As a result, relations between the two Germanys stayed frosty. Indeed, the integration of the two Germanys into the different blocs had highlighted one vital issue, namely the ongoing clash of interests over Berlin. That was to come to a head in the Berlin crisis, 1958–61, and led to the construction of the Berlin Wall (see pages 387–9).

 **KEY TERM**

Warsaw Pact The USSR viewed NATO as an offensive alliance, and Soviet concern was highlighted when the FRG was rearmed and brought into NATO. In response, in 1955, the Warsaw Pact was created as a defensive alliance of the USSR and the countries of central and eastern Europe under Soviet regimes.

KEY FIGURE

Walter Hallstein (1901–82)

A senior civil servant in the FRG foreign office who gave his name to the doctrine of isolating the GDR diplomatically. A keen supporter of a federal Europe, he became the first president of the European Commission 1958–67.

SOURCE F

Report from the British permanent undersecretary at the Foreign Office, following a conversation with Adenauer's ambassador on the German question in 1955, quoted in Armin Grünbacher, *The Making of German Democracy, West Germany During the Adenauer Era, 1945–65*, Manchester University Press, 2010, p. 276.

Dr. Adenauer had no confidence in the German people. He was terrified that when he disappeared from the scene a future German government might do a deal with Russia at the German expense. Consequently he felt that integration with the West was more important than the unification of Germany … he would bend all his energies towards achieving this … and hoped we would do all in our power to sustain him in this task. … The Chancellor [believed] it would be quite disastrous to his political position if [his] views … became known in Germany.

According to Source F, what are the reasons why Adenauer would not trust the German people or government over the German question?

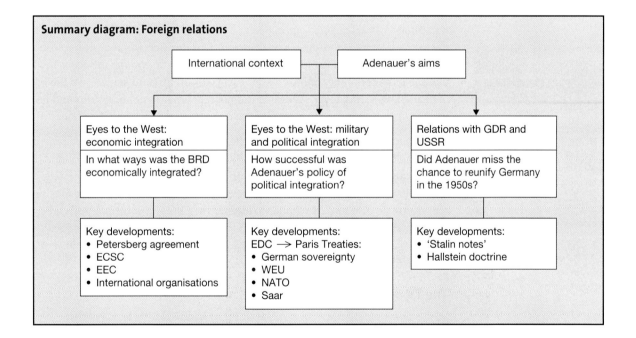

Summary diagram: Foreign relations

International context — Adenauer's aims

Eyes to the West: economic integration	Eyes to the West: military and political integration	Relations with GDR and USSR
In what ways was the BRD economically integrated?	How successful was Adenauer's policy of political integration?	Did Adenauer miss the chance to reunify Germany in the 1950s?

| Key developments:
• Petersberg agreement
• ECSC
• EEC
• International organisations | Key developments:
EDC → Paris Treaties:
• German sovereignty
• WEU
• NATO
• Saar | Key developments:
• 'Stalin notes'
• Hallstein doctrine |

6 Adenauer's final years

▶ *What were the long- and short-term causes of Adenauer's fall from power?*

▶ *How had Adenauer been able to secure such a powerful position for himself?*

In the 1957 election, with the slogan 'No experiments – vote Adenauer', the CDU/CSU had triumphantly won an absolute majority, which secured the ageing Adenauer a third term in office. Yet, his authority soon started to wane, partly accelerated by his own poor judgement and stubbornness in his old convictions on home and foreign affairs.

Adenauer's fall from power

In spring 1959 the first president, Heuss, was obliged to retire and the chancellor, urged by leading members of the CDU, first signalled his willingness to become a candidate for the presidency. Yet, he caused much irritation when a few weeks later he withdrew his nomination. This decision was mainly because he had recognised that the new office would not give him enough influence to guarantee the continuity of his policies, especially on his hard stance over the GDR and USSR. Moreover, Adenauer did not rate Erhard's political skills and he was becoming concerned that the finance minister would become chancellor.

This dithering lost Adenauer a lot of public sympathy, as he was seen as damaging the image of the highest office in the state for the sake of personal interests and strategies. In addition, within the CDU, many were disappointed, as they had assumed that nominating the 83-year-old chancellor was the ideal opportunity to give him the chance to leave at the pinnacle of his political career. Instead, Adenauer seemed to have lost his political instinct and misjudged the long-term consequences of this affair, which delayed his departure for four years.

'The TV dispute'

Adenauer's reputation was also seriously hit by a long-lasting legal conflict during 1958–61. He had set up a national television company, Deutschland-Fernsehen-GmbH, which in effect was to be controlled by the federal government. Of course, he recognised the potential political value of such an organisation, but the SPD claimed that the company was a threat to German federalism and to the freedom of the media. In the end, in February 1961, the company was declared 'unconstitutional' by the constitutional court and it was dissolved. Adenauer had overstretched his competence and his political opponents had used the dispute to accuse him of undermining federalism and of pursuing more government central control.

The 1961 election and the new coalition

Despite the above problems faced by Adenauer and the CDU, and the threat posed by the revived SPD, the polls suggested that they could win the 1961 election. The economy was still going well, and many Germans remained cautious of supporting the youthful SPD leader, Willy Brandt, compared to the experienced Adenauer.

When the GDR erected the Berlin Wall during the election campaign (see pages 387–9), Adenauer significantly misjudged the situation. Most West Germans were appalled by the events in Berlin, but instead of hurrying to the scene of the emerging concrete wall along the border, he carried on campaigning and did not visit Berlin until a week later. Moreover, although his response was reserved, he continued to attack Brandt, who was the mayor of West Berlin and had won much public sympathy.

In the end, the CDU/CSU won the election again, with a vote of 45.3 per cent. Yet, without an absolute majority, they were obliged to enter into negotiations with the FDP, who had considerably increased their vote to 12.8 per cent. Also very significantly, the FDP had publicly opposed a fourth period in office for Adenauer. Therefore, after difficult negotiations, the FDP agreed to join a coalition government under Adenauer's leadership on the condition that he would step down before the end of the four-year period. It was a humiliating condition and it was only a question of time before the old chancellor retired, although the government crisis of 1962 brought things to a head rather more quickly.

Der Spiegel affair

Der Spiegel (*The Mirror*), a rather left-wing political weekly magazine, had long criticised **Franz-Joseph Strauss**, the leader of the CSU, since his appointment as minister of defence. It had attacked him for various dubious financial dealings, but its main focus was his political stance on foreign relations. Strauss was a hardliner, who believed strongly in the concept of 'a massive deterrence' to fight against the threat of communism; and it seemed that he was in favour of a pre-emptive nuclear strike by NATO in case of danger.

On 10 October 1962 (the same month as the **Cuban Missile Crisis**), *Der Spiegel* published an article with information about planned NATO military manoeuvres in the event of an attack by the Warsaw Pact, which questioned the integrity of Strauss. Soon all hell broke loose. The offices of the magazine in Hamburg and Bonn were searched and closed down; Augstein, the publisher, and some journalists were arrested; and Ahlers, the writer of the article, who was in Spain on holiday, was seized by Spanish authorities and sent back to Germany. In the end, the defendants were charged with public treason and corruption on the grounds of publishing highly secret information. Obviously, the whole affair revolved around the freedom of the press, and Strauss was

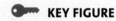

KEY FIGURE

Franz-Joseph Strauss (1915–88)
A leading figure in the CSU of the FRG until 1982. He served various posts under Adenauer, most notably as defence minister 1956–62. He was forced to resign in 1962 over the *Der Spiegel* scandal, but continued to be a powerful influence in Bavarian politics.

KEY TERM

Cuban Missile Crisis
The most serious flashpoint in the Cold War between the superpowers, in October 1962. The dispute was over the installation of nuclear missiles by the USSR on Cuba, a short distance from the US mainland.

harangued widely for endorsing censorship methods reminiscent of the Nazis. At first, Adenauer publicly defended Strauss and amazingly resorted to attacking Augstein in the *Bundestag* by suggesting that the country was on the 'abyss of treason'.

This triggered a government crisis. Five FDP members left the cabinet demanding the resignation of Strauss. Adenauer only managed to rescue the coalition by sacking Strauss and by his own promise to step down in the following year. Moreover, Adenauer was never really prepared to accept any personal responsibility or blame over the *Der Spiegel* affair, even when the government's charges were kicked out by the court. The scandal showed him at his worst as lacking political judgement and behaving arrogantly; he was seriously politically wounded.

Foreign relations

Although domestic factors and Adenauer's advancing age eventually brought about the end of his political career, it should be noted that his inflexible policy towards the 'Eastern bloc' also contributed to his demise.

Despite the opposition of the SPD, Adenauer's foreign policy had generally enjoyed great success. Yet, in the latter 1950s the international context was changing and he failed to adapt to the new environment. For example, he remained unashamedly committed to:

- the non-recognition of the GDR
- the Hallstein doctrine
- Strauss's leadership as defence minister.

Moreover, Adenauer's suspicions of the intentions of the USA and Britain over the Berlin crisis 1958–61 (see page 390) contributed to problems within the coalition. Adenauer's stance was opposed by the coalition partner FDP and also by a strong pro-American faction within the CDU led by Erhard, which became known as the 'Atlanticists'. They made Adenauer's position within the party and the government more difficult in his last few years, pushing for him to be replaced by Erhard as chancellor.

Resignation

Adenauer's days were now numbered. In the *Länder* elections in West Berlin and Rheinland-Pfalz in early 1963 the CDU lost many votes, and voices within the party started to call for a grand coalition with the SPD. In April 1963 Adenauer had to accept the nomination of Erhard as his successor and, in October, aged 87, he resigned as promised from office. However, he kept his seat in parliament and his position as leader of the CDU, from which he only resigned in 1966, a year before his death. Like other great leaders in their final years, he could not accept the changing times and found it very difficult to withdraw from power.

'Chancellor democracy'?

Even during his time in office, Adenauer's style of government and leadership was labelled 'chancellor democracy', a term which was interpreted in positive and negative terms. Although already 73 years old when he became chancellor for the first time, he was still a very agile, far-sighted and, more importantly, politically experienced man. His long years as the mayor of Cologne in the Weimar Republic had taught him everything he needed to know about democratic processes and the need to lobby support. As a committed Catholic, he had disapproved of the political ideologies of communism and Nazism and had kept his moral and political integrity throughout. He was not easily impressed by 'opinion polls' or by 'expert comments'. Instead, his rather pragmatic, sober approach to politics and a good instinct for the feasible helped him to integrate different interest groups in government and in parliament.

Adenauer's style of government was framed not only by his personality, but also by the circumstances of the time:

- As the first chancellor of a new state with no precedents, he felt entitled to interpret the law as he saw fit as a means of strengthening the new democracy. He described this as 'an extensive interpretation of the Basic Law'.
- In the years up to 1955, when the FRG's sovereignty was still restricted, his personal role in the negotiations with the Western powers made his position particularly significant – even dominating. Under the Occupation Statute he combined the role of chancellor and foreign minister and oversaw foreign and defence policies.
- Another advantage that strengthened his position was the amount of freedom he had in the choice of his personnel in the formative early years. He left the economics to Erhard, but otherwise he looked for a group of loyal people around him. Quite controversially, he also appointed a number of Nazi sympathisers to support his policies, for example Hans Globke, the state secretary in the chancellery, was one of Adenauer's most trusted and important men.
- Clearly, success led to success. The SPD failed to provide a real political alternative until the 1960s and Adenauer's electoral victories reinforced his political status as party leader and chancellor. The decade of economic success strengthened the feeling of trust in his government and his patriarchal image fitted in nicely with the rather conservative culture.

Adenauer did face criticism for some of the above factors, as his leadership was seen as undisputed in his first ten years. His powers were untrammelled by the traditional mechanisms of parliamentary democracy and it left a feeling that the first chancellor had left his mark permanently stamped on the office. Yet, he always stayed within the constitutional limits and acted strictly on the majority decisions in parliament. Also, it is telling that his successors were not to rule so effectively. Consequently, the term 'chancellor democracy' did not become permanently institutionalised; it referred to a transient phase, which really could only be applied to Adenauer's years in office.

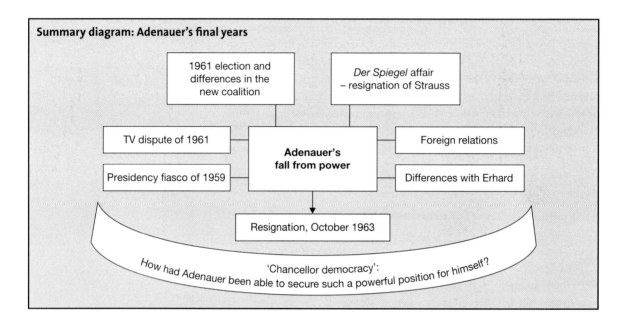

Summary diagram: Adenauer's final years

- 1961 election and differences in the new coalition
- *Der Spiegel* affair – resignation of Strauss
- TV dispute of 1961
- Presidency fiasco of 1959
- **Adenauer's fall from power**
- Foreign relations
- Differences with Erhard
- Resignation, October 1963
- 'Chancellor democracy': How had Adenauer been able to secure such a powerful position for himself?

Chapter summary

Although the FRG was created in 1949 out of the most difficult circumstances, Germany's second attempt at parliamentary democracy proved to be more stable than the first one. The new constitution in the Basic Law was astutely drawn up, bearing in mind the criticisms of the role of the president and the electoral system from the Weimar constitution. In many ways the very environment of the 1950s favoured the FRG. The 'economic miracle' with long-term growth and low unemployment provided many Germans with stability, even prosperity. While real security was created through the integration of the FRG into western Europe through the *rapprochement* with France, the creation of the EEC and the joining of the NATO, this was at the expense of rejecting any co-operation with the GDR.

Adenauer and the CDU politically dominated the early years of the FRG. His 'chancellor democracy' was very much framed by his personality and the circumstances of the time. However, by the early 1960s he was an old man and his position was in decline, especially after the *Der Spiegel* crisis. Moreover, his conservatism and paternalistic approach were no longer in tune with the social and economic developments in Germany.

Refresher questions

Use these questions to remind yourself of the key material covered in this chapter.

1 What were the safeguards in the Basic Law to strengthen democracy?

2 What was Adenauer's vision for the CDU?

3 How did Adenauer and the CDU politically stabilise Germany in the 1950s?

4 What were the aims of the SPD in the 1950s?

5 When and why did the SPD change its political outlook?

6 What is the 'social market economy'?

7 How and why did the FRG become an 'economic giant' in the 1950s?

8 Why was the German education system not improved after the war?

9 Were the lives of German women improved?

10 In what ways was the FRG economically integrated into western Europe by 1963?

11 How successful was Adenauer's policy of integration with the West?

12 Did Adenauer miss the chance to reunify Germany in the 1950s?

13 How successful was Adenauer's foreign policy?

14 Why has Adenauer's leadership been described as 'chancellor democracy'?

 # Question practice

ESSAY QUESTIONS

1 Assess the reasons for the success of Erhard's economic policies.

2 How far did German society change in the twenty years after the Second World War?

3 Which of the following had the greater impact in ensuring prosperity for the FRG between 1949 and 1963? i) Integration with the West. ii) The economic miracle. Explain your answer with reference to both i) and ii).

4 'West Germany proved to be an unqualified success under Adenauer's chancellorship.' To what extent do you agree with this statement?

CHAPTER 10

East Germany 1949–63

The purpose of this chapter is to consider how successfully the new communist state in East Germany, the GDR, developed in its early years, 1949–63. Although it made some progress in those years, it still faced fundamental problems and the challenges for the country were immense. The question was whether it could be seen as a viable state. The main themes considered are:

★ The creation of the SED dictatorship

★ The political survival of Ulbricht's GDR

★ The GDR economy

★ East German society

★ The Berlin Wall

Key dates

1949	Jan. 25–28	First SED Party Conference: it became a 'party of a new type'
	Oct. 7	Foundation of the German Democratic Republic (GDR) in East Germany
1950	Feb.	Creation of State Security Service (*Stasi*)
	Oct.	Elections to the first People's Chamber
1952	July	*Länder* in GDR dissolved
1953	March 5	Death of Stalin
	June 17	Uprising in GDR
1955	May 11–14	Warsaw Pact concluded with GDR as a member
	Sept. 20	USSR recognised sovereignty of GDR
1956	Feb.	Khrushchev's speech denounced Stalin and his methods
1958	Nov. 27	Khrushchev's Berlin ultimatum
1960		Collectivisation of agriculture in GDR completed
1961	Aug. 13	Creation of Berlin Wall
1963	June	Introduction of the New Economic System

1 The creation of the SED dictatorship

▶ *How did the leaders of the GDR control their people?*

The formation of the German Democratic Republic (GDR) in October 1949 was unequivocally shaped by the years of the occupation and particularly by:

- The influence of the German Communist Party (KPD) and the Soviets in the early months of the administration (see pages 287–8).
- The nationalisation of key industries and land reform (see page 290).
- The collapse of Allied co-operation and the growing Cold War (see pages 298–301).
- The declaration of the FRG (May 1949) (see page 302).

In theory, the new constitution of the GDR was a multi-party system with two parliamentary chambers, like the FRG:

- The *Volkskammer*, the highest institution in the state, with free and secret general elections on the basis of proportional representation; its purpose was to represent the people.
- The *Länderkammer*, to represent the interests of the five *Länder*.

The constitution of the GDR claimed it to be a democratic state with its power coming from the people and with guaranteed civil rights, such as freedom of speech and freedom of the press. It looked as if democracy could flourish. Like the FRG, the GDR's constitution was meant to be a temporary measure, pending German reunification.

In reality, the GDR as directed by the Soviets quickly developed into a totalitarian state, shaping its politics, economy and society on the model of the USSR. At no time did the leaders of the new system really have the support of the majority of their people behind them and, therefore, in order to maintain their power, they made use of:

- the SED and the party system
- the judiciary
- the **Stasi** – the GDR state secret service
- Soviet troops and SMAD (see page 287).

The transformation of SED and the party system

Already, before the GDR had been created, the SED, under directives from Moscow, had begun to reform itself into a so-called 'party of a new type'. The new principle introduced was that of 'democratic centralism', as practised by the CPSU, the Communist Party of the Soviet Union (see page 289). Under this system, there was a formal head of state in the role of the president, and a prime minister as head of government, but the main power force was the general

KEY TERM

Stasi *Staatssicherheitsdienst* (SSD). The state security service, the GDR's secret police. Created in February 1950, it was modelled closely on Soviet secret intelligence.

secretary of the SED. In short, from the outset, the real decision-making was made by the **Politbureau**, led by:

- Walter Ulbricht, the party leader 1946–71 (general secretary or first secretary)
- Wilhelm Pieck, president of the GDR 1949–60
- Otto Grotewohl, prime minister of the GDR 1949–60.

The democracy outlined may not have appeared to be in line with Western democracy, but there were many people in the GDR who believed that they were building a new socialist and anti-fascist society that would shake off the horrors of the Nazi past that had arisen from the capitalist system. The new Communist Party, they were told, would be a 'Vanguard Party' that would re-educate the working class away from the old capitalist and bourgeois interests towards understanding their real political interests and building a better Germany.

SOURCE A

From the Resolution of the First Party Conference of the SED (28 January 1949). Available from German History in Documents and Images (http://germanhistorydocs.ghi-dc.org/)

The Marxist–Leninist party is founded on the principle of democratic centralism. This means strictest adherence to the principle that leading bodies and officers are subject to election and that those elected are accountable to the membership. This internal party democracy is the basis for the tight party discipline which arises from members' socialist consciousness. Party resolutions are binding on all party members, particularly for those party members active in parliaments, governments, administrative bodies, and in the leadership of the mass organizations. …

Toleration of factions and groupings within the party is not consistent with its Marxist–Leninist character.

Absolute loyalty to the USSR and the leaders of the SED was the guideline for all party members, and it was thoroughly cleansed of unreliable and critical elements. In the first two years after the foundation of the GDR, Ulbricht, with the backing of the Soviet secret police, removed over 150,000 party members (mainly ex-SPD people). Moreover, some communists, even those in quite high-level positions, who were not sympathetic to the Stalinist line were put on show trials and expelled from the party, or even imprisoned. A new Party Control Commission was established to watch over the right ideological attitude of all party members, which in effect meant it removed critics of Ulbricht. Power remained in the hands of a small circle of top-ranking officials.

Unlike the USSR, the GDR did allow a certain degree of party pluralism, although this measure was only tolerated to give the image of a democratic system. In reality, all parties and other mass organisations had to accept the SED's monopoly of power as 'the undisputed leader of the workers' movement' (see Figure 10.1). Although the leading figures of the CDUD (Otto Nuschke)

> Why did democratic centralism require such party loyalty, according to Source A?

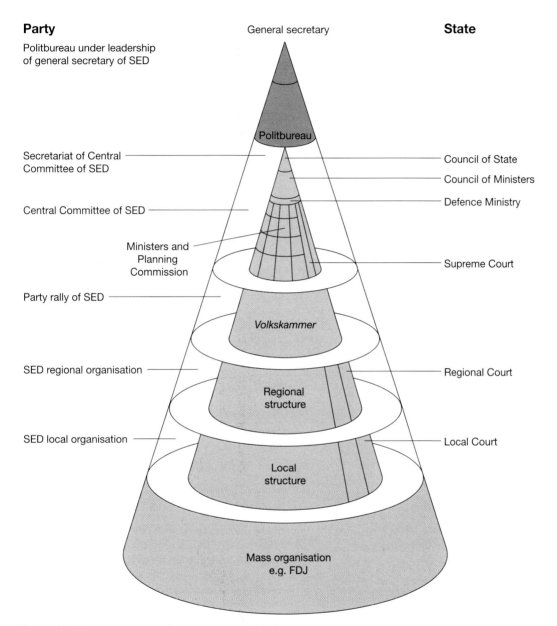

Party

Politbureau under leadership
of general secretary of SED

General secretary

State

Politbureau

Secretariat of Central
Committee of SED

Council of State

Council of Ministers

Defence Ministry

Central Committee of SED

Ministers and
Planning
Commission

Supreme Court

Party rally of SED

Volskammer

SED regional organisation

Regional
structure

Regional Court

SED local organisation

Local
structure

Local Court

Mass organisation
e.g. FDJ

Figure 10.1 Dualism: party and state in the people's democracy.

and the LDPD (Hermann Kastner) did join the government, they had little real
influence. From the start, within those parties all voices critical of the SED were
eliminated through various degrees of intimidation. By 1952–3 the two parties
had officially accepted the leading roles of Ulbricht and the SED and the Soviet
High Commission (see page 360).

In addition, in 1948 the SMAD had allowed the foundation of two other
officially non-communist parties, the NDPD and the DBD. As instruments of

Walter Ulbricht

1893	Born into a poor working-class family in Leipzig and trained as a carpenter
1919	Joined the KPD and elected as a *Reichstag* representative (1928–33)
1933–45	Fled from Germany and remained in Moscow from 1937
1945–9	Returned to Germany with the Red Army and worked closely with SMAD in the Soviet zone
1946	Fully supported the formation of the SED by merging the East German SPD and KPD
1950	Appointed general secretary of the SED, making him party leader
1953	Strengthened his political position in the wake of the uprising (see pages 360–5)
1956	Survived Khrushchev's de-Stalinisation
1960	Became chairman of the Council of State following the death of President Pieck; in effect, leader of the party and head of state until 1971
1961	Ordered the building of the Berlin Wall (see pages 387–90)
1971	Forced to resign on health grounds and replaced by **Erich Honecker**
1973	Died

Ulbricht was never an imposing charismatic revolutionary; he lacked personality and deliberately kept his distance from the people. He was a committed communist who blindly followed the party line and only survived his years in the USSR by being an unquestioning Stalinist, unlike many other German communists. In that way, he was well prepared for his return to Germany in 1945, as the leader of a group of elite German Stalinists, to build up a new socialist system.

In conjunction with SMAD, it was he who efficiently managed the early stages of the establishment of the communist structures in the Soviet zone. He achieved this through:

- the merger of the SPD and the KPD into the SED
- the land reform and the nationalisation of industry
- the foundation of the GDR in October 1949.

As the general secretary of the SED 1950–71, Ulbricht became the most powerful man in the GDR and despite all the crises, showed himself to be a great survivor. This can be put down to two things: his single-minded loyalty to the USSR and his ruthless control of the party and the state apparatus, supported by frequent purges and the actions of the *Stasi*. Ulbricht also oversaw the development of the GDR economy along socialist principles regardless of the costs to the population or the environment. In 1961 he was the driving force behind the building of the Berlin Wall, even though a few weeks before he had famously stated: 'No one intends to build a wall.'

With his goatee beard and high squeaky voice, Ulbricht was regularly caricatured and he was ousted from office unloved and not even respected. Nevertheless, he proved to be a very shrewd and intelligent political operator, who was committed ruthlessly to the communist cause and was responsible for shaping East Germany for a quarter of a century. Further in his defence, one might point out that under him the GDR achieved a degree of prosperity and that his totalitarian methods did not resort to the brutality of Hitler and Stalin.

🔑 KEY FIGURE

Erich Honecker (1912–94)

A lifelong and committed member of the KPD from the 1920s and imprisoned by the Nazis. A founder of the Free German Youth (FDJ); he became its chairman 1945–55. As a member of the Politbureau from 1958 he was responsible for military and security issues and was in charge of the construction of the Berlin Wall. He replaced Ulbricht as general secretary of the SED from 1971, a post which he held until the last few weeks of the fall of the Berlin Wall.

the SED they were to exert influence among the rural and conservative areas of society. Like the CDUD and the LDPD, they were to camouflage the one-party dictatorship of the SED and support government ideas in non-communist circles.

A similar role was given to major mass organisations, like the Free German Federation of Trade Unions (FDGB) and the Free German Youth (FDJ) (see also pages 379–80). They were to implement the will of the SED and to spread its political ideology.

> ## Major political organisations in the GDR
>
> - SED: *Sozialistische Einheitspartei*. Socialist Unity Party of Germany. The new party created in April 1946 by the merger of the KPD and SPD.
> - CDUD: *Christliche Demokratische Union Deutschlands*. Christian Democratic Union in the GDR.
> - LDPD: *Liberaldemokratische Partei Deutschlands*. Liberal Democratic Party in the GDR.
> - NDPD: *National-Demokratische Partei Deutschlands*. National Democratic Party of Germany.
> - DBD: *Demokratische Bauernpartei Deutschlands*. Democratic Farmers' Party of Germany.
> - FDGB: Free German Federation of Trade Unions. Formed in 1945 in the Soviet zone to create a single trade union for all German workers.
> - FDJ: *Frei Deutsche Jugend*. Free German Youth. A communist-inspired youth group which encouraged support for the state.

As a result, all the parties and the mass organisations were integrated in the 'National Front of the GDR' as a broad umbrella organisation (see Figure 10.2). Elections were held on the basis of a unified single list of candidates presented to the *Volkskammer*. This process exerted considerable pressure on the electorate and effectively 'fixed' the results by pressurising people to vote and massaging the figures. Not surprisingly in 1950, the election to the first People's Chamber resulted in the participation of 98 per cent of the electorate and a 99.7 per cent support of the approved list of candidates. The SED and its mass organisations together held an absolute majority of seats.

The judiciary

De-Nazification in the Soviet zone was used by the communist leaders to reform the judiciary and to centralise the system. As a result, the large majority of judicial appointments were replaced on political grounds and, by 1950, half of judges and 86 per cent of public prosecutors were members of the SED.

Many of those new judges were 'retrained' on short intensive courses and many lacked good legal qualifications. Indeed, the real criteria required to become a people's judge (*Volksrichter*) were a good political reputation and a solid record as a political official of the communists. Contrary to the constitution, judges were not independent, but were guided and controlled by the Supreme Court and the SED's institutions.

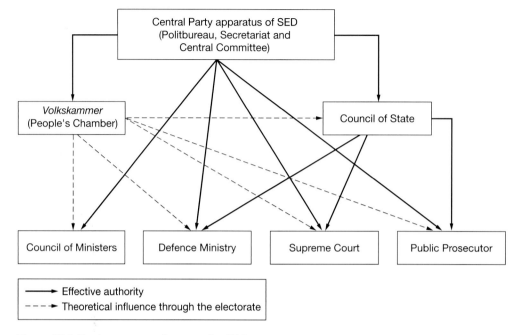

```
┌─────────────────────────────────┐
│   Central Party apparatus of SED │
│   (Politbureau, Secretariat and  │
│        Central Committee)        │
└─────────────────────────────────┘
```

Volkskammer
(People's Chamber)

Council of State

Council of Ministers   Defence Ministry   Supreme Court   Public Prosecutor

⟶ Effective authority
⇢ Theoretical influence through the electorate

Figure 10.2 Dualism: party and state in the GDR.

In many ways, criminal law was adapted over the years by the communists to suppress all opposition. Accusations of 'Nazi crimes' or 'agitation against democratic institutions', or, even more vaguely, 'subversive agitation' or 'disturbance of public and social activities' were used to control dissent. It is estimated that in 40 years about 200,000 people were prosecuted in the GDR for political reasons, and the process served to intimidate and criminalise any kind of opposition.

The Politbureau also played a central role in political trials. Show trials against higher ranking critics of Ulbricht were staged publicly. In these cases, members of the Politbureau often gave minute instructions to the court as to the proceedings and the sentence.

In addition to criminal law, civil, labour and family law were all controlled by the GDR political authorities. Critics of the SED and their families were hindered in their career aspirations and their freedom to travel. For more severe 'crimes' against the state, parents could have their children taken away from them, which created a climate of fear and insecurity reinforced by the secret police, the *Stasi*.

The secret police

The SED leaders had one more very effective means of keeping down any opposition, the state security service, which was commonly called the *Stasi*. It was founded in February 1950 and in the official propaganda the *Stasi* was called 'the sword and shield of the party'. Its stated aims were 'to fight against "saboteurs" and "capitalist agents" who were trying "by order of the American imperialists to undermine the progress of the young socialist state".' It was closely modelled on the Soviet secret intelligence service and from the start the two organisations were closely connected.

The structure and organisation of the *Stasi* were like those of an army, with military-like hierarchy, ranks and punishments. It started with only 1000 permanent members of staff, but by 1955 the number had grown to 13,000. The real expansion of the system and the extent of its surveillance can be seen by the dominating influence of Erich Mielke as the *Stasi* minister. He remained in power until 1989, by which time 91,000 people worked full time for the organisation, including its own paramilitary units. This made it far bigger than the Nazi *Gestapo*, which had overseen a much larger country (see pages 164–5).

Informal members

In addition, there were informal members (known as IMs). These comprised citizens from all walks of life who could be trusted to spy on and denounce colleagues, neighbours, friends or even family. They were contacted and guided by a *Stasi* officer and for each IM a file was kept meticulously under a pseudonym and code. By the time of the fall of the regime, the *Stasi* had 175,000 IMs to help spy on the population of 16.1 million people.

Extent of *Stasi* powers

The *Stasi* worked under the strictest secrecy and with direct authorisation from the SED Politbureau. In reality, there was no legal restraint on its aims or methods. To control and suppress the opposition the *Stasi* stopped at nothing: private letters were opened, homes bugged and searched secretly, bank statements and patients' records combed through to criminalise or ruin critics of the state. People could be arrested and questioned without charge and kept in prison under psychological torture. Over the years the *Stasi* developed into an omnipresent organisation used for the surveillance and control of the whole population.

Military forces

The last line of defence for the SED dictatorship was the use of military forces:

- The People's Police (*Volkspolizei*, *VP* or *Vopo*) was founded in 1949 with traditional policing roles, but also with uniformed paramilitary rapid response units. It proved quite ineffective in the 1953 uprising (see pages 361–5) and was then closely monitored by the *Stasi*. Its most obvious function was to oversee frontier checks, especially after the erection of the Berlin Wall (see pages 388–9).
- The National People's Army (*National Volksarmee*, *NVA*) was founded in 1956 after the creation of the *Bundeswehr* (see page 341) and the Warsaw Pact in

1955 (see page 344). Its doctrine and structure were strongly influenced by the Soviets. It was not only a traditional army, but also a means of controlling the population; it described itself as 'the instrument of power of the working class'.

- SMAD (see page 287) was renamed the Soviet High Commission in October 1949 and Soviet troops remained stationed in barracks throughout the GDR. Their role was to defend the USSR in the event of a NATO attack, but they also served as the last line to crush internal disturbances, most obviously during the 1953 uprising and the creation of the Berlin Wall.

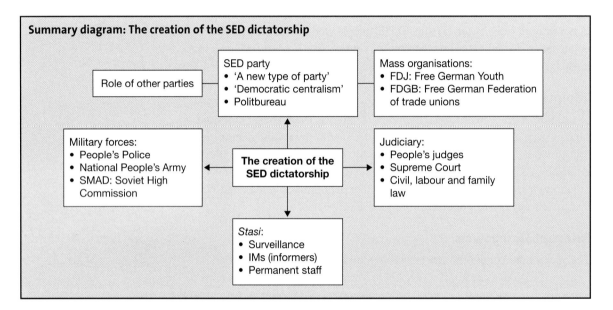

Summary diagram: The creation of the SED dictatorship

2 The political survival of Ulbricht's GDR

▶ *What were the causes and consequences of the workers' uprising?*

▶ *How and why did Ulbricht survive de-Stalinisation?*

The events of 17 June 1953 grew out of the decision by Ulbricht and the SED to accelerate 'the systematic building of socialism'. In practice, this meant policies of rapid industrialisation and collectivisation supported by state centralisation and control. For example:

- The *Länder* states were abolished in 1952 and replaced by smaller units known as *Bezirke* that were easier to administer and control.
- The Churches were intimidated and hampered in their activities.
- Direction of education and media was increased.
- The *Stasi* was expanded to suppress any political criticism.

Wide circles of the population were increasingly alienated from the government, not only by the ruthless nature of the regime, but also by consequences of the GDR economic policies:

- For the remaining middle classes involved in private businesses and shops there was extremely high taxation, administrative harassment and political persecution. It seemed that their position was undermined in favour of rapid expansion of the large nationalised industrial plants (see pages 289–91).
- The majority of farmers were still independent in the early 1950s, but they resented the low prices paid for their agricultural produce and the state's strict directives. Above all, they feared the ongoing threat of forcible collectivisation.
- The workers faced rising prices and food shortages, yet their wages were strictly controlled.

The GDR presented an austere environment in the early 1950s characterised by growing popular dissatisfaction. Basic foods, like bread and fresh vegetables, were still only to be obtained through ration cards, and sometimes not at all. Consumer goods were not being produced, even though the controlled press continuously proclaimed new successes in industrial production levels. One symptom of public attitude, which could not be disguised, was the number of refugees from the GDR to FRG, especially via the 'island' of West Berlin. The number of GDR citizens who had 'voted with their feet' had increased from a figure of 75,000 in 1949 to 171,000 in 1952.

The workers' uprising of 17 June 1953

The emerging crisis was brought to a head in early 1953 by two coinciding events: one external and one internal. First, Stalin's death on 5 March resulted in the new Soviet leaders quickly recommending an easing of the strict Stalinist course for the SED. This signified an attempt to overcome the catastrophic economic situation and the bitter mood of the population. Secondly, in May 1953, in an effort to meet the planned economic targets more quickly and to match the industrial development in the FRG, the GDR government proposed a ten per cent rise in the norms (productivity and working hours). This policy triggered strikes in some big cities. Even when Ulbricht and **Grotewohl** were summoned to a special meeting with the new Soviet leadership in Moscow, they failed to defuse the crisis and on 13 June the GDR leadership reaffirmed that the rise in norms would *not* be withdrawn. This decision proved to be a major mistake.

On 16 June building workers in East Berlin assembled for a peaceful protest march against the norms. The march was quickly joined by workers from all over East Berlin and radicalised into a general protest against the government and the party. Political demands, such as more democracy, German reunification and even the resignation of Ulbricht, dominated the protests, alongside complaints about the shortages of goods. During the protest a worker made

 KEY FIGURE

Otto Grotewohl (1894–1964)

A member of the SPD from 1925, he worked with the KPD in the Soviet zone to create the SED. He served as prime minister of the GDR from 1949 until his death, but the real power always lay with Ulbricht.

a loudspeaker demand for a general strike for the following day, which was reported by a West Berlin radio station. The protest and the call for action were broadcast across the GDR – and it proved impossible to stop the momentum.

By noon on 17 June, it is reckoned that there were 100,000 protestors on the streets of East Berlin. Despite the broad discontent of the middle classes and the farmers, the great majority of demonstrators were industrial workers. Within a few hours the protests had spread like wildfire to over 500 cities, towns and communities with between a further 200,000 and 300,000 protesters (amounting to between five and seven per cent of the workforce). Ulbricht and the SED Politbureau were helpless – and it seemed as if the regime could collapse.

The failure of the workers' uprising

Although the SED leadership was in a weak position and lacking direction, the hopes of East Germans for a real change were short lived. The uprising was not put down by the GDR's forces; instead its failure was caused by the following factors.

Soviet intervention

By midday Ulbricht had appealed for help from the Soviets and a state of emergency was declared. This gave the Soviet commander in East Berlin the right to send Soviet tanks and troops to crush the uprising. Similar orders were given throughout the country imposing martial law. The Soviets met only feeble resistance.

Poor organisation

The uprising was spontaneous, without any effective national co-ordination or planning. Some strike committees of workers were formed, as at Magdeburg and Halle, and they did formulate statements of political and economic objectives, which were printed on the day.

SOURCE B

The manifesto of a building site in East Berlin, dated June 1953.

The building site … in connection with the East Berlin building workers. We demand:

1. Full protection for the strike speakers

2. Free speech and freedom of the press

3. The abolition of the norms

4. The revision of the whole price level for foodstuffs and consumer goods

5. Free elections for all Germany

6. The abolition of zone boundaries

7. Withdrawal of all occupation troops

What do the demands in Source B tell you about the concerns of workers in the GDR?

8. *The abolition of the militarised People's Police*

9. *The immediate resumption of the rebate workers' return tickets*

10. *The release of all political prisoners*

11. *The repatriation of all prisoners of war*

12. *The abolition of the 'People's Controls'.*

But no arrangements were made to seize power by taking control of key strategic points, such as radio stations, railway lines or roads. The demonstrators had no effective weapons to support their cause against the Soviet Army.

Non-intervention by the West

The demonstrators had been naïve to expect support from the West. Although the Western powers paid lip service to the idea of the liberation of the suppressed people in eastern Europe, none would risk direct military involvement in the highly charged atmosphere of the Cold War. The fact that Adenauer also did nothing led many East Germans to feel abandoned by the West.

By the evening of 17 June the Soviet forces had re-established order on behalf of Ulbricht's government, although a few strikes and protests carried on until 21 June. There were an estimated 20–50 fatalities across the country.

The consequences of the 17 June uprising

The claim of the GDR to be a democratic workers' state had been exposed as a sham by the events, and yet amazingly in the wake of the insurrection Ulbricht's regime was strengthened. The main 'ringleaders' were identified and about 1300 people were put on trial: most received long prison sentences and two the death penalty.

Official propaganda blamed the uprising on 'Western agents' and described it as a 'fascist *putsch*' instigated and directed by the imperialist Western powers. Yet, although the uprising did not end Ulbricht's power, he was astute enough to recognise the inadequacies of his regime's power base, and introduced the following changes to bolster it.

The purge of the party

Two of Ulbricht's critics, Zaisser and Herrnstadt, were expelled from the Politbureau and later, in January 1954, from the party itself. Shortly afterwards, an extensive purge within the party at all ranks took place, especially focusing on many previous SPD members, who were charged with slowing the development of socialism. Altogether, it is estimated that 20,000 leading SED officials were removed in the months after the uprising and replaced by thousands of new 'party activists'.

The security apparatus

The uprising highlighted the inadequacy of the security services and their failure to detect and prevent the unrest. So, in the wake of the uprising military and security forces were reformed and strengthened. The *Stasi* was given the authority to suppress any opposition and the number of agents was significantly increased. It was at this time that the extensive surveillance started.

Concessions

Ulbricht did not publicly back down, which might have suggested weakness or error, but the SED did decide to slow down the pace for a while to appease the frustration of the population:

- the work norms were withdrawn
- controlled prices of basic foods were lowered
- more consumer goods were introduced
- the taxes and administrative constraints of farmers and private businessmen were reduced.

SOURCE C

In Source C, why would the cartoonist want to portray the USA in such a negative light?

A cartoon from 17 June 1953. 'The "poison of sedition" harms the troublemaker himself.' The uprising against the SED regime is seen as a 'counter-revolutionary *putsch*'. It puts the main responsibility for it on the USA.

The significance of the uprising

Although the uprising was a major embarrassment to Ulbricht and his clique, in some ways it actually consolidated Ulbricht's position as leader. He had been facing criticism within the party, but if he had been forced to step down following the uprising, it would have been seen as a victory for the demonstrators. The uprising also proved to be a milestone in the evolution of the GDR. It showed that the one-party structure and the development of its mass organisations had become established, and that the presence of Soviet troops could never be ignored. Consequently, Ulbricht had to find a way to work with the Soviet leadership, whoever was in power. Moreover, the GDR was politically recognised by the USSR in 1955 and joined the Warsaw Pact (see page 344). Also, there was a slight improvement in living standards and the regime was able to take some consolation from the fact that the number of refugees declined in the five years from 1953 (see Table 10.6 on page 388). However, this new stability was threatened in 1956 by a crisis generated by the new Soviet leader, **Nikita Khrushchev**.

De-Stalinisation

Ulbricht and the SED leadership had shown themselves keen to preserve and expand the Stalinist structures of the GDR, even after the death of Stalin. So, when, in his speech in February 1956, Khrushchev officially proclaimed the end of Stalinism and denounced his terror methods (de-Stalinisation), it caused turmoil among SED members and in other European communist parties. Official propaganda had always held up Stalin as an idol. Stalin's policies and ideology had been the founding principles of the new state and party, and had secured Ulbricht's power.

Khrushchev's declaration of de-Stalinisation generated an atmosphere of change throughout eastern Europe:

- Poland had riots in Posen. With Khrushchev's agreement, the Polish Communist Party appointed Gomułka in June 1956 to introduce moderate reform.
- In Hungary, in October, a reforming communist leader, Imre Nagy, was pushing for Hungary to withdraw from the Warsaw Pact.

In the GDR, within the SED, hopes were raised for a new communist intelligentsia which would combine Marxism with a more democratic and humane socialism. Well-known philosophers and writers, such as Ernst Bloch and Wolfgang Harich, started to criticise the system of the GDR, openly demanding a 'third way' between anti-capitalism and anti-Stalinism. Such prominent Marxist rebels clearly threatened the structure and direction of the party shaped by Ulbricht.

KEY FIGURE

Nikita Khrushchev (1894–1971)

Khrushchev was a strong supporter of Stalin from the mid-1930s and became general secretary of the Russian CPSU 1953–64. He denounced the excesses of Stalin in 1956 and introduced a policy of de-Stalinisation, creating domestic reforms and a less repressive regime. However, he remained committed to a hardline policy of USSR power; he backed the building of the Berlin Wall and approved the placing of nuclear weapons on Cuba.

The Hungarian uprising

The dramatic events in eastern Europe in 1956 came to a head in November when Soviet troops invaded Hungary to crush Nagy's government of reforms. Over 3000 people died in the conflict and Nagy was captured and executed along with 2000 others. However, three things prevented the Hungarian crisis from triggering a new uprising in the GDR:

- Ulbricht had learned lessons from the 1953 uprising and party discipline had become much stricter, with greater power of the *Stasi*.
- The concession of shortening the working day and the freeing of 21,000 political prisoners in October 1956 reduced public discontent.
- The brutality with which the Hungarian uprising was put down deterred any rebellious tendencies.

Nevertheless, Ulbricht's personal authority was not certain. He was 'a reluctant de-Staliniser', who faced dangerous opposition within the highest ranks of the party, particularly from Karl Schirdewan and Ernst Wollweber. They wanted far-reaching reform of the party's policies over the direction of the economy and the relationship between the GDR and the FRG. During 1956 their support from high positions in the party had increased. It was even rumoured that Khrushchev had considered the replacement of Ulbricht by Schirdewan in order to give stronger backing to the new direction.

Ulbricht's supremacy

Despite all odds, Ulbricht survived. First, the intellectual Marxist rebels were quickly removed from public life. Bloch was forced to resign his post at Leipzig and later escaped to the West. The philosopher Harich fared worse, as he was arrested and given a long prison sentence in 1957. Secondly, it seems that by the early months of 1957 Khrushchev had begun to have doubts about removing Ulbricht in the wake of the USSR's problems within the 'Eastern bloc'. Ulbricht's hardline leadership at least gave a degree of stability in that vital Soviet satellite. Thirdly, Ulbricht showed great skill and ruthlessness in the internal party battle. He bided his time and, eventually, in February 1958, Schirdewan and Wollweber were removed from their posts in the Politbureau. This prompted yet another purge within the party of all elements sympathetic to moderate policies. 'Ulbricht successfully dealt with factionalism in the higher ranks of the SED, such that by the end of the 1950s he was in command of a well-disciplined party of committed Communists' (Mary Fulbrook).

As a postscript, the concentration of power in the GDR and the rigid hierarchy of the SED organisation of the party were confirmed when President Pieck died. The office of president was abolished and, instead, Ulbricht became the chairman of the Council of State; as he was general secretary of the SED and also a member of the Politbureau, he held all-encompassing powers. He and his supporters had managed to suppress or drive out all opposition within and outside the party.

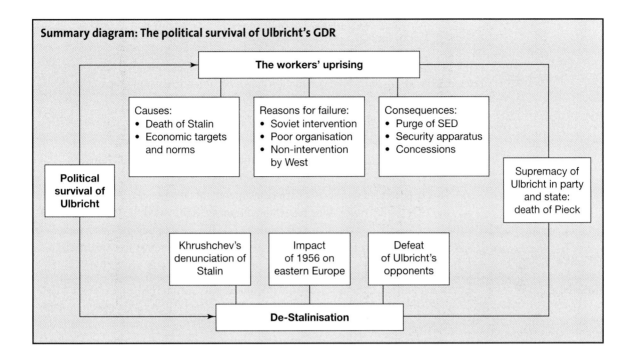

Summary diagram: The political survival of Ulbricht's GDR

3 The GDR economy

▶ *To what extent was communism an economic failure for the GDR?*

The Soviet zone enjoyed some economic benefits (see page 289), but these were outweighed by a number of clear disadvantages:

- a shortage of raw materials
- the loss of provinces to Poland
- the dislocation of population
- the limitations of industrial development.

By the time the Soviet zone had become the GDR, the economic consequences of the years 1945–9 were dramatic:

- dismantling and reparations
- nationalisation
- land reform.

It was no wonder that the GDR's path to economic stability and development was problematic.

The international context

Before the war Germany had been one economic unit with close economic ties between the eastern and western parts of the country. Industry in eastern

Germany had relied on resources from western Germany and it could sell its products in the larger Western markets.

After 1945, and with the onset of the Cold War, the economic development of the Western and Soviet occupation zones became increasingly separated. By 1950 this led to the evolution of two Germanys with different economic and political systems. Not surprisingly, trading links became rather complicated because of the GDR's unique position.

Even though Stalin had refused to let the GDR join the Marshall Plan, the country still looked to the West because of its ongoing shortage of hard currency. This decision led to a sort of bartering agreement between the two Germanys in the 1951 Berlin Treaty, which facilitated trading. It provided the GDR with tariff-free access to the West German market and allowed it to pay in goods, rather than currency. In addition, the GDR was given some interest-free overdraft privileges.

In September 1950 the GDR joined **Comecon** and from that time was gradually economically integrated into the Eastern bloc. The GDR could not keep up with the pace of development of modern technology in the West and its methods of production were far too expensive to compete in free markets anyway. So the possibilities of breaking into the Western markets became rather limited and, consequently, it had to gear its products increasingly to the demands of the USSR and the other Eastern bloc countries.

Within Comecon the GDR was the second largest industrial power after the USSR and came to play a crucial economic role. Foreign trade between the GDR and its brother countries trebled between 1950 and 1955, and by 1954 three-quarters of it was conducted with the socialist bloc countries, of which 40 per cent was with the USSR alone.

Although the GDR was emerging as the most economically developed country in the Eastern bloc, the advantages associated with its membership of Comecon were limiting in other respects. From the start, the GDR's industrial production was geared to the demands of the USSR, which aimed to gradually merge the national economies of the two states. Most obviously, the GDR's Seven-Year Plan in 1958 (see page 371) was formulated within guidelines laid down by the USSR for all countries within Comecon. In that way, engineering machinery, such as agricultural tools, ships and railway wagons, were dispatched to the USSR in return for natural resources, like oil or iron ore. The USSR never really paid the real-world market prices for goods and so it was a rather unprofitable business for the GDR. Until the mid-1960s the USSR and GDR continued to have a very close economic relationship; in that year the introduction of the **New Economic System** (NES) reforms dislocated the closeness of the two states.

KEY TERMS

Comecon Council for Mutual Economic Assistance. Formed in 1949 to facilitate and co-ordinate the economic policy of Soviet states in the Eastern bloc. The GDR joined in 1950.

New Economic System Name given to the economic policy adopted by the SED in 1963. It rejected the Seven-Year Plan in favour of decentralisation in the management of the economy and even the consideration of market criteria. In the late 1960s economic and social reforms did improve living standards.

Industry

Even before the foundation of the GDR, the SED had started discussions for a centralised, planned economy, based on a Stalinist model, in its declaration 'Planned Construction of Socialism'. Then, in response, the SED publicly announced its own slogan: 'To learn from the Soviet Union means learning to win.'

The first Five-Year Plan 1951–5

A short transitional Two-Year Plan steered the GDR economy to extend nationalisation and, by 1950, 76 per cent of industrial production was already under the control of the VEBs and SAGs (see page 290), and banking and insurance was completely directed by the state. It also directed the economy into the appropriate channels, in order to raise the low levels of industrial productivity. The first Five-Year Plan from 1951 to 1955 had ambitious aims, particularly for heavy industry: fuel and power, iron and steel, chemicals, metallurgy and building. As with Stalin's Five-Year Plans in the USSR, the objectives were drawn up by a State Planning Commission, which intended to supervise every aspect of the operation. Indeed, it was determined to prove its success.

SOURCE D

An extract from a GDR Statistical Report on the Development of the Standard of Living in the GDR and in the FRG (1956).

… Average gross hourly wages for industrial workers in the GDR are higher than wages for industrial workers in West Germany, both in the Socialist industries and in industry overall.

Average weekly work hours of male industrial workers [in West Germany] exceeded 50-hours … in 1955. … The average weekly work period in the GDR does not deviate from the 48-hour week.

… Expenses for food and semi-luxury goods as a percentage of overall income are 48.4% in West Germany and 51.5% in the GDR. The share for rent and for education, entertainment, and recreation is significantly higher in West Germany.

> According to Source D, why would the State Planning Commission be so concerned with comparisons between the FRG and GDR in 1956?

On one level the first Five-Year Plan can be seen as a great success. It was officially proclaimed as over-fulfilling its many targets and overall industrial production had doubled since 1950. As Table 10.1 (overleaf) shows, particularly successful were production of iron, sulphuric acid and cement, whereas production of steel and lignite, although dramatically increased, fell short of their targets. So, as a result of the fierce efforts and privations suffered by the GDR population, the SED leaders managed to expand the economy. However, it is tempting to say that the imitation of the Soviet Union model proved to be a mistake, as the performance of the first Five-Year Plan still raised fundamental problems.

Table 10.1 Industrial production in the GDR 1950–5

Product	1950	1955 Plan	1955 Actual
Coal	2,805	3,500	2,667
Lignite	137,050	205,000	200,612
Electricity	19,466	31,600	28,695
Iron	337	1,250	1,517
Steel	999	3,000	2,507
Sulphuric acid	245	400	483
Cement	1,412	2,600	2,971

Note: lignite was easily accessible in East Germany, but it is much dirtier than black coal. The environmental cost has been very great.

Overdependence on heavy industry

Despite the lack of natural resources in the country, the SED leaders set an ambitious target to build up heavy industry, particularly coal and steel. However, many of the newly created industrial enterprises were established at inappropriate locations and were often unprofitable. The emphasis on heavy industry was achieved at the expense of consumer goods, whose production would have helped to revive the domestic market more quickly and keep the people happier. A more realistic alternative would have been to modernise the economy by investing in more modern technologies and lighter industry.

Centralised planning

The dominance of centralised planning discouraged private initiatives and investment. Moreover, the planning processes were often too slow and inflexible to react to short-term necessities and problems. The system meant that production pursued quantity at the expense of quality.

Productivity

Despite the workers' legal rights and the promise of better working conditions, the productivity quotas put pressure on the workforce. Not surprisingly, many workers were sceptical of the system and were tempted to go to the West, where their skills would be welcomed.

These points suggest that the very idea of complete central planning in a relatively advanced economy was ineffective. Moreover, ideological influences carried more weight than expertise or knowledge. The bungling happened at the core of the planning process and things could have worked out much better with less ideology and more pragmatism.

Later plans

A second Five-Year Plan was initiated in 1956 and it aimed to combine the production of capital and consumer goods. Indeed, it even put some stress on technological progress, with the slogan 'Modernisation, Mechanisation and Automation'. It backed the development of nuclear energy and the first nuclear reactor in the GDR was activated in 1957.

Economic planning

1949: Two-Year Plan (1949–50).

1951: Five-Year Plan (1951–5).

1956: Five-Year Plan (1956–60). Aborted in 1958.

1959: Seven-Year Plan (1959–65). Aborted in 1962.

1963: New Economic System (1963–8).

By the late 1950s it seemed as if the GDR's economy and its citizens were making real advances, and in the years 1958–9 the GDR economy grew by twelve per cent per annum. Consumer goods were at last being produced and living standards improved, but not to the extent that was being enjoyed by the 'economic miracle' of the FRG. In 1958 the rationing cards for meat, fat and sugar disappeared. The new 'achievements of socialism' allowed for the creation of workers' cultural centres and polytechnics (see pages 378–9) Housing and basic goods, such as bread, milk and potatoes, were set at low prices. Even the numbers of refugees to the West dropped substantially and it seemed as if Ulbricht's GDR had at last stabilised.

These stabilising social improvements were bought at high cost to the economy and the state could not invest this money into other needy sectors, such as the development of infrastructure for transport and energy, and the modernisation of industry. Also, the GDR was desperately short of hard currency and it had created an artificial exchange rate between the East German *Ostmark* and the West DM, which was kept at one to one; this was an artificial rate which had been created out of pride (the real rate was about four to one).

The fundamental problems were not confronted and were further exacerbated when the SED leadership took a change of direction. At the Fifth Party Congress Ulbricht proudly proclaimed that the GDR aimed 'to catch up and overtake' West Germany by 1961 in per capita consumption. As a result, the second Five-Year Plan was aborted and in its place an ambitious Seven-Year Plan was outlined (1959–65) to co-ordinate GDR economic development more closely with the USSR. Its aims were:

- To increase industrial production by 188 per cent.
- To increase consumer goods production by 177 per cent.
- To extend collectivisation.

These figures were unrealistic. The GDR economy had expanded so quickly that the industrial growth rate declined sharply from 1960 and the number of refugees to the West began to climb again to up to 1000 per day in 1960–1. The results were dramatic, with the building of the Berlin Wall (1961) and the introduction of the NES from 1963. This was to enable more devolution in the management of the economy and even give some freedom to the VEBs to reinvest profits.

Agriculture

There had been immediate dramatic changes in agriculture under the Soviet occupation (see also pages 290–1). These meant that:

- All owners of estates larger than 100 hectares (250 acres) were dispossessed without any compensation, regardless of their political standing. Altogether this land represented about one-third of the agricultural area of the Soviet zone.
- The majority of the land seized was handed over in smallholdings of up to seven hectares to landless farm workers and refugees from the East (nearly 4 million settled permanently or temporarily).
- The remainder was given to local communities for cultivation to create the first early state-owned farms.

This meant that the other two-thirds of agricultural land was still in the hands of small- and middle-sized farmers.

On one level, the land reforms seemed quite positive, as they reinforced the egalitarian spirit. However, by 1949 the new state faced fundamental problems in the agricultural sector. There were hardly any modern machines, fertilisers or even sufficient seeds with which to work the land. Many of the new refugee farmers had little or no agricultural experience. Most significantly, agriculture was dominated by small landholdings, too small to survive independently, let alone make a profit. By 1948 crop and livestock yields had fallen dramatically, so farmers were moving to the cities for work, or to the West.

Collectivisation

The idea of collectivisation of agriculture was a fundamental principle of developing a communist planned economy. Yet, the first Five-Year Plan had unequivocally put its emphasis on trade and industry. It had not deeply invested in agriculture and, at first, it was politically and economically cautious about proceeding with collectivisation. However, by 1952 the SED leadership was so concerned about the difficulties with food supplies that it decided to start introducing voluntary collectivisation through the creation of agricultural production co-operatives called **LPGs**.

The introduction of the LPGs meant that collectivisation actually proceeded slowly. It attracted the small-scale farmer, who was given financial incentives to join, whereas it alienated the larger farmer, who declined to participate. By 1953, the year of the 17 June uprising (see pages 361–5), thirteen per cent of all agricultural land was *not* being farmed, which contributed to the number of refugees to the West reaching high levels.

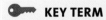 **KEY TERM**

LPGs *Landwirtschaftliche Produktionsgenossenschaft.* Agricultural production co-operatives. The name LPG was given to the large collectivised farms.

The political crises of the uprising and de-Stalinisation served to ease the pace of collectivisation, and by 1958 two-thirds of GDR agriculture was not collectivised, leaving farming still largely independent. However, partly because of the economic pressures, and partly because Ulbricht had secured his personal political supremacy, the SED leadership decided in 1959 to confront the issue of collectivisation once and for all. In 1960–1 the second wave of collectivisation was pushed in an attempt to create a socialist society on the land. This was strongly enforced, mainly by denying farmers access to collective machinery unless they joined the collective. Ideologically committed SED officials were sent into the villages to convince the population of the merits of collectivisation schemes. When many did not give in by not fulfilling the high productivity quotas, arrests and land confiscations were used to speed up the process of collectivisation.

Table 10.2 Collectivisation of East German agriculture 1952–62

Year	Number of collectives	Percentage of farmed area
1952	1,906	3
1954	5,120	14
1956	6,281	23
1958	9,637	37
1960	19,261	84
1962	17,860	85

Results

In the short term collectivisation was a disaster:

- Farmers voted with their feet by going to the West and refugee figures reached a peak in 1961, which was a key reason for building the Berlin Wall in August 1961 (see Table 10.6 on page 388).
- Food production declined markedly.
- Rationing was reintroduced in 1961.

Yet, in a political sense, the GDR communist government achieved its ideological aim of collectivising agriculture. Moreover, in the longer term, agricultural matters did improve. By achieving economies of scale, collectivisation did make agriculture more efficient. From 1963 the SED leadership started to invest substantially more money into the agricultural sector. Therefore, by the 1970s the productivity of LPGs was higher than in most other east European countries. The low fixed prices for basic food meant that the LPGs had to be highly subsidised, just like many farms in the EEC, and the GDR was actually more efficient than the smaller farms in the West.

Conclusion

The basic principles of the GDR state economy were those of nationalisation, centralisation and planning. And for such a small state its achievements stand out. By the early 1960s the GDR had by far the highest level of consumer goods production within the Eastern bloc, and the country was officially ranked tenth in economic production in the world. Yet, the GDR slogan of 'The Building Up of Socialism' did not amount to a new modern beginning. To a large extent, the GDR economy was a kind of 'state capitalism' adapted to match the backward-looking system of the USSR. It could really have done so much better, and its failure had fatal consequences for the country.

Ideological inflexibility

The key problem was that economic policies had to be drawn up under the supremacy of fixed Stalinist ideology, making it extremely difficult for the GDR to build up a balanced economy and to sustain permanent high economic growth. Consequently, hardly any room was left for economic flexibility or individual initiatives, which led to economic mismanagement and inefficiency. Even after the start of the NES reforms (see page 368) there was no real preparedness to overcome the structural imbalance of the national economy.

Effect of the Cold War on world trade

The problems were heightened by the Cold War, which largely cut off the GDR economy from Western markets and forced it to direct its production to the demands of the USSR and the Eastern bloc, with the unfortunate consequences already discussed. This policy led to an almost autarkic mentality.

The 'brain drain'

Probably the biggest failure made by the GDR leadership in the 1950s was that its economic policies did not effectively win over its people. The neglect of consumer industries and the enforced process of collectivisation and nationalisation proved to be catastrophic, as the citizens of the GDR continually compared their lives with the 'capitalist heaven' of West Germany. Although GDR citizens were economically better off than those in all other Eastern bloc countries, the option of moving 'next door' was just too attractive. The ongoing drain of refugees right up to 1961 – more often the young and able – cost the GDR economy dearly.

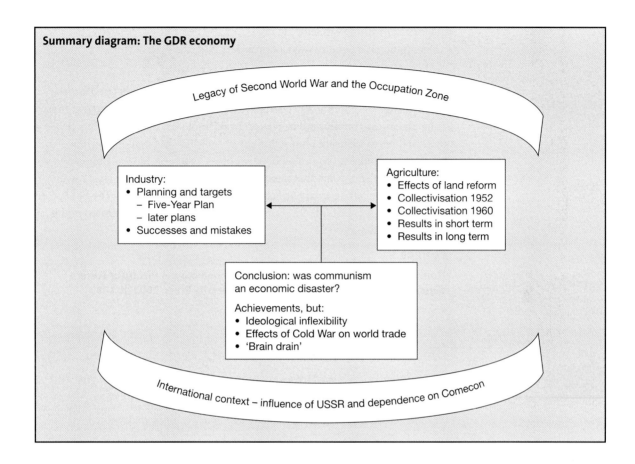

Summary diagram: The GDR economy

Legacy of Second World War and the Occupation Zone

Industry:
• Planning and targets
  – Five-Year Plan
  – later plans
• Successes and mistakes

Agriculture:
• Effects of land reform
• Collectivisation 1952
• Collectivisation 1960
• Results in short term
• Results in long term

Conclusion: was communism an economic disaster?

Achievements, but:
• Ideological inflexibility
• Effects of Cold War on world trade
• 'Brain drain'

International context – influence of USSR and dependence on Comecon

East German society

▶ *To what extent did the GDR become a fairer society for everyone?*

Welfare and housing

The GDR developed its social welfare in a very different way from the FRG. The FRG was built on the principle of social insurance (see page 331). In contrast, the SED, running a communist state, had complete control over the social institutions of welfare. By 1956 the GDR had developed a system which was compulsory and centrally controlled; and it provided universal flat-rate benefits (although special provision was given for state employees, including the army and the police). Although there were compulsory insurance contributions by all people, welfare was very heavily subsidised (unlike in the FRG). Its main features were:

• Health care: free for all from state hospitals and medical centres.
• Pensions: available to all men aged 65 and women aged 60.

- Accident insurance: free for all.
- Unemployment benefit: was not provided, as some kind of work was found for all citizens.

Accommodation was a particular problem in the GDR because its two largest cities, Dresden and Berlin, had been devastated by bombing. Moreover, at first the emphasis of economic policy was on heavy industry, not on housing. It was not until the late 1950s that house building really took off, peaking in 1959–62. However, the impressive number of new homes, reaching 100,000 built per year, could not disguise the fact that many of them were flats in Soviet-style tower blocks and were rather dreary, functional buildings. Nevertheless, the SED had the best of socialist intentions and its aims could be well illustrated in the following 'commandments'.

SOURCE E

According to Source E, what key principles run through these commandments?

From J. Rodden, *Repainting the Little Red Schoolhouse: A History of Eastern German Education, 1945–1995*, Oxford University Press, 2002, p. 108.

The Ten Socialist Commandments of the GDR

1. You should always stand up for the international solidarity of the working classes and workers as well as the close bonds of all socialist countries.

2. You should love your mother country and always be prepared to give all your strength and abilities for the defence of the workers and farmers.

3. You should help to stop the exploitation of one man by another.

4. You should perform good deeds for the socialist movement because socialism leads to a better life for all working people.

5. For the building up of the socialist society you should act in the spirit of mutual help and comradely co-operation, whilst respecting the community and heeding its criticism.

6. You should protect the people's property.

7. You should continuously strive to enhance your performances and to consolidate socialist working discipline.

8. You should bring up your children in the spirit of peace and socialism to become educated, highly principled human beings.

9. You should lead a clean and respectable life and respect your family.

10. You should show solidarity with the peoples fighting for their national liberation and defending their national independence.

Education and youth

All schools were officially opened on 1 October 1945 with the stated purpose of cleansing from them all elements of racism, militarism and reactionary forces.

As a result, 80 per cent of teachers were dismissed and emergency teacher-training classes were organised. Nazi textbooks were thrown away and in their place old ones from the Weimar era were reintroduced (when available). Not surprisingly, for the next few years, the schools in the Soviet zone had to contend with great shortages of staff, books and materials.

Schools and higher education

The communist leaders of the GDR were committed from the start to overhauling the education system, unlike the approach in the Western zones. They wanted to abolish the old school system, since it mirrored the old bourgeois social classes and values which they believed had contributed to the rise of Nazism. In its place they wanted to build up a new socialist society. Their aims were:

- To give all children equal opportunities by creating a centrally state controlled school system, based on socialist ideals and not tarnished by educational privileges.
- To extend technical and practical skills, especially in the sciences, with schools closely linking theory and practice to the requirements of modern industry. Indeed, many schools were 'twinned' with factories to enable students to gain regular hands-on training and skills. Moreover, the students could help with production, particularly when there was a shortage of labour, which would make them identify with the workers who were building the new socialist Germany.
- To establish a strong commitment to socialism and to ensure that future generations would serve the socialist cause.

To these ends, SMAD and the emerging SED imposed dramatic changes within a few months. The Law for the Democratisation of German Schools was put into effect in 1946, offering:

- The expansion of pre-school education (*Kindergarten*).
- The abolition of private and religious schools.
- The introduction of a centralised curriculum with new textbooks.
- The abolition of selective schools and the reorganisation of the system to establish co-educational comprehensive schools for all children aged six to fourteen, *Grundschule*. This policy then provided the chance for the more able to go on to further education at *Oberschule*.

However, as well as these structural changes in the school system, the GDR in the 1950s wanted to go further and establish a real socialist ethos. It wanted to increase social mobility and egalitarianism and to satisfy the demands of the people in a workers' and peasants' state rather than satisfying the academic and professional classes. This ideology prompted a period of great debate in political and educational circles within the GDR, and over the years 1956–65 three major laws were passed which created a system of 'polytechnic education'. The main features of this system were:

POS *Politechnische Oberschule*. The acronym given to the ten-year school system for children aged from six to sixteen years.

- The creation of Polytechnic Upper Schools (**POS**) based on a ten-year system for children from six to sixteen years. (Pupils' education could then be extended for two more years to achieve their *Abitur*, like A-levels, for university and college.)
- Education was centralised and uniform throughout the country, so POS was the compulsory type of school for all children.
- The curriculum was amended substantially to have an emphasis on sciences and technological skills, moral and ideological indoctrination, and Russian as the first foreign language.
- Compulsory practical work for one day a week from the age of fourteen.
- Sport and paramilitary training to raise the general fitness and performance levels of the population and to achieve success in international competition. For boys it was seen as a preparation for military service, which was made compulsory in 1962.
- Adult education was also encouraged, as many East Germans from poorer backgrounds had not had the opportunity to study at university or technical colleges.

Impact of educational policy

Of course, critics of the GDR education structure focused on the negative effects of the highly centralised system. It did not encourage individual self-expression, and there was limited choice involving the parents. Moreover, a pupil's equal opportunity in the GDR was constrained if he or she did not conform to the state's ideology. For example, those who did not join the youth associations (see below) or those who were actively engaged in church congregations could be discriminated against. Most famously, the regime's response to critical thinking is shown in the case of the pupils at Werdau school who openly protested against the voting list for the first election of *Volkskammer* (see page 357). They received prison sentences of two to fifteen years.

Most obviously, the school administration could block career advancement and/or further training. Entry to university was dependent on a commitment to the political system. In this way, the schools became an effective tool for the state to influence and control its youth, and young people learned from very early on to conform and pay at least lip service to the system. Nevertheless, the co-ordinated education system achieved a great deal through the investment of money, time and effort. Indeed, as a percentage of GNP the GDR spent seven per cent on education compared with the FRG's five per cent. Over the years it considerably raised educational standards and eliminated selective schools, which were still very prevalent in West Germany.

The emphasis was placed on providing opportunities for students of working-class and farming backgrounds, which definitely had positive results:

- In the first years after 1945 the percentage of university students from working-class backgrounds rose from nineteen per cent in 1946 to 36 per cent in 1949.
- From 1951 to 1958 the number of universities and colleges had risen from 21 to 46 and the number of students had doubled to 60,000.
- Whereas in 1951 only sixteen per cent of pupils attended school for more than eight years, by 1970 this number had grown to 85 per cent.

Moreover, the improvement was not just quantitative. The initially low standards in maths and natural sciences were gradually raised and the practical advice from the POS helped less gifted pupils, thereby reducing the percentage of dropouts. By the 1970s the GDR came to be a victim of its own educational success because there was a significant glut of graduates who were forced to accept jobs of a much lower standard. The primary aims of the educational policies of the SED had at least been fulfilled in the main.

Youth organisations

As well as the changes imposed on the schools system to direct its young people, the GDR aimed to extend its influence into their private lives through the youth organisation, the FDJ, with its subdivisions, the Young Pioneers and the Ernst Thälmann Pioneers, named in honour of the murdered communist leader (see page 106).

Table 10.3 East German youth organisations

Abbreviation	Title	Year formed	Age range (years)	Membership
FDJ	Free German Youth – *Freie Deutsche Jugend*	1946	14–25	Boys and girls
JP	Ernst Thälmann Pioneers – *Thälmann Pioniere*	1948	10–14	Boys and girls
JP	Ernst Thälmann Young Pioneers – *Junge Pionere*	1948	6–10	Boys and girls

From 1957 the FDJ and the JP became the only officially acknowledged and promoted youth organisations in the GDR and were built on the principles of 'Marxist–Leninist ideology'. They were therefore very much led and controlled by the party leaders in line with the principles of 'democratic centralism' (see page 289).

The aims of the FDJ were to:

- indoctrinate the youth with a socialist education
- fight against capitalist Western influences
- give military and paramilitary training
- organise recreational activities, especially sports
- support community projects to build up the socialist economy, for example through harvest work and basic building work
- provide the training ground for future leadership positions in the GDR.

Its political status was underlined by the fact that the FDJ, like other socialist mass organisations, had a fixed number of seats in the *Volkskammer*, which helped to secure the dominating position of the SED. The FDJ never became compulsory, but in 1950 it already had a membership of over 3 million people. The percentage of non-members became increasingly small as the fear of discrimination over jobs and university places became greater.

Pictures of FDJ members marching and singing evoked memories of the Hitler Youth. The structure and activities were very similar to **Komsomol** in the USSR. For example, members were told heroic tales of communist resistance and struggle; outings also reinforced the message, for instance a visit to Buchenwald concentration camp in honour of Ernst Thälmann (see page 106)). The FDJ had solemn rituals, including an oath of allegiance to the state and an initiation rite taken at the age of fourteen (see page 381). In reality, for young people to get on in life, they literally had to march in the party's step and join the organisation.

The FDJ did have a great deal to offer. The range of activities, sports and trips was extensive. Strategic military training took place in the FDJ, including sailing, gliding, learning to shoot and amateur radio skills. Some members even learned to drive and many young people enjoyed the opportunities offered. At the same time, their socialist consciousness was being developed through working on state construction projects and being trained in surveillance practices.

While some young people accepted the activities and demands of the youth organisations, others found them repressive. Moreover, their rather prudish, old-fashioned and socially conforming approach could not prevent the growing Western influence via the modern media of magazines, radio and, later, television (see pages 334–7). By the early 1960s many young East Germans admired and tried to copy the Western lifestyle through wearing jeans and listening to rock 'n' roll. In an attempt to engage with young people, the SED set up DT64 radio station in 1964, which played popular music that included 40 per cent from Western artists. The FDJ even ran guitar-playing competitions for a short time, before they were banned in 1965. For the most part, young people learned to lead a kind of 'double life', one officially aligned with the state and one in which they privately more or less rebelled against the state expectations and official ideology through their lifestyle.

Churches

According to the GDR constitution, all citizens were granted religious freedom, and it is estimated that in 1950 over 80 per cent of the population were Protestants and ten per cent were Catholics. However, the ideology of an atheistic state claimed that religious beliefs were nothing but superstition, and assumed that religion would gradually disappear in a socialist community. The SED therefore saw the Christian Churches with their anti-communist stance as natural adversaries and it viewed the Churches' links with the outside world with great suspicion: the Catholic Church had international connections and the Protestants had Church councils reaching across the FRG and GDR.

KEY TERM

Komsomol The Communist Union of Youth. The youth wing of the CPSU, founded in 1918.

Churches and state

The Churches in the GDR were allowed to manage their own affairs to some extent, but there was a governmental Department for Ecclesiastical Affairs which laid down a strict division between the Church and the state. For example:

- Religious education was abolished in all schools and gradually the curriculum was replaced by Marxist–Leninist ideology.
- Religious matters were deliberately ignored by the media.
- No financial support was given to Churches from the state (whereas in the FRG a Church tax raised revenue). Consequently, it became very difficult to maintain religious buildings in the GDR; the cathedral in East Berlin was not restored until 1990 and some were simply blown up, for example the famous Potsdam garrison church (see page 139).

In the Ulbricht years, life for Christians in the GDR was difficult. Young people who did not conform to the system and remained strong Christians were pressurised by schools and universities with the threat of barring them. Careers and promotions were later blocked for Christians. The *Stasi* started to tightly control the clergy and often positioned IMs within the congregations to keep a close eye on their activities.

The most severe cases of repression came in the years 1952–3 (and have been closely linked to the months before the uprising of 17 June). Over 50 clergymen and youth leaders were arrested and a Christian youth organisation, the Young Congregation, was defined as anti-socialist and subversive.

Jugendweihe

Further pressure was put on East German youth by the introduction from 1955 of the *Jugendweihe*, which can only be seen as an atheist initiation ceremony with a pledge to the GDR and socialism. Every fourteen-year-old, regardless of denomination, was expected to make the pledge and be inducted into adulthood when they received their identity papers. Those who did not take part had to face the usual consequences for their careers. However, as the 1960s progressed people took a more pragmatic view of the *Jugendweihe* and Christians no longer saw it as completely incompatible with their faith.

GDR society was increasingly de-Christianised and there was a significant reduction in the number of Church members over the years. It is estimated that in the 1970s only about half of the population were professed Christians and they became more marginalised as fringe groups. Nevertheless, the Churches still managed to retain sufficient support for them to be the most significant **niche** in a 'society of niches'. In addition, the emergence of the peace movement in the 1980s and the final days of the GDR demonstrated that the Churches did play an important social and even political role within the state.

 **KEY TERM**

Niche The private space of people as a refuge from the GDR's state power. A term coined by Günter Gaus, Bonn's first representative from the FRG to the GDR.

SOURCE F

? What image of the youth of the GDR is being presented in the poster in Source F?

A poster of a 1959 _Jugendweihe_ ceremony. The title of the book held by the girl is _Space, Earth, Man_.

The socialist woman

Female emancipation was seen as an essential feature of socialist ideology and a self-perpetuating consequence of the establishment of a socialist society. So, the 1949 constitution of the GDR proudly proclaimed:

> _Men and women are equal before the law. All legislation and regulations that are opposed to this principle are repealed. … Women are entitled to the same wages as men for the same work._

Yet, real advantages for women were not so clear-cut in the first twenty years of the GDR because of the legacy from the war:

- The shortage of working men meant that it was necessary to increase the employment of female labour, adding to the hardship of many women.
- In order to relieve the desperate public finances in 1947, the Soviet zone repealed the pensions of hundreds of thousands of widows, thereby forcing women to look for jobs to support themselves.
- Many of the refugees leaving to head West were younger people with families, leaving many elderly women to fend for themselves.

Family

In the 1950s and 1960s a number of measures were put in place in the GDR to help women and families. At the centre of policy was the need for women to produce and reproduce. Therefore, the state offered financial support for working mothers, childcare and crèches, and improved health care. Pregnant and nursing mothers enjoyed additional rations before 1958 and child benefit payments were introduced thereafter. Abortion was strictly limited until 1972, much to the dismay of many women. Despite the propagandist image of women enjoying their work, free from the drudgery of domestic chores, the reality was very different. Many mothers were working in unskilled, low-paid jobs while still taking the responsibility of looking after the children and the household. It was not until 1966 that the Family Law offered more state help and protection for families and stressed the equality of men and women.

Education and career advancement

Again, in terms of education, the GDR aspired to offer equal opportunities between the sexes. From the start, much was achieved for girls in schools, yet in the 1950s the number of female students as a percentage increased quite slowly (see Table 10.4).

Table 10.4 Percentage of female students at East German universities and higher colleges 1953–61

1953	1955	1957	1959	1961
20.4	25.7	25.5	26.9	25.4

Although the figures tended to favour the GDR over the FRG, it seems that the priority of the SED leadership was to support those students from lower social backgrounds and those with strong political beliefs at the expense of female equality. Nevertheless, as a result of a much greater drive in the 1960s and 1970s nearly half of students in higher education were women by 1980.

Women who graduated successfully from university generally had to put up with fewer chances for career advancement and much lower salaries in all fields. The aspired equality between genders was not enforced by special supportive measures within the job market. So while there were some small changes in traditional attitudes towards gender roles in the GDR, they were not primarily to the advantage of women. Many women joined the workforce out of economic necessity, rather than because they were offered equal opportunities.

Active support for the emancipation of women was not really given by the SED until a critical survey in 1961 highlighted the position of women in the GDR. It was backed by the Politbureau and published as *Women – Peace and Socialism*, which revealed the poor progress in the equality process and demanded changes. However, major advances in the laws regarding women's rights were not to be introduced until the late 1960s and 1970s.

Social change

The twenty years after the war were a time of dramatic political change, but the period raised issues about the kind of social change faced by the citizens in the GDR.

Standard of living

Table 10.5 Consumer goods and the percentage of East German households owning them in 1955 and 1966

Item	1955	1966
Cars	0.2	9
Televisions	1.0	54
Fridges	0.4	31
Washing machines	0.5	32

KEY TERM

HO-shop State-owned store where goods could be bought with foreign currency.

In statistical terms it is clear that the growth in the GDR economy had a limited effect on the people until the late 1950s, and it was not until the mid-1960s that there was a marked improvement in material standards of living with the introduction of the NES (see page 368).

Despite the increasing material benefits of life in the GDR there was no real 'feel-good factor'. Life was still quite austere in the 1950s. The economy was one of scarcity, with long queues in front of shops for all kinds of products, from fresh vegetables to spare parts for bicycles. And many other goods were either not available or only of poor quality. All meat and sugar was rationed until 1958. Although the government established state-owned **HO-shops** to sell food and other dearer consumer goods beyond the rationing system, for many people the overpriced goods in those shops were unachievable luxuries. Nevertheless, the issue of standard of living needs to be put into perspective on various levels. People in the GDR in 1963 had definitely become more affluent compared to the citizens living in eastern Germany in 1953 and 1943. Moreover, the GDR was by far the most well-off of the Eastern bloc states. Certainly, a visitor from Poland would have been impressed with what was available in the GDR shops. Also, the state provided extensive subsidies for all citizens for basic foods, rent and public transport. So all of these were maintained at very low prices, and there was no threat of unemployment as the state guaranteed full employment.

Despite the eventual material improvements in the 1960s, the GDR could not escape from its reduced status and condition. The cities of Dresden, Leipzig and Berlin had been great international commercial centres and the GDR could not re-create this past. It was just too obvious that the GDR's material standard of living was inferior to the FRG, and in the end that is why many East Germans voted with their feet.

A 'workers' state'?

Although the GDR was portrayed as a 'workers' state' the vast majority of historians have been able to agree that it was no paradise for the working class. Real democratic participation by workers in workers' councils or free trade unions was effectively blocked from above after the war. Instead, the SED supplanted the capitalist middle classes and quickly formed a privileged bureaucratic 'intelligentsia', which directed the workforce. The interests of this new leadership and its technocrats clashed with the interests of the workers, who were denied any real open participation. The trade unions in the FDGB

(Free German Unions' Association) were purged several times in the first years to make certain that their organisation became a loyal instrument of the SED. In fact, the FDGB became the largest mass organisation of the SED and all of its leading positions were held by SED members. In that way, it could be said that the GDR was not so much a 'dictatorship *of* the proletariat' as a 'dictatorship *over* the proletariat'. That said, the FDGB did look out for its workers when it came to matters like poor working conditions, health and safety or bad management. Furthermore, many members did enjoy some of the benefits that the FDGB offered, especially the holiday resorts run by the organisation.

Equality?

In terms of the GDR's social structure and living standards it is clear that it was becoming much closer to a classless society than the FRG. The wealth and authority of the landed classes and big business were broken once and for all in the occupation years. Moreover, the socialist ideology and economy distinctly levelled the income and social status between the traditional working classes and the middle classes.

Although general income levels in the GDR were well below the average of the FRG, the disparities in wealth were much more marked in the FRG. Certainly, the GDR elite looked after its own interests by acquiring financial privileges, for example, access to good cars and Western currency, but there were far fewer people earning significantly higher incomes. Also, in the GDR it was possible for anyone to improve their position and cross the line from the ruled to the rulers, as long as they conformed to the system.

Conformity and dissent

Officially in the GDR there was no opposition or fundamental criticism in the 'workers' state', as the interests of the state and of its population were claimed to be identical. Of course, the SED leadership recognised that this was by no means the reality, so it imposed an all-encompassing system of control and suppression after the 1953 uprising (see pages 358–9 and 365–7). As it became more dictatorial it started to criminalise any criticism of the state.

The active and most dangerous political and cultural dissent developed among small groups of people, mainly from the 'intelligentsia' and the Churches. They were not prepared to accept the SED monopoly of power and thought, and they started to express their criticism, gaining public attention at home and abroad. Artists and scientists enjoyed a special privileged status within the system, but as soon as they voiced dissent they met all its institutional repression. After 1961 and the building of the Berlin Wall (see pages 387–90), intellectuals such as Professor Robert Havemann had to smuggle their censored texts into the West to get them published.

Yet, the system could not totally enforce conformity; political, social and cultural criticism, however marginal, could be expressed in all sorts of ways, for example by:

- refusing to vote or to join the SED mass organisations
- listening to Western radio or watching Western television stations (which were difficult to block)
- youngsters adopting alternative youth cultures, especially the American lifestyle
- Nazi sympathisers showing their anger by writing graffiti and slogans on walls
- farmers resisting the establishment of collective farms.

Until 1961 people could most obviously show their dissent by emigrating to the West. However, from 1961 it became more apparent that dissent was growing and that most GDR citizens were increasingly living in parallel worlds with private and public lives. People recognised that the surveillance by the *Stasi* had become more imposing; and so learned to withdraw with their families, good friends and common interests into private refuges in a world which was later described by Günter Gaus as a 'niche society'.

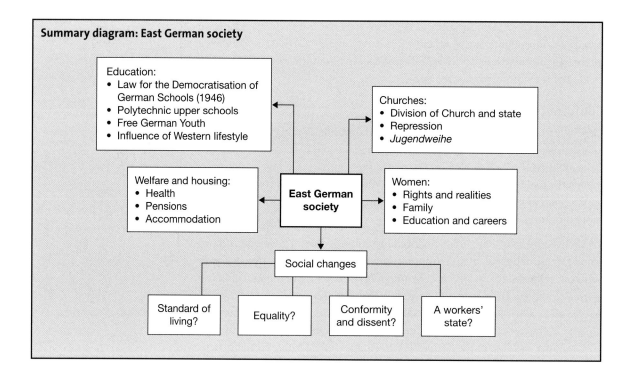

Summary diagram: East German society

The Berlin Wall

▶ *Why was the Berlin Wall built and what was its significance?*

Berlin had remained, since 1945, in a unique status guaranteed by the agreements of the Allied powers in 1945 and confirmed in the wake of the Berlin blockade and the airlift (see pages 298–300).

The divided city

The four Allied military governors of Berlin had far-reaching rights in their own sectors. Their troops were stationed there and their military patrols were guaranteed free movement throughout the whole city. The Western powers still had access to their sectors via the guaranteed air-corridors, and the connections via rail and motorways had been reopened after the crisis in 1949.

The division of Berlin into West and East had been deepened by the foundation of the two German states. The constitutional laws of the FRG applied to West Berlin, with some exceptions. It elected members to the *Bundestag*, but they were only observers and had no right to vote. Meanwhile, East Berlin was named as the capital of the GDR in 1949 and the USSR handed back its authority over the city to the GDR government (although this was not recognised by the Western powers, which insisted that Berlin was still an occupied city under four-power control and therefore not eligible to be called the capital of the GDR).

Despite the existence of the four sectors and the division between East and West, communication and transport were not restricted. The city's underground, trains and buses travelled quite freely, and people could even live in the East and work in the West (or the reverse). Control across the borderline of the sectors was difficult to implement.

'The Berlin fuse'

Since 1949 the USSR had been very aware of the problem of West Berlin; it was seen as an 'isle of the imperialist enemy' in the heart of a socialist state. Most obviously, it provided an escape route for potential refugees, which posed a serious threat to the stability of the GDR.

In the late 1950s it seemed as if the GDR was stabilising and the Berlin problem was receding. The economy reached a high point of economic growth in 1958–9 (see pages 370–1) and the number of refugees actually declined. However, the Berlin problem reached crisis point in 1961, as a result of three major factors.

Khrushchev's Berlin ultimatum

The Berlin crisis, 1958–61, was sparked off by an ultimatum from the Soviet leader which demanded that the three Western powers withdraw from the city within six months in order to create a demilitarised free city-state. The

USA did not accept the ultimatum but seemed prepared to negotiate on European security, so the Soviet ultimatum was quietly dropped. At the same time, Ulbricht announced that West Berlin was part of the sovereign territory of the GDR. This claim was promptly rejected by its mayor, Willy Brandt. Although tensions initially mellowed a little when Khrushchev visited the USA in September 1959, the superpowers' fundamental differences over the German question and the status of West Berlin did not change. Moreover, the international atmosphere was exacerbated by the **U-2 crisis** in 1960 and so Khrushchev remained determined to take a firm stand over Berlin in the interests of the USSR and the GDR.

KEY TERM

U-2 crisis An international flashpoint in the Cold War when a US spy plane was shot down in 1960 in Soviet air space.

The GDR Seven-Year Plan

In 1959 Ulbricht decided to abort the existing Five-Year Plan and launch a Seven-Year Plan to accelerate the process of nationalisation. This policy set extraordinary targets and also new regulations to tighten worker discipline in the factories. However, by 1960 it was clear that the GDR economy had expanded too quickly and the industrial growth rate had declined sharply.

Forced collectivisation

Somewhat surprisingly, Ulbricht decided, despite the political and economic pressures, to proceed in 1960 with the second wave of collectivisation. (It has been suggested that he deliberately prompted the crisis.) It was enforced quite brutally and, as a result, food production declined and in 1961 rationing was reintroduced.

Table 10.6 Number of refugees from East Germany in West Germany (in thousands)

1949	1951	1953	1955	1957	1959	1961
75.0	161.4	331.3	252.9	261.6	143.9	207.0

'No one intends to build a wall'

In the summer of 1961 the Berlin problem came to a head. Khrushchev met the new US president, John Kennedy, in June in Vienna and things went very badly. Khrushchev threatened war unless there was a Berlin settlement. In contrast, in a public statement, Kennedy claimed that he would guarantee the status of West Berlin and free access to the city (although his careful defensive wording made it clear to the USSR that he had no intention of threatening the Soviet sphere of influence in eastern Europe, including the GDR and East Berlin).

At the same time, the GDR government faced real pressure as the number of refugees rose sharply. In April 1961 alone 30,000 left, most via West Berlin, and it was clear that this was threatening the very survival of the young state (see Table 10.6). Ulbricht was desperate to find a solution; the most obvious was to seal the border with West Berlin, but he needed to convince Khrushchev to that end. When rumours began to circulate that the GDR was going to close the border, Ulbricht publicly announced on 15 June, 'No one intends to build a wall'.

SOURCE G

The Berlin Wall from the west looking to the east of the city, 1975.

After intensive and secret consultations with the leaders of the Warsaw Pact and with the agreement of Khrushchev, the SED leaders decided that isolating West Berlin was the only possible step to end the danger to their state. The preparations for this action were conducted with the greatest secrecy and, during the night of 12–13 August 1961, 'Operation Rose' took place. The NVA and police sealed off the western sectors of Berlin with barbed wire and barricades. In the following months a 45-km long wall was erected along the border of the Soviet sector of Berlin and similar barricades were built around the whole 160-km perimeter to cut off West Berlin from the surrounding GDR territory. The 'hole' in the East German border was closed (see the maps on pages 275 and 299).

How does Source G show the effectiveness of the Berlin Wall as a barrier between East and West Berlin?

A turning point for FRG, GDR and the world?

The construction of the Berlin Wall in 1961 encapsulated the history of post-war Germany's division. It was an act which emotionally and physically split the country's capital, ultimately reinforced Germany's political division and tangibly symbolised the iron curtain between the East and the West. It was, therefore, a turning point, confirming the geopolitical position of post-war Germany which did not fundamentally change until November 1989, when the fall of the Berlin Wall marked the collapse of communism, and the ensuing reunification of Germany in 1990.

Western powers

The Western powers were taken by surprise and protested sharply against the breach of the agreement of 1945, but as the wall had been built on Soviet-sector territory their occupation rights were legally limited and they did not interfere. It is interesting to note that despite the public protests, President Kennedy's aides did not think it was even necessary to inform him that the city had been divided until over fourteen hours after the event. The other Western leaders were just as lacklustre over the news: President de Gaulle did not return to Paris from his holiday home until 17 August and Britain's Prime Minister Macmillan was more concerned about the economy. He had been planning to reduce troops in Berlin and still believed that 'we are more likely to be bankrupted than blown up'.

There was, however, one major flashpoint in October, with a stand-off between US and Soviet tanks just 100 metres apart at the Checkpoint Charlie border crossing. But it became clear that no one wanted to risk an escalation over West Berlin as long as the *status quo* of power was guaranteed. In a way, therefore, the creation of the wall underlined the superpowers' lines of authority established during the Cold War. In the words of Kennedy: 'It's not a nice solution, but a hell of a lot better than war.'

GDR

In their propaganda the GDR described the wall as 'the anti-fascist protection wall'. Yet, even some communists felt that it reinforced the failings of the GDR and the Soviets. Forty-two GDR citizens died in 1962 trying to escape across the divide. Nevertheless, in the political sense the wall was a success for the SED leadership, as it achieved its aim and the numbers of refugees dropped sharply. This stabilised the country, giving the GDR a 'second chance', and according to Mary Fulbrook, the 1960s proved to be a 'decade of transition'.

FRG

The FRG could not remain unaffected by the wall. Its construction was a real shock to West Germans and a frustration to the government. Of course, Adenauer's 'magnet theory' had been very successful and he had stubbornly insisted that he was only prepared to accept German unification on his terms, that is, a capitalist West-orientated Germany. Yet, he seemed thrown by the creation of the wall – he did not even visit West Berlin until 22 August – as if events were beyond the control of the aged chancellor. This reluctance brought him much criticism from Berliners. Willy Brandt, after touring West Berlin on 13 August, called for restraint from his own people and for Western help, but to no avail. While Kennedy did eventually go to Berlin in June 1963 and made his famous *'Ich bin ein Berliner'* speech, it was clear that 'German unification' was no longer to play a major role in international politics, but it did so in the propaganda war.

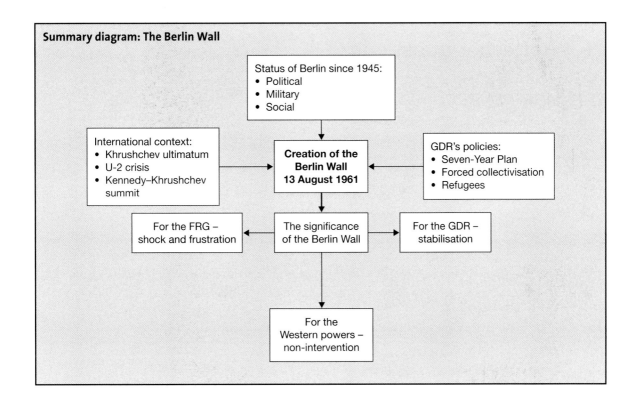

Summary diagram: The Berlin Wall

Chapter summary

The GDR became a very repressive system; indeed, in many respects the dualism of the party and the state was more effective than the Nazi regime. Because the Soviets made little attempt at reconstruction after the war, discontent in the GDR came to a head in the 17 June uprising. It was crushed relatively easily and, despite the widespread atmosphere of de-Stalinisation in 1956, there was no internal threat. By the end of the decade, Ulbricht and the SED with an increasingly powerful *Stasi* had created a disciplined party of loyal communists.

The GDR created its economy on the 'Soviet model' of central planning and agricultural collectivisation. These policies at first were not so effective: in the short term collectivisation was, in fact, a disaster. Nevertheless, the GDR economy did grow rapidly and became the most productive in the Eastern bloc.

The provision for welfare and education in the GDR was generous in many senses, and the 'feel-good factor' with more consumer goods was set to improve in the 1960s. Yet, the regime placed a lot of emphasis on social control and for its citizens there was no room for dissent at all. In the end, the flow of refugees to the West proved to be decisive; the Berlin Wall enabled the GDR to stabilise in the 1960s, albeit as a committed Soviet satellite without any chance of a unified Germany.

Refresher questions

Use these questions to remind yourself of the key material covered in this chapter.

1 How did Ulbricht and the SED establish political supremacy in the GDR?

2 To what extent was the GDR a totalitarian regime?

3 Why did the 17 June uprising fail and with what consequences?

4 To what extent were the GDR's economic problems created by the SED's planning?

5 What did the SED leadership learn from the mistakes of its economic planning after the first Five-Year Plan?

6 What were the consequences of the GDR government's decision to implement collectivisation?

7 To what extent was communism an economic disaster for the GDR?

8 How successful was GDR educational policy?

9 How and why was education radically reformed in the GDR?

10 Did the FDJ really achieve its aims?

11 How well did the Churches survive in the GDR?

12 How emancipated were women in the early years of the GDR?

13 To what extent did East Germans become better off?

14 What opportunities were there to hold alternative views in GDR society?

15 Why was the building of the Berlin Wall so significant?

 Question practice

ESSAY QUESTIONS

1 To what extent did the GDR build a 'socialist paradise' by the mid-1960s?

2 Assess the consequences of the June 1953 uprising for the citizens and politicians in the GDR.

3 Which of the following was more responsible for the GDR's economic failures? i) Ideological inflexibility. ii) The 'brain drain'. Explain your answer with reference to both i) and ii).

4 'Despite its limitations the GDR created a fairer society for its citizens.' To what extent do you agree with this statement?

OCR A level History

Essay guidance

The assessment of OCR Units Y221 and Y255: Democracy and Dictatorships in Germany 1919–1963 depends on whether you are studying it for AS or A level:

- for the AS exam, you will answer one essay question from a choice of two, and one interpretation question, for which there is no choice
- for the A level exam, you will answer one essay question from a choice of two and one shorter essay question, also from a choice of two.

The guidance below is for answering both AS and A level essay questions. Guidance for the shorter essay question is at the end of this section. Guidance on answering interpretation questions is on page 398.

For both OCR AS and A level History, the types of essay questions set and the skills required to achieve a high grade for Unit Group 2 are the same. The skills are made very clear by both mark schemes, which emphasise that the answer must:

- focus on the demands of the question
- be supported by accurate and relevant factual knowledge
- be analytical and logical
- reach a supported judgement about the issue in the question.

There are a number of skills that you will need to develop to reach the higher levels in the marking bands:

- understand the wording of the question
- plan an answer to the question set
- write a focused opening paragraph
- avoid irrelevance and description
- write analytically
- write a conclusion which reaches a supported judgement based on the argument in the main body of the essay.

These skills will be developed in the section below, but are further developed in the 'Period Study' chapters of the *OCR A level History* series (British Period Studies and Enquiries).

Understanding the wording of the question

To stay focused on the question set, it is important to read the question carefully and focus on the key words and phrases. Unless you directly address the demands of the question you will not score highly. Remember that in questions where there is a named factor you must write a good analytical paragraph about the given factor, even if you argue that it was not the most important.

Types of AS and A level questions you might find in the exams	The factors and issues you would need to consider in answering them
1 Assess the reasons why Hitler was appointed chancellor in Germany in 1933.	Weigh up the relative importance of a range of factors as to why Hitler was appointed chancellor in January 1933.
2 To what extent was the Nazi Party's economic policy successful in achieving its aims in the period from 1933 to 1939?	Weigh up the relative success of a range of issues in relation to the main aim of being prepared for war.
3 'Terror was the most important reason why the Nazi Party was able to consolidate its power in Germany in the period from 1933 to 1939.' How far do you agree?	Weigh up the relative importance of a range of factors, including comparing the importance of terror with other issues, to reach a balanced judgement.
4 How successful was Adenauer as leader of West Germany?	This question requires you make a judgement about Adenauer as leader of West Germany. Instead of thinking about factors, you need to think about issues such as: • Adenauer's success in restoring the economy • his ability to restore social stability • foreign policy and rapprochement with France, EEC and rearmament, policy towards the USSR • his handling of particular issues and crises • his election victories • his decline, *Der Spiegel*.

Planning an answer

Many plans simply list dates and events – this should be avoided as it encourages a descriptive or narrative answer, rather than an analytical answer. The plan should be an outline of your argument; this means you need to think carefully about the issues you intend to discuss and their relative importance before you start writing your answer. It should therefore be a list of the factors or issues you are going to discuss and a comment on their relative importance.

For question 1 in the table, your plan might look something like this:

1 Backstairs intrigue – Papen, who wanted to remove Schleicher, appointed Hitler as he thought he could control him; without the persuasion of Hindenburg this would not have happened.
2 Popularity of Nazis – although support had declined in earlier elections, after the chaos of 1932 the only alternative to the Nazis was a regime supported by the military.
3 Germany's economic and political crisis –impact of the Great Depression and failure of the Weimar Republic to manage it.
4 Limited support for Weimar – popular support for Hitler, link to points 2 and 3, inability of Weimar governments to maintain a majority in the *Reichstag*.
5 Fear of communism and the Nazi Party's opposition to it.
6 Nazi organisation, methods and message – appeal to elites who feared communism, so link to point 5.
7 Hitler's character and leadership style.

The opening paragraph

Many students spend time 'setting the scene'; the opening paragraph becomes little more than an introduction to the topic – this should be avoided. Instead, make it clear what your argument is going to be. Offer your view about the issue in the question – what was the most important reason why Hitler was appointed chancellor in January 1933 – and then introduce the other issues you intend to discuss. In the plan it is suggested that backstairs intrigue was the most important reason. This should be made clear in the opening paragraph, with a brief comment as to why – perhaps that the elites saw in Hitler an escape from the threat of communism and a solution to the political chaos that had been present since 1932. This will give the examiner a clear overview of your essay, rather than it being a 'mystery tour' where the argument becomes clear only at the end. You should also refer to any important issues that the question raises. For example:

There are a number of reasons why Hitler was appointed chancellor in January 1933, including both Nazi strengths and the inability of Weimar governments to deal with the political and economic problems[1]. However, the most important reason was the backstairs intrigue that took place between December 1932 and January 1933[2]. This was particularly important as it was this that ultimately led to Papen convincing Hindenburg to back the plan to appoint Hitler[3].

1 The student is aware that there were a number of important reasons.
2 The answer offers a clear view as to what the student considers to be the most important reason – a thesis is offered.
3 There is a brief justification to support the thesis.

Avoid irrelevance and description

Hopefully, the plan will stop you from simply writing all you know about why Hitler was appointed chancellor and force you to weigh up the role of a range of factors. Similarly, it should also help prevent you from simply writing about the events of 1919–33. You will not lose marks if you do that, but neither will you gain any credit, and you will waste valuable time.

Write analytically

This is perhaps the hardest, but most important skill you need to develop. An analytical approach can be helped by ensuring that the opening sentence of each paragraph introduces an idea, which directly answers the question and is not just a piece of factual information. In a very strong answer it should be possible to simply read the opening sentences of all the paragraphs and know what argument is being put forward.

If we look at the third question, on the role of terror in the consolidation of Nazi power in the period

1933–9 (see page 394), the following are possible sentences with which to start paragraphs:

- Terror was crucial in the consolidation of Nazi power as it removed those who could lead opposition to the regime.
- Without creating jobs and reducing unemployment, the Nazis would not have been able to consolidate the regime as …
- The Nazis were able to consolidate their power through the use of propaganda.
- It was only as a result of the legal revolution in 1933–4 that the Nazis were able to consolidate their power.

You would then go on to discuss both sides of the argument raised by the opening sentence, using relevant knowledge about the issue to support each side of the argument. The final sentence of the paragraph would reach a judgement on the role played by the factor you are discussing in the consolidation of Nazi power. This approach would ensure that the final sentence of each paragraph links back to the actual question you are answering. If you can do this for each paragraph you will have a series of mini-essays, which discuss a factor and reach a conclusion or judgement about the importance of that factor or issue. For example:

Terror was important in the consolidation of Nazi power as it silenced those who could not be won over by propaganda or were willing to compromise their beliefs in return for the reduction in unemployment[1]. Terror was also particularly important in destroying potential opposition within the Nazi Party itself and culminated in the Night of the Long Knives, which consolidated Hitler's position as leader. Moreover, it was also important in the legal revolution, as intimidation was used to ensure the passage of the Enabling Act, which allowed the Nazis to establish a dictatorship[2].

1 The sentence puts forward a clear view that terror was important in dealing with sections of Nazi society.
2 The answer shows how terror was linked to other factors, such as the legal revolution.

The conclusion

The conclusion provides the opportunity to bring together all the interim judgements to reach an overall judgement about the question. Using the interim judgements will ensure that your conclusion is based on the argument in the main body of the essay and does not offer a different view. For the essay answering question 1 (see page 394), you can decide what was the most important factor in Hitler's appointment as chancellor, but for question 3 you will need to comment on the importance of the named factor – the importance of terror in the consolidation of power – as well as explain why you think a different factor is more important, if that has been your line of argument. Or, if you think the named factor is the most important, you would need to explain why that was more important than the other factors or issues you have discussed.

Consider the following conclusion to question 3 (see page 394): 'Terror was the most important reason why the Nazi Party was able to consolidate its power in Germany in the period from 1933 to 1939.' How far do you agree?

Although terror was important in the Nazi consolidation of power it was not the most important factor[1]. Terror undoubtedly silenced many who could not be reconciled to the regime, but for many it was the benefits of a job and the improvement in living standards, or the apparent improvement, which propaganda emphasised, that gave the Nazis popular support among many which allowed them to consolidate their power. As a consequence, many people were willing to turn a blind eye to many of the Nazis' policies after the horrors of the Great Depression. Terror was therefore important in silencing critics, but was less important in controlling the majority of the population[2].

1 This is a strong conclusion because it considers the importance of the named factor – the role of terror – but weighs that up against a range of other factors to reach an overall judgement.
2 It is also able to show links between the other factors to reach a balanced judgement, which brings in a range of issues, showing the interplay between them.

How to write a good essay for the A level short-answer questions

The short-answer question will require you to weigh up the importance of two factors or issues in relation to an event or a development. For example:

> Which was more important in ensuring stability in the Federal Republic in the years 1949–63?
>
> (i) The Basic Law.
>
> (ii) The economic miracle.
>
> Explain your answer with reference to both (i) and (ii).

As with the long essays, the skills required are made very clear by the mark scheme, which emphasises that the answer must:

- analyse the two issues
- evaluate the two issues
- support your analysis and evaluation with detailed and accurate knowledge
- reach a supported judgement as to which factor was more important in relation to the issue in the question.

The skills required are very similar to those for the longer essays. However, there is no need for an introduction, nor are you required to compare the two factors or issues in the main body of the essay, although either approach can still score full marks. For example, an opening paragraph could be:

The Basic Law was important in ensuring stability in the Federal Republic as it upheld the key principles of democracy, republicanism and social responsibility which could not be removed by the normal amendment process[1]. The law therefore ensured that the Federal Republic was committed to democracy and that a dictator, who would destroy stability, could not be installed in power, as had happened previously under Weimar[2]. It also reinforced the key principle of democracy by allowing only parties that were committed to democracy, once again preventing the existence of parties such as the Nazis which had destroyed democracy in the 1930s[3].

1 The answer explains one of the important ways in which the Basic Law ensured stability.
2 The implications of upholding democracy are considered.
3 The wider implications are hinted at and there is some development of the point by comparing the situation in the Federal Republic with the 1930s.

The answer could go on and argue how the complex voting system and the five per cent hurdle prevented a large number of small parties from gaining representation, which would have made it harder for a government to achieve a majority and therefore threaten stability.

Most importantly, the conclusion must reach a supported judgement as to the relative importance of the factors in relation to the issue in the question. For example:

Both of the issues had a significant impact in ensuring the development of stability. The Basic Law was important as it provided the Federal Republic with a constitution which protected democracy and banned parties that wanted to destroy it; however, although the Basic Law provided the conditions under which democracy could be established, it was the economic miracle that won the new state popular support among the mass of the population through increased living standards[1]. Although the Basic Law offered the opportunity for stability it was the economic miracle that created enthusiasm for the regime and ensured that it would not only survive but flourish[2].

1 The response explains the relative importance of the two factors and offers a clear view.
2 The response supports the view offered in the opening sentence and therefore reaches a supported judgement.

Interpretation guidance

How to write a good essay

The guidance below is for answering the AS interpretation questions on Unit Y251 Democracy and Dictatorships in Germany 1919–1963. Guidance on answering essay questions is on page 393.

The OCR specification outlines the two key topics from which the interpretation question will be drawn. For this book these are:

- The establishment and development of the Weimar Republic: 1919 to January 1933.
- The impact of war and defeat on Germany: 1939–49.

The specification also lists the main debates to consider.

It is also worth remembering that this is an AS unit and not an A level historiography paper. The aim of this element of the unit is to develop an awareness that the past can be interpreted in different ways.

The question will require you to assess the strengths and limitations of a historian's interpretation of an issue related to one of the specified key topics.

You should be able to place the interpretation within the context of the wider historical debate on the key topic. However, you will *not* be required to know the names of individual historians associated with the debate or to have studied the specific books of any historians. It may even be counter-productive to be aware of particular historians' views, as this may lead you to simply describe their views, rather than analyse the given interpretation.

There are a number of skills you need to develop if you are to reach the higher levels in the mark bands:

- To be able to understand the wording of the question.
- To be able to explain the interpretation and how it fits into the debate about the issue or topic.
- To be able to consider both the strengths and weaknesses of the interpretation by using your own knowledge of the topic.

Here is an example of a question you will face in the exam:

Read the interpretation and then answer the question that follows:

'If their job dictated some sort of collaboration in the implementation of racial policy, by and large they [the German people] conformed to the demand.'

(From Martin Housden, *Resistance and Conformity in the Third Reich*, 1996.)

Evaluate the strengths and limitations of this interpretation, making reference to other interpretations that you have studied.

Approaching the question

There are several steps to take to answer this question:

1 Explain the interpretation and put it into the context of the debate on the topic

In the first paragraph, you should explain the interpretation and the view it is putting forward. This paragraph places the interpretation in the context of the historical debate and explains any key words or phrases relating to the given interpretation. A suggested opening might be:

The interpretation puts forward the view that many of the German population, particularly those who were involved in work that involved implementing Hitler's racial policy, did not resist and continued with work without objecting[1]. This interpretation argues that German workers were willing to work with the state and even collaborate with the racial policy, even so far as in the extermination of the Jewish population[2]. The interpretation suggests that many within Germany not only knew about the extreme racial policy that was being pursued but did little to oppose it and learned to live with it[3].

1 The opening sentence is clearly focused on the given interpretation, but there is no detailed own knowledge added at this point.
2 The second sentence explains what the result of this collaboration meant.
3 The last sentence begins to place the concept of collaboration and conformity in the wider historical debate and suggests that this historian's emphasis on it challenges the view that many Germans did not know about the racial policies.

In order to place Housden's view in the context of the debate about the importance of why the Holocaust happened, and who was responsible, you could go on to suggest that some have argued that it was due to clear objectives which were 'intended' because so many Germans were willing to participate, while others have suggested that some became involved only because of the alien context in which they were living. It raises the question of the extent to which the German people were 'fully' involved or were involved in a 'limited way'.

2 Consider the strengths of the interpretation

In the second paragraph, consider the strengths of the interpretation by bringing in your own knowledge that supports the given view. A suggested response might start as follows when considering the strengths of the view:

There is considerable merit to Housden's view as it offers a clear view that it was due to circumstances[1]. The interpretation is correct as those in the administration as well as those in police battalions or working in the camps carried out their duties. The interpretation is also correct to suggest that they conformed even if they did not have a strong anti-Semitic belief. Many were motivated by other factors and were often influenced by peer pressure or careerism, particularly as the circumstances in which they found themselves working were completely alien to their usual environment[2]. These examples show that it was circumstances rather than a genocidal belief among the German population[3].

1 The answer clearly focuses on the strength of the given interpretation.
2 The response provides some support for the view in the interpretation from the candidate's own knowledge. This is quite detailed and precise, but could still be developed further in the remainder of the paragraph.
3 The final sentence brings the material together to support the interpretation.

In the remainder of the paragraph, you could show how the ordinary German was driven by circumstances and issues such as cowardice, a fear of resisting orders and what might happen, or how some co-operated under the influence of alcohol, all of which were exaggerated by the brutalising context of war.

3 Consider the weaknesses of the interpretation

In the third paragraph, consider the weaknesses of the given interpretation by bringing in knowledge that challenges the given interpretation and explains what is missing from the interpretation. A suggested response might start as follows when considering the weaknesses of the view:

However, there are a number of limitations in Housden's interpretation[1]. Most importantly, it fails to consider the view that German culture had developed a violent variant of anti-Semitism that wanted to eliminate Jews[2]. The interpretation also fails to consider the fact that so many Germans were willing to participate in the anti-Semitic actions of the Third Reich[3].

1 The opening makes it very clear that this paragraph will deal with the weaknesses of the interpretation.
2 It explains clearly the first weakness and provides evidence to support the claim. The evidence is not detailed and could be developed, but the answer focuses on explaining the weakness, rather than providing lots of detail.
3 More detail could have been provided about the willingness of the Germans to participate in the anti-Semitic actions.

Answers might go on to argue that many non-Germans also participated in the murder of Jews and might suggest that there were other overtly anti-Semitic cultures in Europe where such actions did not occur. Some might also suggest that the answer ignores the idea of collective national guilt playing a role in the actions. The paragraph might therefore suggest that the interpretation provides a partial answer which needs further development.

There is no requirement for you to reach a judgement as to which view you find more convincing or valid.

Assessing the interpretation

In assessing the interpretation you should consider the following:

- Identify and explain the issue being discussed in the interpretation: the role played by the German people in the Holocaust.
- Explain the view being put forward in the interpretation: the interpretation is arguing that most German workers co-operated with the policy and were fully involved in the attempts to exterminate the Jewish population.
- Explain how the interpretation fits into the wider debate about the issue: the relative importance of whether the German people were involved 'fully' or in a 'mixed way'.

In other interpretations you might need to:

- Consider whether there is any particular emphasis within the interpretation that needs explaining or commenting on, for example, if the interpretation says something is 'the only reason' or 'the single most important reason'.
- Comment on any concepts that the interpretation raises, such as 'total war', 'authoritarian system', 'liberalisation'.
- Consider the focus of the interpretation, for example, if an interpretation focuses on an urban viewpoint, what was the rural viewpoint? Is the viewpoint given in the interpretation the same for all areas of society?

Summary: this is what is important for answering interpretation questions:

- Explaining the interpretation.
- Placing it in the context of the wider historical debate about the issue it considers.
- Explaining the strengths *and* weaknesses of the view in the extract.

Glossary of terms

Alliance   An agreement where members promise to support the other(s) if one or more of them is attacked.

Allied Control Council   The name given to the military occupation governing body of the four Allied occupation zones.

Allies   The nations who were allied against Germany and Austria-Hungary during the First World War. They were Russia, France, Great Britain and later others, including the USA.

Annexation   Taking over of another country against its will.

Anschluss   Usually translated as 'union'. Although the population of Austria was wholly German, the Versailles Treaty outlawed any political union between Germany and Austria.

Anti-capitalism   Rejects an economic system based on private property and profit.

Anti-feminist   Opposing female advancement.

Anti-Marxism   Opposition to the ideology of Karl Marx.

Anti-modernism   Strand of opinion which rejects, objects to or is highly critical of changes to society and culture brought about by technological advancement.

Anti-Semitism   Hatred of Jews. It became the most significant part of Nazi racist thinking. For Hitler, the 'master-race' was the pure Aryan (the people of northern Europe). The lowest race for Hitler was the Jews.

Arbitration treaty   An agreement to accept the decision by a third party to settle a conflict.

Armistice   A suspension of fighting pending a final peace settlement. Here, it refers to the document signed by German representatives led by Erzberger, on behalf of Ebert's government, and the Allies on 11 November 1918.

Article 48   Gave the Weimar president the power in an emergency to rule by decree.

Aryan   Defined by the Nazis as the non-Jewish people of northern Europe. Technically, refers to people whose language has an Indian/European root.

Aryanise   To remove all non-Aryans from office, business and property.

Asocials   The Nazi '*Volksgemeinschaft*' excluded those who were 'socially unfit', as they deviated from the norms of society. The term 'asocial' was applied in an elastic manner: vagabonds, prostitutes, alcoholics, homosexuals, criminals, 'idlers', even grumblers.

Associationism   Having a strong identity or affiliation with a particular group.

Atomic bomb   Western scientists developed atomic/nuclear weapons as part of the Manhattan Project 1942–5. The first bomb was tested in New Mexico in July 1945 and the next two were dropped on Hiroshima and Nagasaki in Japan in August 1945.

Austro-Hungarian Empire   A large multinational empire in central Europe that existed from 1867 to 1918. It was created from the Empire of Austria and the Kingdom of Hungary.

Autarky   The aim for self-sufficiency in the production of food and raw materials, especially when at war.

Authoritarianism   A broad term meaning government by strong non-democratic leadership.

Autocracy   A system where one person (usually a hereditary sovereign) has absolute rule.

Autonomy   The right of self-government.

Avant garde   A general term suggesting new ideas and styles in art.

Balance of trade   The difference in value between exports and imports. If the value of the imports is above that of exports, the balance of the payments has a deficit that is often said to be 'in the red'.

Balanced budget   A financial programme in which a government does not spend more than it raises in revenue.

Balkans   A region taking its name from the Balkan mountains in south-east Europe. It covers mainly Albania, Bulgaria, Greece, Romania and Yugoslavia (Bosnia, Croatia, Macedonia, Montenegro and Serbia).

Basic Law   *Grundgesetz*. Technically, the document approved in May 1949 was *not* a constitution, as it was not permanent because the founding fathers wanted to have the flexibility to amend it if and when Germany became reunified. Thus, all the terms had the features of a constitution but it was called the Basic Law.

Battle of Britain   Name given to the air battle fought over the skies of southern England in July to October 1940.

Battle of the Atlantic   The naval struggle between the Allied convoys and the German U-boats in the northern Atlantic Ocean.

Bavaria   One of the oldest states in Europe and part of Imperial Germany, which maintained its kingdom until November 1918.

Bilateral trade treaty   A trade agreement between two countries or parties.

Bizone   The name given to the two zones of Britain and the USA which were merged into a unified economic zone in January 1947.

Black market   The underground economy where goods are sold at unregulated prices.

Blanket bombing   The military policy of dropping large numbers of bombs to cause devastation of an area.

Blitzkrieg   Literally 'lightning war'. It was the name of the military strategy developed to avoid static war. It was based on the use of dive-bombers, paratroopers and motorised infantry.

Block warden   A low-ranking local party man who provided information for the local office on the people of his neighbourhood.

Blut und Boden   'Blood and Soil'. Nationalist and racist romanticism which glorified the rural role of the peasantry.

Bolshevik Revolution   'Bolshevik' means majority, which was used by Lenin as the leader of the majority Russian Socialist Party from 1903. In October 1917 Lenin and the Bolsheviks seized power to create a communist government.

BRD   Bundesrepublik Deutschland. The Federal Republic of Germany (FRG) was formed on 23 May 1949.

Buffer state   The idea of separating two rival countries by leaving a space between them. Clemenceau believed that the creation of an independent Rhineland state could prevent long-established Franco-German aggression (although Wilson believed this was at odds with self-determination).

Bundesrat   The 'federal council' or upper house of the German parliament. Its members were appointed by members of the *Länder* governments.

Bundestag   The 'federal assembly' or 'lower house' of the FRG parliament. It claimed to be the successor to the *Reichstag*.

Bundeswehr   The name given to the German Army created in the FRG by the Paris Treaties. It was ratified by the *Bundestag* in 1955 and came into effect the following year. It introduced conscription for all men aged over eighteen years.

Cartel   An arrangement between businesses to control the market by exercising a joint monopoly.

Chancellor   *Kanzler*. Prime minister of the German government.

Chinese Revolution   The civil war between the nationalists and the communists 1948–9 led to a communist revolution and the proclamation of the Chinese People's Republic on 1 October 1949, which was led by Mao Tse-tung.

Co-determination   The practice in which employees have a role in the management of a company.

Coalition government   Usually formed when a party does not have an overall majority in parliament; it then combines with more parties and shares government positions.

Cold War   The period of tension between the USA and the USSR, 1945–90, that did not result in open warfare.

Collectivisation   The policy of creating larger and more efficient agricultural units controlled by the state. It was initiated by Stalin in the USSR in the 1930s.

Comecon   Council for Mutual Economic Assistance. Formed in 1949 to facilitate and co-ordinate the economic policy of Soviet states in the Eastern bloc. The GDR joined in 1950.

Concordat   An agreement between Church and state. A Concordat was signed by the papacy and the Nazi government in July 1933.

Conscription   Compulsory enlistment to the armed services by the state. Germany inherited from Prussia the tradition of a large conscript army with a high standard of military readiness.

Constitution   The principles and rules that govern a state.

Constitution court   *Bundesverfassungsgericht*. The main task is to review judicial cases and rule whether they are unconstitutional.

Constitutional monarchy   Where the monarch has limited power within the lines of a constitution.

Cuban Missile Crisis   The most serious flashpoint in the Cold War between the superpowers, in October 1962. The dispute was over the installation of nuclear missiles by the USSR on Cuba, a short distance from the US mainland.

Cult of personality   Using the power and charisma of a political leader to dominate the nation.

Customs union   An association of independent nations, which create a free trade area and remove customs/tariffs between them; also they usually agree on a common tariff for countries outside the area.

Deficit financing   The financial policy of a government to spend more than it receives as revenue, in order to stimulate the economy. In this way, it gives the people more money to spend and so, in theory, increases the demand for goods and thereby creates work.

Demagogue   A leader who plays on the prejudices of the masses with populist emotions.

Demilitarisation   The removal of military personnel, weaponry or forts.

Democratic centralism   Based on the idea from Marxist–Leninist theory of the decision-making practice and discipline of the Communist Party. Any decisions made at the centre should be passed down and accepted as policy below, and free expression from the lower ranks of the party should be passed up to the Central Committee for scrutiny to maintain discipline and control.

Depression   An economic downturn marked by mass unemployment, falling prices and a lack of spending.

Diktat   A dictated peace. The Germans felt that the Treaty of Versailles was imposed without negotiation.

Dualism   A system of government in which two forces coexist, for example the Nazi Party and the German state.

DWK   *Deutsche Wirtschaftkommission*. German Economic Commission. Created in 1947 to administer the economy of the Soviet zone. It was very much in response to the creation of the German Economic Council in the Bizone.

Eastern bloc   A label given to the countries controlled by the USSR in eastern Europe from 1945: Poland, Czechoslovakia, Hungary, Romania, Bulgaria, Albania and the GDR.

ECSC   The European Coal and Steel Community, created in 1951.

Edelweiss Piraten   Edelweiss Pirates. The name given to a loose collection of youth groups who did not conform. Edelweiss is a white alpine flower which served as a symbol of opposition.

EEC   The European Economic Community. Created by the Treaty of Rome in March 1957 and comprising six countries: FRG, France, Italy and the Benelux states.

Ersatzkaiser   'Substitute emperor'. After Marshal Hindenburg was elected president, he provided the *Ersatzkaiser* figure required by the respectable right wing – he was a conservative, a nationalist and a military hero.

Eugenics   The scientific programme for the genetic improvement of the race.

Expellees   Ethnic Germans who either fled their homes in central and eastern Europe, or were forcibly expelled following the Second World War.

European Council An international organisation set up in May 1949 to promote co-operation between European countries on legal standards, human rights and democratic values. It pre-dated the creation of the EEC. Most famously, it established the European Court of Human Rights.

European Defence Community A plan proposed by France's prime minister, Pleven, to form a pan-European defence force. The plan was signed in May 1952 by the FRG, but not ratified by the French parliament.

Euthanasia The practice of putting an end to the lives of people suffering from incurable illnesses.

Exports Goods sold to foreign countries.

Expressionism An art form which focuses on expressing feelings through symbolism, exaggeration or distortion.

Fall of the Berlin Wall The symbolic turning point on 9 November 1989 for the breakdown of the GDR, which led to German reunification and the eventual collapse of the USSR (1991).

Federal president *Bundespräsident*. The head of state.

Federal structure Where power and responsibilities are shared between central and regional governments, for example, the USA.

Final Solution A euphemism used by the Nazi leadership to describe the extermination of the Jews from 1941, although in the earlier years the term had been used more loosely before there was any real overall plan.

'First past the post' An electoral system that simply requires the winner to gain one vote more than the second placed candidate. In a national election it tends to give the most successful party disproportionately more seats than its total vote merits.

Four Ds De-Nazification, to eliminate Nazi influence; demilitarisation, to destroy German armed forces; democratisation, to re-establish democratic institutions in Germany; and decentralisation, to break down the centralised Nazi political structure and restore local/regional government.

Freikorps 'Free corps'. They were right-wing, nationalist soldiers who acted as paramilitaries

and were only too willing to use force to suppress communist activity.

Führerprinzip 'The leadership principle'. Hitler upheld the idea of a one-party state, built on an all-powerful leader.

Fulfilment The policy of conforming to the terms of the Versailles Treaty, while aiming for a moderate revision of the terms. It was initiated by Joseph Wirth in 1921–2 and later pursued by Stresemann.

Gauleiter 'Leader of a regional area'. The Nazi Party was organised into 35 regions from 1926.

GDR German Democratic Republic. (DDR, *Deutsche Demokratische Republik*.) Communist East Germany, 1949–90.

Genocide The extermination of a whole race.

German Federation of Trade Unions DGB (*Deutscher Gerwerkschaftsbund*). The civil service and unions of other professional sectors organised themselves into two large umbrella organisations (*Deutscher Beamtenbund* and *Deutsche Angestellten-Gewerkschaft*).

German romanticism German classicism in art, literature and music.

Gestapo *Geheime Staats Polizei*. The secret state police. A key policing organisation for surveillance and repression.

Ghetto A term used to describe the historic area lived in by the Jews in a city.

Gleichschaltung 'Bringing into line' or 'co-ordination'.

GNP Gross national product is the total value of all goods and services in a nation's economy (including income derived from assets abroad).

Gradualism Changing by degrees; progressing slowly.

Grand Alliance A term initially used by Churchill to describe the alliance of Britain, the USA and the USSR 1941–5.

Great Depression The severe economic crisis of 1929–33 started in the USA by the Wall Street Crash; marked by mass unemployment, falling prices and a lack of spending.

Greek Civil War   A conflict (1946–9) between communists and monarchists, which was backed by British troops until their withdrawal in February 1947.

'Guns or butter'   A phrase used to highlight the controversial economic choice between rearmament and consumer goods.

Hard currency   A currency that the market considers to be strong because its value does not depreciate. In the 1920s the hardest currency was the US dollar.

High treason   The crime of betraying one's country, especially by attempting to overthrow the leader or government.

Hitler Youth   *Hitler Jugend* (HJ). Nazi youth organisation.

HO-shop   State-owned store where goods could be bought with foreign currency.

Holocaust   Term to describe mass slaughter – in this context it refers to the extermination of the Jews.

Horst Wessel   A song written by a young Nazi stormtrooper who was killed in a fight with communists in 1930. The song became a Nazi marching song and later virtually became an alternative national anthem.

Hyperinflation   In Germany in 1923, it meant that prices spiralled out of control because the government increased the amount of money being printed. As a result, it displaced the whole economy.

Imperial Germany   *Kaiserreich*. The title given to Germany from its unification in 1871 until 1918. Also referred to as the Second Reich (Empire).

Imports   Goods purchased from foreign countries.

Indoctrination   Inculcating and imposing a set of ideas.

Intentionalists   Historians who interpret history by emphasising the role (intentions) of people who shape history.

'Iron curtain'   A term used by Churchill in 1946 to describe the border between Soviet-controlled countries and the West.

Junkers   The landowning aristocracy, especially those from eastern Germany.

Kaiser   Emperor. The last Kaiser of Germany was Wilhelm II, 1888–1918.

Komsomol   The Communist Union of Youth. The youth wing of the CPSU, founded in 1918.

Korean War   The first armed confrontation of the Cold War in 1950–3. The FRG was not in a position to give military support, but the war did act as a major boon to the production of German goods.

Kripo   *Kriminalpolizei*. Criminal police responsible for the maintenance of general law and order.

Kulturkampf   A struggle for culture or civilisation. Bismarck's anti-Catholic policy of the 1870s aimed at reducing the role and power of the Catholic Church in Germany.

Labour exchanges   Local offices created by the state for finding employment. Many were created in several countries to counter mass unemployment.

League of Nations   The international body to encourage disarmament and to prevent war.

Lebensborn   Literally, the 'spring' or 'fountain of life'. Founded by Himmler and overseen by the SS to promote doctrines of racial purity.

Lebensraum   'Living space'. Hitler's aim to create an empire by establishing German supremacy over the eastern lands in Europe.

LPGs   *Landwirtschaftliche Produktionsgenossenschaft*. Agricultural production co-operatives. The name LPG was given to the large collectivised farms.

Maginot Line   Extensive defence fortifications built on the Franco-German frontier by the French governments in the 1930s.

'Magnet theory'   The idea that the attraction of a free and prosperous West Germany would sooner or later draw East Germany irresistibly towards it.

Mandates   The name given by the Allies to the system created in the peace settlement for the supervision of all the former colonies of Germany (and Turkey) by the League of Nations.

March converts   Those who joined the NSDAP immediately after the consolidation of power in January–March 1933.

Revolution from below The radical elements in the party wanted to direct the Nazi revolution from a more local level rather than from the leadership in Berlin.

Ribbentrop Bureau The office created by the Nazi Joachim von Ribbentrop, who ran his own personal 'bureau' to oversee foreign affairs.

Rote Kapelle 'Red Orchestra'. Name given to the communist spy network which passed information to the USSR.

RSHA Reich Security Office, which amalgamated all police and security organisations.

Rule of law Governing a country according to its laws.

SA *Sturm Abteilung*. Became known in English as the stormtroopers. They supported the radical socialist aspects of Nazism. They were also referred to as the Brownshirts after the colour of their uniform.

SAGs *Sowjetische Aktiengesellschaft*. Soviet state-controlled companies set up in January 1946 as part of reparations for the USSR.

Schlieffen Plan Its purpose was to avoid a two-front war by winning victory on the Western Front before dealing with the threat from Russia. It aimed to defeat France within six weeks by a massive German offensive in northern France and Belgium.

A second revolution The aims of Röhm and the SA were for social and economic reforms and the creation of a 'people's army' which would merge the German Army and the SA. These aims were more attractive to 'left-wing socialist Nazis' or 'radical Nazis'.

SD *Sicherheitsdienst*. Security service.

SED *Sozialistische Einheitspartei*. Socialist Unity Party of Germany. The new party created in April 1946 by the merger of the KPD and SPD in the Soviet zone.

Self-determination The right of people of the same nation to decide their own form of government. In effect, it is the principle of each nation ruling itself. Wilson believed that it was integral to the peace settlement and would lead to long-term peace.

Show trial A trial held for show with a predetermined judgment.

Siegfriede 'A peace through victory'. Refers to Germany fighting the First World War to victory and making major land gains.

SMAD The Soviet Military Administration in Germany. The name given to the Soviet authorities that supervised the occupation in the Soviet zone. It was renamed the Soviet High Commission in October 1949.

Social Darwinism A philosophy that portrayed the world as a 'struggle' between people, races and nations. Hitler viewed war as the highest form of 'struggle' and was deeply influenced by the theory of evolution based on natural selection.

Social mobility The movement of people between different levels, or classes, of society.

Socialist republic A system of government without a monarchy that aims to introduce social changes for collective benefit.

Soviet A Russian word meaning an elected council. In Germany many of these councils were set up in 1918 and had the support of the more radical and revolutionary left-wing working class.

Soviet republic A system of government that aims to introduce a communist state organised by workers' councils and opposed to private ownership.

SS *Schutz Staffel* (protection squad). Became known as the Blackshirts, named after the uniform.

SS *Einsatzgruppen* SS Special Action Units. First used during the invasion of Poland. After the invasion of the USSR four units were launched in eastern Europe. They were responsible for rounding up local Jews and murdering them in mass shootings.

'Stab in the back' myth The distorted view that the German Army had not lost the First World War and that unpatriotic groups, such as socialists and Jews, had undermined it. The myth severely weakened the Weimar democracy from the start.

Stasi *Staatssicherheitsdienst* (SSD). The state security service, the GDR's secret police. Created in February 1950, it was modelled closely on Soviet secret intelligence.

State within a state A situation where the authority and government of the state are threatened by a rival power base.

Structuralists   Historians who interpret history by analysing the role of social and economic forces and structures. They tend to place less emphasis on the role of the individual in shaping history.

Stunde Null   'Zero hour'. A term used in German society to describe Germany's collapse in the months after 1945.

Supranational   Beyond the authority of one national government, creating a project or policy by a group of nations, for example, EEC, World Trade Organisation.

Tariffs   Taxes levied by an importing nation on foreign goods coming in, and paid by the importers.

Tenant farmer   A farmer who works land owned by someone else and pays rent either in cash or in a share of the produce.

Teutonic paganism   The pre-Christian beliefs of the Germans.

Toleration   Acceptance of alternative political, religious and cultural views.

Total war   Involves the whole population in war, economically and militarily.

Totalitarian   A system of government in which all power is centralised and does not allow any rival authorities.

Truman doctrine   In March 1947 President Truman explained his decision to help the anti-communist forces in Greece. Truman's doctrine was to contain communism by sending money and equipment to any country facing communist influence.

'Turn of the tide'   Used to describe the Allied military victories in the winter of 1942–3, when the British won at El Alamein in North Africa and the Soviets forced the surrender of 300,000 German troops at Stalingrad.

U-2 crisis   An international flashpoint in the Cold War when a US spy plane was shot down in 1960 in Soviet air space.

Unconditional surrender   Roosevelt and Churchill's statement in 1943 that the Allies would not accept a negotiated peace.

Unilateral disarmament   The disarmament of one party. Wilson pushed for general (universal) disarmament after the war, but France and Britain were more suspicious. As a result, only Germany had to disarm.

Unrestricted submarine warfare   Germany's policy of attacking all military and civilian shipping in order to sink supplies going to Britain.

Untermenschen   Subhumans. Covered all races who, according to the Nazis, were 'inferior', or subhuman. Included Jews, Slavs and Gypsies (Sinti and Roma).

USSR   Soviets had been introduced in 1917. At first, Russia was named Soviet Russia (RSFSR) and then renamed the USSR, the Union of Soviet Socialist Republics, in 1922.

V-1 and V-2   The flying pilotless bombs and the long-range rocket developed by scientists in Germany. Used in air raids against Britain 1944–5.

VEBs   *Volkeigener Betrieb*. People-owned companies in the GDR. Factories owned on behalf of the people and managed by the state, which controlled production targets and all worker discipline.

Vernunftrepublikaner   'A rational (pragmatic) republican'. Used in the 1920s to define those people who really wanted Germany to have a constitutional monarchy but who, out of necessity, came to support the democratic Weimar Republic.

Volk   Often translated as 'people', although it tends to suggest a nation with the same ethnic and cultural identities and with a collective sense of belonging.

Völkisch   Nationalistic views associated with racism (especially anti-Semitism).

Volksgemeinschaft   'A people's community'. Nazism stressed the development of a harmonious, socially unified and racially pure community.

***Waffen* SS**   The armed SS: a paramilitary organisation of elite troops.

Wall Street Crash   The collapse of share prices on the New York Stock Exchange in October 1929.

War bonds   To pay for the war, Imperial Germany encouraged people to invest in government funds in the belief that they were helping to finance the war and their savings would be secure.

Warsaw Pact   The USSR viewed NATO as an offensive alliance, and Soviet concern was highlighted when the

FRG was rearmed and brought into NATO. In response, in 1955, the Warsaw Pact was created as a defensive alliance of the USSR and the countries of central and eastern Europe under Soviet regimes.

Wehrmacht   The name of the combined armed forces 1935–45. During 1921–35 the term *Reichswehr* had referred simply to the German Army. In 1935 the German armed forces were reorganised and given the name *Wehrmacht*. It consisted of the army, the navy and the air force.

Weimar Republic   Took its name from the first meeting of the National Assembly in Weimar, which had moved from Berlin because of many disturbances. Weimar was chosen because it was a town with a great historical and cultural tradition.

Welfare state   The idea of the state playing a key role in the protection and promotion of the economic and social well-being of its people.

Weltpolitik   'World policy'. The imperial policy of Kaiser Wilhelm II to make Germany a great power by overseas expansion.

White-collar workers   Workers not involved in manual labour.

White Russians   Opponents of the Bolsheviks after the creation of the Soviet state.

White Terror   The 'Whites' were seen as the opponents to the Reds. The term 'White Terror' originated from the suppression of the soviet republic in Bavaria in May 1919, although it became a general name for the murders and violence of 1919–22.

Wiedergutmachung   Literally means making good again. The policy introduced by Adenauer of paying reparations, or restitution, to the victims of Nazism.

'Without me'   A phrase used to describe the tendency of many West Germans in the 1950s to put politics to one side. This mentality saw politics in terms of work, home and family, with little interest in international and military issues.

Further reading

Books relevant to the whole period

V. Berghahn, *Modern Germany* (Cambridge University Press, 1987)
Puts its emphasis on social and economic history with an excellent selection of statistics

W. Carr, *A History of Germany, 1815–1990* (Edward Arnold, 1991)
A clear and informative narrative that puts nineteenth- and twentieth-century German political history into perspective

M. Fulbrook, *History of Germany 1918–2000: The Divided Nation* (Blackwell, 2002)
A broad summary of German history including the explanation of different interpretations

General texts on Weimar Germany

E.J. Feuchtwanger, *From Weimar to Hitler: Germany 1918–33* (Macmillan, 1995)
Highlights the positive achievements of the Weimar Republic and argues that Weimar's failure was not inevitable

E. Kolb, *The Weimar Republic* (translated by P.S. Falla and R.J. Park) (Routledge, 2004)
A thorough and clear historical survey with an excellent overview of the main historiographical interpretations

A. J. Nicholls, *Weimar and the Rise of Hitler* (Palgrave, 2000)
The clearest and most accessible overview which emphasises how the weaknesses of Weimar paved the way for Nazism

General texts on Nazi Germany

K.D. Bracher, *The German Dictatorship* (Penguin, 1973)
Still probably the best one-volume history of the Nazi dictatorship

M. Burleigh, *The Third Reich: A New History* (Cambridge University Press, 1993)
A recent – and demanding – analysis which radically re-examines the Third Reich, and puts emphasis on racial doctrine and policies

I. Kershaw, *The Nazi Dictatorship: Problems and Perspectives of Interpretation* (Routledge, 2000)
A thorough review of historiographical interpretations

General texts on post-war Germany

M. Fulbrook, *Interpretations of the Two Germanies, 1945–1990* (Macmillan, 2000)
A clear historical survey of the two regimes with a review of the historiographical interpretations

P. O'Dochartaigh, *Germany Since 1945* (Palgrave Macmillan, 2004)
The clearest and most accessible overview of post-war Germany

D. Williamson, *Germany from Defeat to Partition, 1945–63* (Longman, 2001)
A comprehensive survey of the period 1945–63 with a range of documents

Chapter 1

R. Bessel and E. Feuchtwanger, editors, *Social Change and Political Developments in Weimar Germany* (Croom Helm, 1981)
Ten detailed but interesting essays on Weimar Germany. The first one on the German Revolution is particularly helpful

R. Henig, *Versailles and After* (Methuen, 1984)
A short narrative of the treaty with analysis of its consequences

Chapter 2

A. de Jonge, *The Weimar Chronicle* (Paddington Press, 1978)
Not really a historical interpretation, but more an attempt to explore the mood and culture of Weimar

J. Wright, *Stresemann, Weimar's Greatest Statesman* (Oxford University Press, 2002)
A major recent biography of Stresemann's life and career which portrays him in a positive light

Chapter 3

I. Kershaw, editor, *Weimar: Why Did German Democracy Fail?* (Weidenfeld & Nicolson, 1990)
An excellent collection of essays on the political and economic causes of the collapse of Weimar democracy

H. Mommsen, *The Rise and Fall of Weimar Democracy* (University of North Carolina Press, 1996)
A comprehensive analysis of the collapse of the Weimar Republic which focuses on the bringing together of domestic and international forces

Chapter 4

I. Kershaw, *Hitler 1889–1936: Hubris* (Allen Lane, 1998)
I. Kershaw, *Hitler 1936–1945: Nemesis* (Allen Lane, 2000)
A two-volume *tour de force* biography of Hitler, which aims to synthesise the intentionalist and structuralist interpretations

Chapter 5

M. Broszat, *The Hitler State* (London, 1981)
An authoritative study by the leading structuralist historian which examines the nature of government in the Third Reich

R. Gellately, *The Gestapo and German Society* (Clarendon, 1990)
A detailed study which shows the effectiveness of the *Gestapo*, despite its policing constraints

R.J. Overy, *The Nazi Economic Recovery, 1932–1938* (Cambridge University Press, 1996)
A concise and very clear overview of the economic material. He argues that, despite the expansion of the Nazi economy, it had become stagnant by 1939

Chapter 6

M. Burleigh and W. Wippermann, editors, *The Racial State: Germany 1933–45* (Cambridge University Press, 1991)
A thorough analysis of Nazi racial policies, which covers not only the Jews, but also Gypsies, asocials and mentally ill people

D. Crew, editor, *Nazism and German Society 1933–45* (Routledge, 1994)
A collection of articles which questions the image of totalitarian control of the regime over the German people

D. Welch, *The Third Reich* (Routledge, 1993)
An account of the relationship between politics, public opinion and propaganda. It focuses on how the regime mobilised and controlled the masses

Chapter 7

R.J. Evans, *The Third Reich at War* (Penguin, 2009)
The best up-to-date text on the overall impact of the war. The last volume of his trilogy on Nazi Germany

M. Housden, *Resistance and Conformity in the Third Reich* (Routledge, 1997)
A good study of the range of opposition forces in the Third Reich. Also contains an extensive range of primary sources

Chapter 8

C. Eisenberg, *Drawing the Line: The American Decision to Divide Germany* (Cambridge University Press, 1996)
Concentrates on the years 1944–9, and dismisses the myth that the division of Germany was Stalin's fault

M. McCauley, *The Origins of the Cold War, 1941–49* (Routledge, 2008)
An excellent introduction that puts German developments in the international perspective

Chapter 9

A.J. Nicholls, *The Bonn Republic: West German Democracy, 1945–1990* (Longman, 1997)
Clearly written and with some style – especially strong on political and economic developments

C. Williams, *Adenauer: The Father of the New Germany* (Abacus, 2003)
Probably the best biography of Adenauer in English

Chapter 10

M. Fulbrook, *Anatomy of a Dictatorship: Inside the GDR, 1945–1989* (Oxford University Press, 1995)
A thorough survey of the power structure and the patterns of public opinion in the GDR dictatorship

C. Ross, *The East German Dictatorship* (Arnold, 2002)
A helpful survey of the debates in the historiography about the GDR

Index